THE HEALTH CARE SUPERVISOR'S LEGAL GUIDE

Karen Hawley Henry, J.D.
Littler, Mendelson, Fastiff & Tichy
San Francisco

AN ASPEN PUBLICATION®
Aspen Systems Corporation
Rockville, Maryland
Royal Tunbridge Wells
1984

Library of Congress Cataloging in Publication Data

Henry, Karen Hawley.
The health care supervisor's legal guide.

"An Aspen publication."
Includes index.
1. Health facilities—Employees—Legal status, laws, etc.—United
States. 2. Health services administrators—Legal status, laws, etc.—
United States. I. Title. [DNLM: 1. Collective bargaining—Legislation.
2. Health Facility Administrators. 3. Labor Unions—Legislation.
4. Personnel Administration, Hospital—Legislation. WX 33.1 H522h]
KF3580.H4H46   1984   344.73'03211   84-14664
ISBN: 0-89443-598-1   347.3043211

Publisher: John Marozsan
Associate Publisher: Jack W. Knowles, Jr.
Editor-in-Chief: Michael Brown
Executive Managing Editor: Margot G. Raphael
Managing Editor: M. Eileen Higgins
Editorial Services: Scott Ballotin
Printing and Manufacturing: Debbie Collins

Library of Congress Catalog Card Number: 84-14664
ISBN: 0-89443-598-1

Printed in the United States of America

1 2 3 4 5

A Note

The author has made every reasonable effort to ensure that this text contains accurate summaries of the relevant law and legal principles as they existed at the time the final manuscript was submitted for publication. The reader should be aware, however, that the statements, summaries, and guidelines of legal and other principles contained herein can be affected by minor changes in the factual circumstances, by differences in interpretive judgments, and by changes in the law itself. Furthermore, the statements, summaries, guidelines, and other contents of this text are not to be construed as legal advice or opinion and they are not a substitute for the advice of counsel.

Table of Contents

Foreword   ix

Preface   xi

Introduction   xiii

PART I— THE SUPERVISOR   1

Chapter 1— Your Role As a Supervisor   1
    Profile of a Good Supervisor   1
    Supervisory Characteristics To Avoid   8
    Problems and Rewards of a Supervisor   10

Chapter 2— Your Legal Status   14
    The Supervisor's Dual Role   14
    Supervisors As Management   15
    Supervisors As Employees   20
    Reconciliation of Your Dual Status   21

PART II— EMPLOYMENT LAW   23

Chapter 3— The National Labor Relations Act   23
    The Need To Know the Act   23
    Structure of the Act—An Overview   23
    Health Care Institutions   26
    Section 7 Employee Rights   27
    Section 9 and Representative Questions   30
    Unfair Labor Practices   40

Topics of Particular Significance 49
Appendix 3-A 72

Chapter 4— Collective Bargaining Agreements **75**
What Are Collective Bargaining Agreements? 75
Typical Contract Provisions 75
Negotiations: Practical Conditions and Pointers 82
Strike Issues and Law 85
Reducing the Agreement to Writing 88
Common Contract Provisions 89
Enforcement of Union Contracts 99
Contract Interpretation 104
Topics of Particular Significance 109
Appendix 4-A 115

Chapter 5— Public Employment Labor Relations Laws **138**
Distinctive Characteristics of Public Employment 138
Federal Employment and Executive Orders 139
State Laws 141

Chapter 6— Discrimination in Employment **150**
Fair Employment Practices 150
Federal Nondiscrimination Requirements 150
State Laws 157
A Look Ahead 159
Appendix 6-A 162

Chapter 7— Race, National Origin, Sex and Religion **165**
An Introduction to Title VII 165

Chapter 8— Age, Handicap, and Veterans **195**
Age 195
The Handicapped 206
Veterans' Rights 218

Chapter 9— Wage and Hour Requirements **225**
Federal and State Laws 225
Fair Labor Standards Act (FLSA) 225
Equal Pay Act 236
State Wage-Hour Laws 238
Topics of Particular Significance 239
Appendix 9-A 251

Chapter 10—Regulation of Employer-Employee Relationships **257**
Disability Programs 257
Unemployment Insurance 259
ERISA 262
Terminable-at-Will Contracts 264
Blacklisting and Strikebreaking 265
Licensure Laws 266
Employment References 267
Access to Employer Files 267
Detention and Search of Employees 268

PART III— WORKING AT SUPERVISION **271**

Chapter 11—A Suggested Methodology for Supervision **271**
The 3 Areas of Supervision 271
What Is Supervision? 272
A Methodology for Decision-Making 275
Appendix 11-A 281

Chapter 12—Procedure: Notice, Notice, and More Notice **285**
A Review 285
Procedure Equals Notice 285
Purpose of Notice 286
Types of Notice 287
Appendix 12-A 303

Chapter 13—Substance: Proving Your Case **312**
Types of Issues 312
Dealing with Performance Problems 315
Handling Conduct Problems 321
Handling Attendance Problems 340

Chapter 14—Using Your Knowledge and Skills **352**
Introduction 352
Case Study #1: Substance vs. Procedure 353
Case Study #2: The Reluctant Patient 357
Case Study #3: The Delayed Lab Reports 361
Case Study #4: The Case of the Salary Increase 364
Case Study #5: Quit or Discharge? 366
Case Study #6: The Case of the Schedule Changes 369

Index **373**

Foreword

The health care industry is changing rapidly and dramatically. Rather than pursuing continual expansion, the industry must focus now on selective growth and on maximizing its use of existing resources—most notably, its work force—through improved efficiency and productivity. Yet health care is a labor-intensive industry and its human resources are governed and protected by a myriad of state and federal regulations. Administering human resources in this increasingly complex and changing environment is perhaps more difficult and confusing than it needs to be because of the lack of a definitive guide or roadmap. This need has finally been met.

The Health Care Supervisor's Legal Guide by Karen Hawley Henry, J.D., is based on the premise that "good supervision" is simply good risk management and it reflects her conviction that the necessary supervisory skills can be acquired and consistently applied through the use of an organized and analytical knowledge base. The result is a highly readable, interesting, and helpful handbook for the health care supervisor at any level.

The usefulness of the book, one that will become a standard reference source for the health care manager, comes as no surprise. Ms. Henry has been involved in health care labor relations for 15 years, and is chief counsel for the Affiliated Hospitals of San Francisco, a multiemployer association of hospitals and medical centers. These experiences have given her a first-hand familiarity with, and sensitivity to, the problems faced by health care employers and supervisors.

Whether or not you work in the health care industry, if you manage and supervise human resources, this comprehensive and practical book will fill a basic need. With it, the supervisor can learn how to manage most successfully while operating within the constraints imposed by employment law.

<table>
<tr><td>*William C. Hoffman, Jr.*</td><td>*Ira Warm*</td></tr>
<tr><td>Associate Director—Human Relations</td><td>Vice President, Personnel Services</td></tr>
<tr><td>Children's Hospital</td><td>Seton Medical Center</td></tr>
<tr><td>Boston, Massachusetts</td><td>Daly City, California</td></tr>
</table>

Preface

The legal framework governing the employee-employer relationship and the supervision of employees has grown tremendously over the past two decades. The impact of federal, state, and local statutes and regulations, and of interpretive decisions issued by the courts and governmental agencies, now affects almost every aspect of employee and labor relations, supervision, and human resource management in a health care institution. As a result, effective supervision (and the effective management of those with supervisory responsibilities) requires both a working knowledge of these laws and general principles and the ability to apply them in the work setting.

These two elements—a working knowledge of the applicable legal principles and a suggested method for applying these principles—are the primary focus of this book. The material emphasizes the practical implications of the law and is designed to be of assistance to all members of health care supervision, management, and administration, from the first-line supervisor to the human resource administrator to the chief executive officer. As a practical and legal guide to health care supervision, *The Health Care Supervisor's Legal Guide* also is of value to students of the health care professions and of health care administration.

Many of the suggestions presented are the result of the author's experiences in health care labor relations as a staff member of a state nurses association, as labor relations staff and then labor counsel for the Affiliated Hospitals of San Francisco, and currently as a shareholder (partner) with the law firm of Littler, Mendelson, Fastiff & Tichy with a practice focusing on health care labor law.

A very special "thank you" goes to all members of hospital supervision and management with whom I have shared these experiences and from whom I have received a great deal of support and friendship. For making these experiences possible, I also extend a special note of appreciation to Arthur Mendelson of Littler, Mendelson, Fastiff & Tichy who, throughout it all, has taken the time and interest to be a mentor and a friend. And finally, another debt of gratitude and acknowledgment must be expressed to Gregory W. McClune of Littler, Mendelson, Fastiff & Tichy who is a very special member of our health care labor law team and who provided valuable assistance and suggestions during the preparation of this book.

Karen Hawley Henry, J.D.
San Francisco, California
August 1984

Introduction

WHY THIS BOOK

The Health Care Supervisor's Legal Guide is the result of two separate but complementary motivations.

First, employment practices have become heavily regulated, with an accompanying increase in employers' potential liability for what is done or not done in such matters. This potential liability can be reduced or controlled only if employers view good supervision as a critical necessity, not a luxury.

Yet frequently employers overlook the importance of supervision and the legal constraints imposed on supervisory action. This neglect often is accompanied by a belief that "legalese" cannot be allowed to stand in the way of doing what is "right" from a management perspective or what is dictated by operational needs. Although this belief may be widely held, its underlying assumption simply is not true.

Admittedly, compliance with supervisory principles (including legal considerations) can affect "how" and "when" you take action but it does not preclude effective and unequivocal action. To the contrary, observance of these principles can aid strong supervision by reducing the number of successful employee challenges to employers' actions and by enhancing employers' credibility. Thus, a primary motivation behind this book is to encourage employers to recognize that effective supervision is simply good risk management and that they must place a priority on its achievement.

A second motivation was to provide a practical tool to aid supervisors in performing their responsibilities. Too often for comfort, supervisors have taken disciplinary or other action, then learned to their dismay that it was inappropriate (or even unlawful). These kinds of hindsight difficulties can and should be avoided. They not only are distressing to the individual supervisor involved and to

xiii

the attorney or labor representative who must be the bearer of bad tidings but they also can be very costly to the institution.

Furthermore, most of these errors in supervisory decision making are not caused by a lack of concern among individuals with supervisory responsibilities as to how they perform their functions. The truth actually is the opposite. Experience has demonstrated time and time again that supervisory personnel do want to perform their responsibilities competently and effectively. They care about how their actions are perceived by employees and how those actions impact on the work setting; conversely, they do not enjoy the prospect of rescinding decisions they already have made, whether reinstating a terminated employee, reducing a suspension to a written warning, granting a promotion that had been denied, etc.

Notwithstanding these good intentions, major errors continue to occur. In large part, this is because the academic approach to supervision has not kept up with the increasing importance of its functions or the needs of individuals who possess supervisory responsibilities. Few schools (or employers) offer practical coursework in supervision.

Yes, courses or materials in management skills, communication techniques, and a whole host of other "human resource development" topics often are included in professional, technical, or administrative programs offered in academic settings or through continuing education. But these programs often deal in generalities while supervision also must be concerned with specifics. Although competent legal or labor relations assistance can be helpful to supervisors, or even critical or mandatory in some instances, these resources are supplemental only. They cannot take the place of knowledgeable supervision: supervisors who know what the problem is, what the facts are, when and what questions to ask (of their employees and of their legal or labor relations personnel), and how to analyze what action should be taken before it is taken.

For these reasons, and in the hope that it can provide some practical assistance, *The Health Care Supervisor's Legal Guide* has been written.

THE APPROACH TAKEN

The twin motivations that led to this book also resulted in the development of an approach to supervision that has appeared helpful to individuals with supervisory responsibilities, whether they be on the first line or are department heads or chief executive officers. Specifically, it is suggested that supervision can be approached in a deliberate fashion, with supervisors developing the ability to analyze—or doublecheck, if you will—their own decisions or recommendations before taking any final action. Essential to this approach is that you possess a good common-sense understanding of the legal framework governing employers and that you:

- have the ability to apply your understanding of the legal framework
- know what functions are included within the term supervision
- know how to perform those functions on a daily basis and within the constantly evolving legal framework

FORMAT OF THE BOOK

The format of *The Health Care Supervisor's Legal Guide* divides this approach to supervision into three equally important parts:

- Part I, The Supervisor, introduces the importance of the supervisory role by describing and placing in context the role and status of supervisory personnel. When are you "the employer" and for what purposes are you "an employee," remembering that the emphasis (or bias, if you will) of this book is toward your actions on behalf of an employer.

- Part II, Employment Law, summarizes the laws, court decisions, and regulations that affect your actions on behalf of your employer. To provide both a general understanding of this legal framework, as well as a more detailed appreciation of the do's and don'ts governing the problems you probably encounter most frequently, each chapter describes the general principles that control discrimination law, wage-hour law, and labor relations law, etc. In addition, Chapters 3, 4, 7, and 8 contain a final section, "Topics of Particular Significance," devoted to addressing many of the recurring issues supervisors face.

- Part III, Working at Supervision, describes a "how" method for approaching your supervisory functions within the legal framework. This suggests that you analyze what action should be taken and whether it is warranted by checking first whether it complies with your employer's procedural or due process obligations and whether it is warranted substantively. For example, can you prove that the employee did or did not do whatever you claim to be the case, have you avoided any legal prohibitions that apply, etc.? To help you develop this ability to double-check your own decision or recommendations before you proceed to implementation, Chapter 14 presents a variety of case studies accompanied by suggested answers, responses, or issues to note.

Admittedly, the approach to supervision advocated here, as reflected by the format and division of topics, puts heavy emphasis on legal do's and don'ts. This emphasis was not selected arbitrarily but is a natural consequence of the reality facing all of us today: employers are subject to extensive legal regulation and can face substantial adverse consequences (financial and otherwise) from employment actions that are challenged successfully. Under these circumstances, reality dictates that supervision occur within, and take account of, the applicable legal framework.

HOW TO USE THIS BOOK

The Health Care Supervisor's Legal Guide is designed to be useful to supervisors in two ways: (1) it provides a basic foundation needed by anyone with such responsibilities and (2) it can serve subsequently as a reference source when you encounter actual problems on the job.

Use As a Reference

As a reference source, the following may be of particular interest:

- The Table Of Contents and the Index provide a detailed listing of the subject matter. Since cross-references are included, these should be used for ready access to specific issues. For example, the page location for issues concerning overtime payment appears under all of the following headings: Wage-Hour Law, Fair Labor Standards Act, Overtime, and Disciplinary Action (Violation of Overtime Policies).
- Topics Of Particular Significance are included in Chapters 3, 4, 7, 8, and 9. These discuss issues that arise frequently in the health care setting.
- Legal citations to legislation, administrative regulations, and court decisions are listed at the end of each chapter should you wish to refer to the full text of the legal authority mentioned.

A Cautionary Note

It must be remembered that the legal framework governing your actions always is in a state of flux. Two weeks . . . or six months . . . or a year after this book is completed, the law may be altered dramatically by new legislation, new regulations, or court decisions that almost daily are refining and reinterpreting employer legal obligations.

For this reason, after reviewing the entire chapter or Topic of Particular Significance applicable to your issue, you should check with your employer's labor relations or legal resources as to any changes in the legal framework, any differing interpretation they might have, or any twist in the law that could affect the general summary presented here.

Part I

The Supervisor

Chapter 1

Your Role As a Supervisor

PROFILE OF A GOOD SUPERVISOR

Good supervisors are made, not born. Being an excellent accountant, or registered nurse, or housekeeper, or in one of the numerous other occupations in a health care facility (even the administrator) does not automatically give you all the knowledge and skills required of competent and effective supervisors. To the contrary, a whole new set of skills and a very different way of thinking may be required for functioning in a supervisory capacity and you may have received little (if any) training to help you meet these new expectations.

As a result, some supervisors, whether they are newly promoted or of long tenure, become frustrated, dissatisfied, or they experience a feeling that things are "out of control." With this in mind, the question is, "How do I avoid a similar fate?"

As a start, it must be recognized that supervision requires a strong commitment in terms of time and energy plus a great deal of personal self-confidence. With this commitment, you then need to acquire (or strengthen) your skills and knowledge in three major areas:

1. You must be knowledgeable in, or develop a knowledge of, the variety of functions included under the heading of supervision.
2. You must have a working knowledge of the legal framework that governs an employer's relationship toward employees.
3. You must know how to apply your knowledge of supervisory functions and the legal framework to your day-to-day performance.

Supervisory Functions

Supervision includes many different types of tasks and functions. Depending upon your level of authority and your employer's organizational scheme, your functions may include any or all of the following:

- hiring employees
- assigning employees and setting work standards
- handling the approval, or assignment, of work schedules, overtime, days off, etc.
- evaluating employees on a periodic or as-needed basis
- developing a joint "action plan" with an employee to identify goals and objectives for future progress, the means to be used to achieve these goals, etc.
- taking disciplinary action as necessary
- counseling employees concerning their performance, new work methods or practices, etc.
- ensuring employees' compliance with employer policies, standards, and procedures
- initiating suggestions for changes, modifications, or additions to your employer's policies, procedures, etc.

In turn, each of these (and any other supervisory functions) may be composed of many subfunctions or sequential steps. For example, if you have the supervisory responsibility for hiring new employees, this may require that you:

- review employment applications to determine whether candidates meet minimum hiring standards and whether an interview would be appropriate
- conduct employment interviews
- seek references from prior employers and verify other critical information provided on the employment application or during the interview
- make a final or recommended decision and, if hiring is to result, subsequently extend an appropriate offer of employment.

During this entire process, and in other supervisory functions, you need to keep in mind not only your employer's policies and procedures but the relevant framework of legal obligations and how to apply it to the task at hand.

Legal Framework

Employers are subject to many restrictions and requirements in their relationships toward employees or applicants. (As Chapter 2 discusses what you do or don't do can incur liability for your employer if your actions violate these legal standards.) Accordingly, and because federal and state requirements now extend to practically every aspect of the employment relationship, you need to develop a working knowledge of what the laws require and how they affect your supervisory decision making.

Working knowledge means that you need to be acquainted with the basic concepts and do's and don'ts that apply to the following major categories of employment law:

- labor relations laws controlling the relationships among employers, employees, and unions
- discrimination laws prohibiting employer action "because of" race, sex, religion, national origin, handicap status, veterans status, etc.
- wage-hour laws regulating how, and how much, you pay employees
- other regulation of the employment relationship such as federal statutes governing health, welfare, and retirement plans, state laws on unemployment, disability, and worker compensation, the legal principles affecting whether employment can be terminated at will and for any reason not specifically prohibited by law, etc.

The practical implications of this legal framework, and the necessity for possessing a common-sense appreciation of its impact on your employment-related decisions, can be illustrated readily:

Example #1: The Facts

1. A union is attempting to organize your employees. During this organizing drive, you decide that you must finally take the step of terminating Ms. Jones.
2. Ms. Jones' work performance has been unsatisfactory for some time and she is still employed only because you consider it to be a personal failure if you have to terminate anyone. Now you find, however, that she is using her worktime to seek union support from other employees and you decide that this misuse of her paid time is the last straw so you proceed to terminate her.
3. Two days later, an NLRB election is held to determine whether the employees wish to be represented by the organizing union, and they vote for "no union."
4. The union, after her termination and the election, files an unfair labor practice charge with the National Labor Relations Board (NLRB) claiming that Ms. Jones was discriminated against, and terminated, for engaging in union activity.

When you are told that an NLRB charge has been filed, your reaction is that it is totally frivolous; after all, Ms. Jones was not terminated for favoring the union, she was terminated for not working during worktime.

However, during the NLRB hearing to determine whether your employer has violated the National Labor Relations Act (NLRA or the Act) by terminating Ms. Jones' employment, the Board attorney introduces evidence showing that you did not discharge (or take any lesser disciplinary action) against other unsatisfactory employees who violated your employer's policy prohibiting solicitation on worktime. This evidence still causes you no concern. Why should it since those other employees were engaging in worthwhile causes such as asking other employees to purchase Girl Scout cookies, tickets to church raffles, or to your annual picnic, or engaging in activities that aided employee morale such as soliciting money to buy a gift for another worker, setting up a football pool, etc.?

Example #1: The Outcome

Three months after the hearing the NLRB administrative law judge (ALJ) hearing the case issues her decision. To your amazement, the ALJ finds that your employer did violate the Act by terminating Ms. Jones. To make matters worse, the recommended decision ultimately is upheld by the Board itself. Why? Because an employee who violated your solicitation policy to engage in union activities was terminated while similarly situated employees who committed violations by using worktime for other purposes were not. This means, legally, that union activities were treated differently or subjected to unlawful discrimination.

What is the end result of this chronology for your employer? Among other things (including legal defense costs), the Board may order that the NLRB election (in which your employees voted against union representation) be set aside and a second election held. The NLRB also has ordered your employer to reinstate Ms. Jones in employment and to give her back pay with interest.

The direct consequences for you as a supervisor are equally onerous. First, you now have to deal with a reinstated employee whose work performance is unsatisfactory but who is dramatic proof to other employees that they may be able to successfully challenge terminations or other supervisory actions that you take. Second, if you now seek to improve Ms. Jones' unsatisfactory work performance (and that of any other employees), you have made your task doubly difficult.

How could these consequences have been avoided?

First, you should know, and follow, applicable legal standards through uniformly enforcing a valid policy prohibiting solicitation or distribution during worktime for union and nonunion activities alike and by ensuring that all employees are aware of, and comply with, this policy.

Second, and of equal importance, if you previously had taken timely and appropriate action concerning Ms. Jones' poor work performance, the problem might never have arisen. Why not? Because she could have corrected her ways (or transferred her allegiance to another employer) before the events in question. Or, if she persisted in violating your employer's policies and legitimate expectations and was then terminated, you could have demonstrated to the NLRB that her discharge was not discriminatory. How? By showing that it was simply the last step in a documented process of progressive discipline and that the final incident triggering her termination was not discriminatory in any way since the policy was enforced consistently and even-handedly with regard to all activities, including unions, Girl Scout cookies, etc.

If this example, which is not atypical, does not convince you of the necessity for knowing the applicable legal framework and consequences before you act, then you will get additional reinforcement by taking a few moments to complete the following "test."

Example #2: A Test on Federal Law

As you read the following questions, mentally answer them True or False in accordance with your understanding of federal law:

	True	False
1. An employment application should ask the following questions of candidates:		
• What is your marital status?	___	___
• If you have children under 12, do you have child-care arrangements?	___	___
• What is your date of birth?	___	___
• Do you have any disabilities that prevent you from performing all of your work functions, and, if yes, what are they?	___	___
2. Employees must be paid overtime for work in excess of 40 hours in a week, but there is no requirement to pay overtime for work in excess of eight hours in a day.	___	___
3. An employer can lawfully enforce a policy that requires retirement after age 65.	___	___
4. You cannot tell employees, during a union organizing drive, that you believe a union is unnecessary.	___	___
5. You can safely refuse to pay an employee who actually works half an hour of overtime without first seeking prior approval from you if your employer requires advance authorization of overtime.	___	___

Now, compare your answers against the correct responses. This is easy enough since, if you answered True to any of the questions, you could be violating federal law. Specifically:

Example #2: The Outcome

Question 1: Under the interpretation given to Title VII by the Equal Employment Opportunity Commission, you should not inquire into marital status since it could lead to discrimination against women; for the same reason, you should not inquire into an applicant's child-care arrangements. You should not request an applicant's age since this is viewed as information that could lead to age discrimination. Asking applicants to specify their disabilities during the application procedure would violate the Rehabilitation Act of 1973 as interpreted by federal regulations if your employer receives federal financial assistance or is a federal contractor.

At this point you may be asking, ''What can I do lawfully since I need some of this information?'' The answer is, ''a great deal,'' provided it is done or asked at the proper time and in the proper way. For example:

- You cannot, as noted, ask applicants about child-care arrangements (which usually is asked only of women and contains an assumption that problems will arise) but can and should apply the same standards of attendance and punctuality to all employees, regardless of their child-care or other personal reasons for poor attendance or lack of dependability.
- You can ask individuals any of the information that an employer legitimately needs to know after they are employed if you provide assurances that it will be used only for permissible purposes, e.g., to know marital status for purposes of health insurance coverage, to know age for purposes of pension plan participation, etc.

Question 2: It is true that federal law does not require that overtime be paid after eight hours in a workday if you use a 40-hour workweek for purposes of overtime calculation. However, if a hospital or other facility primarily engaged in caring for the sick, aged, or mentally ill elects to go to an ''8 and 80'' option, which means that overtime is paid after 80 hours in a biweekly pay period, then federal law does require overtime for work in excess of eight hours in a day. You also should ascertain whether your state requires overtime payment after eight (or another specified number of) hours in a day.

Question 3: This is false since federal law generally allows mandatory retirement only after an employee has reached age 70.

Question 4: The employer can and should tell employees, through their supervisors, what its position is toward unionization in general or one union in particular. This generally does not violate federal law unless accompanied by threats, interrogation, promises, or surveillance.

Question 5: Since federal law requires that employees be paid for overtime actually worked, you should not refuse to pay it simply because a person worked the extra hours without complying with an employer policy that requires advance approval. What you can do, however, is to use progressive discipline to enforce the policy; in other words, you can inform employees through written and verbal notice of the policy (counselling, written warnings, and perhaps even suspension or termination) that they must receive advance approval before working overtime. Unless such a policy is enforced in this fashion, an employer could very quickly lose any financial control over overtime costs.

As these examples illustrate, it is very easy to run afoul of federal and/or state prohibitions applicable to employers; it is just as easy, once you know the basic rules, to avoid these violations and to find other permissible ways of enforcing or fulfilling the employer's fundamental objective or purpose.

Working at Supervision

Knowing what supervisory functions you should perform, and the legal framework of do's and don'ts imposed on employers, is helpful but not sufficient. You also must know how to apply this knowledge to your daily supervisory functions.

Simply stated, the key to knowing how to apply these principles is to think before you act. As basic as it sounds, many errors in supervisory decision making occur because of a belief that you must act—now. To the contrary, in the vast majority of instances, you will have sufficient time to:

- think through the nature of the problem you are facing
- check your employer's policies and procedures to determine those that apply, and how they apply
- review any applicable legal standards
- analyze whether the action you want to take is warranted and whether it can be defended successfully if it is challenged
- seek assistance as needed.

As you approach this thinking process, however, you need a method to ensure that you have not forgotten something and that your action, once taken, can be defended. One such method—and the one advocated in Part III—is to check whether you have met all procedural and substantive requirements applicable to the problem you are facing. As discussed more fully in Chapters 11, 12, and 13:

- *Procedure* means whether the employee has received reasonable notice of your employer's policies, standards, and expectations; notice of your dissatisfaction with the person's conduct or performance; notice as to what the consequences will be if there is no improvement; and whether you have conducted a fair and sufficient investigation of pertinent facts, including asking the employee's version of the events.
- *Substance*, by contrast, focuses on whether you or your employer can prove that the employee did or did not do whatever it is that resulted in the disciplinary action. In a case of termination for sleeping on the job, for example, can you prove that the employee was in fact sleeping and that it was during worktime? Or will the employee be able to claim successfully that the eyes were closed momentarily because they were being "rested"? If your analysis of the facts establishes that you cannot prove a sleeping allegation, then you need to reconsider what, if any, action is warranted.

As this discussion implies, it is both possible and beneficial to approach supervisory problems from an organized and deliberate fashion. Good supervisors do it every day. Without such an approach, it is easy to lapse into hasty or emotional decisions that are influenced by how things appear rather than how they really are.

SUPERVISORY CHARACTERISTICS TO AVOID

By contrast to competent and effective conduct there are numerous supervisory styles to be avoided.

First and foremost, some supervisors become adept at passing the buck. Under this approach, you never take the responsibility for anything that the employer does. If you terminate an employee, make it clear that this is being done only because that department head or that administrator insists that it be done. This way, you will be able to testify truthfully, if the action is challenged, that you played no role in the decision and that you did not recommend that the person be terminated even though you had numerous prior difficulties with the individual's performance while an employee.

A different approach, but one that is just as effective for divorcing yourself from the unpleasantries of being a boss, is to adopt the "buddy system." This style allows you to demonstrate your human relations skills by forming personal ties with favorite employees, who then become your confidants or confidantes and recipients of all sorts of management information and favors. In return, these employees can be counted upon to support your actions or viewpoint (at least when you are within earshot). The only difficulty with this approach is that you may begin to encounter increasing resistance from other employees when you attempt to enforce standards of performance and conduct that you do not apply to your favored few.

Another type that is all too common can be called, for want of a better term, the schizoid supervisor. Matching the profile is quite simple: you apply the basic elements of due process to employees covered by a collective bargaining agreement but you do not use these same standards in dealing with employees who are not covered by a union contract. The rationale is an assumption that those irritating due process technicalities exist only because of a union contract and therefore you are free to do as you think best when there is no contract.

However, this schizoid approach is disastrous from an employee relations perspective and its underlying assumption is wrong. Why? Because a variety of legal constraints can dictate that you comply with basic due process requirements, even for those not covered by a union contract and even if they also are supervisory or administrative employees. Even more importantly, this approach is wrong because:

- It tells your employees that their only means of obtaining fair and consistent treatment is to organize and secure a union contract. It thus may encourage unionization that might not otherwise occur because employee dissatisfaction with treatment by supervisors is a major reason underlying votes for union representation.
- It ignores the fact that compliance with good supervisory decision making, including complying with substantive and procedural considerations, is the fair way to treat employees, just because they are your employees.

A final example from this nonexclusive list of supervisory styles to avoid is the "complainer" method of supervision. As a complainer, you never can be faulted for failing to take or to recommend any corrective action toward employees since you are the first one to point out that such action cannot be taken because of the union, or because top administration will not support you, or because of various laws, or because of any other convenient reason.

The depicted scenario becomes a self-fulfilling prophecy but not because of the reasons cited by the complainer. True, this style often is accompanied by supervisory inaction or, if action is taken, by a high frequency of reversals. However, this happens only because once action finally is taken, it lacks a proper foundation of progressive discipline; or it does not take into account an employer's own past practices, policies, or procedures; or it violates some basic legal prohibition; etc.

Fundamentally, then, what the complainer style conveniently forgets is that employers can take appropriate employment action even in times of extensive governmental regulation and even if a union contract applies so long as there is consistent and deliberate supervision. This means that competent supervision requires time, knowledge, and a recognition that you are accountable only for taking reasoned action; you are not responsible for guaranteeing the impossible, namely, that there will never be any challenges or any successful challenges by employees to your supervisory decisions.

PROBLEMS AND REWARDS OF A SUPERVISOR

The fact that a knowledgeable and competent supervisor still is able to take appropriate and timely action does not mean that problems will never arise or that things will always go smoothly. Particularly in the health care setting, specialized issues can arise that on occasion may make your life more difficult. Most of these problems can be dealt with or avoided if you are forewarned.

The Complexity of Health Care Institutions

Health care institutions can be complex organizations. This means that decisions may have to be filtered through many layers of authority or take into account multiple priorities or considerations. As an illustration, assume that you wish to establish or modify a policy on how employees should handle the storage and dispensing of medications. If you anticipate a speedy completion of the project, then you may be in for some disappointment since it may require that:

- you first develop a draft of your proposed policy or modification, taking into account the various work units or departments affected (nursing, pharmacy, etc.)
- you take into account all of the legal restrictions applicable to prescribed drugs, which may require review by legal counsel at various steps
- you obtain approval from administration, including nursing and pharmacy, as well as the medical staff, which may mean numerous revisions, with another review by all those affected after each revision
- you provide for communicating the final policy to all employees who must comply with it, and that you provide for monitoring the policy to encourage consistent enforcement by all individuals who supervise the affected employees.

This process can be very time consuming, to say the least, but it is dictated by the levels of authority and multiplicity of professions, classifications, and legal standards involved. Your accompanying frustration may be minimized, however, if you recognize these considerations and take them into account during your initial planning process.

The 'Doctor Problem'

This is not the place (and it would not be particularly pertinent) to attempt to describe the obvious fact that physicians, whether they be attending staff, employed physicians, or house staff, play an integral role, direct and/or indirect, in the administration of a hospital. The points that do need to be stated, however, are that:

- your supervision of employees must take into account the somewhat unique actions and reactions of physicians, and
- your own actions, while recognizing the physicians' authority and expertise as medical care providers, should avoid any tendency to accord special standards or deference when physicians are involved in the disciplinary process.

For example, if a physician complains loudly about an employee's work performance and demands that the person be terminated, and if you then take disciplinary action without following the same supervisory process and procedure you use for complaints initiated by other individuals, you are setting yourself up for trouble. Why?

First, the mere fact that a physician has complained about an employee, or even demanded that the individual be terminated, does not necessarily mean that the physician is correct. Second, if you have not investigated the facts, obtained written witness statements to the extent possible, talked to the employee, and otherwise established for yourself that a termination is proper, then (if your action is challenged) how are you going to be able to explain or sustain why you believed the termination was necessary?

It must be remembered that the physician who is complaining today may be supportive of the employee tomorrow. This is not intended as criticism of physicians, it is simply stating an empirical reality: many physicians are not familiar with the needs and requirements of supervisory action and do not enjoy (and who does?) being known as the reason an employee was terminated.

Thus, for example, if you take action without following your normal process, then (1) you may be faced with a subsequent letter stating that the physician never intended that the employee be terminated (and the letter has a convenient way of surfacing at the most inconvenient time); or, (2) the physician's testimony concerning the complaint or the underlying facts may be critical (since you did not conduct your own investigation) if an arbitration or administrative hearing (NLRB, EEOC, etc.) becomes necessary and the physician may have lost interest by then or may refuse to give full cooperation; or, (3) with the passage of time, the physician may have developed a very hazy recollection of events that you cannot supplement because you did not complete an adequate investigation and documentation.

To put it in a nutshell, therefore, the only way to preclude these or other problems from arising is to ensure that you handle supervisory matters appropriately on all occasions, even when a physician is involved.

Professional and Technical Classifications

The myriad of classifications found in health care institutions presents another consideration or problem to be taken into account, one that may affect how you, as an individual, perceive and perform your own supervisory functions.

This problem is twofold: (1) supervisors from professional occupations tend to negate the need for corrective supervisory action, believing it to be unnecessary when you deal with highly skilled and educated employees and (2) many supervised employees believe corrective disciplinary action is inappropriate when applied to them.

Both of these reactions can cause you innumerable difficulties since they ignore the external requirements imposed on you and your employer—e.g., professionals covered by a union contract (or who file NLRB or EEOC charges) have been reinstated because there was no progressive discipline, or they were not told clearly and unequivocally that a failure to improve could lead to termination, or because of other defects in supervisory action. Moreover, these beliefs can be a disservice to supervised employees since they may deprive them of clear and unequivocal communication from you that their performance or conduct is unsatisfactory and must be improved at the risk of termination.

Admittedly, there is no necessity (and little if any benefit) to order employees around and invent excuses for exercising your disciplinary authority. Instead, employees should have input into the development of professional standards. You also should provide assistance by teaching, counselling, and suggesting improved methods of performance or the use of outside resources.

However, this does not eliminate the necessity for adhering to basic supervisory principles applicable to all employees: clearly telling employees what your employer's policies are, what you consider to be satisfactory or unsatisfactory work performance or conduct, what the consequences are if the employee does not improve, etc. In summary, therefore, it still is critical that you take clear and unequivocal corrective and disciplinary action if and when your efforts at counselling and assistance become ineffective.

Special Rewards

If supervisors in the health care setting face all of these specialized problems, what do they get in return, what are the special rewards? Aside from the satisfaction that many individuals derive from being recognized and promoted, and from possessing greater responsibility and opportunity for management participation, other unique or special rewards do exist. .

While the nature of these rewards will vary from individual to individual (and you will be the expert in answering this question), they include, in brief:

- the satisfaction that results from improved employee performance, recognizing that proper supervision can make a difference even with excellent employees who have superb skills and superior performance
- the opportunity to broaden your own skills and knowledge by incorporating into your functioning the additional elements required of competent supervisors, and
- the increased opportunity to assist your employees in making a greater contribution to the goals of your institution by improving their understanding of these objectives, how they can be met, and the role played by your service or work area.

Chapter 2

Your Legal Status

THE SUPERVISOR'S DUAL ROLE

From both a practical and legal standpoint, your status as a supervisor is unique. On the one hand, the law generally considers you to be an agent of your employer, and as its agent your acts or omissions can be binding on your employer even when it has no knowledge of your actions. On the other hand, the law considers you for many purposes to be an employee. This chapter discusses your dual status, or the law's split personality toward you. Again, remember that the emphasis of this manual and of this chapter is upon the critical role you fulfill on behalf of your employer.

You Are Management

Unless the facility that employs you is exceptionally small, its chief executive officer could not possibly supervise and direct the entire work force. Key functions must be delegated to others. As one of those "others," you act on behalf of the facility—you are its agent—and thus you come to be viewed as "management" by the employees you supervise. Since employees regard you as their employer's spokesperson and rely upon you as a source of direction, it follows that the facility should be bound by your actions.

You Are an Employee

Since just about everyone has a boss, each of you, no matter how great your responsibilities and authority, is reminded occasionally that you also are an employee. As an employee, you are entitled to many of the same rights and protections enjoyed by the employees you supervise. For example: (1) racial or sexual discrimination by a facility is equally unlawful whether it is committed against the employees you supervise or against supervisory, administrative, or managerial employees; (2) you are covered by Social Security and other programs intended to benefit employees in general.

You Are a 'Management' Employee

The dual status of supervisory employees (from first-line supervisors through the chief executive) sometimes causes a feeling that a conflict exists; that you have two inconsistent allegiances, one to the employees you supervise, another to your employer, and that you are caught in between these two obligations. Yet no perceived or actual conflict exists if you remember your legal status as a supervisor, the purpose of supervision, and the role you fulfill on behalf of your employer.

Whenever these feelings of conflict arise, remember that:

- As a supervisor, your action or inaction can bind your employer.
- Since you can bind your employer, or create liability, then your employer has a legitimate interest in determining what you do, how you do it, and what the scope or limits of your authority should be.
- For the same reasons, your employer also should be able to expect that you will uphold its policies and procedures (even if you disagree) since it, and not you, generally will be responsible for any resulting liability.
- As a supervisory employee, you have the obligation and right to advocate, within management, any revisions or changes in policies you believe to be necessary or appropriate.
- Since your employer is totally dependent on you and other managerial personnel for carrying out its mission and philosophy, this means that your dual status gives you a unique opportunity to make a valuable contribution to your employees by demonstrating a management approach consistently reflected throughout the institution.

SUPERVISORS AS MANAGEMENT

Your Agency Status: An Illustration

The National Labor Relations Act (the NLRA or the Act)—a federal statute that governs the relationships among private employers, their employees, and unions—provides a good illustration of your agency status. Under the Act, you are an agent of your employer and, so viewed, you are an extension of management for labor relations purposes.

The NLRA's perspective that you and your employer have a single identity means that your employer can be bound by and liable for your actions even if it did not authorize your conduct and even if it had told you in advance to not engage in the objectionable conduct.

As an example, suppose that you decide to "help" your employer win an NLRB election by telling your employees that they will be fired for union activities. Assume also that in a prior management meeting, the do's and don'ts of election activity were reviewed with all supervisors, including you, and all persons present at the meeting were told to make no threats to employees. Under these circumstances, will your employer have any responsibility for your actions? Yes.

Your employer will be responsible for your words unless it subsequently tells your employees (not just you) that you had no authority to make those statements and it expressly disavows your statements by also telling them that they will not be fired or otherwise discriminated against for union activities. If your employer does not do this, then it will be liable for your actions since the employees are justified in relying upon your apparent authority to make and carry out those threats.

The moral is that because you are your employer's agent, and because you can bind your employer by what you say and do (or fail to do), it is important to understand:

- where your authority comes from
- what the scope of your authority is
- what is beyond your authority
- what liability can result from your actions.

How You Get Authority

There are five basic ways in which your authority to act can be established: (1) expressly, (2) impliedly, (3) through apparent authority, (4) by ratification, and (5) because of an emergency.

Express Authority

This is the most direct and safest way for all concerned. It simply means that your employer has expressly told you that you have certain authority. This can be stated in some written document such as a policy statement or job description (an appropriate method for describing your basic authority), or orally (which can be subject to misinterpretation or tricks of memory but frequently is the most workable method for granting special authority). For example: a letter or memo to you, or your official job description, or written policies, may set forth the things you are empowered to do on the facility's behalf and, just as importantly, they may contain restrictions or limitations on your authority.

Implied Authority

Since it is virtually impossible to predict all of the situations you might face in your daily work—and equally impossible to spell out all the express powers you might need in those situations—the law has come to recognize the concept of implied authority. In fact, most authority is created by implication. It is the authority that may be inferred from

- the wording of your express authority
- the customs of your workplace
- the relationship between you and your superiors
- the authority you must have to perform your job properly.

An example of how implied authority can arise: Suppose that after a number of years in your facility's laundry you are promoted to department head. As such, you have the responsibility for ensuring that the laundry is operating efficiently and without breakdowns. Although you never have been given any express instruction on the matter, you also believe that this primary responsibility would include the authority to arrange for any necessary repairs of laundry equipment. Based upon common practices and the nature of your position, such a conclusion concerning your authority would be correct. Remember, however, that the safest (and best) way to handle questionable areas of your authority is to ask first, then act.

Apparent Authority

Even when you exceed your actual express or implied authority, your actions still can bind your employer. This may occur in two ways, apparent authority and ratification. The doctrine of apparent authority arises when your employer's actions, whether intentional or unintentional, cause others to conclude mistakenly that you possess certain authority. Your employer can either do something that misleads others to believe that you have authority and that causes them to rely on that authority, or your employer might fail to act, thereby allowing others to rely on a mistaken belief concerning your authority. In either event, your employer can be bound by your actions.

As an example, in that laundry just discussed, assume that it is customary for the department head to have the authority to purchase laundry detergent. Two weeks after you are appointed, however, the administration issues clear instructions to you that detergent and other supplies can be ordered only by the purchasing department—but no one tells the detergent supplier of this new arrangement.

If you then ignore your express instructions and purchase detergent from the supplier, and your employer subsequently seeks to cancel the sale, what will happen?

The answer is: Your facility will be bound because you had apparent authority to purchase the supplies. Since laundry department heads normally possess such authority, it was reasonable for your supplier to conclude (in the absence of contrary information) that you also possessed the necessary authority, so the purchase will be binding.

Ratification

Ratification, the second way in which your unauthorized acts can bind your facility, occurs only after you have acted and requires your employer's approval or acceptance of the act. Strictly speaking, ratification does not confer authority; instead, it is based on the view that if, upon learning of your unauthorized act, your employer accepts it or fails to disavow it, your facility will be bound.

Emergency Authority

In your work an emergency situation may arise in which you may be required to act in an area where you have uncertain authority. In these circumstances, and unless you have received different instructions to the contrary, you are authorized to do what is necessary to prevent substantial loss to your facility. Your actions in response to the emergency are impliedly authorized and will bind your facility.

Exceeding Your Authority

Because your actions may have a great effect on your employer, it is important to both the facility and yourself that you act within the limits of your authority. If you are unsure of the scope of your authority and feel that you may be treading on thin ice, do not be afraid to ask. A quick clarification from a knowledgeable superior may save your employer and you a great deal of trouble.

Written policies and procedures, job descriptions, etc., may impose limitations on your authority, specify operating standards and procedures, and/or identify the supervisory or administrative personnel authorized to approve deviations from those standards. Should you receive an order that conflicts with any such limitations or restrictions—or, for that matter, should you give such an order—then it should be questioned in a reasonable manner.

Common sense will tell you that certain orders should not be obeyed. If, for example, you are told that you can falsify timecards or take medical supplies home for your own personal use, then you are expected to know that the order is invalid. Under these circumstances, reliance on the order given to you, or a claim that you are "only following orders," clearly would not be justified.

Personal Liability

Another important issue to keep in mind, without becoming paranoid about it, is that you may be individually liable for a wrongful act that you commit in performing your job. While variations in state law, in the type of claim filed, and in the pertinent facts all can affect the generalizations stated here, if your employer is required to compensate someone for financial or physical injury resulting from your acts, it then "may" be able to recover that sum from you. Different rules apply to financial and physical injuries; they are considered next.

Financial Injuries to Others

Generally, if you act as an agent for your facility and enter into a contract or other commercial dealing on its behalf (with authority to do so), the facility alone is liable. If, however, you exceed your authority, then you as well as your facility may be personally liable. To avoid this personal liability, you would have to explain clearly to the other party to the contract that you are making no guarantees concerning your own authority. If you enter into a contract on behalf of your employer, however, knowing that you do not have the authority to do so, then your employer would have legitimate concerns about your judgment and actions. So again, the best way to avoid personal liability (and the best way to safeguard your employer's interests) is to act within your known authority.

Physical Injuries to Others

With regard to physical injuries that you cause others while acting in the scope of your employment, both you and your facility are liable. Much of this liability will be covered by your employer's workers' compensation insurance if the individual injured was an employee and it occurred in the course of employment. Even so, you are not always relieved of personal liability just because you are acting for your employer. Also, if an injury occurs when you are acting outside the scope of your employment, then you alone may be liable.

A Preventive Approach

In the case of both financial and physical injury, your facility may be able to recover from you the money it is required to pay a third party. However, most employers want to be supportive of you and of your supervisory actions, particularly where you acted in good faith. For this reason, they are hesitant to seek recovery from you unless exceptional circumstances exist, even though legally they may be entitled to do so.

This discussion of your potential liability is not intended to terrorize you, paralyze you on the job, or turn you into an overly cautious supervisor. It is intended only to put you on notice as to the potential consequences of your acts and to emphasize the importance of acting within the scope of your authority and of asking the employer for clarification rather than assuming that you have certain powers.

SUPERVISORS AS EMPLOYEES

The law also recognizes that you and other supervisory and administrative personnel are employees and that you are covered appropriately by certain legislation and legal principles. Examples of the protections offered to you as an employee include the following.

Equal Pay Act

The portion of the Fair Labor Standards Act (FLSA) that is commonly known as the Equal Pay Act applies to you even though you are exempt from the FLSA's minimum wage and overtime provisions. The Equal Pay Act, which is administered by the Equal Employment Opportunity Commission (EEOC), prohibits your facility from paying different salaries to men and women for jobs of equal skill, effort, and responsibility unless the difference is based on (1) length of service, (2) the quantity and quality of performance, or (3) other factors not related to sex. Thus, women supervisors must be paid at the same rate as men occupying equivalent positions unless one of those factors applies.

Discrimination Laws

Various federal and state laws prohibit discrimination at the workplace. Title VII of the Civil Rights Act of 1964 and the Age Discrimination in Employment Act are examples of federal legislation in this area; many similar state laws also are on the books.

As a general rule, these federal and state statutes prohibit discrimination against all employees and apply equally to supervisory and nonsupervisory personnel. For example:

- Title VII prohibits employment discrimination based upon race, color, national origin, sex, or religion. The Act provides no exclusions or exemptions for administrative, executive, or supervisory personnel and applies to applicants for employment as well as those with jobs. But always remember,

Title VII cuts two ways. While it prohibits discrimination against you in your supervisory position, it also treats you as an agent of the facility, so any discriminatory act you commit against supervised employees will be attributed to your employer.

- The Age Discrimination in Employment Act (ADEA) also treats you as both an employee and an employer. Like Title VII, the ADEA provides no general exemption for supervisory, administrative, or managerial employees. In fact, such employees may especially benefit from the ADEA coverage since they may be promoted to their positions only after long years of service and thus a higher proportion are in the age group protected by that Act.

Insurance Programs

As a supervisory employee you are covered by the Social Security Act, which provides retirement and other benefits to eligible persons; by federal and state unemployment insurance programs, which provide a minimum level of economic protection if you are out of work; and perhaps by a state workers' compensation program, which provides compensation if you are injured on the job or permanently disabled.

Descriptions of these and other programs are available from the federal and state agencies that administer them and you should familiarize yourself with their provisions. They are designed to benefit both you and the employees you supervise.

RECONCILIATION OF YOUR DUAL STATUS

Once you accept a supervisory, administrative, or managerial position, your employer should be entitled to rely (and to do so confidently) upon an assumption that you will advance its interests and goals. But this assumption will be true only if you are able to successfully reconcile your dual status of being ''the employer'' for some purposes and ''an employee'' for other purposes.

Where such a reconciliation does not occur, a we-they relationship can develop within management ranks. This may be perceived by, and influence, the reactions of your supervised employees and of the individuals to whom you report. Once this happens, you may find that your effectiveness as a supervisor, as a leader, and as a manager becomes eroded.

These comments are not designed to persuade you that you must be a company person who never questions and who identifies totally with the employer. Instead, the only points to be made are:

- The existence of your dual status is a reality that must be recognized.
- The existence of dual status does not mean that it must create divided loyalties; reviewing again this chapter's introductory comments may be helpful in resolving any contrary feelings you may have.
- The dual status issue exists for all supervisory, managerial, and administrative personnel and most of them have been successful in resolving any mixed feelings this may have created.
- The dual status can produce conflicts on a recurring basis or you consistently may find yourself more comfortable in an employee rather than an employer role. If this happens, then only you can decide whether it is possible to resolve the conflicts or whether you would prefer to not have the stress, strain, and challenge of a supervisory position.

But be cautious. Do not jump too hastily to the conclusion that the supervisory life is not for you or that you will never be able to resolve the problem of being pulled in two directions. Particularly for supervisors promoted from employee ranks, there are many changes in role, in employees' perceptions of you, and in others' expectations of you.

Frequently, these changes cannot be accommodated instantaneously so if difficulties develop, seek assistance. The experiences of others—managerial programs on role conflict, or stress, or other related topics—and the support of your peers and of those to whom you report can be of tremendous help and should be sought out.

Part II

Employment Law

Chapter 3

The National Labor Relations Act

THE NEED TO KNOW THE ACT

Whether you are in public or private employment, familiarity with the National Labor Relations Act (the NLRA or the Act) is a definite asset. While the NLRA—a federal statute governing relationships among unions, employers, and employees—covers only private employers, its provisions and concepts have been adopted in modified form by many public employment entities.

In addition, a basic knowledge of the NLRA is critical even if your facility has no union contracts because, as is discussed later, the Act's protections are not limited to union employees. To the contrary, the Act can require that you reinstate nonsupervisory employees who are not covered by a union contract if, for example, you terminate them "because of" union activity or if, as a second example, you terminate them because they collectively decide to stop working to enforce demands for improved working conditions.

This chapter analyzes:

- who the Act covers
- what the Act requires
- what the Act's enforcement agency and procedures are
- what specific issues are of importance to health care employers.

STRUCTURE OF THE ACT—AN OVERVIEW

The Act's Evolution

The NLRA in its present form actually represents a series of federal statutes. In 1935, Congress passed the National Labor Relations Act, also known as the

Wagner Act, as a means of encouraging collective bargaining and protecting employees who engage in such activities. Only employer "unfair labor practices" were prohibited by the original Act.

In 1947, Congress passed the Labor Management Relations Act—the Taft-Hartley amendments. These attempted to fine-tune the NLRA by prohibiting union abuses or unfair labor practices, deleting supervisors from coverage, guaranteeing employers the right of free speech, etc. These amendments also excluded nonprofit hospitals from coverage.

In 1959, the Labor Management Reporting and Disclosure (Landrum-Griffin) Act was passed. These amendments to the NLRA were designed in part to encourage union democracy by providing some regulation of unions' internal procedures and actions toward members.

Finally, in 1974, the Health Care Amendments to the NLRA were passed to bring nonprofit hospitals under the Act's coverage again.

Unless a precise reference to one of the previously mentioned federal statutes is required for clarity, the obligations imposed on employers, employees and labor organizations under this series of federal legislation are collectively referred to here as simply the NLRA or the Act.

Basic Structure of the Act

The Act as now constituted provides the basic framework, or ground rules, for labor relations in private health care institutions across the country. This objective is implemented primarily by sections 7, 8, and 9 of the Act:

- Section 7 defines the protected rights of employees.
- Section 8 prohibits the commission of certain unfair labor practices by employers or unions.
- Section 9 establishes the rules governing the determination of appropriate bargaining units and the conduct of elections.

The National Labor Relations Board (the NLRB or the Board) is the federal agency responsible for ensuring compliance with the Act. The Board is assisted by the enforcement and remedial provisions in section 10 of the Act.

Coverage of Employers

The Act covers all employers engaged in interstate commerce; however, to avoid inconsistent assertions of jurisdiction, the Board has developed written jurisdictional guidelines. These list, for each industry, the amount of revenues, purchases, or other monetary transactions that will lead to the assertion of Board jurisdiction on the basis that the employer significantly affects interstate commerce.

If your employer is covered by the Act, then your facility is not subject to any parallel labor relations legislation your state may have enacted. The Act preempts or takes over the entire field of labor relations for covered employers. Thus, states cannot regulate issues relating to an employer's recognition of unions, peaceful strikes, unfair labor practices, or other areas arguably falling within matters subject to the Act.

Role of the Supervisor

Since most private health care employers, particularly hospitals, are covered by the Act, you should have a general familiarity or a working knowledge of its provisions and requirements. In addition, and as a supervisor, you are considered an agent of your employer and thus what you do or do not do can be attributed to your employer. Accordingly, your actions could result in a Board finding that your employer has committed an unfair labor practice, including any resulting financial liability. Your actions could even result in an NLRB election's being set aside based upon illegal or improper employer activity.

However, an encouraging note is in order: Do not be paralyzed into total silence and inaction because you are afraid of violating the Act's ground rules or because you are concerned that some risk might result. The filing of unfair labor practice charges or other claims under the Act does not automatically mean that they are meritorious or that any liability exists.

Supervisors should not believe that they have failed in some way simply because a charge has been filed, or even because the Board may have found a violation of the Act. Many of its provisions are technical in nature, and violations can be inadvertent and in good faith. The main error to avoid is a studied ignorance of the Act's requirements; and, the primary point to be emphasized is that a basic knowledge of your employer's obligations under the Act can help reduce the number of charges, invalid or valid, and lessen the cost and time consumed by Board proceedings.

For these reasons, this chapter is designed to cover the most common features of the Act, the mechanics of its provisions, and topics of particular interest to health care supervisors. This material is not designed to turn you into a labor lawyer; its purpose is to give you the ability to identify and avoid potential problems and to seek further assistance as necessary.

In view of changing Board and court interpretations of the Act's provisions, no one should apologize for seeking labor relations or legal assistance as necessary. The only mistake to be avoided is the failure to identify the problems and to seek out appropriate help in a timely fashion.

HEALTH CARE INSTITUTIONS

Definition of Health Care Employer

When passed in 1935, the Act contained no exemption for health care employers but in 1947 the Taft-Hartley Amendments specifically excluded nonprofit hospitals from the definition of an employer. After 1947, the Board voluntarily declined to assert jurisdiction over proprietary hospitals and did not change that position until 1967.[1] A primary rationale for the Board's change in position was its conclusion that the growth in the number of proprietary facilities substantiated their impact on interstate commerce.

The Health Care Amendments of 1974 again redefined an employer to include nonprofit health care institutions. Thus, the Act's current definition of health care institutions is: "The term 'health care institution' shall include any hospital, convalescent hospital, health maintenance organization, health clinic, nursing home, extended care facility, or other institution devoted to the care of sick, infirm, or aged persons."[2]

With these amendments, the Act now covers all private health care institutions falling within that definition and without regard to whether the employer is a proprietary "for-profit" institution or a nonprofit facility. The only condition is that the employer be engaged in interstate commerce. The Board's monetary guidelines for the assertion of jurisdiction over health care institutions are as follows:

- nursing homes, visiting nurse associations, and related facilities with gross revenues of more than $100,000 per year
- proprietary and nonprofit hospitals and other health care institutions with gross revenues above $250,000 per year.[3]

Federal, state, municipal, and other public hospitals are exempt.

Private health care employers who do not meet these jurisdictional guidelines are not subject to the Act and may or may not be covered by state labor relations laws. Some courts have held that states cannot regulate labor relations for employers not covered by the Act but others have ruled to the contrary, believing that a no man's land should not exist.

Unique Health Care Provisions

The 1974 Health Care Amendments also added to the Act the following provisions specifically adapted to the unique characteristics of the health care industry:

1. Unions must give at least ten days' advance written notice of the date and time for a threatened strike.[4]
2. The Federal Mediation and Conciliation Service (FMCS) has the authority to conduct mandatory mediation of contract negotiation disputes.[5]
3. The FMCS also can appoint a Board of Inquiry to make recommendations on issues in dispute during contract negotiations.[6]
4. Unions that wish to renegotiate collective bargaining agreements must give health care employers 90 days' notice of their intention to terminate or modify the agreement as well as a 60-day notice to the FMCS. For new contract negotiations, however, a union need only give a 30-day notice to the FMCS.[7]
5. Employees objecting to mandatory payment of union dues on religious grounds have the option of donating equivalent monies to a nonreligious charity, an option subsequently extended to nonhealth care employees covered by the Act.[8]

SECTION 7 EMPLOYEE RIGHTS

What the Act Protects

Section 7 is the foundation of the Act. It protects the rights of employees to band together by stating that:

> [e]mployees shall have the right to self-organization, to form, join, or assist labor organizations, to bargain collectively through representatives of their own choosing, and to engage in other concerted activities for the purpose of collective bargaining or other mutual aid or protection. . . .[9]

Section 7 also provides that employees shall have the right to refrain from any or all of these same concerted activities except to the extent that a collective bargaining contract may require membership in a labor organization (or payment of dues) as a condition of employment. Section 7, then, is an industrial guarantee of employee rights to be protected by section 8's prohibition of employer or union conduct that infringes on those rights.

Protected Concerted Activity

The kind of employee rights protected by section 7 include the right:

- to complain about working conditions with, or to, or on behalf of other employees

- to discuss, advocate, and actively strive toward unionization by soliciting other employees and/or distributing literature, subject to consistently enforced no-solicitation, no-distribution policies
- to strike on their own behalf, or to honor a picket line established by another group of employees or unions, even if the employees striking or honoring another picket line are nonunion.

These examples illustrate the varied kinds of activities protected by the Act; however, countless other kinds of activities also are protected. Although there is no set definition for what constitutes a protected employee activity, it must contain two elements:

1. The activity must be concerted.
2. The activity must be, in the language of section 7, "for the purpose of collective bargaining or other mutual aid or protection."

Concerted Activity

If a group of employees act together, or if one employee expressly acts as the representative of a group, this clearly would be concerted activity. Yet until 1984, the NLRB also followed the doctrine of implied concertedness.[10] Under that doctrine, an employee acting alone whose actions were unknown to other employees (and perhaps even of no actual interest to them) could be engaging in concerted activity where, for example, the employee had:

- filed a complaint concerning the employer's alleged violation of state safety provisions[11]
- attempted to enforce rights contained in a collective bargaining agreement[12]
- claimed state workers' compensation benefits from a state tribunal[13]
- filed a claim for state unemployment benefits[14]
- requested receipt of an individual pay increase where a common pay system was in effect,[15] etc.

The Board's concept of implied concerted activities was not received enthusiastically by all appellate courts and in 1984 it abandoned this concept, adopting the following standard:

> In general, to find an employee's activity to be "concerted," we shall require that it be engaged in with or on the authority of other employees, and not solely by and on behalf of the employee himself. Once the activity is found to be concerted, an 8(a)(1) violation will be found if, in

addition, the employer knew of the concerted nature of the employee's activity, the concerted activity was protected by the Act [i.e., was for mutual aid or protection], and the adverse employment action at issue (e.g., discharge) was motivated by the employee's protected concerted activity.[16]

Even under the Board's new standard, one that requires some factual evidence of group or collective activity, steps by an individual employee to enforce a collective bargaining agreement still may be concerted activity.[17] For this reason, and also because the Board may change its standard again or apply the new standard in varying ways depending upon the facts of a particular case, the exercise of extreme caution would be appropriate.

If the existence of concerted activity is arguable, you may wish to avoid becoming a test case by ensuring that no disciplinary or other retaliatory action is taken because of an employee's activities concerning terms and conditions of employment, even if only one individual is involved.

Mutual Aid or Protection

To be protected concerted activity, your employee(s)' activity not only must be concerted, it also must be one engaged in for purposes of self-organization, collective bargaining, or other mutual aid or protection. While the phrase "mutual aid or protection" is difficult to define with any great precision, the following are examples of actions previously found to be legitimate subjects of concerted activity:

- distributing literature concerning legislation indirectly affecting working conditions[18]
- criticizing the employer publicly during organizational efforts[19]
- protesting changes in operating room assignments and on-call procedures[20]
- seeking improvements in wages, hours, and other terms and conditions of employment
- refusing to use an employer's grievance procedure as the sole mechanism for resolving disputes with the employer[21]
- hiring an attorney to present the employees' concerns regarding the assignment of a single registered nurse to an emergency department night shift.[22]

For the health care industry, the Board appears to be attempting to draw a distinction between concerted activity by health professionals that impacts on wages, hours, and terms or conditions of employment in contrast to generalized protests concerning patient care or the quality of such care.[23] Yet since patient care issues also can be characterized as involving employee workload, employee safety, ability to function, etc.,[24] determining what kinds of health care employee activities constitute protected concerted activity frequently calls for additional or outside labor relations or legal advice.

Section 7 Rights for Nonsupervisory Employees

While it is customary to think of section 7's "protected" rights as being exercised in the union context, they clearly apply to nonunion employees as well.[25] Therefore, you must take care not to penalize any nonsupervisory employee who engages in protected concerted activities and that you observe the same standards and guidelines as outlined above for all such employees.

SECTION 9 AND REPRESENTATION QUESTIONS

An Employer's Perspective

Employers generally prefer a nonunion work force, not because it saves money (it can be as costly as unionization, if not more so), but because it allows for management flexibility and the opportunity to treat employees as individuals rather than as common denominators under a collective bargaining agreement. The practical and philosophical arguments behind unionization or resistance to unionization are not debated here, however. Instead, you should be aware that:

- A key problem leading to unionization often relates to supervisory-employee relationships.
- Employers must honor certain guarantees established by the Act if unionization is attempted (e.g., employers cannot violate employee rights protected by the Act or the laboratory conditions that must prevail during NLRB elections).
- The Act contains certain procedures and requirements for holding an NLRB election to determine whether employees do or do not want to be represented by a labor organization.

To Organize or Not To Organize

A union is not just a group of employees, it is a political and business institution, with needs and goals of its own. Thus, a union's attempt to organize a group of employees may reflect a variety of causes. One or more of your employees may be discontented and approach the union directly. Or, the union may have targeted a group of your employees as a potential source of additional income or your employer as a base from which to engage in further organizing. More rarely, an already organized employer may exert pressure on a union to organize competitors who still are union free.[26] Whatever the reason, the union's approach most likely will be a pragmatic one based on a realistic assessment of the probabilities of success.

Methods for Achieving Employer Recognition

If a union can persuade a substantial portion or a majority of your employees in a potential bargaining unit that they need or should have a union, it may demand recognition from your employer. Recognition can be achieved in three ways:

1. The union can request that the employer voluntarily agree to recognize it as the exclusive bargaining agent of the employees in that unit.
2. The union can file a petition for an election to be conducted by the NLRB; if it wins a valid election it will be the employees' exclusive bargaining representative.
3. The NLRB, in the much more infrequent case in which an employer has committed flagrant unfair labor practices that preclude a fair election, can order the employer to bargain with the union even if the union lost an NLRB election and even if, at the time of the Board's order, the union does not have majority status.

First Method: Voluntary Recognition of Unions

An employer may learn of an attempt to organize its employees well before the union makes a formal approach or contact. Indeed, you might even be approached by employees who tell you of the union's drive or their interest in unionization. Sometimes, and even before the union has succeeded in organizing many employees, it may formally notify the employer of its organizing effort. Eventually, however, the employer will receive a formal request for recognition from the union. When this happens, the union frequently offers to "prove" its claim of majority authorization by what is known as a card check.

Authorization cards are the most common organizational tactic. Basically, the union organizer (who could be but need not be employed by your facility) asks your employees to sign a card designating the union as their collective bargaining representative and authorizing the union to request recognition from your employer. The United States Supreme Court has recognized that authorization cards may be a valid indication of union majority status sufficient to impose upon your employer the duty to bargain with the union.[27]

There are two types of situations in which a union may be able to use authorization cards to become your employees' collective bargaining representative without winning an NLRB election:

1. Where your employer has committed unfair labor practices that make a fair election unlikely and that tend to undermine the union's majority status, the cards are considered to be a better indicator of majority employee preference than a tainted election.[28]
2. Where your employer agrees to determine the union's majority status by a card check, this can reveal whether the union has gathered validly signed authorization cards from a majority of your employees.[29]

There are drawbacks to the use of authorization cards. A card check usually consists of comparing the signed authorization cards with your employer's personnel records, W-2 forms, or other documents containing the employees' signatures. For a number of reasons, an employer acts unwisely by agreeing to voluntarily recognize a union based on such "proof" of majority status. The chief problem with authorization cards from an employer's perspective, however, is that they often are the products of misrepresentation and consequently seldom reflect the employees' true sentiments:

- Union organizers have been known to tell employees that the cards will be used only to get an election, or to gather information, or that the employee must sign the card to vote, yet the last is untrue and the first two representations are misleading since the card actually can be used by the union to seek exclusive recognition without an election.
- An employee may have signed as a favor to a coworker or to stop another employee from pestering about the cards, or the phrasing of the card may be ambiguous, or the employees may have been coerced into signing.
- Some employees may have changed their minds after signing.

Another drawback is that the cards generally are signed before the employer has had an opportunity to respond to the union's charges. This means that use of the cards to establish union representation deprives the employer of its right to communicate with employees concerning the underlying issues and it deprives your employees of an opportunity to make an informed decision.

Another danger from this type of "proof" is that it can result in premature recognition of a union as an exclusive bargaining agent, thus violating the Act. If, for example, you recognize a union that does not actually represent a majority of your employees in the bargaining unit, an unfair labor practice is committed, and another union still can attempt to organize the same group of employees. Your good faith but erroneous belief that a union does in fact represent a majority of your employees is not a defense to premature recognition.[30]

Thus, on balance, when employers have not committed unfair labor practices in response to organizing, they are legally and practically safe in refusing to honor a demand for voluntary recognition and can insist that they will grant no recognition unless and until the union has been certified in an appropriate bargaining unit following an NLRB election.[31]

Rival Union Situations

A particularly dangerous situation occurs when one union demands voluntary recognition and a rival union also claims employee support from the same group of employees. The NLRB has held that an employer violates section 8(a)(2) of the Act when it recognizes and negotiates a contract with one union at a time when a rival union has raised a "real question concerning representation."[32] The NLRB has modified this doctrine to:

1. allow for employer recognition of a majority union unless the rival union files an NLRB petition,[33] and to
2. allow for continued negotiations between an employer and an existing union during the processing of the NLRB petition and NLRB election.[34]

Since the NLRB's modified doctrine may be subject to further change, and since variations in facts may affect your employer's legal status, legal counsel is essential whenever claims from rival unions exist.

Perils and Pitfalls

When faced with a demand for recognition from a union, the safest approach is a blunt but unambiguous refusal to recognize the union or any proof it offers in support of its demand, saying that the question should be decided through the NLRB election processes. Any other action could prejudice your own employees' right to an election and make your employer vulnerable to subsequent unfair labor practice charges.

Do not even attempt to poll your employees to determine their sentiments. Everyone is curious, and an employer—or you—may react to knowledge of an organizing drive by conducting an employee poll to find out how much support the union has and what your employees' feelings are. Such polls are unwise for two reasons: (1) the Board rules for conducting polls are very strict and any deviation can result in a violation of the Act[35] and (2) should your poll confirm the union's claim of majority status, then your employer may, by that fact alone, be obliged to recognize and bargain with the union without any opportunity to present the employer's perspective.[36]

Second Method: NLRB Secret Ballot Elections

The preferred and most widely used method for a union to become the employees' recognized representative is by an NLRB-supervised secret ballot election.

Types of Representation Elections

The NLRB election process is commenced by the filing of a request for an election, called a "petition" (Exhibit 3–1), at the nearest NLRB regional office. A petition can be filed for:

- an election to determine the employees' exclusive collective bargaining representative, if any, which is the most common type of election petition filed (RC case)
- an election at the request of the employer where a union has claimed that it represents a majority of the employees (RM case)
- decertifying, or having recognition withdrawn from, an existing labor organization (RD case)
- removing a union shop (mandatory dues) agreement from an already recognized labor organization (UD case).

Petition Requirements

The petition for an election must be in writing and signed and either be notarized or contain a declaration that its contents are true and correct. It also must contain certain formal information regarding the employer, the number of employees affected, and a description of the bargaining unit sought by the union. The bargaining unit description is extremely important: it may be an improper employee group (which should be challenged by the employer) but if it is proper, it will determine who has the right to vote and to be represented if the union wins.

If the petition is filed for an election to select a collective bargaining representative, to decertify a representative, or to withdraw the union's authority to negotiate union shop contract provisions, it must be accompanied by a showing of interest, which is proof acceptable to the NLRB that at least 30 percent of the employees in the bargaining unit support the petition. This rule does not apply to a union that is a party to a current or recently expired contract, to a union intervening in an election already requested by another union, or in expedited elections held under section 8(b)(7) of the Act.

As a practical matter, a union seeking to become recognized by your employer is unlikely to file a petition unless it has signed up at least 50 percent of the employees in the appropriate bargaining group. Experience has shown that most of the unions are at their peak strength at the time the petition is filed. The real issue, therefore, is whether the union can prevent its support from being eroded below 50 percent-plus of those employees who eventually vote.

NLRB Processing of Petition

When a petition is filed and supported by the 30 percent showing of interest, the Board will set a tentative date for a representation hearing. A hearing may not actually be held, however, since it is possible for the employer and union(s) involved to consent to an election if all issues pertinent to the election can be resolved such as the scope of the bargaining unit (who can vote and who would be represented by a union), supervisory status of individual employees, whether an existing contract bars the union's request for an election, the date for the voting, etc. This procedure allows both parties to avoid a representation hearing at the NLRB regional office.

If the parties do not consent to an election, an NLRB representation hearing will be held, generally within three weeks after the filing of the petition, to receive evidence on the disputed issues. The regional director (administrative head of the applicable NLRB regional office) then issues findings and, if appropriate, will direct that an election be held on a certain date (again, generally within three weeks from the date of the "Direction of Election"). Less frequently, the regional director may elect to transfer the hearing record and case to the NLRB in Washington.

If a consent election is held, the advantages of this method are: (1) each party has a degree of control over the determination of the election issues, which they might not have if the Board decided the issues, and (2) the expense and delay of a representation hearing are avoided. Consent elections are favored by the Board, and regional offices are encouraged to facilitate them wherever possible.[37]

There are two types of consent agreements: (1) "Agreement for Consent Election," or (2) "Stipulation for Certification under Consent Election." Under both approaches, the parties agree that the election will be conducted by a regional director. However, under the Agreement all disputed issues arising out of the election are decided by the regional director while under a Stipulation, and for most issues, the parties preserve their right of appeal to the Board in Washington.[38]

The Stipulation has the advantage of protecting the parties from a perceived bias of a particular regional office, while an Agreement, by cutting off the right of NLRB review, limits costs. Since the consequences of a consent election or the type of consent election can be far-reaching, however, no decision should be made as to which type of agreement, if either, you should enter into without consulting with someone knowledgeable about election procedures, the legal issues pertinent to the election, and your NLRB regional office.

Within seven days after the NLRB regional office approves an election agreement or directs an election, your employer must submit what is called an "excelsior list" containing the names and addresses of all eligible employee voters who will participate.[39] The regional director then makes this list available to all parties.

Scope of Bargaining Units

The scope of the bargaining unit—who will and will not vote in the election and be represented by the union if it wins—frequently is the most important single issue to be resolved before the voting takes place. What is and what is not an appropriate bargaining unit is a difficult and complex subject. The NLRA contains

Exhibit 3-1 Sample of an NLRB Election Petition

PETITION

DO NOT WRITE IN THIS SPACE
CASE NO.
DATE FILED

INSTRUCTIONS.—Submit an original and four (4) copies of this Petition to the NLRB Regional Office in the Region in which the employer concerned is located.
If more space is required for any one item, attach additional sheets, numbering item accordingly.

The Petitioner alleges that the following circumstances exist and requests that the National Labor Relations Board proceed under its proper authority pursuant to Section 9 of the National Labor Relations Act.

1. Purpose of this Petition (*If box RC, RM, or RD is checked and a charge under Section 8(b)(7) of the Act has been filed involving the Employer named herein, the statement following the description of the type of petition shall not be deemed made.*)

(*Check one*)

☐ RC—CERTIFICATION OF REPRESENTATIVE —A substantial number of employees wish to be represented for purposes of collective bargaining by Petitioner and Petitioner desires to be certified as representative of the employees.

☐ RM—REPRESENTATION (EMPLOYER PETITION)—One or more individuals or labor organizations have presented a claim to Petitioner to be recognized as the representative of employees of Petitioner.

☐ RD—DECERTIFICATION—A substantial number of employees assert that the certified or currently recognized bargaining representative is no longer their representative.

☐ UD—WITHDRAWAL OF UNION SHOP AUTHORITY—Thirty percent (30%) or more of employees in a bargaining unit covered by an agreement between their employer and a labor organization desire that such authority be rescinded.

☐ UC—UNIT CLARIFICATION—A labor organization is currently recognized by employer, but petitioner seeks clarification of placement of certain employees: (*Check one*) ☐ In unit not previously certified
☐ In unit previously certified in Case No. _____

☐ AC—AMENDMENT OF CERTIFICATION—Petitioner seeks amendment of certification issued in Case No. _____

Attach statement describing the specific amendment sought.

2. NAME OF EMPLOYER	EMPLOYER REPRESENTATIVE TO CONTACT	PHONE NO

3. ADDRESS(ES) OF ESTABLISHMENT(S) INVOLVED (*Street and number, city, State, and ZIP Code*)

4a. TYPE OF ESTABLISHMENT (*Factory, mine, wholesaler, etc.*)	4b. IDENTIFY PRINCIPAL PRODUCT OR SERVICE

5. Unit Involved (*In UC petition, describe PRESENT bargaining unit and attach description of proposed clarification.*)

Included

Excluded

6a. NUMBER OF EMPLOYEES IN UNIT:
PRESENT _____
PROPOSED (BY UC/AC)

6b. IS THIS PETITION SUPPORTED BY 30% OR MORE OF THE EMPLOYEES IN THE UNIT?

(If you have checked box RC in 1 above, check and complete EITHER item 7a or 7b, whichever is applicable)

YES ☐ NO ☐

Not applicable in RM, UC, and AC

7a. ☐ Request for recognition as Bargaining Representative was made on .... (Month, day, year) and Employer declined recognition on or about .... (Month, day, year) (If no reply received, so state)

7b. ☐ Petitioner is currently recognized as Bargaining Representative and desires certification under the act.

8. Recognized or Certified Bargaining Agent (If there is none, so state)

NAME .... AFFILIATION ....

ADDRESS .... DATE OF RECOGNITION OR CERTIFICATION ....

9. DATE OF EXPIRATION OF CURRENT CONTRACT, IF ANY (Show month, day, and year) .... 10. IF YOU HAVE CHECKED BOX UD IN 1 ABOVE, SHOW HERE THE DATE OF EXECUTION OF AGREEMENT GRANTING UNION SHOP (Month, day, and year)

11a. IS THERE NOW A STRIKE OR PICKETING AT THE EMPLOYER'S ESTABLISHMENT(S) INVOLVED?   YES .... NO .... 11b. IF SO, APPROXIMATELY HOW MANY EMPLOYEES ARE PARTICIPATING?

11c. THE EMPLOYER HAS BEEN PICKETED BY OR ON BEHALF OF .... (Insert name) .... A LABOR ORGANIZATION, OF .... (Insert address) .... SINCE .... (Month, day, year)

12. ORGANIZATIONS OR INDIVIDUALS OTHER THAN PETITIONER (AND OTHER THAN THOSE NAMED IN ITEMS 8 AND 11c), WHICH HAVE CLAIMED RECOGNITION AS REPRESENTATIVES AND OTHER ORGANIZATIONS AND INDIVIDUALS KNOWN TO HAVE A REPRESENTATIVE INTEREST IN ANY EMPLOYEES IN THE UNIT DESCRIBED IN ITEM 5 ABOVE.   (IF NONE, SO STATE.)

NAME	AFFILIATION	ADDRESS	DATE OF CLAIM (Required only if Petition is filed by Employer)

I declare that I have read the above petition and that the statements therein are true to the best of my knowledge and belief.

.... (Petitioner and affiliation, if any)

By .... (Title, if any)
   (Signature of representative or person filing petition)

Address .... (Telephone number)
   (Street and number, city, State, and ZIP Code)

WILLFULLY FALSE STATEMENT ON THIS PETITION CAN BE PUNISHED BY FINE AND IMPRISONMENT (U.S. CODE, TITLE 18, SECTION 1001)

Source: National Labor Relations Board, Washington, D.C. 20570.

certain basic rules that the Board must follow. For example, professional and nonprofessional employees must be in different units (unless a majority of the professional employees agree otherwise); guard employees cannot be put into a unit containing nonguards, and guards cannot be represented by a labor organization that admits nonguards as members.[40]

Aside from these minimum statutory requirements, the Board has relied on certain factors to determine the appropriateness of a bargaining unit. Generally speaking, there must be a "community of interest" among the employees in the proposed unit concerning terms and conditions of employment, as well as some geographical and physical proximity. Since the NLRB has ruled that the unit must only be *an* appropriate one, not necessarily *the* most appropriate, the Board generally has wide latitude in determining the unit's scope. The only way an employer generally can appeal the Board's bargaining unit determination is to proceed to an NLRB election and then, if the union wins, refuse to bargain. If the Board subsequently seeks enforcement of its bargaining order against the employer by a United States Court of Appeals, the employer can defend on the basis of the improper bargaining unit.

Campaign Conduct

The period prior to the election is used by both employers and unions for vigorous campaigning. Although what you have and have not done before the petition's filing may be the determining factor, you never should underestimate the value of discussing the employer's position with your staff. To do so, you should be aware that the Board and the courts have developed general rules for deciding what is and what is not acceptable conduct during this critical phase. Your failure to follow these rules can result in an election's being set aside, and a second (or even third) one's being held.

The primary rule of thumb is that there can be no threat of reprisal, promise of benefits, or similar action. [41] Brief examples of the types of conduct falling within this rule of thumb—and conduct you should avoid—are as follows:

- asking employees about their union activities or how they are going to vote (even if they initiate the conversation or say that it will be off the record)
- giving the impression that you are spying on the employees' union activities (driving by their meeting location is not a good idea)
- having an overly broad (invalid) solicitation and distribution policy
- cracking down on employees when your employer's policies were not enforced consistently before the campaign
- taking disciplinary action against employees because of their union activities, or changing working conditions, compensation, etc., when it is not in accordance with a previously established and regular practice

- soliciting employee grievances or problems that you then correct
- granting additional or new benefits to induce employees to vote against the union (but you can implement a regularly scheduled wage increase or an increase decided upon before, but implemented after, the petition is filed).

In addition, actions such as forging campaign materials (which does not allow the employee-voters to recognize the materials as campaign propaganda) or altering official Board documents to reflect endorsement of either party constitute objectionable conduct.[42]

However, if you observe these and other related guidelines (described more fully in Appendix 3–A), then you and your employer are free to tell employees why you believe they should not vote for unionization, to inform them of known facts, and to express your opinions concerning the issues raised by the election. Furthermore, you should do so because if you do not, your employees will not have access to all pertinent information and considerations before voting.

Election Procedures

The election itself is always conducted by an NLRB agent and almost invariably at the workplace. In health care institutions, polling may be held at different times and even on different days to enable all employees to vote.

The election is always by secret ballot and each side has the right to be represented at the polling by designated observers. These observers cannot be supervisory employees (and supervisors cannot be present in the polling area); this is because the NLRB views your mere presence as inherently coercive or threatening. In addition to ensuring a fair election by monitoring objectionable conduct, observers have the duty to challenge voters who, for example, have not sufficiently identified themselves. Objectionable conduct at the polls includes campaigning in the vicinity; such activity often will lead to the election's being set aside.

To win the election, the union must receive more than 50 percent of the votes actually cast, not 50 percent of those employees eligible to vote. The ballots are counted at the closing of the polls and the parties have five days to file objections to the election with the NLRB. The ballots, the eligibility list, and the list of challenged voters are retained by the Board to prevent recrimination and harassment by any party.

Postelection Rights and Remedies

If any party to the election files objections within the five-day period and the objections are factually disputed, the regional director may hold a hearing to resolve them. If the regional director determines that the objections are valid, the election is set aside and a new one ordered. If, on the other hand, the regional director determines the objections are without merit, the election is certified. If any party is unhappy with the regional director's decision, it may appeal to the NLRB in Washington, D.C.

Third Method: Bargaining Order Remedy

The third major method by which a union is legally recognized as the exclusive representative of the employees occurs far less frequently than either of the two others. It arises when a union demands recognition and/or an election is held and the employer engages in activity that the Board considers so unfair that a rerun election would be futile.

In such circumstances, the Board may order the employer to bargain with the union.[43] While generally the union must demonstrate that it had majority support among the employees at some point during its demand for recognition, the NLRB has issued orders to bargain even where the union never attained majority status among the employees. The Board's right to issue such orders, absent a showing of union majority status at some point in time, has not been upheld unanimously by the federal courts.[44]

UNFAIR LABOR PRACTICES

Section 8 of the Act is designed to protect the employee rights guaranteed in section 7 by outlawing certain unfair labor practices. Section 8(a) lists employer unfair labor practices and section 8(b) unlawful union conduct.

Section 8(a) and Employer Unfair Labor Practices

Restraining, Coercing, or Interfering with Employees' Rights—
Section 8(a)(1)

The essential element of an 8(a)(1) unfair labor practice is its emphasis on interference with the section 7 rights of employees. An employer is prohibited from interfering with, restraining, or coercing employees who are exercising their right to engage in activities protected by section 7, such as forming, joining, or assisting labor organizations, or engaging in collective bargaining.[45] The terms "interfere, restrain, or coerce" are not defined but they clearly include such actions as deliberate attempts to prevent employees from voting in an election, making express or implied threats of reprisal for joining a union, and subjecting employees to surveillance or questioning concerning their union interests and activities.

The critical factor is: Does your action, objectively speaking, have a tendency to interfere with employees' rights? If it does, then 8(a)(1) may be violated, no matter how innocent your intentions. This is not to say that all employer action that potentially could inhibit union activity is prohibited. Section 8(c) guarantees an employer the right to express its point of view and to attempt to persuade employees to reject a union, provided that your expression of views contains no threat of reprisal or force or promise of benefit.

Assistance to Labor Organization—Section 8(a)(2)

The Act does not simply prohibit interference with union activities; it also bars employer domination or interference "with the formation or administration of any labor organization" as well as precluding employer contributions of financial or other aid.[46]

An employer must remain neutral and not materially assist a union in any way whatsoever if it is to avoid charges of domination, interference, or assistance. Evidence of unlawful activity can include a suggestion by you that an in-house union limited to the employees of a hospital should be formed after an outside union has commenced organizing, or if you provide or pay for a meeting place for the union, or if supervisors assist with the filing of NLRB election petitions or provide other types of aid such as drafting constitutions and bylaws, etc.

Your good faith will be no defense to this charge. Even greater caution is warranted when you note that for a labor organization to exist, the basic element required is that a group of employees get together for the purpose of discussing or dealing with their employer concerning wages, hours, and working conditions. Thus, forming or aiding "employee associations," employee advisory committees, and similar employee groups can be a violation of 8(a)(2) under many circumstances.[47]

Discrimination Based on Union Membership—Section 8(a)(3)

This unfair labor practice occurs where there is intentional discrimination "because of" union activities. One obvious example is granting general wage increases but manipulating them in such a way that union leaders do not get them. As another example, you might be tempted to tighten up on your rules because a union is attempting to organize or has been recognized. It is no defense to say that the policy has always existed on paper if in fact it was never enforced prior to unionization.

Still another example, and a frequent allegation by employees and unions, occurs when a worker is discharged, reputedly because of union activities. Two facts can lead the Board to a conclusion that the Act may have been violated: (1) the employee is a known union adherent, and (2) the individual has been fired.

If these two facts are present, you must be prepared to show a legitimate motivation for your disciplinary action if a charge is filed. The best way to avoid 8(a)(3) charges, therefore, is to apply your working conditions uniformly, without favoritism, and to adequately investigate and support your reasons for taking disciplinary action.

Reprisal for Participating in NLRB Procedures—Section 8(a)(4)

If the Act is to be enforced, the Board's processes must be available to employees without fear of retribution. This is accomplished by 8(a)(4), which makes it an unfair labor practice for employers to discharge or otherwise discriminate against employees simply because they have filed charges or given testimony under the Act. So broad is this prohibition that an employer can violate the Act for taking action against an employee who files charges even though it is clearly demonstrated that the charges are false.

A further example of prohibited conduct would be if you insisted that a striker withdraw an unfair labor practice charge before reinstatement to employment. However, if you are involved in an NLRB hearing, you may pay any normal wages lost by employees subpoenaed by your employer without being required to make the same payment to union witnesses who are employees.

Refusal To Bargain—Section 8(a)(5)

Once a union has legally established itself as the exclusive bargaining representative of your employees, the Act imposes the obligation for your employer to bargain in good faith with the recognized union. Although simply stated, this unfair labor practice is perhaps the most complex in its application, for two reasons:

1. The Board, in determining whether there has been a refusal to bargain, must examine your employer's attitude, its willingness to meet at reasonable times and confer in good faith, the entire course of negotiations and surrounding circumstances, etc. However, the law only requires your employer (and the union) to bargain in good faith. It does not, indeed cannot, compel an employer to make concessions, to agree to any particular union proposal, or actually to reach agreement on a collective bargaining contract.
2. The duty to bargain exists not only when a union is first recognized and bargaining commences for a contract, but also (a) when a contract is expired and is being renegotiated, and (b) even during the life of an existing contract.

A more detailed treatment of what is and what is not good faith bargaining—and the critical issue of what bargaining is, and is not, required during the term of a contract—is discussed in Chapter 4.

Section 8(b) and Union Unfair Labor Practices

While section 8(b) lists a variety of union unfair labor practices, the primary and most common ones for purposes of this discussion are sections 8(b)(1), (2), (3), (4) and (7).

Restraint of Employees or Employer—Section 8(b)(1)

Just as the Act guarantees employees the right to engage in union activities, section 8(b)(1)(A) also guarantees them the right to not engage in union activities. A union can violate this section in a number of ways. Thus, coercive union statements such as "We have ways of handling people like you that argue against the union" are an unfair labor practice.[48] Likewise, physical threats to or actual violence against employees who refuse to cooperate with the union is prohibited even where the threats are directed against the employer and the employer's agents since they contain an implied threat of harm against employees.[49]

A good example of the distinction between lawful and unlawful conduct includes picketing. While the Board and the courts regard picketing as a lawful means of exerting pressure, mass picketing calculated to deter nonstrikers from working may violate the Act. Thus, if a union strikes your facility and blocks the entrances of your premises, that conduct may be unlawful even though done in a peaceful way.[50]

By contrast, section 8(b)(1)(B) recognizes that employers must be free to choose their own collective bargaining and grievance-handling representatives without any unlawful coercion by the union. As a result, if you are designated to handle grievances at any level of the procedure, the union cannot lawfully refuse to deal with you and attempt to force your employer to choose another representative. Similarly, a union may not refuse to participate in bargaining because of objections to individual members of the employer's bargaining team, just as you are precluded from selecting or objecting to the union's negotiating committee.

Discrimination Based on Union Membership—Section 8(b)(2)

Some examples of conduct prohibited by this section are obvious, such as insisting that an employer discharge an employee for not joining the union or paying dues when the union contract does not impose such an obligation. However, prohibited conduct often is more subtle, such as insistence on a provision in the contract giving the union total control over seniority or granting "superseniority" to employee union stewards where this has no relationship to their responsibilities on behalf of the union. A union also violates 8(b)(2) if it causes or attempts to cause "an employer to discriminate against an employee" in violation of 8(a)(3). This means, for example, that a union cannot lawfully force or attempt to force you or your employer to discriminate against an employee because of the person's activity on behalf of a rival union.

There is an important exception to your employees' right to support (or not support) their recognized union: it is not a violation of 8(b)(2) for a union to enforce union shop or other union security provisions in a collective bargaining contract. (Chapter 4 covers the most typical forms of union security provisions.) Section 8(b)(2) specifically allows a union to discriminate, for example, by requesting or demanding an employee's termination where the person has failed to "tender the periodic dues and the initiation fees uniformly required as a condition of acquiring or retaining membership." The only constraints in section 8(a)(3) are that (1) any such union security provisions must be by agreement between an employer and a properly recognized exclusive bargaining representative (union), and (2) the employee's obligations cannot arise prior to the 30th day of the agreement.

Refusal To Bargain—Section 8(b)(3)

The obligations imposed upon an employer to bargain in good faith apply equally to unions. A typical 8(b)(3) refusal to bargain charge arises when the union strikes over a permissible subject of bargaining (see Chapter 4) or conditions a settlement on the employer's agreement to permissible or illegal bargaining subjects.

Secondary Boycotts—Section 8(b)(4)

The right to strike and to picket have become firmly established principles of federal labor law yet certain types of strikes are forbidden. Thus, strikes and picketing directed against an employer who is a genuine neutral in a labor dispute constitute an unfair labor practice. The simplest example of such a secondary boycott arises in the following manner:

- Union X has a labor dispute with employer A, a blood bank.
- Employer B, a hospital, does business with employer A but has no other connection to employer A.
- Union X strikes the blood bank.
- Union X then pickets the hospital to encourage its employees to join them in a sympathy strike. This is an attempt to persuade the hospital to cease doing business with the blood bank and a means of exerting more pressure on the blood bank.

In this scenario, union X has violated 8(b)(4) since the hospital is a neutral employer and the union may lawfully picket only the blood bank, the employer with which it has a dispute. (See Ally doctrine, *infra,* which is the most notable exception to this general principle.)

Illegal Picketing—Section 8(b)(7)

In certain circumstances, picketing an employer with the object of organizing its employees can be an unfair labor practice. Such picketing is unlawful where:

- The employer has lawfully recognized another union and the picketing occurs at a time when an election would not be appropriate (generally, within one year after the first union has been certified by the NLRB pursuant to an election, or where an existing collective bargaining agreement precludes an NLRB election).
- A valid election has been conducted by the NLRB within the preceding 12 months and the union lost.
- The union fails to file an NLRB representation petition requesting that an election be conducted within a reasonable time after the start of the picketing; but note, a "reasonable period" cannot exceed 30 days.[51]

You should be alert to the fact that such picketing violates the Act only where it is organizational (to persuade employees to join the union) or recognitional (to achieve recognition from the employer). Where the picketing is in protest against an employer's unfair labor practice, or is informational in nature, then 8(b)(7) is not violated even if one of those three circumstances exists.

NLRB Unfair Labor Practice Proceedings

The NLRB's unfair labor practice proceedings are triggered by the filing of an unfair labor practice charge. The Board has standard forms for filing charges. The most commonly used are "Charge Against Employer" (Exhibit 3–2) and "Charge Against Labor Organization or Its Agents" (Exhibit 3–3).

Filing the Charge

An unfair labor practice charge can be filed by an individual, an employer, or a union (called the "charging party"). An individual does not have to be your employee to file a charge against your employer. Regardless of who files the charge, the Act requires that this be done within six months of the alleged unfair labor practice. This time requirement is met where the practice is continuing in nature.

For example, if on January 1, 1985, you enter into a two-year collective bargaining contract that contains two different wage rates for hospital attendants, depending upon whether they do or do not belong to the union, a charge filed on December 1, 1986, will still be timely where you have followed this discriminatory pay practice during the six months prior to December 1.

Processing the Charge

Once an unfair labor practice charge is filed, the Board's procedure generally follows these steps:

Exhibit 3–2 NLRB Form for Charge Against Employer

	DO NOT WRITE IN THIS SPACE
INSTRUCTIONS: File an original and 4 copies of this charge with NLRB regional director for the region in which the alleged unfair labor practice occurred or is occurring.	Case No.
	Date Filed

1. EMPLOYER AGAINST WHOM CHARGE IS BROUGHT

a. Name of Employer		b. Number of Workers Employed	
c. Address of Establishment (Street and number, city, State, and ZIP code)	d. Employer Representative to Contact		e. Phone No.
f. Type of Establishment (Factory, mine, wholesaler, etc.)	g. Identify Principal Product or Service		

h. The above-named employer has engaged in and is engaging in unfair labor practices within the meaning of section 8 (a), subsections (1) and _____ of the National Labor Relations Act,
                                         (List subsections)
and these unfair labor practices are unfair labor practices affecting commerce within the meaning of the Act.

2. Basis of the Charge (Be specific as to facts, names, addresses, plants involved, dates, places, etc.)

By the above and other acts, the above-named employer has interfered with, restrained, and coerced employees in the exercise of the rights guaranteed in Section 7 of the Act.

3. Full Name of Party Filing Charge (If labor organization, give full name, including local name and number)

4a. Address (Street and number, city, State, and ZIP code)	4b. Telephone No.

5. Full Name of National or International Labor Organization of Which It Is an Affiliate or Constituent Unit (To be filled in when charge is filed by a labor organization)

6. DECLARATION

I declare that I have read the above charge and that the statements therein are true to the best of my knowledge and belief.

By _____   _____
   (Signature of representative or person filing charge)   (Title, if any)

Address _____
                              (Telephone number)   (Date)

WILLFULLY FALSE STATEMENTS ON THIS CHARGE CAN BE PUNISHED BY FINE AND IMPRISONMENT (U.S. CODE, TITLE 18, SECTION 1001)

Source: National Labor Relations Board, Washington, D.C. 20570.

Exhibit 3–3 NLRB Form for Charge Against Union

INSTRUCTIONS: *File an original and 3 copies of this charge and an additional copy for each organization, each local and each individual named in item 1 with the NLRB regional director for the region in which the alleged unfair labor practice occurred or is occurring.*	DO NOT WRITE IN THIS SPACE
	Case No.
	Date Filed

1. LABOR ORGANIZATION OR ITS AGENTS AGAINST WHICH CHARGE IS BROUGHT

a. Name	b. Union Representative to Contact	c. Phone No.

d. Address (Street, city, State and ZIP code)

e. The above-named organization(s) or its agents has (have) engaged in and is (are) engaging in unfair labor practices within the meaning of section 8(b), subsection(s) _____ (List Subsections) _____ of the National Labor Relations Act, and these unfair labor practices are unfair labor practices affecting commerce within the meaning of the Act.

2. Basis of the Charge (Be specific as to facts, names, addresses, plants involved, dates, places, etc.)

3. Name of Employer		4. Phone No.
5. Location of Plant Involved (Street, city, State and ZIP code)		6. Employer Representative to Contact
7. Type of Establishment (Factory, mine, wholesaler, etc.)	8. Identify Principal Product or Service	9. No. of Workers Employed

10. Full Name of Party Filing Charge

11. Address of Party Filing Charge (Street, city, State and ZIP code)	12. Telephone No.

13. DECLARATION

I declare that I have read the above charge and that the statements therein are true to the best of my knowledge and belief.

By _____ _____
   (Signature of representative or person making charge)   (Title or office, if any)

Address _____
          (Telephone number)   (Date)

WILLFULLY FALSE STATEMENTS ON THIS CHARGE CAN BE PUNISHED BY FINE AND IMPRISONMENT (U.S. CODE, TITLE 18, SECTION 1001)

Source: National Labor Relations Board, Washington, D.C. 20570.

- The regional office where the charge was filed conducts an investigation and requires that the charging party submit proof in support of the allegations.
- The charged party (which will be your employer if an individual or union files a charge against your facility) also will be requested to submit evidence. Frequently, a Board agent will want to speak to your witnesses directly and/or obtain sworn affidavits. Whether you do or do not provide evidence often is a practical question. For example, if the truth of the allegations hinges on a credibility question (what you said or asked an employee), then the region still may decide to issue a complaint, regardless of the evidence you provide, and your evidence will simply help the attorney prosecuting the case against you to prepare for the unfair labor practice hearing. If, on the other hand, your evidence can demonstrate that in fact no violation occurred, you may wish to provide the evidence in the hope that the charge will be withdrawn by the charging party or, absent withdrawal, that it will be dismissed by the region.
- The region may conclude there is reason to believe the Act has been violated. If so, it will prepare a complaint and serve it on the charged party. This complaint is similar to one in a civil lawsuit in that it sets out the basis for the Board's jurisdiction, a statement of the allegations (usually in very summary fashion), and the sections of the Act allegedly violated. A hearing date also will be set. The charged party then must file its reply or "answer" to the complaint.
- The region may discuss settlement with the charged party before or after a complaint is issued. While the Board has several different kinds of settlement procedures and forms, a common requirement is that the charged party is required to post an NLRB notice stating that it no longer will engage in the prohibited conduct. The settlement agreement also might contain a nonadmission clause stating that the charged party is not admitting a violation of the Act by entering into the settlement.
- An unfair labor practice hearing is held before an administrative law judge if no settlement is reached. An attorney for the general counsel (the prosecuting arm of the Board) has the responsibility for presenting the case. Legal counsel or other representatives of the charging party also may be present and participate. The hearing is very similar to a trial: the general counsel puts on witnesses and evidence, subject to cross-examination, then the charged party puts on its witnesses and evidence, again subject to cross-examination. A transcript or record of the hearing will be made and briefs (each party's written summary of the evidence and its arguments) can be filed.
- The administrative law judge is responsible not only for conducting the unfair labor practice hearing but also for issuing a recommended decision on the allegations in the complaint. If the general counsel or charged party disagrees with that recommended decision, exceptions (a form of appeal) may be filed

with the Board in Washington. The Board then can either adopt the administrative law judge's decision without change, modify it, or reverse it entirely.

- The Board can file a petition for enforcement of its decision with a federal court of appeals if its decision and order are not complied with by the charged party. This simultaneously gives the charged party the opportunity for judicial review. A charged party who loses before the Board also may appeal to the federal appellate courts and subsequently to the United States Supreme Court.

It should be remembered that this listing of the NLRB's unfair labor practice proceedings is only a summary. While the Act imposes some procedural requirements, and there are still more in the Board's own rules and regulations and case-handling manuals, the actual procedure can vary. You should not attempt to use self-help by personally representing your own facility since knowledgeable representation by counsel well versed in NLRB procedures and the Act is a must.

TOPICS OF PARTICULAR SIGNIFICANCE

Definitional Problems

House Staff and Employee Status

The Act covers only "employees," as statutorily defined. There has been a question whether hospital house staff members (interns, residents, and clinical fellows) are students or employees. In the leading case of *Cedars-Sinai Medical Center*,[52] the NLRB held that house staff members are students, not employees, and thus are not protected by the Act. The Board's rationale emphasized the educational nature of internships and residencies and that such individuals participated in the program as a requirement for the practice of medicine, not for the purpose of earning a living.

The Board also noted that the number of hours worked and the quality of care they provided did not change the monetary compensation paid to the house staff members. They also chose their programs for the quality of the educational experience rather than because of the amount of stipend offered. From the hospital's point of view, the Board concluded, the programs were not designed to meet its staffing requirements but to allow the students to develop, in a hospital setting, the clinical judgment and proficiency necessary to the practice of medicine. Moreover, the tenure of house staff members was limited to the training program and few expected to remain, or did, after completing their programs. After *Cedars-Sinai* was issued, there was an attempt in Congress to amend the definition of "employee" to specifically include house staff members but that effort failed.[53]

Several notes of caution are in order, however. First, this discussion concerns only the "employee" status of house staff for NLRA purposes. If the issue involves house staff status for other purposes, such as workers' compensation, payroll taxes, etc., then a contrary conclusion "may" be possible.[54] Furthermore, any physicians actually employed (such as employee health, department heads, etc.) would be employees for purposes of the NLRA unless they are in supervisory roles, etc. Second, the fact that interns and residents are not deemed employees under the NLRA does not prohibit such a group from engaging in an unprotected strike or other concerted activity to force recognition from a health care employer.[55]

Clinical Supervision and Supervisory Status

A complex issue under the Act is the supervisory status of registered nurses who are charge nurses, head nurses, shift supervisors, or some other type of "nurse in charge." Section 2(11) of the Act provides:

The term "supervisor" means any individual having authority, in the interest of the employer, to hire, transfer, suspend, lay off, recall, promote, discharge, assign, reward, or discipline other employees, or responsibly to direct them, or to adjust their grievances or effectively to recommend such action, if in connection with the foregoing the exercise of such authority is not of a merely routine or clerical nature, but requires the use of independent judgment.[56]

Persons who fall within the definition of "supervisor" are not "employees" for purposes of the Act and the NLRB cannot conduct an election or otherwise require an employer to recognize a unit including supervisors. Furthermore, other features of the Act (such as the right to engage in concerted activity, etc.) are inapplicable since they are limited to employees.

In the 1974 Health Care Amendments, Congress specifically declined to enact any special definition of "supervisor" for the health care industry. The Senate committee noted that the Board had carefully avoided applying the definition of "supervisor" to a health care professional who gives direction to other employees in the exercise of professional judgment when the direction is incidental to the professional's treatment of patients and not an exercise of supervisory authority in the interest of the employer.[57]

Following the Health Care Amendments, the Board has continued to adhere to the distinction between the exercise of supervisory functions and authority and the exercise of professional direction and judgment and has applied this distinction in numerous cases since. From a review of many such cases,[58] it is possible to extract the factors and considerations supporting supervisory status:

- The positions are permanent rather than being rotated among numerous R.N.s.
- The individuals exercise the authority to grant time off or to authorize overtime.
- They exercise the authority to call in replacements to cover absences rather than merely reporting shortages in staffing to someone else.
- They are compensated at a higher rate of pay than nonsupervisory R.N.s rather than simply receiving a premium for the occasions when additional duties are performed.
- They exercise the authority to hire other R.N.s or effectively to recommend such hiring through the use of their own discretion.
- They exercise the authority to terminate other R.N.s or effectively to recommend such termination through the use of their own discretion.
- They have the authority to take, or effectively to recommend, other disciplinary action concerning R.N.s rather than having authority limited to counselling them on nondisciplinary matters.
- They attend meetings not open to nonsupervisory personnel where supervisory issues (personnel management) are discussed.
- They have been told by the employer that they are supervisors and that they have supervisory authority.
- Their recommendations concerning personnel matters (hiring, firing, disciplinary action, transfers, etc.) generally are followed rather than their superiors' being free to disregard their recommendations.
- They perform personnel evaluations of other R.N.s independently, particularly when the ratings are used for disciplinary or pay purposes, rather than just offering their input to a superior who determines the content of the actual evaluation.
- They spend a majority of their time performing supervisory and administrative functions rather than direct patient care.
- They have the authority to adjust employee grievances.
- They possess several of the above-listed characteristics.

The Board also will take note of the ratio of individuals claimed to be supervisors to unit employees. Where the number of claimed supervisors is unrealistically high, the Board will closely examine their supervisory status.[59] Finally, the fact that a registered nurse, whether called a charge nurse or a head nurse, supervises non-R.N. personnel such as licensed vocational nurses is not determinative, in the NLRB's view, unless they spend more than 50 percent of their time in such supervision.[60]

Definition of a Health Care Institution

The Act defines "health care institution" very broadly. Hospitals, health clinics, health maintenance organizations, nursing homes, convalescent hospitals, extended care facilities, and others "devoted to the care of the sick, infirm, or aged person(s)" are specifically included within its coverage.[61] The Board's interpretation of "health care institutions" is equally broad. Accordingly, a health care employer will be covered if the services provided are local in nature and even if it is a nonprofit charitable institution.[62]

The Board has included in the term health care institution, a number of types of facilities such as those that provide:

- an outpatient therapy service for drug and alcohol abusers[63]
- outpatient clinics for family care[64]
- outpatient clinics for gynecological services and abortions[65]
- residential care and treatment for neglected, abandoned, or mistreated children[66]
- care and services for the mentally retarded[67]
- educational and vocational rehabilitation for retarded and developmentally disabled individuals.[68]

However, if the programs provided by your employer are vocational rather than medical in nature, and are designed to prepare the "patients" for an independent self-sufficient life away from the facility, the Board has held that such places are not health care institutions.[69] Similarly, the Board has decided that facilities that merely provide blood processing service, or blood banks, do not constitute "health care institutions."[70] The same is true of medical laboratories that test human medical specimens,[71] a diagnostic medical laboratory,[72] and a medical college in which the provision of health care services was ancillary to the primary function of training physicians and promoting research.[73]

Labor Unions with Supervisor Members

The two essential points to consider when the question is one of supervisors' membership in a labor organization are that:

1. An employer can prohibit membership in a labor organization by its supervisory personnel. This prohibition can be enforced by disciplinary action, including termination from employment, if a supervisory employee joins or refuses to resign.[74]

2. Supervisors may belong to an organization that also functions as a collective bargaining representative (a common occurrence with state registered nurse associations) but the mere fact of such supervisory membership will not disqualify the organization from serving as a collective bargaining representative of nonsupervisory employees. However, such membership may create the potential for active participation by supervisors and a conflict of interest that can lead to disqualification (see following discussion).

On various occasions the NLRB has considered the difficult problem of supervisors' involvement in labor organizations by supervisory personnel and whether that could preclude the union from serving as the exclusive bargaining representative of nonsupervisory employees. The critical determinants on this issue are that (1) statutory employees (those covered by the Act, a term that excludes supervisors) "have the right to be represented in collective bargaining negotiations by individuals who have a single-minded loyalty to their interests;"[75] and (2) the reciprocal right of an employer to have the individual loyalty of its own supervisors.[76]

This means that if supervisors are actively in control of the labor organization (are a significant proportion of its membership, actively participate as members, serve as officers, take part in its collective bargaining functions, etc.) the entity may be disqualified because of a conflict of interest where it seeks to represent employees of an employer whose own supervisors are participating members. However, where the organization is seeking to represent employees of an employer whose own supervisory members do not participate significantly in the labor entity, then the employer must show that there is a clear and present danger of a conflict of interest interfering with the collective bargaining process.[77]

Encouragement of 'Professional Organizations'

Health care employers frequently encourage their employees' membership in professional organizations. This encouragement—or even a requirement—has taken various forms: paying for members' annual subscriptions, making available meeting rooms and other hospital facilities without charge, paying dues, and other tangible support. However, once a nurses' or other employee association becomes a "labor organization," as many have, then any such employer activity can quickly lead to allegations that your facility is "dominating or assisting" the labor entity within the meaning of 8(a)(2) of the Act, or that you are coercing or restraining employees in violation of 8(a)(1). The risk of such allegations is sufficiently great to cause your review and elimination of any such encouragement.

Bargaining Unit Issues

Traditional Bargaining Unit Criteria

Unless an employer and the union agree upon an "appropriate unit," the Board is required to make this determination.[78] The scope of the bargaining unit is of critical importance since (1) only that group of employees will be permitted to vote in the election to determine whether a union will become the exclusive bargaining representative, and (2) if the union wins, that same group of employee classifications generally will be the workers covered by any collective bargaining contract subsequently negotiated.

Traditionally, the Board has attempted to include within the same bargaining unit those employees who share similar interests in wages, hours, and other conditions of employment. The Board frequently describes this as a "community of interest." In determining which employees share a sufficient community of interest, a number of factors are taken into consideration, including:

- broad similarity in wages and the method of calculating them
- similar hours of work
- similar employment benefits
- common supervision
- similar features in qualifications, training, skills, and job functions
- the amount of interchange among the employees in the performance of their duties
- geographic proximity
- whether the group has a history of collective bargaining
- whether the entire group has been organized
- the desires of the employees themselves
- the organizational structure of the employer.[79]

The 1974 Health Care Amendments, however, clearly reflected Congress' intent that the Board should not apply its traditional bargaining unit criteria to the health care industry. As was argued by Senator Robert Taft, Jr. (Republican, Ohio) and Congressman Paul J. Fannin (Republican, Arizona), among others, hospitals and other types of health care institutions offer diversified medical services to patients, and if each professional interest and job classification could form a separate bargaining unit under the Board's traditional criteria, the resulting proliferation of units would create numerous administrative and labor relations problems affecting the delivery of health care. Unwarranted unit fragmentation also could lead to crippling jurisdiction disputes and numerous work stoppages.[80]

Similarly, the Senate report accompanying the bill leading to these amendments noted that "due consideration should be given by the Board to preventing proliferation of bargaining units in the health care industry."[81]

Presumptively Appropriate Units

Since the passage of the amendments the Board has identified at least six groups of health care employees it considers to be appropriate bargaining units:

1. registered nurses
2. salaried physicians (not house staff)
3. all other professionals
4. technical employees (this unit could include psychiatric technicians, x-ray technicians, licensed vocational or practical nurses, histology technicians, and other technical employees identifiable by the requirement of licensure, certification, or registration in order to perform their work)
5. service and maintenance employees, a designation that includes all employees who are not technicals, professionals, or office clericals
6. business office clericals, a unit that does not include clerical employees who work in "production areas" such as ward or unit clerks but only those in the administrative areas of the hospital.[82]

Appellate Court Reaction to Board Position

The Board, in some instances, also has allowed other units such as maintenance employees or stationary engineers (boiler operations).[83] This fragmentation of a health care facility's employees into numerous units has resulted in frequent reversal of the Board's determination by federal courts of appeal.[84]

Thus, considerable controversy surrounds the question of whether the Board has carried out Congress' instructions that it avoid undue proliferation of bargaining units and whether the Board is required to reduce the number of appropriate units for health facilities. As a result, this area of the law still is somewhat uncertain, and only a clear statement from the United States Supreme Court is likely to resolve the situation.

Professionals and Scope of Unit

The Act prohibits the Board from including professionals and nonprofessionals in the same bargaining unit unless a majority of the former vote for such inclusion. The question then arises: What is a "professional" for NLRA unit purposes? Section 2–(12) of the Act provides a partial answer by defining a professional employee as:

one engaged in work predominantly intellectual in character as opposed to routine; involves independent judgment in its performance; is not susceptible to standardization; requires knowledge of an advanced type personally acquired by prolonged study in an institution of higher learning or in a hospital.[85]

Apart from registered nurses and physicians, the Board also considers the following to be professional employees:

- audiologists
- cardiopulmonary technologists
- chemists
- dietitians
- medical technologists
- pharmacists
- physical and occupational therapists
- pulmonary function technologists
- radioisotope technologists
- radiologic paramedics
- recreation therapists
- speech therapists.[86]

Separate R.N. Representation

In 1975, the Board issued a decision greatly affecting representation of R.N.s and creating considerable controversy. It concluded that if R.N.s sought to be represented in a separate bargaining unit, apart from all remaining professional employees (who would constitute a second professional unit), they were entitled to do so. The Board's ruling was based on its conclusion that R.N.s had sufficiently distinct interests, duties, and qualifications to warrant such separation and that they had a preexisting history of separate representation, both of which factors supported deviation from the express admonition of Congress that bargaining units should not be fragmented.[87] Several courts of appeal have refused to uphold the Board's position, however, concluding instead that a per se separate unit for R.N.s ignores a clear congressional mandate to avoid the proliferation of units.[88]

The resultant situation is unsatisfactory. The Board continues to take the position that a separate unit limited to registered nurses is appropriate[89] except for very special circumstances[90] but the appellate courts are reversing with great frequency if the employer raises the issue by refusing to bargain after an NLRB election in such a unit.

The Board argues that a "tradition" of separate representation makes such units appropriate. Yet there is little statistical support for that position as a national proposition and, in any event, many hospitals voluntarily recognized separate registered nurse units prior to the 1974 amendments when different considerations, such as recognitional strikes, applied. Again, this is an area that will be resolved only by litigation and, in all probability, by a clear statement from the United States Supreme Court.

Strikes in the Health Care Industry

The Law of Economic Action

The term "strike" as defined in the Act includes "any strike or concerted stoppage of work by employees . . . and any concerted slowdown or other concerted interruption of operations by employees."[91] Although never elevated to the status of a constitutional right, the use of economic weapons by employees or labor organizations has been recognized as part and parcel of the process of collective bargaining.[92] Economic action by unions typically takes the form of strikes, picketing, and boycotts; employers in turn can legally engage in such economic action as the replacement of strikers and lockouts.

It always must be remembered that striking, picketing, and other economic action by employees is "protected activity" under section 7 and thus any employer attempt to interfere unlawfully with such action will constitute an unfair labor practice. Several exceptions to the employees' right to strike do exist, however:

- A labor organization in certain circumstances must comply with notice requirements in the Act before it strikes. If the union does not do so, the strike will be illegal and the employees may lose their section 7 protected status, thereby subjecting them to the possibility of discharge or other employer action.[93]
- Many collective bargaining agreements contain no-strike clauses and a strike in violation of such a clause generally is unprotected activity, with the same consequences.

You must exercise caution in this area, however. Unless a strike is illegal because of noncompliance with the Act's notice requirements, or is in violation of a no-strike clause, or illegal for some other specific reason, strikers retain their status as employees. As a result, they cannot be terminated.

Strikers also generally are entitled to reinstatement at the conclusion of the strike. An exception is that strikers who have been permanently replaced (not terminated, please; the terminology is important) during an economic strike only have the more limited right to return to work as job openings arise.

In contrast to economic strikes, however, an unfair labor practice strike occurs where the employer's unfair labor practices have caused or prolonged the strike. If this happens, you cannot permanently replace the unfair labor practice strikers.

Special Notification Requirements

Where a collective bargaining contract exists between a health care institution and a labor organization, the Act requires that the party seeking termination, modification, or renegotiation of the contract must:

1. provide written notice to the other party of its intention to terminate or modify the contract at least 90 days prior to its expiration date
2. give at least 60 days' advance notice of the existence of a dispute to both the Federal Mediation and Conciliation Service (FMCS) and any state agency with similar functions
3. refrain from engaging in a strike or lockout until 90 days after the first notice has been given and 60 days after the notice to the mediation services
4. provide at least ten days' written advance notice of the date and time it intends to engage in striking, picketing, or other concerted activity if the employer is a health care institution;[94] it should be noted, however, that the ten-day strike notice requirement applies only to labor organizations, not to a group of employees exercising their right to participate in concerted activity.[95]

The Act also provides, in section 8(d), that employees engaging in a strike in violation of those notice periods, unlike lawful strikers, are subject to discharge without the right to reinstatement.[96]

Where the union is negotiating its first collective bargaining agreement with an employer, the modified notice requirements are as follows:

1. Both the FMCS and any similar state agency must be given at least 30 days' notice that a dispute exists between the parties.
2. A labor organization must give a health care institution at least ten days' written advance notice of the date and time it intends to engage in striking, picketing, or other concerted activity. Moreover, the ten days' notice cannot be given within the 30-day notice period to the FMCS. This means that at least 40 days must elapse between the notice to the FMCS and any lawful strike.[97]

Mandatory Mediation

Mediation must be distinguished from the several types of arbitration:

- "Rights" arbitration is a determination of a dispute arising under an existing contract by any mutually selected neutral "umpire" whose decision is final and binding.
- "Interest" arbitration is a determination of the content of a new collective bargaining agreement and, again, is final and binding.
- Mediation, by contrast, is where an individual or mediator assists the union and employer in negotiating a new contract and attempts by persuasion and logic to effect a compromise. The compromise can be accepted or rejected by the parties at will but it is hoped that it will result in a settlement of a new contract. The mediator's suggestions are not binding on the parties.

While mediators may be from the private sector (sometimes arbitrators are selected to function in a mediation role as, for example, in the 1982 National Football League strike), the Act itself established the FMCS as an independent agency in recognition of the fact that a skilled mediator can be valuable in resolving labor disputes by avoiding or settling strikes.

Subsequently, because of congressional concern about the unique disruption caused by strikes in the health care industry, the 1974 Health Care Amendments contained new provisions allowing for mandatory mediation in that industry.[98] Mandatory means only that the FMCS can require that the parties to a health care dispute accept the services of a federal mediator, not that the mediator can require acceptance of any recommendations.

Board of Inquiry

The possible establishment of Boards of Inquiry (BOI) also is provided for by the Act's provisions applicable to the health care industry. Under those provisions:

- The director of the FMCS, upon concluding that a threatened or actual strike or lockout involving a health care institution will interfere substantially with patient services available in a particular locality, may appoint a special Board of Inquiry to investigate the issues in the dispute.
- The BOI, at the conclusion of the investigation, makes a written report containing findings of fact and making recommendations for settling the dispute.
- The FMCS must establish a BOI within certain time constraints imposed by the statute.[99]

If an employer or union fails to cooperate with an appointed BOI, it is vulnerable to an 8(a)(5) or 8(b)(3) charge that it is not bargaining in good faith, unless the FMCS director fails to comply with the Act when establishing the BOI.[100]

Ally Doctrine

A union that pickets a neutral employer uninvolved in the dispute commits an 8(b)(4) unfair labor practice. However, your employer is not protected against such secondary picketing if, by its actions, it has become an "ally" of the primary employer. A typical situation would be as follows:

- Union X has a labor dispute with employer A and strikes and pickets employer A.
- Employer A, in order not to lose business, asks employer B to service A's customers while the strike is in progress.
- Union X thereafter pickets employer B. That activity will be protected since B has lost its neutrality by becoming an ally of A.

The Senate report accompanying the legislation indicated, however, that a special exception to the ally doctrine should be recognized for health care institutions. This said that a secondary health care institution, employer B in the example, would not become the ally of the primary institution (employer A) by accepting patients or by otherwise providing life-sustaining services to A through the furnishing of employees who possessed critical skills, such as an EKG technician. However, the report held that the ally doctrine would apply if employer B supplied supervisory nurses or other staff who did not provide life-sustaining services.[101]

Employee Resignations from Union during Labor Dispute

Some of your employees who are union members may want to continue working during a strike by their labor organization, or during a strike by another union that is recognized by their own union (a sympathy strike). If this happens, a natural question is, "What, if anything, can a union do to stop employees from resigning their union membership or to punish union members who cross a line?"

The answer begins with the fact that while employees technically have the right to refrain from participating in strikes and unions may not restrain or coerce them in the exercise of this right,[102] unions' bylaws may allow fines against members who cross their lawful picket lines to work during a strike, and the union can enforce these fines in state court.[103] To escape the possibility of such a fine, employees desiring to work during a strike must resign their union membership before they work or cross the picket lines and, once their resignation is effective, the union should have no authority to assess fines.[104] Such a resignation will not affect an employee's employment status since any union membership requirement in the existing or renegotiated collective bargaining agreement can be satisfied by the employees' payment to the union of periodic amounts equal to the union dues and initiation fees required of actual members.[105]

Many union constitutions, in an attempt to prevent this sort of strike-related resignation, place limitations on their members' rights to resign. For example, a union's bylaws may prohibit resignation where the member has any outstanding union dues owing or may say that a member cannot resign within a 90-day period prior to contract expiration. However, the Board has held that a union may not unreasonably restrict a member's rights to resign, so the question is, ''What's unreasonable?''

One of the Board's answers is that a limitation is unreasonable if it restricts the right to resign for more than 30 days after written notice of resignation is given to the union.[106] If the Board adheres to this answer, this means that in evaluating your employees' right to work (if they desire to stay on the job) and their right to resign, you should keep the following guidelines in mind:

- If a union does attempt to restrict resignations, employees who want to continue working during a strike still may do so freely, at the very latest, 30 days after they have sent a written notice of resignation to the union.
- If the union has not established any strike-related or other restrictions on resignations, then an employee's resignation may be made effective immediately.
- If the union has no provisions for assessing fines (or other penalties) against members who work during a strike, then it can impose no fines or take other disciplinary action even if your employees retain their membership.
- If the union's restrictions are for less than 30 days (for example, a member must give ten days' notice of resignation) then the union's own provision (not the Board's 30-day rule) would apply, assuming that the bylaws' restriction on the right to resign was otherwise valid.
- If the employer wants to lawfully inform its employees of their legal right to work, to resign, or to do neither, it may do so. However, an employer cannot encourage its employees to resign their membership, or to not join the union, since this would be an unfair labor practice under section 8(a)(3).

The Board's 30-day rule, as described above, has been accepted by one federal court of appeals and rejected by another.[107] As a result, the union-resignation rules allowed in your geographical area and the current state of the law must be checked with legal counsel before any information is distributed to employees concerning their rights and obligations.

Solicitation and Distribution Policies

The right of employees to engage in concerted activity is not absolute. Prior to the Health Care Amendments, the Board and courts developed certain guidelines governing an employer's right to restrict solicitation (verbal discussions, including soliciting employee signatures on authorization cards) and distribution of written materials by employees and nonemployees. Under this traditional approach, an employer generally may adopt and enforce the following types of restrictions if they apply to all solicitation and distribution, not just to solicitation and distribution for union-related purposes:

1. Nonemployees (including nonemployee union organizers) may be prohibited from engaging in any solicitation or distribution in the employer's facility (the nonemployee still could do so, however, on public property surrounding your facility) where reasonable efforts by the union will allow communication with employees.
2. Employees can be proscribed from soliciting on worktime (rest breaks, meal periods, etc., generally are not worktime).
3. Employees may be prohibited from distributing on worktime or in work areas.[108]

Health care institutions have argued that stricter limitations on employee activity should apply in their facilities because of the unique type of service provided and the need to avoid any disruption, stress, or inconvenience to patients.

The United States Supreme Court resolved the issue by ruling that hospitals may legitimately impose stricter policies in only one way: that an employee, even if on nonwork time, can be restricted from soliciting other employees in "immediate patient care areas." Operating rooms, patient rooms, and areas where treatment is provided are examples of "immediate patient care areas." Cafeterias, gift shops, and lobbies generally are not immediate patient care areas unless a health facility can show that patient care services would be affected directly and adversely.[109]

Exhibit 3–4 illustrates one way in which a solicitation-distribution policy can be worded. Neither this example, nor any other model policy you might find in other resource materials, should be used "as is." What constitutes worktime, nonworking time, work areas, immediate patient care areas, etc., can vary from facility to facility, and the law can change. As the sample notes, any policy governing solicitation and distribution by employees should be prepared and/or reviewed by labor or legal counsel before adoption or enforcement.

Once adopted, however, the policy cannot be enforced validly against union solicitation or distribution or access by nonemployee organizers unless it is done without discrimination. Even if the policy is valid on paper, you cannot enforce it just with regard to union activities while allowing unrestricted solicitation and

Exhibit 3–4 Sample Policy on Solicitation and Distribution of Written Material

The policy described here governs the solicitation and distribution of materials on Hospital property by employees and nonemployees.

The reasons for the Hospital's solicitation and distribution policy are as follows: to prevent disruption in the operation of the Hospital, to avoid interference with patient care, to prevent disturbances or inconvenience to our patients and their visitors, and to control litter problems that could result if the distribution of written materials was unregulated. The importance of these reasons requires that all employees and nonemployees observe the policies set forth below. A violation of these policies by employees will result in disciplinary action, the precise nature of such disciplinary action to be determined by all surrounding circumstances.

Distribution or Solicitation by Outsiders on Hospital Property

Persons not employed by the Hospital may not solicit or distribute literature on Hospital property for any purpose at any time.

Distribution or Solicitation by Hospital Employees

1. *Solicitation:* Employees may not solicit for any purpose during working time. Employees may not solicit for any purpose during nonworking time in patient rooms or in immediate patient care areas such as x-ray and therapy, nursing stations, the corridors of patient treatment areas or patient rooms, and sitting rooms for patients and visitors.
2. *Distribution:* Employees may not distribute written literature for any purpose in working areas or during their working time. Distribution of literature can be done only in areas that are not work areas, and the employee must not be on working time.
3. *Working Time:* Working time does not include your rest breaks or your lunch period. Working time does, however, include the working time of both the employee doing the solicitation or distribution and the employee to whom it is directed. Therefore, even if you are on your lunch period, rest break, or other nonworking time, you cannot distribute to or solicit another employee who is on working time.
4. *Working Areas:* Working areas are all areas of the Hospital except cafeterias, employee lounges and locker rooms, lobbies, the gift shop, and outside areas, including parking lots.
5. *Remember:* Solicitation or distribution by employees must not impede access in or out of the Hospital or impede physical movement within the Hospital.

If you have any questions as to the meaning of working time, working areas, or any other portions of this policy, please contact your Personnel Office.

It is important that all employees follow these rules on solicitation and distribution. A violation of these rules by an employee can lead to disciplinary action, including the possibility of termination.

(*Note:* These suggested guidelines should not be used without review and/or revision by legal counsel.)

distribution by employees on other issues such as social events, sale of personal items, etc.

The only notable exception is that activities such as Red Cross drives, hospital volunteer group postings, or displays of pharmaceutical products that are related to the health care facility's functions and community services may not preclude continued enforcement of a solicitation and distribution policy that is valid in other respects.[110]

In summary, great caution is called for in this area. The reason is that if you adopt an overly broad policy (one that imposes too many restrictions), it not only is an unfair labor practice, it also can result in the Board's setting aside an election lost by a union and scheduling a new vote.

The Weingarten Rule

Union Employees

Under the Weingarten Rule (a statement of employees' rights named after one of the two companion United States Supreme Court decisions announcing the rule), an employee is entitled to have a union representative present:

- upon request
- at an investigatory interview by the employer
- if the employee reasonably believes that the investigatory interview will result in disciplinary action.[111]

Since the original rule was issued, it has been subjected to further interpretation and clarification. The following is a summary of its general principles and application:

- An employee does not have a right to the presence of a union representative if discipline is imposed without an investigatory interview and the employee simply asks the reasons why previously determined disciplinary action has been imposed.[112]
- An employee may subjectively but erroneously believe that discipline will be imposed but an employer still can conduct an interview (such as a non-disciplinary counseling session) without union representation and avoid a meritorious unfair labor practice charge if you correctly tell the employee in advance that the interview is not investigatory and that no disciplinary action will be taken for the incidents or issues to be discussed at the interview.[113]
- The employee or the union has the burden of asking a representative to be present and the employer has no duty to raise the subject or to ask whether the

employee desires union representation[114] (unless a collective bargaining agreement imposes such an affirmative obligation upon your employer).

- The employee may request representation and the employer may respond by (1) terminating the interview, (2) allowing attendance by the union representative, or (3) advising the worker that the interview will not be continued with the union representative present, that the employee may leave if so desired, and that the employer will make its decision without an interview.[115] Once so informed, the employee could waive the right to representation if the person voluntarily agrees to continue the interview without such representation.[116]

- The employee has no right to representation if no investigatory interview is held and an employer meets with the worker solely to inform the person of a decision already reached that disciplinary action will be taken.[117]

- The employee must request representation but the union or employee may ask for a preinterview opportunity to consult together where the timing of the interview otherwise precludes such consultation.[118]

- The employee must be told, in advance, the general nature of the charges to facilitate the individual's right to meaningful representation during the interview.[119]

- The employer need not wait until a particular union representative is available, only for so long as any representative is reasonably available.[120]

- The union representative may advise and aid the employee during the interview and speak in order to clarify the facts, yet the employer has the right to insist upon hearing from the employee directly during the meeting.[121]

Nonunion Employees

The *Weingarten* case concerned a union employee's request for union representation during an investigatory interview. The issue before the Supreme Court was whether the request constituted protected concerted activity (see prior discussion of section 7 and protected activity). The Court's answer was that the activity was concerted because the union representative would be protecting the rights of other employees in the bargaining unit in addition to the rights of the individual employee seeking representation.

While it is clear that section 7 applies to all covered employees, whether or not there is union representation, the narrower issue of the extent to which *Weingarten* applies to nonunion employees has not been resolved definitively. Some of the answers that appear to be emerging are that:

- If a request for the presence of a union representative or of a fellow employee is made after a union wins an NLRB election but before the election results are certified, the *Weingarten* rule would apply.[122]

- If the request occurs in the context of other protected activity, or is related in some way to other protected activity (for example, during an organizing drive, where the employees have engaged in a work stoppage and the employer is considering potential disciplinary action, etc.), then again, the request for representation may be viewed as "concerted," and if so, *Weingarten* would apply.[123]
- If an individual employee seeks the presence of a coworker, but is acting alone and there is no connection with preceding or contemporaneous group activity, then the request may be viewed as concerted by the NLRB if it adheres to its precedent, but the court of appeals for your area may not agree.[124]

Since the question of *Weingarten's* applicability to nonunion employees may be influenced by differing facts, and since the law is evolving and subject to reversals and the establishment of new rules and principles, legal assistance should be sought whenever a problem arises.

Duty of Fair Representation

The essence of collective bargaining is that the employer must negotiate with the employee's exclusive bargaining agent, the union; an employer cannot deal with a second union, or employees directly, if an exclusive bargaining representative exists. Yet the granting of these exclusive rights to recognized unions has resulted in labor law's placing corresponding duties upon unions to prevent abuses. Thus, the union has a duty to represent fairly and impartially all employees in the bargaining unit, whether or not they are members of the union.[125] This "duty of fair representation" arises from the need to protect minority and individual interests from domination and abuse by the majority and applies to both contract negotiations and contract administration.

A common area for allegations that the union has not fairly represented the employee is in the processing of grievances. If the union fails to process a grievance as a result of bad faith, discrimination, or arbitrary conduct, it breaches its duty to the employee.[126] Under some circumstances (notably, a union's failure to timely demand arbitration if an employee is discharged), negligence may be sufficient to constitute a breach.[127]

If an employee can allege a breach of the union's duty that precluded the worker from securing a remedy for the employer's violation of the union contract, then the employee can sue your employer directly for breach of contract. The willingness of employees to file such claims in federal or state courts, and the possibility that the union may be found financially liable to the employee in damages,[128] has impeded some unions' ability to resolve cases short of arbitration and can increase the number of grievances a union takes to arbitration.

NOTES

1. Butte Medical Properties, 168 N.L.R.B. 266 (1967).

2. 29 U.S.C. § 152(14).

3. Butte Medical Properties, 168 N.L.R.B. 266 (1967); University Nursing Homes Inc., 168 N.L.R.B. 263 (1967); Ochsner Clinic, 196 N.L.R.B. 10, *enforced*, 474 F.2d 206 (5th Cir. 1973); East Oakland Community Health Alliance, Inc., 218 N.L.R.B. 1270 (1975).

4. 29 U.S.C. § 158(g).

5. 29 U.S.C. § 158(d)(C).

6. 29 U.S.C. § 183.

7. 29 U.S.C. § 158(d).

8. 29 U.S.C. § 169.

9. 29 U.S.C. § 157.

10. Alleluia Cushion Co., 221 N.L.R.B. 999 (1975), *overuled by* Meyers Inds. Inc., 268 N.L.R.B. No. 73 (1984).

11. *Id.*

12. NLRB v. Interboro Contractors, Inc., 388 F.2d 495 (2d Cir. 1967).

13. Krispy Kreme Donut Corp., 245 N.L.R.B. 1053 (1979), *enforcement denied*, Krispy Kreme Development Corp. v. NLRB, 635 F.2d 304 (4th Cir. 1980); Farrens Tree Surgeons, Inc., 264 N.L.R.B. No. 90 (1982); *but see*, Central Georgia Electric Corp., 269 N.L.R.B. No. 123 (1984) (under 1984 holding of Meyers Inds. Inc., 268 N.L.R.B. No. 73 (1984), an individual employee's pursuit of a worker's compensation claim does not constitute protected concerted activity since the Board will not presume that the activity is of interest to other employees).

14. Self-Cycle and Marine Distributor Co., 237 N.L.R.B. 75 (1978).

15. Hansen Chevolet, 237 N.L.R.B. 584 (1978).

16. Meyers Ind's. Inc., 268 N.L.R.B. No. 73, 12 (1984).

17. *Id.* at 4, 11.

18. Eastex, Inc. v. NLRB, 437 U.S. 556 (1978).

19. Roanoke Hosp. v. NLRB, 538 F.2d 607 (4th Cir. 1976).

20. NLRB v. St. Anne's Hosp., 648 F.2d 67 (1st Cir. 1981).

21. Dominican Sisters of Ontario, 264 N.L.R.B. No. 158 (1982).

22. *Id.*

23. *Id.*

24. NLRB v. Parrlance Ambulance Co., 115 L.R.R.M. 2193 (7th Cir. 1983).

25. NLRB v. Washington Aluminum Co., 370 U.S. 9 (1962).

26. Robert Lewis & William A. Krupman, Winning NLRB Elections 28 (1972).

27. NLRB v. Gissel Packing Co., 395 U.S. 575 (1969).

28. *Id.*

29. Snow & Sons, 134 N.L.R.B. 709 (1961), *enforced*, 308 F.2d 687 (9th Cir. 1962).

30. ILGWU v. NLRB (Bernard-Altmann Corp.), 366 U.S. 731 (1961).

31. Linden Lumber Div. v. NLRB, 419 U.S. 301 (1974).

32. Midwest Piping & Supply Co., 63 N.L.R.B. 1060 (1945).

33. Abraham Grossman, 262 N.L.R.B. No. 115 (1982).

34. RCA Del Caribe, Inc., 262 N.L.R.B. No. 116 (1982).

35. Sullivan Electric Co., 199 N.L.R.B. 809 (1972), *enforced*, 479 F.2d 1270 (6th Cir. 1973).

36. Struksner Constr. Co., 165 N.L.R.B. 1062 (1967).

37. NLRB CASE HANDLING MANUAL, § 11084.2.

38. *Id.* at 11084.1.

39. Excelsior Underwear, Inc., 156 N.L.R.B. 1236 (1966); NLRB CASE HANDLING MANUAL, § 11312.

40. 29 U.S.C. § 159(b).

41. Midland Nat'l Life Ins. Co., 263 N.L.R.B. 24 (1982).

42. *Id.*

43. NLRB v. Gissel Packing Co., 395 U.S. 575 (1969).

44. Conair Corp., 261 N.L.R.B. 1189 (1982), *enforced in part, denied in part*, Conair Corp. v. NLRB, 721 F.2d 1355 (D.C. Cir. 1983) (bargaining order improper where union never attained majority status); *but see*, United Dairy Farmers Coop. Ass'n v. NLRB, 633 F.2d 1054 (3d Cir. 1980) (nonmajority bargaining order permissible).

45. 29 U.S.C. § 158(a)(1).

46. 29 U.S.C. § 158(a)(2).

47. *See* Cabot Carbon v. NLRB, 360 U.S. 203 (1959).

48. Lane v. NLRB, 186 F.2d 671 (10th Cir. 1951).

49. Operating Engr's, Local 542 v. NLRB, 331 F.2d 99 (3d Cir.), *cert. denied*, 379 U.S. 826 (1964).

50. Western Wirebound Box Co., 144 N.L.R.B. 912 (1963).

51. 29 U.S.C. § 158(b)(7).

52. 223 N.L.R.B. 251 (1976); *see* Physicians Nat'l House Staff v. Fanning, 642 F.2d 492 (1981), *cert. denied*, 450 U.S. 917 (1981).

53. H.R. 2222; DAILY LAB. REP. (BNA) No. 231 at, A-4 (1979).

54. *See, e.g.*, Einstein Medical Center v. Labor Bd., 87 L.R.R.M. (BNA) 2778, 2780 n.5 (1974).

55. 29 U.S.C. § 164.

56. 29 U.S.C. § 152(11).

57. S. Rep. No. 766, 93rd Cong., 2d Sess. 4, *reprinted in*, 1974 U.S. CODE CONG. & AD. NEWS 3946, 3951.

58. *E.g.*, A. Barton Hepburn Hosp., 238 N.L.R.B. 95 (1978); Eventide South, 239 N.L.R.B. 287 (1978); Tryon Nursing Home, 223 N.L.R.B. 769 (1976); Morristown-Hamblen Hosp. Assn., 226 N.L.R.B. 76 (1976); St. Rose de Lima Hosp., 223 N.L.R.B. 1511 (1976); Bishop Randall Hosp., 217 N.L.R.B. 1129 (1975); Gnaden Hutten Memorial Hosp., 219 N.L.R.B. 235 (1975); Meharry Medical College, 219 N.L.R.B. 488 (1975); Newton-Wellesley Hosp., 219 N.L.R.B. 699 (1975); Presbyterian Medical Center, 218 N.L.R.B. 1266 (1975); Trustees of Noble Hosp., 218 N.L.R.B. 1441 (1975); St. Mary's Hosp., 220 N.L.R.B. 496 (1975); Valley Hosp., 220 N.L.R.B. 339 (1975); Victor Valley Hosp., 220 N.L.R.B. 977 (1975).

59. McAlester Hosp. Found., Inc., 233 N.L.R.B. 589 (1977).

60. A. Barton Hepburn Hosp., 238 N.L.R.B. 95, 96 (1978), *citing* New York Univ., 205 N.L.R.B. 4, 8 (1973); Adelphi Univ, 195 N.L.R.B. 639, 643–644 (1972).

61. 29 U.S.C. § 152(14).

62. East Oakland Community Health Alliance, Inc., 218 N.L.R.B. 1270 (1975); Rhode Island Catholic Orphan Asylum (St. Aloysius Home), 224 N.L.R.B. 1344 (1976).

63. Sodat, Inc., 218 N.L.R.B. 1327 (1975).

64. East Oakland Community Health Alliance, Inc., 218 N.L.R.B. 1270 (1975).

65. Charles Circle Clinic, Inc., 215 N.L.R.B. 382 (1974).

66. St. Peter's School, 220 N.L.R.B. 480 (1975).

67. Beverly Farm Found., Inc., 218 N.L.R.B. 1275 (1975).

68. Chicago School & Workshop for the Retarded, 225 N.L.R.B. 1207 (1976).

69. Abilities & Goodwill, Inc., 226 N.L.R.B. 1224 (1976).

70. San Diego Blood Bank, 219 N.L.R.B. 116 (1975).

71. Boston Medical Laboratory, Inc., 235 N.L.R.B. 1271 (1978).

72. Damon Medical Laboratory, Inc., 234 N.L.R.B. 333 (1978).

73. Albany Medical College of Union Univ., 239 N.L.R.B. 853 (1978).

74. Florida Power & Light Co. v. IBEW Local 641, 471 U.S. 790, 812–813 (1974); *see also,* 29 U.S.C. § 164(a).

75. Nassau & Suffolk Contractors' Ass'n, Inc., 118 N.L.R.B. 174 (1957).

76. Sierra Vista Hospital, Inc., 241 N.L.R.B. 631 (1979).

77. *Id., accord,* Abington Memorial Hosp., 250 N.L.R.B. 682 (1980).

78. 29 U.S.C. § 159.

79. *See, e.g.,* Kalamazoo Paper Box Corp., 136 N.L.R.B. 134 (1962).

80. 120 Cong. Rec. 6936–42, 6990–91.

81. S. Rep. No. 776, 93rd Cong., 2d Sess. 4, *reprinted in,* 1974 U.S. Code Cong. & Ad. News 3946, 3950.

82. Barnett Memorial Hosp. Center, 217 N.L.R.B. 775 (1975); Mercy Hosp. of Sacramento, Inc., 217 N.L.R.B. 765 (1975), *rev'd and remanded in part on other grounds,* 589 F.2d 968 (9th Cir. 1978), *cert. denied,* 440 U.S. 910 (1979), *decision on remand,* 244 N.L.R.B. 229 (1979); Ohio Valley Ass'n, 230 N.L.R.B. 604 (1977); St. Catherine's Hosp. of Dominican Sisters, 217 N.L.R.B. 787 (1975); *see generally,* Gerald Morales, *Unit Appropriateness in Health Care Institutions,* 30 Lab. L.J. (BNA) No. 3 at 174 (March 1974).

83. *E.g.,* Eskaton Am. River Health Care Center, 225 N.L.R.B. 755 (1976); St. Vincent's Hosp., 223 N.L.R.B. 638 (1976).

84. *E.g.,* NLRB v. HMO Int'l, 678 F.2d 806 (9th Cir. 1982); NLRB v. St. Francis Hosp. of Lynwood, 601 F.2d 404 (9th Cir. 1979); St. Vincent's Hosp. v. NLRB, 567 F.2d 588 (3d Cir. 1978); NLRB v. West Suburban Hosp., 570 F.2d 213 (7th Cir. 1978); NLRB v. Mercy Hosp. Ass'n, 606 F.2d 22 (2d Cir. 1979), *cert. denied,* 446 U.S. 971 (1980); Beth Israel Hosp. & Geriatric Center v. NLRB, 677 F.2d 1343 (10th Cir. 1982).

85. 29 U.S.C. § 152(12).

86. Samaritan Health Servs., 238 N.L.R.B. 629 (1978); Chicago School & Workshop for the Retarded, 225 N.L.R.B. 1207 (1976); Sutter Community Hosp., 227 N.L.R.B. 181 (1976); Mercy Hosps. of Sacramento, Inc., 217 N.L.R.B. 765, 768 n.15 (1975); Newington Childrens Hosp., 217 N.L.R.B. 793 (1975).

87. St. Catherine's Hosp. of Dominican Sisters, 217 N.L.R.B. 787 (1975).

88. *E.g.,* NLRB v. St. Francis Hosp. of Lynwood, 601 F.2d 404 (9th Cir. 1979); NLRB v. HMO Int'l, 678 F.2d 806 (9th Cir. 1982); St. Vincent's Hosp. v. NLRB, 567 F.2d 588 (3d Cir. 1978); Presbyterian/St. Luke's Medical Center v. NLRB, 653 F.2d 450 (10th Cir. 1981).

89. Addison-Gilbert Hosp., 253 N.L.R.B. 1010 (1981); Newington-Wellesley Hosp., 250 N.L.R.B. 409 (1980).

90. St. John of God Hosp., Inc., 260 N.L.R.B. No. 117 (1982); Mt. Airy Psychiatric Center, 253 N.L.R.B. 139 (1981).

91. 29 U.S.C. § 142(2).

92. NLRB v. Ins. Agents' Union, 361 U.S. 477, 495 (1960).

93. 29 U.S.C. § 158(d).

94. 29 U.S.C. §§ 158(d), (g).

95. West Jefferson Medical Group, 264 N.L.R.B. No. 196 (1982).

96. 29 U.S.C. § 158(d).

97. 29 U.S.C. § 158(d), (g).

98. 29 U.S.C. § 158(d)(C).

99. 29 U.S.C. § 183.

100. Affiliated Hosps. v. Scearce, 418 F. Supp. 711 (N.D. Cal. 1976), aff'd, 583 F.2d 1097 (9th Cir. 1978).

101. S. Rep. No. 93–776, 93rd Cong., 2d Sess., reprinted in, 1974 U.S. CODE CONG. & AD. NEWS 3946, 3951.

102. 29 U.S.C. §§ 157, 158(b)(1)(A).

103. NLRB v. Allis Chalmers Mfg. Co., 338 U.S. 175 (1967); Pattern Makers League v. NLRB, ___ F.2d ___, 115 L.R.R.M. 2264 (7th Cir. 1983), but see, Machinists Local 1327 v. NLRB, No. 82–7580 (resignation within 14-day period preceding a strike or lockout does not preclude union's assessment of fines for working during the strike).

104. NLRB v. Granite State Joint Board, 409 U.S. 213 (1972).

105. NLRB v. General Motors, 373 U.S. 723 (1963).

106. NABET, Local 531, 265 N.L.R.B. 213 (1982); Pattern Makers League, 265 N.L.R.B. No. 170 (1982), enf'd, ___ F.2d ___, 115 L.R.R.M. 2264 (7th Cir. 1983); but see, Machinists Local 1327 v. NLRB, No. 82–7580 (9th Cir. 1984), denying enforcement, 263 N.L.R.B. 984 (1982).

107. Compare Pattern Makers League v. NLRB, ___ F.2d ___, 115 L.R.R.M. 2264 (7th Cir. 1983) (union rule fining members who resign to work for struck employer is invalidated), and Machinists Local 1327 v. NLRB, No. 82–7580 (9th Cir. 1984) (union rule precluding resignation and allowing fines against resigning members from 14 days before strike through duration of strike, is reasonable).

108. E.g., NLRB v. Babcock & Wilcox, 351 U.S. 105 (1956); Stoddard-Quirk Mfg. Co., 138 N.L.R.B. 615 (1962); United Aircraft Corp., 139 N.L.R.B. 39 (1962), enforced, 324 F.2d 128 (2d Cir. 1963), cert. denied, 376 U.S. 951 (1964), but see Republic Aluminum Co. v. NLRB, 374 F.2d 183 (5th Cir. 1967); NLRB v. Rockwell Mfg. Co., 271 F.2d 109 (3d Cir. 1959).

109. Beth Israel Hosp. v. NLRB, 437 U.S. 483 (1978), accord, NLRB v. Baptist Hosp., 442 U.S. 773 (1979); see also NLRB GEN. COUNSEL GUIDELINES FOR HANDLING NO-SOLICITATION NO-DISTRIBUTION RULES IN HEALTH-CARE FACILITIES, Memorandum 79–76 at (October 5, 1979).

110. Rochester Gen. Hosp., 234 N.L.R.B. 253 (1978).

111. NLRB v. Weingarten, Inc., 420 U.S. 251, 257–260 (1975); Garment Workers v. Quality Mfg. Co., 420 U.S. 276 (1975).

112. Baton Rouge Water Works Co., 246 N.L.R.B. 995, 997 (1979).

113. Amoco Chemical Corp., 237 N.L.R.B. 394, 396 (1978); see Albert M. Lewis, Inc. v. NLRB, 587 F.2d 403, 410–411 (9th Cir. 1978), enforcing in part, 229 N.L.R.B. 757 (1977).

114. Lennox Indus., Inc., 244 N.L.R.B. 607 (1979).

115. Roadway Express, Inc., 246 N.L.R.B. 1127 (1979).

116. U.S. Postal Serv., 241 N.L.R.B. 141 (1979).

117. Baton Rouge Water Works Co., 246 N.L.R.B. 995, 997 (1979).

118. Climax Molybdenum Co. v. NLRB, 584 F.2d 360 (10th Cir. 1978), *denying enforcement,* Climax Molybdenum Co., 227 N.L.R.B. 1189 (1977); Appalachian Power Co., 253 N.L.R.B. 931 (1980).

119. Pacific Tel. & Tel. Co., 262 N.L.R.B. No. 127 (1982).

120. Coca-Cola Bottling Co., 227 N.L.R.B. 1276 (1977).

121. Southwestern Bell Tel. Co. v. NLRB, 667 F.2d 470 (5th Cir. 1982), *denying enforcement,* 251 N.L.R.B. 612 (1980).

122. ITT Corp. v. NLRB, 719 F.2d 851 (6th Cir. 1983); Anchortank, Inc. v. NLRB, 618 F.2d 1153 (5th Cir. 1980).

123. NLRB v. Columbia Univ., 541 F.2d 922 (2d Cir. 1976); *see also,* E.I. du Pont de Nemours & Co. v. NLRB, 707 F.2d 1076 (9th Cir. 1983).

124. Materials Research Corp., 262 N.L.R.B. 1010 (1982) (nonunion employee's request for coworker is concerted activity), du Pont Co. v. NLRB, _____ F.2d _____, 115 L.R.R.M. 2157 (3rd Cir. 1983) (refusal to honor nonunion employee's request for presence of coworker violates 8(a)(1)); *see also,* Anchortank v. NLRB, 618 F.2d 1153 (5th Cir. 1980) (although not presented by evidence of that case, court stated that a request for presence of coworker is concerted activity); *but see,* E.I. du Pont de Nemours & Co. (DuPont Co.) v. NLRB, 707 F.2d 1076 (9th Cir. 1983) (absent other concerted activity, no 8(a)(1) violation for employer's refusal to allow presence of coworker).

125. Vaca v. Sipes, 386 U.S. 171 (1967).

126. *Id.*

127. Dutrisac v. Caterpillar Tractor Co., _____ F.2d _____ (9th Cir. 1983).

128. Bowen v. U.S. Postal Serv., _____ U.S. _____, 74 103 S.Ct. _____, L. ED. 2d 402 (1983).

Appendix 3–A

Basic Guidelines for Supervisory and Management Personnel

The first thing to remember is that there is no rule of law that prevents an employer from communicating its views concerning a labor organization to employees, or from taking the position that the employees' best interest would be served by not having a labor organization, or from campaigning actively for a "No" vote. To the contrary, section 8(c) of the National Labor Relations Act specifically guarantees the right of free speech to employees.

A note of caution: You should never ask employees how they will vote, how they feel about the union, whether they do or do not prefer union representation, or any other questions related to union activity or preferences. Furthermore, if the employee volunteers this information, you can listen but you should not inquire further. The reason for this caution is that the NLRB believes that asking questions related to employees' preferences, activities, or how they will vote is inherently coercive. Even where an employee initiates this type of discussion, you run the risk that such individuals subsequently will change the story and say that you asked the questions and they only answered your questions. Therefore, you should merely listen and make no direct comments and you also should report or make a memo of the correct facts: For example, that employee Jones came up to you and said the following, "_____," where and when the employee approached you, and who else was present.

With all of this in mind, the following are examples of what you can and cannot tell to or discuss with employees. REMEMBER: If you have any questions or doubts, do not act until you seek and receive clarification.

1. *An Employer or Supervisor Can Legitimately Do All of the Following:*

    1. Tell employees how their wages, benefits, and working conditions compare with other employers (whether unionized or not) and how those factors in your facility are superior to those in union contracts negotiated with other employers.

2. Tell employees of the disadvantages that may result in belonging to a union, such as loss of income because of strikes, requirements to serve in picket line, expensive dues, fines, and assessments.
3. Tell employees that the law permits the employer to hire a permanent replacement for anyone who engages in an economic strike.
4. Tell employees that no union can make the employer pay more than it is willing or able to pay.
5. Tell employees about the benefits they enjoy now as nonunion employees but be sure to avoid any veiled threats or promises as to how your employer will react if a union wins the election.
6. Tell employees that merely signing the union authorization card or application for membership does not mean that they must vote for the union in an NLRB election but that they are free to cast a vote that is in their own best interests. Furthermore, tell employees that NLRB elections are determined by the majority vote of the employees *actually voting*—not the total number of employees who are eligible. Therefore, it is essential that all employees vote.
7. Tell employees about the NLRB election procedures, the importance of voting, and the secrecy of the ballots.
8. Tell employees that the employer opposes the principle of compulsory union membership but that the union would have the right to request that a collective bargaining contract require employees to pay dues or be terminated from employment.
9. Hold group meetings of employees to explain the employer's position. These meetings can be held on worktime without having to give equal time for union-scheduled meetings. However, these meetings cannot be held during the 24-hour period immediately preceding the election and they should never be held unless they have been planned and scheduled by management.

2. *An Employer or Supervisor Cannot Do Any of the Following:*

1. Promise employees a pay increase, promotion, benefit, or special favor if they stay out of a union or vote against it.
2. Threaten loss of jobs, reduction of income, discontinuance of any privileges or benefits, or use any intimidating language that may be designed to influence employees in the exercise of their right to belong, or refrain from belonging, to a union.
3. Threaten, through a third party, any of the above acts of interference.
4. Spy on union meetings or conduct yourself in a way that would indicate to the employees that you are watching them to determine whether or not they are participating in union activities. Surveillance of an employee's union activities is considered to be inherently coercive or threatening.

5. Engage in any partiality favoring nonunion employees over employees active on behalf of a union.
6. Discipline or penalize employees actively supporting a union for an infraction that nonunion employees are permitted to commit without being similarly disciplined. REMEMBER: You can discipline employees for violating a valid employer policy in accordance with your normal procedures *if* the violation is the real reason for the employer's action. The violation cannot be a pretext for a real reason of antiunion motivation because of the employee's union activities. It is suggested that legal counsel be consulted before any disciplinary action is taken against any employee during preelection time.
7. Select employees for layoff or reclassification with the intention of curbing the union's strength or of discouraging affiliation with it.
8. Ask employees for an expression of their thoughts about a union or its officers.
9. Ask employees at the time of hiring or thereafter whether they belong to a union or have signed a union application or authorization card.
10. Ask employees about the internal affairs of unions, such as meetings, etc. Refer back to the introductory discussion of what to do if employees, of their own accord, walk up and tell you of such matters. Remember that it is not an unfair labor practice to listen but you must not ask questions to obtain additional information.
11. Make a statement that you will not deal with a union or that the employer will shut down if the union wins.
12. Enforce an invalid solicitation-distribution policy—for example, by preventing employees from soliciting union membership or discussing the election or union activities during their nonworking time, including breaks and lunch periods.

Note: Guidelines for supervisory conduct during union organizing drives or NLRB election campaigns should be reviewed with your employer's legal counsel.

Chapter 4

Collective Bargaining Agreements

WHAT ARE COLLECTIVE BARGAINING AGREEMENTS?

A collective bargaining agreement is simply a written contract between an employer and a union setting forth their agreement as to wages, hours, and other terms and conditions of employment. You should not take the word "contract" too literally, however. This is because a collective bargaining contract will not be interpreted exactly the same way, and under exactly the same rules, as are commercial contracts.

You also should note that a collective bargaining agreement is not a contract of employment. It typically does not guarantee continued employment to the covered employees and it does not create an employer-employee relationship. To the contrary, a collective bargaining agreement (1) can preclude you from entering into enforceable employment contracts with individual employees, and (2) serves only as the general framework for governing the terms of any employer-employee relationship that may be created by your decision to hire a particular applicant.

TYPICAL CONTRACT PROVISIONS

It is difficult to define "typical" union contract provisions since every one should be drafted to fit the needs, operations, and practices of the affected employer. For this reason, health care employers are wise to avoid any standard-form contracts drafted by a union and equally wise to avoid simply borrowing language from other contracts without first analyzing what the employer wants to do and how it fits into an employer's existing practices and any existing contract provisions.

These cautions should be kept in mind in reading Appendix 4-A, which is a copy of the 1983–85 collective bargaining agreement between the California Licensed

75

Vocational Nurses' Association, Inc., and Lakeside Community Hospital in Lakeport, Cal. This contract is typical in that it addresses two major types of subjects:

1. It sets forth the contractual relationship between the union and employer. For example:
   - The employer recognizes the union as the exclusive bargaining representative of the employees within the bargaining unit (Article 1).
   - The employer agrees to notify the union of new hires covered by the contract and of covered employees who are terminated; both the union and the employer agree that employees covered by the contract are free to engage or not engage in union activities (modified open shop, Article 4).
   - Both the union and employer agree to resolve disputes concerning the interpretation of the contract through a final and binding grievance and arbitration procedure (Article 13).
   - Reciprocal no-strike, no-lockout provisions are included (the union will not strike and the employer will not lock out during the life of the contract in return for final and binding arbitration of contract disputes, Article 13, Section G).
2. It also governs the relationship between the employer and its employees, and even among employees themselves. It does this by specifying, for example, the employees' wages (Article 7), hours (Articles 7 and 9), fringe benefits (Article 8), working conditions (such as Article 10's provisions concerning performance evaluations), and the employees' seniority rights, layoffs, and vacancies (Article 12).

Negotiation of Union Contracts

Collective bargaining is the process by which an employer and union negotiate the contents of a collective bargaining agreement. Collective bargaining is subject to certain legal guidelines but when operating within those parameters, a variety of practical considerations can affect how you negotiate and what positions you should adopt.

Legal Framework

The obligation to bargain in good faith is imposed by section 8(d) of the NLRA:

> [T]o bargain collectively is the performance of the mutual obligation of the employer and the representative of the employees to meet at reasonable times and confer in good faith with respect to wages, hours, and

other terms and conditions of employment, or the negotiation of an agreement or any question arising thereunder, and the execution of a written contract incorporating any agreement reached if requested by either party, but such obligation does not compel either party to agree to a proposal or require the making of a concession. . . .[1]

Section 8(d) is enforced by sections 8(a)(5) and 8(b)(3) of the Act, which make it an unfair labor practice for an employer or union to refuse to bargain in good faith.

You will note that the definition in section 8(d) has several separate elements:

Obligation To Bargain

An employer has no obligation to bargain with a union unless and until:

- the union is designated as the exclusive bargaining representative for a group of employees (how a union becomes recognized is discussed in Chapter 3)
- the employer receives a request from the union to commence collective bargaining negotiations; while no strict formalities must be met by this union request, it must convey clearly to the employer that bargaining is being sought.[2]

Bargaining in Good Faith

The requirement imposed by section 8(d) ''to meet at reasonable times and confer in good faith'' often is referred to in shorthand fashion as the ''obligation to bargain in good faith,'' or your ''bargaining obligation.''

The duty to bargain in good faith requires that:

- you enter into negotiations with an open mind (without a predetermined disposition not to bargain)
- you make a sincere effort to reach an agreement on mutually acceptable terms.[3]

The obligation to bargain in good faith is the same for all industries. For example, the Board has held that nursing homes must meet the same bargaining standards as those that apply to other businesses, despite extensive governmental and other regulation of nursing home rates.[4]

The presence or absence of good faith is a state of mind. The Board and courts scrutinize the parties' entire conduct to determine whether they have fulfilled this obligation.[5] A difficult line to draw has been between mere hard bargaining, which is lawful, and bad faith bargaining, which is not.

However, certain characteristics of bad faith bargaining have been identified. One of the most common types is what has come to be called "surface bargaining." This arises when one of the parties, while pretending to negotiate, actually is just going through the motions without any real intention of arriving at an agreement. In a sense, the party is shadow boxing as a tactical maneuver.[6] The kind of conduct that may result in a finding of surface bargaining includes:

- attending bargaining sessions without meaningful participation
- rejecting the other side's proposals without reason
- making no real effort to reconcile differences
- engaging in dilatory conduct such as sudden and unpredictable changes of position when the parties are on the verge of an agreement
- postponing scheduled negotiation sessions repeatedly
- imposing unreasonable conditions or demands.[7]

Bargaining tactics that have the effect of bypassing the union or that tend to undermine its authority also will be classified as bad faith. If, for example, you make proposals directly to the employees and not to the union, you have bypassed the union and violated your bargaining obligation.[8] Similarly, take-it-or-leave-it bargaining may be found to constitute a bad faith refusal to bargain where the totality of the employer's conduct establishes that no real attempt was made to reach agreement.[9]

Good faith bargaining does not require you to agree with every or any union proposal, or that you reach agreement on a new contract, or that a contract must result from collective bargaining. Section 8(d) protects your right to disagree, stating that it "does not compel either party to agree to a proposal or require the making of a concession. . . ."

This means that hard bargaining in and of itself is not bad faith bargaining. As summarized by the Board:

> An employer is not, and may not be, required to yield on positions fairly maintained, but it may not use those positions as a "cloak" behind which to conceal a purposeful strategy to give the union a "runaround" while purporting to be meeting with the union for the purpose of collective bargaining.[10]

An 'Impasse' in Negotiations

The duty to bargain does not require that the parties negotiate forever if, as is their right, they simply cannot agree.[11] This means that if your employer has engaged in exhaustive good faith bargaining but the parties still are stalemated in their respective positions, then the law recognizes that an impasse exists. When that occurs, the duty to bargain is suspended and your employer "may" unilaterally implement terms it offered during negotiations without the union's agreement. Yet caution is in order since:

- Your employer cannot implement terms that are more favorable than those previously offered to the union.[12]
- Your bargaining obligation is not suspended if the impasse results from a party's bad faith bargaining or other unfair labor practices.[13]
- The existence or nonexistence of impasse often is difficult to determine since it generally is a factual question dealt with on a case-by-case basis (and consideration is given to factors such as the number of negotiating sessions, the rigidity of the parties' positions, etc.).[14]
- A strike does not automatically mean that an impasse exists.[15]
- Changes in either party's circumstances, the bargaining climate, etc. (such as a strike, altered business conditions, an actual change in either party's position) can eliminate the legally defined impasse on the theory that such a changed condition renders one or both of the parties more flexible in their negotiating positions, and that the "circumstances which led to the impasse no longer remain in status quo."[16]

Because of these complexities, it is unwise for an employer to conclude that an impasse (or at least, an impasse for purposes of the NLRA) has been reached without seeking expert assistance. This is particularly true if your employer is contemplating some action, such as the unilateral implementation of a salary increase, based on its conclusion that an impasse exists.

Subjects of Bargaining

Another element of section 8(d) you should note is that the obligation to bargain in good faith only exists for certain subjects, namely, "wages, hours, and other terms and conditions of employment." This wording of section 8(d) has led the Board and the courts to distinguish among mandatory, permissive, and illegal subjects of bargaining.

A mandatory subject of bargaining concerns an issue that falls within the phrase "wages, hours, and other terms and conditions of employment." If, for example, a union demands a wage increase, this is a mandatory subject of bargaining and you must bargain in good faith. Similarly, if your employer proposes wage concessions in negotiations for a new contract, the union cannot refuse to discuss the issue but must bargain in good faith. In addition, either a union or an employer can insist upon including a mandatory subject in a contract, even to the point of impasse. If an impasse (or stalemate) is reached in negotiations, then the union can strike in support of its demands.

By contrast, a permissive subject is a demand or proposal falling outside of the phrase "wages, hours, and other terms and conditions of employment." An example would be a union demand that supervisors be covered by the contract. This is not a mandatory subject of bargaining because supervisors are not covered employees for purposes of the Act and an employer cannot be compelled to negotiate concerning them unless it agrees voluntarily to do so. As a result, you could flatly refuse to even discuss the union's demand. Even if you did agree to discuss it, the union could not lawfully strike or take other action to force your employer to agree to the inclusion of supervisors.

An illegal topic is a demand that would cause the other party to violate the law. A clear example would be a union demand that your hospital agree to a closed shop union security clause, which is a demand that all applicants for employment must be union members as a precondition of employment. This is prohibited by section 8(a)(3) of the Act and an employer cannot lawfully agree to this demand.

Section 8(d) does not specifically define "wages, hours, and other terms and conditions of employment." As a result, the Board and the courts have interpreted, on a case-by-case basis, whether a particular demand or proposal represents a mandatory or permissive subject of bargaining:

- Wages: Under these interpretations, the term "wages" includes hourly pay rates, overtime pay, piecework rates, incentive plans, shift differentials, paid holidays and vacations, other fringe benefits, and severance pay. However, wages has been interpreted to mean more than simply the sums of money you pay for work performed; it also extends to other direct forms of compensation or economic benefits that flow from the employment relationship.[17] This means that wages also includes the following further examples of mandatory subjects for bargaining: shift differentials, pensions, profit-sharing plans, regular Christmas and other bonuses that have the attributes of compensation for service rendered (rather than gifts), stock purchase plans, merit wage increases, insurance plans, company-furnished housing, meals, discounts, and other services.[18]

- Hours: As with wages, the term "hours" has been extended beyond its obvious meaning to include the length of the workday, workweek, the days of the week and hours during the day to be worked, compulsory overtime, and related matters.[19]

- Other Terms and Conditions of Employment: The most room for interpretation exists with the section 8(d) phrase "other terms and conditions of employment." It has been interpreted to include a variety of other issues such as the hire, disciplinary action, and discharge of employees; work rules;

safety practices; individual workloads; union security provisions, including the establishment of a union or agency shop and union dues checkoff provisions; and management-union relationships, including grievance and arbitration procedures and no-strike clauses.[20]

As noted, a mandatory subject of bargaining means that either party can insist upon its inclusion in any settlement or written contract and can enforce that demand by economic action such as a strike or lockout. It also means that since you must bargain about the issue, you cannot unilaterally change a mandatory subject without risking a possible refusal-to-bargain charge under section 8(a)(5) of the Act. You should remember that:

- If you have an unexpired contract that directly speaks to and governs a particular mandatory subject, then neither you nor the union has any obligation to bargain about or to change the contract provisions.
- If you have an unexpired contract that does not cover the mandatory subject, you may have the legal obligation to bargain with the union prior to changing any extracontractual practice and you can implement your proposed change only after you have bargained and an impasse has been reached.
- If the contract has expired, you still cannot change mandatory subjects of bargaining unless you have reached an impasse in negotiations; then you can implement the proposed changes even if the union did not accept them. The reason you can do this is that an impasse temporarily defers the obligation to bargain. This is an extremely tricky area of the law and you never act upon your own assumption that an impasse has been reached; consult with counsel.

An example can help in describing these guidelines. Assume that your x-ray technicians now receive a shift differential of 25 cents an hour. This is part of the written collective bargaining agreement between your nursing home and the union, a contract that will not expire for another year. Assume further that you are having difficulty hiring x-ray technicians for the night shift and you want to leave the differential at 25 cents an hour for the P.M. shift but increase it to 50 cents an hour for the night shift as a recruitment aid.

Before you could lawfully implement the change in shift differential:

- You must meet your bargaining obligation toward the union even though the proposed change is an improvement and even though the collective bargaining contract is still in effect and has not been formally opened for negotiations.
- You must, at a minimum, notify the union of the proposed increase in the shift differential.

- You must meet with the union, if it objects, to discuss your proposal and you must make a good faith attempt to reach agreement by considering any union objections, arguments, or suggested modifications.
- You can proceed to implement the higher night shift differential without the union's concurrence when, and only when, the negotiations reach an impasse in the sense that further discussions would not be fruitful.

Now, to change the facts, assume that you are submitting your proposed shift differential change when the contract is open (after it has expired but before a new one has been renegotiated). Under these circumstances, you still are required to bargain in good faith concerning the proposed increase and you still can lawfully implement your action once an impasse has been reached but both you and the union would be free to take economic action in support of a demand or position.

The only legal distinction that hinges on the existence of a current collective bargaining agreement is that neither party can take economic action when an impasse occurs during the life of a contract (assuming the agreement contains a no-strike, no-lockout provision and that flagrant unfair labor practices have not been committed). Economic action can be taken, however, if an impasse occurs in the negotiation or renegotiation of a new contract.

NEGOTIATIONS: PRACTICAL CONDITIONS AND POINTERS

If an employer has union contracts or the labor organization is newly recognized, a priority must be placed upon the process of negotiating and administering those contracts. The employer has just as much interest and stake in the outcome of collective bargaining as the labor organization and employees. You will be required to follow the terms and conditions of the contract and its terms can have an impact on your ability to manage and to get the work done.

The employer should enter collective bargaining by evaluating union demands against existing and future cost constraints, equity considerations among classifications of employees, and the impact of specific union proposals or contract provisions. There also should be awareness that employer proposals may be in order.

Effective collective bargaining requires advance planning, attention to detail, and patience.

Advance Planning and Preparation

A variety of activities should be completed before your employer's negotiating committee even sets foot in the room used for the sessions. While the exact nature of these activities can vary, the more common issues to review or to keep in mind as potentially needing advance preparation are the following:

- determining recent salary increases given by competing employers (and the resulting comparable salaries or salary ranges) as well as the benefit packages offered by those employers
- reviewing grievances that arose during the term of the contract to determine whether your employer should submit its own proposals for changes
- discussing existing provisions (and problems) with the supervisory personnel dealing with the contract on a daily basis; in this way, other areas requiring change (or perhaps just requiring additional clarification) might be identified
- reviewing cost-of-living statistics (or other data) that may be pertinent to formulating your employer's position (or data that may be relied on by the union or that may affect your employees' expectations)
- considering whether your benefit plans (for example, any retirement or health insurance programs) need revision in their eligibility features, benefit levels, etc., and, if so, determining the precise changes that would be most appropriate.

Use of a Chief Spokesperson

Whether an employer uses in-house representatives, paid consultants, or legal counsel, an experienced professional should be the chief spokesperson. Chaos—and a poor bargain—will result if no one individual has the responsibility for negotiations and stating the employer's position. A qualified spokesperson helps not only in evaluating union proposals and recommending a course of action and employer responses but also in drafting language to reflect precisely any employer proposal or any agreements reached. The chief spokesperson generally will be assisted by an employer negotiating committee (or at the minimum one supervisory or administrative employee); the composition of that committee should be chosen carefully.

Who Should Participate on the Negotiating Committee

Depending upon the group of employees represented by the union, the composition of the employer's negotiating committee can vary. If, for example, the bargaining unit covers all professional employees, who work in a variety of departments, not all department heads can or should participate on the committee because such large groups are unmanageable and consume an excessive amount of otherwise productive worktime. Participation by assistant or associate administrators or other individuals who have responsibility for some or all of the departments is one alternative. If, by contrast, a very small unit of employees is involved, perhaps a professional unit in a very small nursing home or a registered nurse unit in a small hospital, the department head or other administrative person in charge of that entity could be involved.

The basic consideration is that, generally, at least one individual on the employer's negotiating committee should be familiar with the operations of the affected departments and at least one should be fully cognizant of the employer's personnel policies and practices. Whatever the composition of the committee, its representatives must ensure that other employer personnel affected by the negotiations are kept informed and give input as appropriate during the course of the contract talks.

In turn, and even if you do not participate physically in the process, all supervisors should remember that they can contribute to the success of the negotiations. They should keep informed of daily developments and be ready to offer constructive suggestions as needed. They also need to alert their own superiors or other employer personnel who are participating as to any rumors circulating among employees or other similar events that could affect the negotiations or how the employer's offers are presented or perceived.

Conduct of the Bargaining Sessions

The conduct of bargaining sessions is the primary responsibility of the chief spokesperson. The purpose of the employer negotiating committee is to assist the spokesperson, not by speaking out on any and all issues as the whim arises but by serving as a resource. During the session, the spokesperson presents the employer's proposals or responses to union requests, explains the justification for the positions presented, and indicates to the union, directly or indirectly, avenues of possible agreement. The spokesperson also should have access to the chief executive officer (who may not, and generally should not, be present during actual negotiating sessions) for decisions.

Strikes

Strikes are not a desirable method for resolving labor disputes but they can and do occur. Legally, and because Congress brought health care institutions under the Act, (1) the states no longer can outlaw or regulate strikes against hospitals and other such facilities, and (2) employees have been granted the right to strike. Practically speaking, this means that employees have the unfettered right to withdraw their services by striking in support of their new demands if the contract has expired and a settlement has not been reached. Faced with such a situation, an employer's only options may be to accept either the union's requests or the fact that a strike may be inevitable because the demands are unrealistic and too costly.

If your health care institution is faced with a work stoppage, it has a number of options, none of which are particularly attractive (but they still may be preferable to accepting the union's demands). You could, for example:

- provide a reduced level of service
- close the facility and transfer your patients
- continue full operations through the use of temporary or permanent replacements.

If your facility reviews its options and decides to remain open during a strike and to maintain its services to the maximum extent possible, a number of difficult decisions have to be made.

> Patients needs, staffing requirements, and supplies must all be examined. It is crucial, therefore, to analyze such factors as the ability to receive supplies during the strike, the ability of strike replacements to cross the picket line, and the willingness of nonstriking personnel to work behind the picket line. In some instances, it may even be necessary to remove the patients to another facility in order to ensure proper care.[21]

All these problems are highlighted if the health care institution is located in a community where alternative services are either nonexistent or in short supply. Furthermore, you cannot make your decisions in a vacuum. You must be guided by the employer's rights and obligations under labor law principles, some of which are outlined next and in Chapter 3. At the same time you must be mindful of the institution's continued duty of care owed to existing patients and those seeking admission to the facility.

STRIKE ISSUES AND LAW

The following list is not all-inclusive but it does discuss briefly some of the most frequent problems that arise when a health care institution is picketed or struck.

Triaging and Transferring Patients

An employer who performs services that would have been done by a struck employer ordinarily becomes the "ally" of the other and, as a result, may be picketed. However, an exception exists that allows hospitals to transfer their patients to other health care facilities without the accepting institutions' becoming allies.[22]

Similarly, a hospital that supplies a struck facility with employees possessing critical skills, such as an EKG technician, retains its neutral status and does not become an ally of the struck institution.

Replacing Strikers

Supervisors and Other Exempt Personnel. If an employer uses its exempt managerial personnel to perform nonexempt, struck work during a strike, legal counsel should be sought so as to maintain such employees' exempt status.[23]

Volunteers. To preserve their voluntary status, volunteers should confine their services to ministering to the comfort of patients.[24] If volunteers are used for other services, as might be necessary, they may need to be treated as employees and if so, the employer must comply with state and federal wage-hour laws and other applicable legislation.

Members of the Striking Union. Members of the striking union who report for work should be assigned their regular duties and their performance of any other work should be voluntary.

Other Employees. Nonsupervisory employees may be requested to perform work that would have been done by striking employees. However, an employee who refuses to perform such "struck work" may not be disciplined.[25]

'Outside Replacements.' An employer is always free to hire temporary employees to replace striking employees and may hire permanent replacements if the strike is "economic" (e.g., after contract negotiations break down and the employer's unfair labor practices have not caused or prolonged the strike) or "unprotected" (e.g., in violation of a no-strike clause and the employer has not committed flagrant unfair labor practices). Unless strikers have been lawfully and permanently replaced, they have a right to reinstatement upon their unconditional request to return to work.

Some state laws require an employer to inform potential applicants that a strike is in progress.[26] In addition, under federal law, it is unlawful to willfully transport employees across state lines for the purpose of "obstructing or interfering by force or threats" striking employees.[27] Some states have enacted antistrikebreaker laws that penalize employers for utilizing professional strikebreakers.[28]

Questioning Employees on Their Strike Intentions

When there is a reasonable belief that a strike is imminent, such as the receipt of a ten-day strike notice, an employer has a limited right to question its employees regarding their intentions to work if a strike occurs.[29] However, the questions must be completely neutral and unaccompanied by threats, promises, or other coercive conduct.[30] To be valid, the health care employer should fully explain the purpose of the questioning, assure employees that no reprisals will be taken against them as a result of their response, and otherwise refrain from creating a coercive atmosphere.[31]

Wages, Benefits, Unemployment, Etc.

Wages. New employees hired either as temporary or permanent replacements for striking workers must be paid at the same wage rate and compensation in effect immediately prior to the strike.[32] An exception to this general rule is that if the employer has implemented its "last offer" after an impasse in negotiations is reached, the same "new" wage can be paid to strike replacements.

Employees are not entitled to any wages for periods when they are out on strike. Applicable wage-hour law, however, may require an employer to pay all unpaid, accrued wages up to the date of the strike.[33]

Health and Life Insurance Issues. Collective bargaining agreements and current health insurance contracts should be consulted to determine when coverage terminates for employees who are not working. In the absence of any provision governing such situations, an employer should follow its regular practice used for employees on an unpaid leave of absence. Some states allow striking employees to maintain coverage under a group life insurance policy by paying the premiums themselves.[34]

Vacations and Sick Leave. A striker who has a previously authorized vacation scheduled to begin on or after the commencement of the strike is entitled to vacation pay for that period.[35] An employee already on paid sick or disability leave at the start of the strike should continue to receive those benefits so long as the person remains disabled and unable to work, even if the employee actively participates in the strike.[36]

Unemployment Compensation. Whether or not striking employees receive unemployment benefits depends upon state law. Generally, they are not entitled to such benefits until (1) they are permanently replaced or (2) they obtain other eligible employment and that job is severed for reasons unrelated to the labor dispute.

Transportation and Lodging. Employees who are concerned about their personal safety and protection may be provided with transportation and lodging by the employer. However, transportation and lodging cannot be used as an inducement to encourage employees to abandon the strike.[37]

Subcontractors. Employees of independent contractors or subcontractors working at a health care facility may be insulated from a strike there by the establishment of separate "reserved" gates.[38] If certain gates or entrances are reserved exclusively for employees and people doing business with the contractor, then a striking union that pickets the gates will be violating the National Labor Relations Act.

It should be noted that advance planning for a strike is critical, and these and related issues should be reviewed with legal counsel so that appropriate modifications and decisions can be made. Review by legal counsel also is imperative since the legal principles do change and geographical variations do exist.

REDUCING THE AGREEMENT TO WRITING

The actual practices followed by particular employers and unions concerning settlement agreements and written contracts vary tremendously. Some parties write up and initial their settlement and identify precisely whether a new provision is to be added to article *X* on page *Y*. By contrast, some other settlements are verbal, with nothing in writing until the new contract has been prepared and is ready for execution (i.e., signing by the parties). Recognizing that variations exist, it still is suggested, at a minimum, that the following be done:

- Each agreement on new language (or modifications to existing language) should be reduced to writing as it is reached (even if it is only handwritten on a slip of paper) and initialled or signed by the chief spokespersons for both parties.
- An outline of the final settlement should be prepared and similarly initialled or signed (and, depending on the sequence of the negotiations, this outline actually may consist of a prior written employer offer with insertions, strike-outs, or other changes noted on the document, or it could be an outline prepared by one party, or the old contract with strikeouts and insertions, etc.).

By reducing the basic components of your settlement to writing, you have eliminated (or at least reduced) the number of ambiguities and uncertainties (or actual disagreements) that might arise when the full contract is drafted. It should be remembered that people ''hear'' things differently so this approach also aids in protecting your employer from unpleasant subsequent disputes over ''who said what'' and ''what was meant by what was said'' during negotiations.

Tentative Settlements

There is no requirement in the NLRA that a contract settlement be approved by the affected employees. This means that a single union representative or a union negotiating committee could reach a final settlement at the conclusion of any particular set of negotiations. In actual practice, however, many unions will reach only a tentative settlement with an employer, meaning that the agreement is not binding until it has been accepted or ratified by a majority of voting employees.

If this happens to your employer, it is important to know whether the union will be presenting this tentative settlement to your employees with a recommendation that it be accepted, with a recommendation that it be rejected, or with no recommendation. These distinctions can be critical since, in many circumstances, a union recommendation against acceptance of the tentative settlement package may convince a majority of the employees voting that they should reject the agreement in favor of continued negotiations or in favor of a strike.

Postsettlement Activity

When a collective bargaining agreement is renegotiated, it often appears as though little has changed. Yet this can be deceptive, particularly if you remember that even a small shift of a sentence or phrase can have great impact on what the contract says and how it may be interpreted. For this reason, and because a settlement simply means that the process of contract administration is beginning (which is how an employer complies with the contract during the term of the contract), it is important to ensure that all supervisory and administrative personnel become familiar with the new agreement immediately after ratification.

Therefore, a meeting or seminar for supervisory personnel should be held to review changes in the agreement and how existing provisions and changes will be interpreted by your employer (if a meeting is not scheduled, it should be requested). Of course, this review session is even more critical when you are confronted with an entirely new collective bargaining agreement.

COMMON CONTRACT PROVISIONS

While contracts can vary tremendously in length and in specific provisions, there is a great deal of commonality concerning the types of subjects addressed.

Variations in Specific Contracts

Collective bargaining agreements contain a variety of provisions on a multitude of subjects. They all have some common features such as wage rates, fringe benefits, hours of work, overtime or other premium pay, and seniority or other provisions governing layoffs or bidding on vacancies. However the exact provisions and how they are worded can vary widely. As a result, you must read and reread any collective bargaining contract that covers the employees you supervise.

As you read the contract, note any limitations, restrictions, or qualifying language. Never assume that the language you see is superfluous or unimportant; it all exists for a reason and if anything at all is unclear, seek assistance. Also remember that the contract's written provisions are continually being interpreted by the employer and the union and that those formal or informal understandings may affect the current meaning of the language you read.

One illustration of how results can differ, based on small variations in language, may be helpful:

Every collective bargaining contract should describe the unit or group of employees it covers, but how this is done can vary. For example, the document might say, "This contract covers Registered Nurses classified as Registered Staff Nurses" or it might refer to functions or work covered by the contract, such as,

"The union's jurisdiction extends to the work performed by all Registered Nurses, excluding only those Registered Nurses who have the authority to hire, fire, take disciplinary action, or to effectively recommend same."

The first statement of contract coverage is quite precise, minimizing disputes as to who is or is not covered. The first example also is narrower, being limited to the staff nurse classification, while the second extends to all nonsupervisory registered nurses and could include employees in specialized or advanced clinical positions where the restrictions and limitations of the bargaining agreement may not be appropriate. Furthermore, the second example gives the union what is called "bargaining work jurisdiction"—the ability to control who does and does not do the work performed by covered registered nurses, both currently and in the future.

The statement of contract coverage will be affected by any NLRB finding as to the appropriate bargaining unit yet the illustration does point out the importance of careful draftsmanship and, equally, of careful reading.

Common Contract Provisions

Some of the provisions you may find in health industry collective bargaining contracts are quite typical of those in most union agreements.

Wages

Collective bargaining agreements state the single wage rate or the range of wages for classifications covered. Schedules of job classifications and the applicable wage rates may appear in the contract or as appendixes to it. The need to maintain health care institutions on a 24-hour basis also may be reflected by the incorporation of provisions for shift differentials, standby or callback pay, guarantees for callback pay, minimum rest periods between shifts, and other similar details.

Hours of Work

Many contracts do not guarantee employees a minimum number of hours of work, or "guaranteed workweek." A guarantee means that employees will be paid for the specified number of hours even if work is not provided or is not available. The fact that the contract defines the workday (for example, an eight-hour day), or workweek (such as five eight-hour days or 40 hours) does not automatically mean that a guaranteed workweek has been agreed upon. The workday and workweek must be defined contractually to serve as a basis for calculating overtime. By contrast, a guaranteed workday or workweek generally exists only when the contract explicitly provides for it.

Fringe Benefits

Fringe benefits generally fall into one of two areas: paid time off and paid benefits such as insurance. Paid time off includes vacations, holidays, sick leave and/or paid leaves of absence, educational leave, and jury duty. Vacations and holidays, however, usually affect the most employees and have the greatest cost impact.

A vacation clause should state who is eligible and how much time is earned at varying years of service. Such clauses also may cover work performed during a vacation period, scheduling of vacations, splitting and deferring them, and the amount of vacation pay due, if any, upon termination from employment. Precise wording in this clause is essential since disputes over vacations are a source of many arbitrations.

Since holiday work cannot be avoided in most health care facilities, your contracts should state clearly whether a premium is to be paid for working a holiday, what day is the holiday for purposes of premium pay, and the employee's rate for such work. Contracts may provide that the employer will attempt to grant certain employees the day off on major holidays (such as Christmas Day or New Year's Day) or to alternate such days off, etc.

Provisions for floating holidays and/or the employee's birthday also are increasingly common. The term floating holiday aptly describes a paid day off that is scheduled by mutual agreement between the employee and employer (which probably means you). Thus, the exact day taken floats, or varies, from employee to employee and from year to year, an attraction to health care institutions with staffing and scheduling needs.

Many employers offer a variety of paid fringe benefits: group health, dental, drug, vision, and life insurance programs. Eligibility standards are critical in this area. Is coverage limited to employees who work a certain number of hours (such as regularly scheduled part-time and full-time personnel)? Is the employee required to pay a portion of the premium as a condition of coverage? If so, these standards and requirements should be stated clearly.

Many health care institutions have retirement programs that may be incorporated in collective bargaining contracts by specific reference. Retirement plans almost invariably are covered by the Employee Retirement Income Security Act of 1974 (ERISA) (see Chapter 10), as are many group health and welfare plans. This means that an employer must administer the plans for the benefit of employee participants, who must meet certain standards in order to participate. In addition, the NLRA imposes certain requirements on jointly administered pension plans (those administered by both employer and union representatives), and the contract cannot conflict with these provisions.

Working Conditions

Working conditions vary from facility to facility and within the same institution. Health care institutions, by their very nature, create a variety of working conditions that reflect real (or perceived) differences in operational needs and/or employee preferences within a particular work area or job classification.

Unions frequently seek provisions to regulate or standardize these varying working conditions. For example, if employees in one area are scheduled to work three out of four weekends while others from the same classification assigned to a different area (and supervisor) are scheduled to work only every fourth weekend (because of the extensive use of relief personnel), the union is certain to present a proposal on weekends off.

While weekend provisions are not unusual in health care collective bargaining agreements, they do pose special problems relating to scheduling, fixed vs. rotating days off, and the proportion of full-time to part-time employees. Any such provisions must be drafted with great care so you will not be penalized for failure to comply with impossible requirements and, equally important, so that you can continue to ensure that the quality of care is maintained.

Seniority

Employees with a greater length of service, or seniority, often are given greater protection or preferential treatment. The concept of seniority may be seen in many contract provisions: job assignments, promotions, layoffs and rehires, transfers, choice of vacation time, choice of shifts and work hours, overtime distribution, and relocations. Health care institutions, with their higher numbers of technical and professional employees, must try to maintain a balance between the seniority claims of long-service employees and the ability to recognize professional qualifications, superior performance, and position requirements.

Here again, note the exact language used. For example, in evaluating seniority in bidding for jobs, does the contract refer to seniority as the sole factor, or is seniority controlling only if competing employees are of equal merit and ability, or must you award the position to the senior employee if that person is qualified when measured against the requirements of the position?

Who determines the qualification or ability of competing employees? The employer (you)? Or is your judgment subject to the grievance and arbitration provisions? Is seniority in the event of a layoff to be exercised within a particular classification or among classifications and is it limited to the work area or is it housewide? While seniority and layoff provisions may seem unimportant during good times, they become critical to your operations and continued efficiency when the need for a layoff arises.

Union Security

Union security, which is demanded by most unions, requires that employees join or pay dues to the union. The principal forms of union security are the following:

- The closed shop: This means that the employer can hire an applicant only if the individual already is a member of the union. The closed shop grants a union control over the labor market but fortunately it is illegal under section 8(a)(3) of the Act and is an unlawful subject of bargaining if proposed by the union. However, if the employer is not covered by the Act, certain states permit such a union demand and contract provision.

- The union shop: In this form, by contrast, the employer may hire a nonunion applicant but the employee must join the union within a specified period time (The deadline for joining cannot be sooner than 30 days after being hired). If the employee does not become or remain a union member, you would be required to terminate the person unless, in accordance with the language of section 8(a)(3) of the NLRA:

    1. you have "reasonable grounds for believing that such membership was not available to the employee on the same terms and conditions generally applicable to other members" or

    2. you have "reasonable grounds for believing that the membership was denied or terminated for reasons other than the failure of the employee to tender the periodic dues and the initiation fees uniformly required as a condition of acquiring or retaining membership."

- The contract and section 8(a)(3), as quoted here, may state the requirement in terms of union membership but you should remember that despite this language, the employee cannot be terminated for refusing to join the union but only for refusal to pay dues and initiation fees equal to those uniformly required of members.

- The agency shop: Under this form, the contract does not state that the employee is required to join or to remain in the union. However, an employee who decides to not join still is required to pay money to the union, but frequently, the amount is less than the union's actual dues.

- Maintenance of membership: This provision does not state that membership or payment of dues is required of all covered employees. Instead, the contract may say that employees who belonged to the union when the agreement was signed must continue to do so during the life of the contract. Frequently, but not always, this provision will be linked with a requirement that all or a certain proportion of new hires be subject to union shop requirements.

Union security is one issue still subject to state regulation. Section 14(b) of the Act,[39] the "right-to-work" provision, gives states the power to prohibit either union or agency shop contract provisions. As a result, do not agree to, or insert, union security provisions in a contract, or terminate an employee under any such provision, unless you know that such provisions are valid in your state.

Grievance and Arbitration Procedures

One of the most (if not the most) important contract provisions is the grievance and arbitration procedure used to settle disputes arising during the life of the agreement. The grievance procedure usually contains a number of steps to be followed by unions (on behalf of employees) and by the employer. An example of a grievance procedure is presented in Exhibit 4–1.

This grievance procedure is from Article X of the 1983-85 Collective Bargaining Agreement between Local 250, Hospital and Institutional Workers' Union, AFL-CIO, and the Affiliated Hospitals of San Francisco, a multiemployer collective bargaining association of seven private nonprofit hospitals in the San Francisco Bay Area. It is only one of the many possible ways in which such a procedure may be worded but it does illustrate common features found in many contracts. Appendix 4–A, the collective bargaining agreement between the California Licensed Vocational Nurses' Association, Inc., and Lakeside Community Hospital in Lakeport, Cal., presents another version of a grievance and arbitration procedure in article 13.

The Affiliated Hospitals' grievance procedure is typical in that it has a series of steps. A Step 1 grievance is unwritten and is directed to the employee's supervisor. If the grievance is not resolved satisfactorily, the union (not the employee) must put the complaint in writing and submit it to the designated hospital representative. If this is not resolved at Step 2 to its satisfaction, the union can demand final and binding arbitration of the issue. As the steps proceed, the person to whom the grievance is addressed and who will be responding on behalf of the employer has progressively more authority. If the dispute cannot be resolved directly by union and employer representatives, the union has the right to demand arbitration.

Several other important and common features of this particular example are as follows:

- The union has retained control over the grievance procedure. The employee does not have the right to file a formal grievance at Step 2 or to demand arbitration. The union itself decides whether to file a grievance and whether to demand arbitration, although it may be influenced to a greater or lesser degree by the employee's desire. Union control over grievances exists because the collective bargaining contract is between the employer and the union, not between the employer and individual employees. The union wants to determine how the contract will be interpreted, including interpretations reached

Exhibit 4–1 Example of a Grievance and Arbitration Procedure

ARTICLE X—GRIEVANCE PROCEDURE

Section 1—Employee Grievance:

If an employee or the Union has a grievance or complaint concerning the interpretation or application of the terms of this Agreement, including a discharge case, it shall be taken up in this manner:

Step 1: The employee or the Union representative may first confer with the department head or with such other person as the Employer may designate and attempt to settle the matter.

Step 2: If the grievance or complaint is not thus settled, it shall be set forth in writing by the Union and submitted to the Hospital and the Affiliation [the employer association]. The authorized representative of the Union shall then confer with the administrator of the Hospital, or his or her designated representative, and with a representative of the Affiliation if desired by the Hospital, and attempt to settle the matter. In making such an attempt, there shall be a full and frank disclosure by both the Hospital and the Union of their position with respect to the grievance, including the supporting rationale for the position taken. The Hospital shall indicate its final Step 2 response as to the granting or denial of the grievance in writing.

Section 2—Employer Grievance:

Step 2: If a Hospital or the Affiliation has a grievance or a complaint concerning the interpretation or application of the terms of this Agreement, it shall be set forth in writing and submitted to the Union. This shall be at Step 2 of the *Grievance Procedure*. The Administrator of the Hospital, or his or her designated representative, and/or the representative of the Affiliation, shall then confer with the authorized representative of the Union and attempt to settle the matter.

Section 3—Arbitration:

Step 3: If any such grievance or complaint has not been settled by any of the procedures described, the question may, at the request of either party, be submitted to arbitration by an Arbitrator to be selected by the representatives of the Affiliation and the Union. The award of the Arbitrator shall be final and binding on all concerned. The Arbitrator may award damages for any breach of this contract; but no such award of damages shall be made for any period earlier than the date when the grievance or complaint was first presented. The Affiliation and the Union shall each pay one-half (½) of the costs of arbitration, including the fees of the Arbitrator and other expenses of the arbitral proceeding, but not including compensation of costs of representation, advocacy or witnesses for either party.

Section 4—Time Limits:

No grievance or complaint shall be considered unless it has first been presented in writing in Step 2 within thirty (30) days of the alleged occurrence thereof.

If the grievance is not settled at Step 1 or Step 2 within fifteen (15) days of presentation in such step, or if the responding party does not reply within fifteen (15) days of presentation in such step, the grievant may take such grievance to the next step. No grievance shall be submitted to arbitration unless the demand for arbitration is presented by a party in writing to the other party within thirty (30) calendar days of the other party's final written response in Step 2 of the grievance procedure.

Exhibit 4–1 continued

Section 5—Power of Arbitrator:

The Arbitrator shall have no power to add to, to subtract from or to change any of the terms or provisions of this Agreement. His or her jurisdiction shall extend solely to claims of violation of specific written provisions of the Agreement and involve only the interpretation and application of such Agreement. The award shall be based upon the joint submission agreement of the parties, or in the absence thereof, the questions raised by the parties in respect to the specific interpretation and application of the Agreement. Without limitation upon the foregoing, if either party shall give notice of a desire to modify this Agreement as provided in Article XI, the Arbitrator shall have no power to determine what modifications or changes, if any, should be made in the Agreement or otherwise to decide any question with respect thereto, other than the sufficiency and effect of the notice itself.

Section 6—Employee's Personnel Files:

With respect to a particular complaint or grievance of an employee concerning the interpretation or application of this Agreement, and on the employee's authorization, the Business Representative of the Union may inspect relevant material in the employee's personnel file upon which the Hospital is or will be relying.

Section 7—Employee Participation:

The Employer and the Union agree that employees should be free to participate on behalf of any party in all steps of the *Grievance* and *Arbitration* Procedure, and should be free from recriminations from either side for so doing.

Section 8—Disaster Clause:

If there should occur any major public catastrophe (such as earthquake, bombing attack on the city or other similar event) as a result of which any Hospital which is a member of the Affiliated Hospitals of San Francisco is required to render unusual services without assurance of compensation to cover the cost thereof, the parties agree immediately to consider whether such event requires modification of this Agreement for the duration of the emergency. For this purpose, the Agreement may be modified by action of the Executive Board of the Union and the Affiliation, and any modification agreed upon shall be binding on the parties. If the parties cannot agree on the subject of modification, then the matter shall be immediately submitted to the Arbitrator appointed under the *Grievance Procedure*. In this instance only shall the Arbitrator have authority to change any term or provision of this Agreement; but in this instance he or she shall have authority to determine wages, hours and working conditions during the emergency resulting from such catastrophe in the light of what is reasonable under all circumstances.

Section 9—No Work Stoppage:

There shall be no stoppage or interruption of work during the life of this Agreement.

Source: Reprinted with permission of both parties from the 1983-85 Collective Bargaining Agreement between the Affiliated Hospitals of San Francisco and Local 250, Hospital and Institutional Workers' Union, Service Employees International Union, AFL-CIO.

through the filing of grievances, through grievance settlements short of arbitration, and through an arbitrator's decision.

- The employer has the right to file grievances protesting a union breach of its own contractual obligations. Section 2, Employer Grievance, of Exhibit 4–1 illustrates this type of procedure. The right to file a grievance gives employers a nonjudicial forum for resolving union breaches of contract. However, the existence of such a clause also means that the employer may be required to submit the dispute to arbitration rather than being able to seek direct judicial relief from a court.[40] As a result, the relative advantages and disadvantages of this clause should be explored with legal counsel before proposing or agreeing upon contract language for employer grievances.

- Time limits for processing grievances are described in Section 4, which states that "No grievance or complaint shall be considered unless it has first been presented in writing in Step 2 within thirty (30) days of the alleged occurrence thereof." Under this provision, if an employee were terminated on May 1 and the union's written grievance were not filed with the employer until June 15, the grievance would be untimely. Similarly, where the union is dissatisfied with the employer's written response to a grievance, the union must demand arbitration within 30 calendar days of the hospital's final Step 2 response. If it does not, an arbitrator should rule that the merits of the termination are not arbitrable since the contract bars untimely grievances.

Unions often say that time limits are simply "technical" requirements and that reasonable employers should not raise them in their defense. This is not true. Time limits have an important function: to ensure that employee complaints or problem areas are corrected as soon as possible and that employer liability does not continue to accrue.

While it is easy to say, and union representatives have said, that employers should not make mistakes, all human beings, including employers, do indeed make mistakes. If an employer does err, and interprets the contract incorrectly (and as a result, e.g., an employee is receiving less money than is due), the union and employee should have some obligation to raise the matter in a timely fashion so that it can be corrected, rather than sitting on their rights.

You should pay particular attention to the time limits in any union contract with your facility because the union's failure to comply with such limits can be waived. Specifically, if the defect is not raised at a preliminary step of the grievance and maintained throughout that procedure, then the employer may be viewed as agreeing to resolve the issue on its merits without relying upon time limit defense.

Refusals To Arbitrate

One note of caution with respect to any refusal to arbitrate untimely grievances: Section 4 of Exhibit 4–1 says, "No grievance or complaint shall be considered unless it has first been presented in writing in Step 2 within thirty (30) days. . . ." Despite that flat ban, an employer could not actually refuse, with impunity, to process a grievance filed three months after the event. Why? Because employers cannot unilaterally refuse to go to arbitration based upon their own interpretation of the contract's time limits. And why not? Because arbitration (not the court's, or the employer's unilateral judgment) is the agreed-upon forum for deciding issues of compliance or noncompliance with time limits (as well as many other issues of contract interpretation).

Thus, if a grievance is not timely filed, you should tell the union that the complaint is untimely and that you are not waiving its untimeliness but that you will discuss it on its merits without prejudicing your position. If the union subsequently demands arbitration, both issues would be presented to the arbitrator for decision. The arbitrator then would decide the merits of the grievance only if it is found that it was timely under the contract.

No-Strike Clause

Unless a strike violates the NLRA or the no-strike clause of an existing contract, it is a legitimate economic tool.[41] While negotiated and agreed to by the union, a no-strike clause is binding on individual employees, who thereby lose their right to strike during the life of the agreement.[42] Breach of a no-strike clause may result in:

- discharge of the employees since those who strike in violation of such a clause lose their protected status under section 8(a)(1)
- a court injunction ordering an end to the strike if the underlying dispute is arbitrable
- the potential of an employer lawsuit against the union for damages caused by the strike, and
- the risk of criminal sanctions for violating an order of the court against employees who continue to strike despite a court injunction.

An employer's right to obtain a court injunction against a union that breaches its no-strike clause in order to honor another union's strike against the same employer (a sympathy strike) is severely limited, however, by a key Supreme Court decision. Under this decision, you generally will not be able to enjoin sympathy strikes unless there is an underlying dispute, other than the scope of the no-strike clause itself, which is arbitrable.[43] Yet you still could proceed against the union engaging in a sympathy strike, in either arbitration or a court action, for breach of contract and any resulting damages.

Union Visitation Clause

As noted in the Chapter 3 discussion of solicitation and distribution policies, an employer has the right to limit (or prohibit) access to its property by nonemployees. This general proposition does not change with the signing of the collective bargaining agreement; to the contrary, a nonemployee union representative still has no independent right of access to your facility's premises. However, collective bargaining agreements may permit union representatives access for limited purposes such as investigating employee grievances and observing compliance with contract provisions. Care should be taken, however, to ensure that the contract also provides that union business with employees is to occur on nonworking time in nonwork areas and that the visits are not to interfere with hospital operations.

If your employer has a collective bargaining agreement allowing union visitation rights, then it is important that you enforce any contract restrictions or limitations on the union's visits, such as requesting advance notification if this is required of the union by the contract.[44]

ENFORCEMENT OF UNION CONTRACTS

Retention of the Right To Strike

Although the vast majority of collective bargaining agreements contain no-strike provisions and equally broad arbitration clauses, some unions specifically retain in their contracts the right to strike over certain issues. If the right to strike is retained during the life of the contract, then economic action—and not peaceful resolution through final and binding arbitration—becomes the union's means of enforcing its position on a disputed issue. Similarly, the employer would retain the right to lock out.

In the health care industry, you would be well advised to reject any union desire to retain the right to strike (in lieu of arbitration) during the life of a contract. This provision could preclude the stability you need from an existing contract and subject your institution to the potential of more strikes, with all of their adverse impact upon patient care.

Final and Binding Arbitration

Jurisdiction of Arbitrator(s)

In 1960, the United States Supreme Court, on the same day, decided three cases that have become landmarks in the law of labor arbitration and are referred to collectively as the Steelworkers Trilogy[45] because they all involved suits brought by the United Steelworkers of America. These three cases, taken as a whole, produced the following major rules:

- If a contract contains no-strike and arbitration provisions, any dispute is subject to arbitration unless the language of the agreement provides otherwise.

- If it is not clear whether the employer has agreed to arbitrate a given issue, doubts are resolved in favor of arbitrability.
- If it is appropriate and helpful, the arbitrator, in reaching a decision, may call upon rules and customs established in the particular shop and industry and may rely upon the negotiating history and other dealings between the parties.

Arbitration is a matter of contract. You cannot be required to submit a dispute to arbitration if you have not agreed to do so.[46] An arbitrator's power and authority are derived from and can be limited by the terms of the collective bargaining contract. The arbitrator's duty is to settle disputes arising under the contract by applying and interpreting that agreement, not by adding to or modifying the parties' agreement as reflected in the contract.[47]

The Arbitration Process

Simply stated, arbitration is a contractual, nonjudicial proceeding in which a neutral third person, usually chosen by the parties, hears evidence and argument by both sides and issues a final and binding award. An arbitrator must be distinguished from a mediator. A mediator is involved in negotiations for a new contract. Frequently working with each party individually, a mediator attempts to bring the two sides together and to fashion a compromise settlement satisfactory to both. An arbitrator, on the other hand, generally renders a decision on a dispute under an existing contract. The arbitrator's decision usually is unsatisfactory to at least one, and sometimes both, of the parties.

Selection of the Arbitrator: The first step is the selection of the arbitrator or the arbitration panel. Some contracts name one arbitrator for the life of the agreement, others may name a group of arbitrators from which the one for a particular case is selected.

Occasionally, the contract provision will allow a government agency such as the Federal Mediation and Conciliation Service or a private organization such as the American Arbitration Association to name an arbitrator or to submit a list to the parties from which they select one. Whichever method is used, the aim is to obtain the services of a neutral third party acceptable to both sides. Arbitrators, who should have experience in labor matters, include college professors, attorneys, judges, public officeholders, and others.[48]

Scheduling the Arbitration: The date, time, and place of the arbitration are the next items to be agreed upon between the parties and the arbitrator. The exact phrasing of the issue(s) to be decided also must be determined. This can be done by the parties' agreeing on a written submission or statement that briefly sets out the subject matter of the dispute. It also can be done by a verbal statement at the commencement of the arbitration hearing.

Sometimes the parties are unable to agree on the exact wording of the issue(s). If this happens, they submit a verbal or written statement reflecting their separate versions and the arbitrator frequently is given the authority to frame the issue for decision. Since the arbitrator is bound by both the contract and the submitted issue(s), the wording is of great significance.

The Arbitration Hearing: Procedural questions growing out of the dispute and influencing its final disposition are left to the arbitrator to resolve.[49] Procedural questions usually involve a claim by one of the parties that the other has failed to follow the required procedure (such as time limits) for processing grievances as established in the collective bargaining contract.

The arbitrator also controls the conduct of the hearing. So long as fundamental due process rights are given to both parties, the arbitrator has a great deal of latitude. For example, unless expressly required by both parties, strict observance of legal rules of evidence is not necessary.[50] Nevertheless, an arbitrator will impose certain basic rules of evidence. Similarly, there are no hard-and-fast rules concerning the burden of proof or the order of presentation of evidence. In discharge and discipline cases, however, you (the health care institution) generally will have the burden of proof (you must prove your case), and thus your evidence will be presented first.

Typically, each side presents its case by briefly outlining its argument and the evidence to be submitted and by introducing documents and calling witnesses in support of its position. Each side has the right to cross-examine witnesses put on by the opposing party. After both sides have presented their evidence, the final arguments may be made orally and the hearing closed. Frequently, the parties may prefer to submit written documents, termed briefs, that summarize their evidence and the legal and factual arguments in support of their case. Finally, the arbitrator, having considered the oral evidence and written briefs, if any, makes an award that is sent to both parties.

Supervisor Participation in Arbitration: As a supervisor, you may be a participant in an arbitration hearing where the union is protesting disciplinary action that you took or recommended or where you were a first-hand witness to some relevant events. If your testimony is required, an employer attorney or other representative of the employer will meet with you in advance to review your potential testimony. Before that meeting, you should be sure to review all pertinent documents; if you do not, the meeting will take twice as long and neither you nor your employer will have any valid objection if your failure to do so means the attorney has to sit there at a cost to your employer while you refresh your recollection.

At that prehearing review, try to control your natural impatience in reviewing (or rereviewing) facts and events with your representative. Your representative wants to present your case persuasively, which requires total familiarity with what happened, why it happened, and the extent to which different witnesses vary in their recollections.

If you have to testify at an arbitration or similar hearing, always keep in mind that you are responsible only for your answers, not for the questions posed. Be responsive to the questions, answer the questions—and do not forget that it is natural to forget. No one has a perfect memory.

Witness Demeanor: Your version of the underlying events or facts frequently will conflict with that presented by union witnesses. When this happens, the arbitrator must decide between the two versions. Of crucial importance in this determination is the arbitrator's observation of a witness's demeanor: Does the witness' conduct and testimony give the appearance of telling the truth and accurately recalling the events?

The best and only rule to follow in maximizing the positive nature of your testimony and of your demeanor is to always tell the truth. If you lie or fabricate, it will show in your testimony and you may get caught in your own web by the union counsel. So, if you do not remember something, say so; if you do remember, testify as you recall it. Do not feel compelled to fill in any gaps in memory with what you think "could have happened," or with what "sounds the best" for the case, or with what you've "heard" from others in preparing for the case. Avoid this tendency since no one has a perfect memory—not you, not the union, not the arbitrator—and if you remember instead to follow the basic principles just reviewed, then you will have done everything that could reasonably be expected of a witness.

The Arbitration Award

The award is the arbitrator's binding determination of the issues presented by the parties. Awards usually are short and ideally they should be "definite, certain and final and should dispose of all matters submitted."[51] While an arbitrator generally will accompany the award with a separate written opinion (called a decision) that states the reasons for the outcome, there is no obligation to do so unless required by the collective bargaining agreement itself.[52] Should an arbitrator attach an opinion that is ambiguous or even faulty, it will not affect the validity of the award.[53]

Finality of the Award

Federal and state courts have jurisdiction under section 301 of the NLRA to set aside (or vacate) an arbitrator's award in certain limited circumstances.[54] If the arbitrator clearly has exceeded the terms of the collective bargaining contract or of the issue submitted for decision, the courts do have the power to set aside or modify the resulting award. In addition, where the award is tainted by fraud; or where the arbitrator has been guilty of misconduct in handling the proceeding; or where the award is irrational, arbitrary, or capricious, the courts have the power to intervene.

Except for these limited grounds, an arbitration award generally is final and binding upon both parties and neither one (nor the employee) has the right to appeal the decision. This finality is another feature that distinguishes arbitration from court procedure. Ordinarily, court orders are appealable and the appellate court can consider not only whether the lower court has jurisdiction but also whether it decided the case correctly in the light of the evidence presented to it and the applicable law.

A note of caution: the finality of arbitration also means employers should take extreme care in drafting the arbitration clause of your contract and in presenting cases to arbitration.

Exceptions to the Finality of the Award

The term "final and binding arbitration of contract disputes" is not always a totally correct description. Sometimes, arbitration is neither final nor binding. The major exceptions are as follows:

- Arbitration awards will be set aside by courts, as noted previously, in the very infrequent circumstances of arbitrators' exceeding their jurisdiction or being guilty of other misconduct.[55]

- The employee has specific rights in certain types of cases. If a contract issue decided by an arbitrator, including a just cause issue resulting from employer disciplinary action, also is the subject of a charge filed with the Equal Employment Opportunity Commission, then an adverse arbitration decision will not preclude the employee from pursuing the discrimination claim, even to the point of filing and pursuing a lawsuit against the employer under Title VII of the Civil Rights Act of 1964. In the case of *Alexander v. Gardner-Denver Co.*,[56] the Supreme Court held that the national labor policy of deferring to final and binding arbitration could not extend to precluding an employee from asserting claims under Title VII.

- A final and binding arbitration decision also will not preclude an employee from filing an unfair labor practice charge with the NLRB concerning the same subject matter but alleging violations of the Act, such as discharges based upon union activity. While under some circumstances the Board will defer to the arbitration process or an arbitration award, it retains the right to process the charge notwithstanding the availability of arbitration or the issuance of an arbitration award.[57]

Practically speaking, however, these exceptions to the finality of arbitration awards do not arise with great frequency and under normal circumstances a decision is in fact final and binding upon employer, union, and employee alike.

Refusals To Arbitrate and Section 301

If a collective bargaining contract provides for arbitration of disputes, and you refuse to do so, the union may obtain an order from a federal court compelling arbitration.[58] The court is limited to deciding whether the dispute is "arguably" subject to the arbitration process under that particular contract. The court cannot become involved in deciding whether either party is right or wrong on the merits of the dispute.[59] Once a court has decided that the issue is not clearly excluded from arbitration by the contract, it will order the resisting party to submit to arbitration.

CONTRACT INTERPRETATION

Various general principles must be kept in mind when reviewing and interpreting the provisions of collective bargaining contracts.

Residual Rights Theory

It is simply not possible for a collective bargaining agreement to contain all policies, rules, and procedures concerning employee performance, employee conduct, employer-employee obligations and rights, and a multitude of other possible issues. A collective bargaining contract, instead, simply describes certain things the parties, but primarily the employer, have agreed to do or not to do. Since the agreement does not cover all issues, the concept of "residual rights" exists to aid in contract interpretation.

The residual rights theory basically says that what management has not given away, it retains. Thus, if employees request paid sick leave and you have a problem concerning the requirements to be met or the procedures to be followed, you may find that the collective bargaining agreement is silent on this issue. This does not mean that the employees do not have to meet any requirements or follow any established procedures when they are ill or claim sick leave. Instead, it means that you should refer to your own facility's policies and procedures on this issue.

Many unions do not agree with the concept of reserved or residual rights yet various arbitrators have relied upon this theory in reaching decisions. While different arbitrators have phrased the concept in varying ways, one of the most complete and clearest statements was made by Arbitrator John Day Larkin:

> Initially, before unions came into the picture, all power and responsibility and all aspects of personnel management were vested in the company and its officials. Except for certain limitations imposed by Federal, state or local legislative enactments, there were no limitations on management's prerogatives. When a union is formed, and a collective bargaining agreement is entered into, the original power and authority of the

company is modified only to the extent that it voluntarily and specifically relinquishes facets of its power and authority. . . . In short, the company does not have to bargain with the Union to get rights which are inherent in the management function; but it may relinquish certain of those rights in the course of bargaining with the Union.[60]

However, you must distinguish between a desire to change certain terms and conditions of employment that are not specifically covered by the contract and the process of determining the present term or condition of employment. To return to the sick leave example:

1. You are interested not just in determining the eligibility requirements currently required of employees but you also want to tighten up your reporting procedures.
2. You first must determine whether the subject of sick leave eligibility and procedures is covered by the contract.
3. You have your answer if the contract completely covers the subject since you cannot change those requirements during the life of the agreement (absent the union's consent to different contract terms).
4. You then look to any written policies and procedures or employer practices (if the issue is not addressed in the agreement), remembering that any proposed change in those policies or practices may be subject to a bargaining obligation with the union prior to implementation, and that implementation of any such change may result in a union grievance or unfair labor practice claiming that the change violates your established "past practice."

Clear Contract Language vs. Past Practice

If contract language is clear and unequivocal, the arbitrator cannot ignore it or give it a meaning other than that expressed. As stated by one arbitrator, an arbitrator is not free to "'ignore clear-cut contractual language . . . and . . . legislate new language, since to do so would usurp the role of the labor organization and employer.'"[61] Arbitration is a creation of the contract, and is designed to interpret, not change, agreements reached by an employer and union.

Only where contract language is unclear, ambiguous, or incomplete should the arbitrator go beyond the literal contract wording by relying upon other indicators of the parties' intent.

Past Practice

If your employer has a consistent and long history of handling similar questions in one way, then that past practice may be admitted to show how the employer has interpreted the contract's language or that the practice has essentially added to (or filled in) the written terms. Factors that will influence the arbitrator in determining whether the past practice does exist and whether the employer's conduct actually assists in interpreting the contract are:

- the consistency of the employer's conduct
- the length of time the practice has been in effect
- the union's knowledge or agreement, if any, and whether that can be shown
- the circumstances under which the practice arose and
- the type of issue involved.

For example, assume that your collective bargaining agreement contains a seniority clause covering (1) layoffs resulting from a lack of work and (2) promotions into vacant or new positions. The contract also contains a vacation provision listing the amount of time employees are to receive but it does not state how the employer is to handle conflicting vacation requests.

Two employees come to you, one from the night shift and one from the day shift, both requesting approval of the same vacation periods. Because you have only one relief person and cannot provide additional coverage on such short notice, you decide to grant the request of the junior employee on the night shift and you deny permission to the senior employee on the day shift. Your decision also is based on the fact that several other day shift workers will be absent during the period requested by the senior employee and you are concerned about having an insufficient number of regular employees to handle the workload effectively.

The senior employee goes to the union, which files a grievance on her behalf. The union's argument at the arbitration hearing is twofold. First, the union argues that the contract's seniority provisions govern the question and that the senior employee is entitled to the requested vacation time where conflicting requests are submitted. Second, the union argues that on prior occasions, you, as the employer, always have honored the request of the senior employee.

When faced with the contract language, the arbitrator should note that it does not clearly cover the issue presented, "Did the employer violate the collective bargaining agreement by denying the day shift employee's vacation request?" The arbitrator will then look at the evidence and arguments submitted by both sides concerning the employer's past method of handling conflicting requests. The arbitrator also should be influenced by the circumstances under which your prior actions occurred. Specifically:

- If your employer establishes that its prior practice was not to use seniority under any and all circumstances, but only where possible, then your action is consistent with that prior practice even if the union can establish that your prior actions occurred over a long enough period of time, and were sufficiently clear and understood by the employees and union, so as to fill in the contract and bind your present actions.

- If the employer's evidence also establishes that sometimes either the senior or junior employee was given the vacation time requested and that sometimes both requests were denied, then the union will have failed to establish that any consistent practice even existed.

Under both of these circumstances, and since your actions have not violated either the contract language or the employer's own past practice, the arbitrator should issue an award denying the union's grievance.

Unions tend to rely upon the concept of past practice whenever contract language does not totally support their positions. Your rule of thumb in handling any such arguments is to remember that:

- The use of past practice, related evidence as to custom or prior dealings, and other aids of interpretation is not appropriate where the contract language is clear and unambiguous.
- The union still has the burden of proving that you have established a consistent and historical method for handling related problems, even where the language is incomplete, unclear, or susceptible to several interpretations.
- The supervisor (you) should determine what the employer's policy or prior practice is before you take action.
- The supervisor should not assume or admit that a past practice exists (particularly since your definition and the one that actually would be used by a arbitrator may differ); instead, you should seek assistance.

Negotiating History

The parties' prior negotiating history may help an arbitrator interpret contract language where the wording is unclear. To return to the past practice example, at the arbitration hearing the employer's chief negotiator testified that during the prior negotiations the union had proposed that the following language be added to the contract's vacation clause: "Where more than one employee requests the same vacation period within a work area, the senior employee's request shall be approved under all circumstances."

The employer's negotiator also testified that the institution had rejected the union's proposal. She explained that she had told the union the proposal could not be accepted because a recognition of seniority could not be guaranteed under all circumstances and because the employer had to retain the right to meet its scheduling and staffing needs. The union then dropped its proposal for the additional contract language.

This testimony would allow the arbitrator two possible grounds for rejecting the union's grievance:

1. that the employer's "past practice" was simply to honor seniority where possible while retaining the right to reject senior employee requests as deemed necessary
2. that the union's request for new contract language reflected its recognition that neither the contract nor the employer's past practice gave senior employees an absolute guarantee of their vacation preference and/or by withdrawing its proposal the union was concurring in a continuation of the status quo.

Prior Arbitration Awards

Sometimes a union and an employer will take an issue to arbitration where the same general situation was the subject of a previous arbitration award, either by that arbitrator or another. The question then arises: What impact, if any, does the prior decision have on the current grievance?

The key point here is that arbitrations are not courts of law and arbitrators are not legally bound by precedent or prior rulings on the same issue. Unlike judges, arbitrators are free, in theory at least, to make a decision contrary to a long line of awards and similar cases. Nevertheless, many arbitrators voluntarily handle cases in the following ways:

- Where a party attempts to arbitrate the merits of the same event or incident, the arbitrator may decline on the basis that the question has been determined by a previous final and binding award.
- Where a new grievance concerns a new incident but presents the same issue or question decided previously, subsequent arbitrators may decline to relitigate the issue and will apply the interpretation of the prior arbitrator even if they rely on "new evidence" to reach the same conclusion.[62]
- Where a permanent arbitrator or panel has made prior awards, subsequent arbitrators frequently consider themselves bound by such awards and have refused to deviate.[63]

Various reporting systems publish arbitration decisions issued throughout the nation. Parties to an arbitration that have not previously arbitrated the issue before them frequently use these reported decisions in their arguments, suggesting that the arbitrator apply the same reasoning to the case now being decided. Arbitrators themselves frequently quote published decisions as supporting their own reasoning or decision.

In short, while arbitrators are not legally required to honor prior arbitration decisions under the same or different contracts or by the same or different arbitrators, a "law" of arbitration appears to be emerging and common principles are being applied to similar fact situations. This allows employers, unions, and you as a supervisor to have a better understanding of the considerations that might influence an arbitrator in interpreting specific contract language.

Grievance Settlements As Contract Law

Where a provision is ambiguous the arbitrator, as an aid to interpretation, may take note of the parties' own actions in handling previous grievances under the same provisions.[64] Indeed, if the case involves an issue identical to one settled by mutual agreement of the parties, an arbitrator ordinarily will not make an award contrary to the previous resolution.[65]

The situation may be viewed differently, however, where a grievance is not being settled but the union has simply declined to take it further in the grievance/arbitration process. If the union has consistently declined to pursue its contract interpretations by pushing grievances to arbitration, and has allowed the employer to continue enforcing a contrary interpretation, then the arbitrator may view this course of conduct as implied acceptance of management's interpretation.[66]

TOPICS OF PARTICULAR SIGNIFICANCE

Negotiation of Professional Standards

Health care institutions have a high proportion of professional and technical employees who express a great desire to participate in fundamental decisions concerning patient care as well as on professional standards and issues. They have attempted (and continue to try) to incorporate a variety of professional issues into collective bargaining contracts. These attempts pose great difficulties for employers.

The employer is responsible for maintaining satisfactory standards of care and service. Failure to do so can subject the employer to potential liability from a variety of sources (licensure agencies, Medicare, Joint Commission on Accreditation of Hospitals, malpractice or other personal injury suits). For this reason, and because of the adversary nature and rigidity of many collective bargaining contracts, including the possibility of final and binding arbitration, many employers have resisted union efforts to include staffing patterns, the right to refuse assignments, joint participation in decision making, etc.

Yet as a practical matter, your rejection of these union proposals may lead to a strike or other economic action by the labor organization. You should know, therefore, that questions exist as to whether these types of matters are mandatory subjects of bargaining. The dividing line between mandatory and permissive patient care issues is not firm and you should review again this chapter's discussion of mandatory topics for bargaining and the concept of "protected concerted activity," as discussed in Chapter 3.

In any event, employers can agree voluntarily to include professional issues in a contract. The permissive nature of your bargaining obligation simply protects employers from being forced to give agreement. Any such provisions must be carefully considered before agreeing that the subjects will be addressed in the contract. The specific language also must be drafted with great care. Generally, disputes concerning these issues should be excluded from arbitration. Unless this is done, you will have turned over to an outside third party the power to finally and conclusively decide issues affecting the fundamental purpose—and perhaps even the structure—of the institution.

Interest Arbitration

There are two distinct types of arbitration: (1) "rights" arbitration involves the interpretation or application of an existing collective bargaining contract and (2) "interest" arbitration occurs when an arbitrator is given the power to determine the provisions of a new contract.

Interest arbitration may be used when the parties are unable to agree on the provisions of a new, renewed, or reopened contract. The parties may find it difficult or impossible to reach agreement by direct negotiation. Rather than resorting to economic force (a strike or lockout), the parties can agree to submit unresolved issues to arbitration, with both sides bound by the arbitrator's decision concerning whether the disputed issues should or should not be included in the contract and, if so, in what form. In some public employment, you may find "advisory" arbitrations where the process is basically the same but where the arbitrator's decision is not legally binding.

Just Cause and Disciplinary Action

Many contracts provide that the employer may not discharge or discipline an employee except "for cause" or for "just cause." Even where the contract is silent, many arbitrators will imply a just cause limitation on the employer's right to discipline or discharge.[67] Some contracts list a number of standards or rules as grounds for disciplinary action but the inclusion of such a list can be dangerous unless it is clear that it does not represent an all-inclusive statement as to the various grounds for discharge.

Where no grounds are listed, or where exclusive grounds are not stated, the arbitrator will note the generally accepted duties owed by employees to management such as honesty, punctuality, sobriety, respect for employer's property, observing directions, and the like.[68] Thus, even where the grounds for disciplinary action are not expressly set out in posted rules, in other employer policies or procedures, or in the contract itself, disciplinary action for employee misconduct or unsatisfactory performance generally will be upheld so long as the employer's standards are applied in a uniform, nondiscriminatory manner.[69]

An employer's obligation to prove just cause generally does not extend to a probationary or new employee. Contracts frequently provide for a probationary period during which the employee has limited rights compared to those of individuals with longer service. For example, the employee might not acquire seniority until the probationary period is completed. Vacation, holiday pay, and even wage rates also may be limited.

Yet the most crucial part of the probationary period (from your standpoint) is the right to discharge a probationary employee without being required to defend a union grievance or prove just cause. Again, however, this general rule has certain exceptions. For example, if the discharge violates other contract provisions prohibiting discrimination based on union activities, race, sex, etc., then it may be possible for a union grievance to be arbitrated. Even under these circumstances, however, you should not have to prove just cause; instead, the union should have the burden of proving that the discharge was for prohibited reasons.

It is important to remember that a Title VII or other legal challenge still can be filed to protest terminations in the probationary period (see Chapter 7) so you should retain the internal documentation as to your reasons and the facts.

The purpose of the probationary period is to give the employer an opportunity to evaluate a new employee's actual performance and conduct before extending certain job rights. As a supervisor, you should ensure that all probationary employees are evaluated during that period, which may be 60, 90, 180 days, etc., depending upon the contract.

Your decision to retain or to terminate the employee should be made well in advance of the probationary period's expiration. If you were to delay in making your decision until after that period had ended—even by just one day—then the employee no longer would be a probationary employee, and you would have to prove just cause if the termination were challenged.

NOTES

1. 29 U.S.C. § 158(d).

2. Steel City Transport Inc. v. NLRB, 389 F.2d 735 (3d Cir. 1968), *citing* NLRB v. Columbian Enameling & Stamping Co., 306 U.S. 292 (1939); NLRB v. Barney's Supercenter, 296 F.2d 91 (3d Cir. 1961).

3. NLRB v. Highland Park Mfg. Co., 110 F. 2d 632, 637 (4th Cir. 1940).

4. Nassau County Health Facilities Ass'n, Inc., 227 N.L.R.B. 1681 (1977).

5. NLRB v. Insurance Agent's Int'l Union, 361 U.S. 477, 498 (1960).

6. NLRB v. Herman Sausage Co., 275 F.2d 229, 232 (5th Cir. 1960).

7. *E.g.*, A.H. Belo Corp. v. NLRB, 411 F.2d 959 (5th Cir. 1969), *cert. denied*, 396 U.S. 1007 (1970); NLRB v. Herman Sausage Co., 275 F.2d 229 (5th Cir. 1960); NLRB v. J.A. Terteling & Sons Inc., 357 F.2d 661 (9th Cir. 1966).

8. Finch Baking Co. v. NLRB, 479 F.2d 732 (2d Cir. 1973), *enforcing,* 199 N.L.R.B. 414 (1972), *cert. denied,* 414 U.S. 1032 (1973).

9. General Electric Co., 150 N.L.R.B. 192 (1964), *enforced,* 418 F.2d 736 (2d Cir. 1969), *cert. denied,* 397 U.S. 965 (1970). Under GE's approach, the company decided in advance what it felt would be a fair contract, publicized its position widely in the media, then dug in its heels in a widely publicized stance of unbending firmness. However, in reaching a conclusion that the company had engaged in a "refusal to bargain" violation of the Act, the appellate court relied upon the company's "totality of conduct" and made it clear that a "take-it-or-leave-it" or "best-offer-first" bargaining method was not in itself unlawful. 418 F.2d 736, 762 (1969).

10. NLRB v. My Store Inc., 345 F.2d 494, 498 (7th Cir. 1965), *quoting* NLRB v. Herman Sausage Co., 275 F.2d 229, 232 (5th Cir. 1960).

11. NLRB v. American Nat'l Ins. Co., 343 U.S. 395, 404 (1952).

12. NLRB v. Katz, 369 U.S. 736 (1962).

13. United Contractors Inc., 244 N.L.R.B. 72, 77 (1979); *see* NLRB v. Herman Sausage Co., 275 F.2d 229, 234 (5th Cir. 1960).

14. *E.g.,* Taft Broadcasting Co., 163 N.L.R.B. 475 (1967).

15. J.H. Bonck Co., Inc., 170 N.L.R.B. 1471 (1968).

16. Boeing Airplane Co., 80 N.L.R.B. 447, 454 (1948).

17. W.W. Cross & Co. v. NLRB, 174 F.2d 875, 878 (1st Cir. 1949).

18. *E.g.,* Inland Steel v. NLRB, 170 F.2d 247 (7th Cir. 1948), *cert. denied,* 336 U.S. 960 (1949) (pensions); General Tel. of Florida v. NLRB, 337 F.2d 452 (5th Cir. 1964) (bonuses); Smith Cabinet Mfg. Co., 147 N.L.R.B. 1506 (1964) (shift differentials); NLRB v. Adams Dairy, Inc., 137 N.L.R.B. 815 (1962), *modified,* 322 F.2d 553 (8th Cir. 1963), *vacated,* 379 U.S. 644 (1965), *on remand,* 350 F.2d 108 (8th Cir. 1965), *cert. denied,* 382 U.S. 1011 (1966).

19. Meat Cutters, Local 189 v. Jewel Tea Co., 381 U.S. 676, 691 (1965).

20. *E.g.,* Winter Garden Citrus Products Coop. v. NLRB, 238 F.2d 128 (5th Cir. 1956) (work rules concerning coffee breaks, lunch periods, smoking, employee discipline, dress); NLRB v. Gulf Power Co., 384 F.2d 822 (5th Cir. 1967) (safety rules and practices); Gallenkamp Stores Co. v. NLRB, 402 F.2d 525, 529 n.4 (9th Cir. 1968) (hiring practices, workloads); NLRB v. Andrew Jergens Co., 175 F.2d 130, 133 (9th Cir. 1949) *cert. denied,* 338 U.S. 827 (1949) (union security); NLRB v. United Nuclear Corp., 381 F.2d 972 (10th Cir. 1967) (layoffs); Shell Oil Co., 77 N.L.R.B. 1306 (1948) (no-strike clauses).

21. District 1199 v. First Health Care Corp., 222 N.L.R.B. 212, 213 (1976).

22. General Counsel Guidelines, Memorandum 74-79, LABOR REL. YEARBOOK (BNA)—1974, at 357.

23. Marshall v. Western Union Tel. Co., 621 F.2d 1246 (3d Cir. 1980).

24. Wage-Hour Opinion Letter No. 626, CCH ¶ 30616 (1967).

25. Valmac Industries, 217 N.L.R.B. 580, 582 (1975), *enforced,* 533 F.2d 1075 (3d Cir. 1976).

26. *See, e.g.,* CAL. LAB. CODE § 973 (West 1971).

27. 18 U.S.C. § 1231.

28. *See, e.g.,* CAL. LAB. CODE § 1134 (West Supp. 1984). The validity of state strikebreaker laws has been questioned and such laws may be preempted by federal law. Illinois v. Archer, 704 F.2d 935 (7th Cir. 1983).

29. Mosher Steel Co., 220 N.L.R.B. 336 (1975).

30. Mobile Home Estates, 259 N.L.R.B. 1384 (1982).

31. Preterm, Inc., 240 N.L.R.B. 654 (1979).

32. Swedish Hosp. Medical Center, 238 N.L.R.B. 1087 (1978), *enforced*, 619 F.2d 33 (9th Cir. 1980).

33. *See, e.g.*, CAL. LAB. CODE § 209 (West 1971).

34. *See, e.g.*, CAL. INS. CODE § 10116 (West 1972).

35. Stokely-Vancamp, Inc., 259 N.L.R.B. No. 128 (1982).

36. Conoco, Inc., 265 N.L.R.B. No. 116 (1982). The situation is less clear where a striking employee falls ill and demands sick pay.

37. Pilot Freight Carriers, 223 N.L.R.B. 286, 298 (1976).

38. Sailors Union of the Pac. (Moore Drydock), 92 N.L.R.B. 547 (1950).

39. 29 U.S.C. § 164(b).

40. Eberle Tanning Co. v. Food & Commercial Workers Int'l Union, 682 F.2d 430 (3d Cir. 1982); Atkinson v. Sinclair Refining Co., 370 U.S. 238 (1962).

41. Iodice v. Calabrese, 512 F.2d 383 (2d Cir. 1975).

42. DeQuoin Packing Co. v. Amalgamated Meat Cutters and Butchers Workmen, Local P-156, 321 F. Supp. 1230 (E.D. Ill. 1971).

43. Buffalo Forge Co. v. United Steelworkers of Am., 428 U.S. 397 (1976).

44. *See, e.g.*, Standard Motor Products, Inc., 11 Lab. Arb. (BNA) 1147 (Hill, 1949); Farah Mfg. Co., 65 Lab. Arb. (BNA) 654 (Cohen, 1975).

45. United Steelworkers of Am. v. American Mfg. Co., 363 U.S. 564 (1960); United Steelworkers of Am. v. Warrior & Gulf Navigation Co., 363 U.S. 574 (1960); United Steelworkers of Am. v. Enterprise Wheel & Car Corp., 363 U.S. 593 (1960). The steelworkers trilogy also reflects that Section 301 of the NLRA, 29 U.S.C. § 1185, gives courts the jurisdiction to enforce agreements to arbitrate by compelling arbitration and to enforce arbitration awards.

46. United Steelworkers of Am. v. Warrior & Gulf Navigation Co., 363 U.S. 574, 582 (1960).

47. Schlesinger v. Building Serv. Employees Int'l Union, 367 F. Supp. 760 (E.D. Pa. 1973).

48. ELKOURI & ELKOURI, HOW ARBITRATION WORKS, at 90 (3d Ed. 1973).

49. John Wiley & Sons, Inc. v. Livingston, 376 U.S. 543 (1964).

50. ELKOURI & ELKOURI, HOW ARBITRATION WORKS, at 252 (3d Ed. 1973).

51. Code of Ethics and Procedural Standards for Labor-Management Arbitration, Part II, Section 5(a), 15 Lab. Arb. (BNA) 961, 964–965.

52. United Steelworkers of Am. v. Enterprise Wheel & Car Corp., 363 U.S. 593, 598 (1960).

53. *Id.*

54. *Id.* at 597, Ludwig Honold Mfg. v. Fletcher, 405 F.2d 1123 (3rd Cir. 1969).

55. A detailed discussion of the various grounds that exist for refusing to enforce or vacating arbitration awards is found in OWEN FAIRWEATHER'S PRACTICE AND PROCEDURE IN LABOR ARBITRATION, ch. XXI, Vacation, Enforcement, or Correction (BNA, 2d Ed. 1983).

56. Alexander v. Gardner-Denver Co., 415 U.S. 36 (1974); *see also*, McDonald of West Branch, ——U.S.——, 52 L.W. 4457(April 18, 1984)(adverse arbitration decision does not preclude subsequent employee lawsuit under §1983 of Civil Rights Act of 1871).

57. Spielberg Mfg. Co., 112 N.L.R.B. 1080 (1955); NLRB v. Huttig Sash & Door Co., 377 F.2d 964 (8th Cir. 1967).

58. Textile Workers Union v. Lincoln Mills of Ala., 353 U.S. 448 (1957).

59. Amalgamated Clothing Workers v. Ironall Factories Co., 386 F.2d 586 (6th Cir. 1967).

60. National Lead Co., 43 Lab. Arb. (BNA) 1025, 1027–28 (Larkin, 1964).

61. Clean Coverall Supply Co., 47 Lab. Arb. (BNA) 272, 277 (Witney, 1966).

62. *See, e.g.,* Celanese Fibers Co., 48 Lab. Arb. (BNA) 502, 504–05 (Altrock, 1966).

63. Bethlehem Steel Co., 43 Lab. Arb. (BNA) 228, 232 (Crawford, 1964).

64. Bendix-Westinghouse Automotive Air Brake Co., 23 Lab. Arb. (BNA) 706, 710 (Mathews, 1954).

65. ELKOURI & ELKOURI, HOW ARBITRATION WORKS, at 162–63 (3d Ed. 1973).

66. *Id.*

67. *See, e.g.,* Velsicol Chemical Corp., 52 Lab. Arb. (BNA) 1164, 1166–67 (Oppenheim, 1969).

68. Worthington Corp., 24 Lab. Arb. (BNA) 1, 6–7 (McGoldrick, 1955).

69. *Id.*

Example of a Collective Bargaining Contract

COLLECTIVE BARGAINING AGREEMENT

This Agreement is by and between the CALIFORNIA LICENSED VOCA-TIONAL NURSES' ASSOCIATION, INC. (hereinafter referred to as the ''Association'') and LAKESIDE COMMUNITY HOSPITAL (hereinafter referred to as the ''Hospital'').

ARTICLE 1

Recognition

The Hospital recognizes the Association as the exclusive collective bargaining representative for Licensed Vocational Nurses covered by this Agreement with respect to wages, hours, and other terms and conditions of employment.

ARTICLE 2

Coverage

This Agreement covers all employees classified as Licensed Vocational Nurses, excluding all other Hospital employees, and guards and supervisors as defined by the National Labor Relations Act. For the purposes of this Agreement, covered Licensed Vocational Nurses will be referred to as ''LVNs.''

Source: Reprinted with persmission from Lakeside Community Hospital, Lakeport, Cal., and the California Licensed Vocational Nurses' Association, Inc., Oakland, Cal.

ARTICLE 3

Hospital Rights

The Hospital will retain and have exclusive right to exercise the customary functions of management, including but not limited to, the right to manage and control the premises and equipment; the right to select, hire, promote, suspend, discharge, assign, supervise and discipline employees; to determine and change starting times, quitting times and shifts; to determine and change the size of, composition of and qualifications of working forces; to establish, change and abolish its policies, practices, rules and regulations and to adopt new policies, rules and regulations; to determine and modify job descriptions, job classifications, job evaluations, and the assignment of particular functions; to determine or change methods and means by which its operations are to be carried on including the right to subcontract; to assign duties to employees in accordance with needs and requirements as determined by the Hospital; and to carry out all functions of management—whether or not exercised by the Hospital prior to execution of this Agreement—subject only to provisions expressly specified in this Agreement.

ARTICLE 4

Association Membership

Section A   Membership Not Required.

LVNs covered by this Agreement are free to join or not join the Association according to their own free will and choice, including whether they wish to remain members or to terminate present or future membership.

Section B   List of LVNs.

The Hospital agrees to provide the Association with a list of all LVNs covered by this Agreement by name, home address, and date of hire within thirty (30) days of the execution date of this Agreement. Thereafter, the Hospital will notify the Association monthly of new hires and terminations occurring the prior month. A copy of such list shall be given to the LVN Representative.

Section C   Materials to New Hires.

The Association shall supply a packet of materials for new hires, and the Hospital then agrees to distribute a packet to each new hire.

ARTICLE 5

Discrimination

There shall be no discrimination by the Hospital or Association against any covered LVN on account of membership or nonmembership in the Assocation, or on account of activity on behalf of or in opposition to the Association.

There shall be no discrimination by the Hospital or the Association against any covered LVN on account of sex, race, national origin, religion, political affiliation, or on the basis of age where an employee is 40 years or older. Any complaint alleging discrimination in violation of this paragraph shall be subject to the provisions of Article 13, Grievance and Arbitration Procedure, except that no such complaint or allegation shall be arbitrable under Step 4 of that procedure.

ARTICLE 6

Employment Categories

Section A   Regular Employees.

1. *Full-Time*. A full-time LVN is one who is regularly scheduled on a predetermined basis for eighty (80) hours in each two-week pay period. A full-time LVN shall be entitled to all of the fringe benefits listed in Article 8 herein.

2. *Part-Time*. A part-time LVN is one who is regularly scheduled on a predetermined basis to work at least forty (40) hours, but less than eighty (80) hours, in each two-week pay period. Part-time LVNs shall be entitled to those fringe benefits listed in Article 8 herein on a prorated basis in accordance with the number of hours worked, except as may be specified to the contrary in Article 8. However, in no event shall a part-time LVN be entitled to additional fringe benefit credit for hours worked in excess of eighty (80) hours a pay period.

Section B   Per Diem and Temporary.

1. A Per Diem LVN is one who is either scheduled to work or is called in to work but on an "as needed" basis.

2. A Temporary LVN is regularly scheduled on a predetermined basis but for less than ninety (90) calendar days.

3. The Hospital reserves the right to establish, change, or modify availability requirements for Per Diem LVNs so long as the requirements are not arbitrary or capricious. The Association will be notified of any such requirements.

4. Per Diem and Temporary LVNs are not entitled to any of the fringe benefits listed in Article 8. The sole exception is that Per Diem and Temporary LVNs shall

be entitled to payment at the rate of time-and-one-half (1½) for all hours worked on a recognized holiday (Article 8, B-1), other than the LVN's birthday.

Section C   Change in Status.

1. *Per Diem/Temporary to Regular.* If a Per Diem or Temporary LVN becomes a Regular employee, the date of such change in status shall be used to determine eligibility and accrual of fringe benefits. The only exceptions are that (a) if a Per Diem or Temporary LVN was previously a Regular employee, with continuous service, then the LVN's regular employee hire date shall be adjusted forward for the period of time the LVN was a Per Diem or Temporary employee, and (b) the Per Diem/Temporary shall be given credit, toward vacation accrual, for hours worked as a Per Diem or Temporary, and 173 hours worked shall equal one (1) month.*

2. *Regular to Per Diem/Temporary.* If a Regular LVN becomes a Per Diem or Temporary LVN, then (a) the LVN will be paid any remaining vested and prorated vacation, and/or all earned unpaid holidays; (b) sick leave shall not be paid off, but shall be retained for a period of one (1) year for the LVN's future use in the event that the LVN again becomes a Regular employee within such one (1) year; and (c) the LVN will be paid the hourly rate applicable to Per Diem and Temporary LVNs on and after the date of such change in status.

ARTICLE 7

Compensation and Hours of Work

Section A   Salary Schedule.

The salary schedule for LVNs covered by this Agreement is found in Appendix A.

Section B   Credit for Prior Experience.

A newly hired LVN shall start at Step 2 of the applicable salary range if the LVN has three (3) or more years of acute care Hospital experience within the last five (5) years prior to date of employment at the Hospital and a newly hired LVN shall start at Step 3 of the applicable salary range if the LVN has five (5) or more years of acute care Hospital experience within the last seven (7) years prior to the date of employment at the Hospital. This provision shall be effective on and after the date of contract execution.

---

*The provision for credit toward vacation based on hours worked shall be effective on and after January 1, 1981. For Per Diem and Temporary employment prior to January 1, 1981, the LVN will be credited with 75 hours of work for each calendar month of such employment.

Section C   Tenure Step Movement.

LVNs will move from step to step within the salary schedule each year on the LVN's anniversary date of employment; however, the Hospital may withhold a tenure step increase if the LVN receives an unsatisfactory evaluation. In order to withhold a pay increase, pursuant to this Section, the evaluation must be performed on a timely basis (no later than two weeks after the anniversary date), unless precluded by an emergency.

Should an LVN receive an unsatisfactory evaluation, he or she shall be allowed thirty (30) calendar days to correct the deficiencies and to achieve satisfactory performance. If a satisfactory evaluation is given after the completion of the thirty (30)-day period, the LVN shall move to the next step retroactive to the LVN's anniversary date. In the event of an unsatisfactory evaluation, the LVN shall be given an additional thirty (30) calendar days to correct the deficiencies and to achieve satisfactory performance, and shall again be reevaluated after the completion of this second thirty (30)-day period. If the LVN receives a satisfactory evaluation, the effective date of the step increase shall be the date of satisfactory evaluation shown on the evaluation form.

This Section shall not preclude or otherwise prejudice the Hospital's right to take disciplinary action for unsatisfactory performance or other reasons without following the procedure outlined above.

Section D   Overtime.

1. An LVN shall be paid at the rate of one and one-half (1½) the LVN's straight-time rate of pay for all hours worked in excess of eight (8) consecutive hours or in excess of eight (8) hours in a workday, or for work in excess of eighty (80) hours during a two-week pay period. The "workday" and the "two-week pay period" shall be a standard period of time for all employees and shall be as designated by the Hospital.

2. An LVN shall be paid at the rate of two (2) times the LVN's straight-time rate of pay for all hours worked in excess of twelve (12) consecutive hours or twelve (12) hours in a workday.

3. Time taken for vacation, holiday, sick leave, funeral leave or education leave shall not count as time worked for overtime purposes.

4. Overtime and other premium pay shall not be duplicated or pyramided for the same hours worked.

Section E   Shift Differential.

1. *PM Shift.* A PM Shift is a straight time or overtime shift of 4 or more hours beginning on or after 3:00 p.m. The PM Shift differential shall be $.75 an hour.

2. *Night Shift.* A Night Shift is a straight time or overtime shift of 4 or more hours beginning on or after 11:00 p.m. The Night Shift differential shall be $1.50 an hour.

3. An LVN who works a PM or Night Shift shall receive the applicable shift differential for hours actually worked.

Section F   Standby and/or Callback.

1. LVNs assigned to standby status shall be paid at the rate of $1.50 an hour for each hour of such standby time.

2. If called to work when on standby, the LVN shall be paid at the rate of time and one-half for all hours worked with a minimum guarantee of one hour's work or pay in lieu thereof.

3. If called to work when not on standby, a Regular LVN shall be paid at the rate of time and one-half for all hours worked, with a minimum guarantee of four (4) hours. If an LVN is called back under this Paragraph 3, again leaves the Hospital and is called back within the period covered by the minimum guarantee, an additional guarantee(s) shall not be applicable but the LVN shall receive payment for all hours worked or the first minimum guarantee, whichever is greater.

Section G   Meetings.

1. LVN attendance at meetings announced by nursing service, including inservice-education meetings, shall be considered time worked.

2. Full-time LVNs will not be required to attend meetings on a scheduled day off.

3. LVNs attending meetings on a scheduled day off shall be guaranteed a minimum of one (1) hour's pay at straight time or time and one-half, whichever is applicable.

Section H   Ambulance Duty.

LVNs shall not be required to accompany patients being transported by an ambulance. If the Hospital requests an LVN to so accompany a patient, and the LVN agrees, the LVN shall be paid at straight time or time and one-half, whichever is applicable. In addition, the LVN will receive any additional compensation then received by other Hospital employees who perform ambulance duty.

Section I   Reporting Pay.

If an LVN reports for work as scheduled or called, and the Hospital does not put the LVN to work, the LVN will be paid for one-half (½) the LVN's normal shift. However, no pay is required under this provision if the Hospital has attempted to contact the LVN at least twice by telephone (which calls shall be documented) at least two (2) hours prior to the start of the shift, to inform the LVN not to report, or if the LVN has been told to not report.

ARTICLE 8

Fringe Benefits

Section A   Sick Leave.

1. *Eligibility and Rate of Accumulation*. LVNs will accrue paid sick leave at the rate of one (1) day for each month of employment, accumulative to a maximum of 480 hours. LVNs will not be eligible for sick leave pay until the first of the month following thirty (30) days of employment.

2. *Sick Leave Usage*. Sick leave shall be payable on the first day of illness and shall continue to be paid until the LVN returns to work or uses all of the LVN's accumulated sick leave. Sick leave shall only be paid for regularly scheduled workdays.

3. *Integration of Sick Leave*. Sick leave shall be integrated with State Disability Insurance and Workers' Compensation.

4. *Proof of Illness*. As a condition of sick leave payment, the Hospital shall have the right to request verification or proof of illness or injury, including but not limited to a doctor's certificate from the LVN's personal physician and by verification rights contained in Section E below, Leaves of Absence, where the LVN is absent for more than three (3) days or where the Hospital has other grounds for questioning the legitimacy of the sick leave claim.

5. *Return from Sick Leave*. The Hospital may request verification of the LVN's ability to return to work, including but not limited to the following: (a) if an LVN is absent for less than four days, the LVN may obtain clearance through the Emergency Room Nurse, or (b) if the LVN is absent for four (4) or more days, clearance must be obtained from the LVN's personal physician or from the Emergency Room Physician.

6. *Pay Out of Sick Leave*. Sick Leave in excess of 480 hours, which an LVN does not otherwise earn or is entitled to use for sick leave purposes, shall be paid to the LVN on the LVN's next anniversary at the LVN's straight-time rate of pay.

Section B   Holidays.

1. *Paid Holidays*. The following shall be recognized as paid holidays:

New Year's Day	Veterans Day
Presidents' Day	Thanksgiving Day
Memorial Day	Christmas Day
Independence Day	LVN's Birthday
Labor Day	

2. *Inclusion of Shift Differential.* Holiday pay shall include the LVN's shift differential, if applicable.

3. *Day Off on a Holiday.* If a holiday falls on the LVN's regular day off, the LVN shall receive an additional paid day off, at the straight-time rate including the LVN's applicable shift differential, within a period of thirty (30) days before or thirty (30) days after the holiday. An LVN's request for a particular day off will be granted whenever possible. Alternatively, if the LVN requests, the day off may be taken at any time within a year of the holiday and may be added to the LVN's next vacation provided that the LVN complies with Section C, 3 of this Article.

4. *Work on a Holiday.* A Regular LVN who works on one of the scheduled holidays shall receive an additional paid day off, at the straight-time rate including the LVN's applicable shift differential; and, in addition, time and one-half (1½) for all hours worked. The Regular nurse shall be entitled to take the paid day off during a period of thirty (30) days before or thirty (30) days after the holiday worked. An LVN's request for a particular paid day off within that period will be granted whenever possible. Alternatively, if the LVN requests, the day off may be taken at any time within a year of the holiday worked and may be added to the LVN's next vacation provided that the LVN complies with Section C, 3 of this Article.

5. *Definition of a Holiday Shift.* When an LVN's shift overlaps two calendar days, the day on which a majority of the shift is worked shall be the holiday shift.

Section C   Vacation.

1. *Vacation Schedule.* LVNs shall receive the following paid vacations:

After the completion of the first, second, third and fourth years of employment: two weeks;

After the completion of the fifth, sixth, seventh, eighth, and ninth years of employment: three weeks;

After the completion of the tenth year of employment, and each subsequent year thereafter: four weeks.

2. *Prorated Vacation.*

(a) After completing one (1) year's employment, an LVN may request prorated vacation time accrued, but not yet vested, since the last anniversary date. In such event, the LVN will authorize a deduction from his or her termination paycheck in the event that the LVN takes the requested prorated vacation and terminates prior to the completion of the anniversary year without giving two weeks' notice in accordance with Paragraph 4 below.

(b) After completing six (6) months of employment, an LVN may request prorated vacation time accrued, but not yet vested. In such case, the LVN will authorize a deduction from his or her termination paycheck in the event that the

LVN takes the requested prorated vacation and terminates prior to the completion of one (1) year of employment.

3. *Scheduling of Vacation.*

(a) LVNs shall submit their vacation requests in writing to the Nursing Office at least thirty (30) days prior to the start of the requested vacation time. The Nursing Office shall approve or deny the vacation request in writing within ten (10) days after the submission of the LVN's request. Vacation time shall only be approved in minimum increments of eight (8) hours, unless the Nursing Office agrees otherwise.

(b) There shall be no automatic seasonal ban on vacations. However, the Hospital retains the right to determine the number of vacation requests, if any, which can be granted for any period of the year.

(c) Where more than one LVN requests the same or overlapping vacation times, and all current requests within a given work area cannot be granted, the Hospital shall give preference to requests for vested vacation time earned as of the last anniversary date. If all such requests cannot be granted, seniority shall determine which vacation requests can be approved. The foregoing is subject to the proviso that previously authorized vacations shall not be subject to change based upon requests subsequently submitted for the same vacation time, whether those later requests are for vested vacations or are submitted by more senior LVNs.

(d) Where a full-time LVN requests vacation time in increments of a week, each week will be defined as five days with pay and two days without pay.

4. *Termination Vacation Pay.* Upon termination or resignation, an LVN shall receive all vested vacation pay for vacation earned as of the last anniversary date. If the LVN gives at least two (2) weeks advance written notice of resignation, excluding vacation or other paid or unpaid time off, then the Hospital will grant prorated vacation pay based upon months of employment since the last anniversary date.

5. *No Carryover of Vacation.*

(a) All vacation must be taken as time off within the anniversary year following the date it was earned. Vacation pay in lieu of time off will not be granted.

(b) If an LVN has not taken all such vacation time by two months prior to the completion of the anniversary year, the LVN will be asked to submit a vacation request. If the LVN does not do so within two (2) weeks, the vacation time off will be scheduled by the Nursing Office for the current or following anniversary year.

(c) The only exceptions to (a) and (b) above are: (1) if an LVN cancels an authorized vacation at the request of the Hospital; (2) if the Hospital cancels an authorized vacation due to an emergency, or (3) if the LVN requests cancellation of authorized vacation due to a personal emergency necessitating the cancellation, and the Nursing Office approves in writing, a carryover of all or part of the LVN's vacation time to the following anniversary year.

Section D   Jury Duty and Court Appearances.

1. An LVN called for jury duty (or subpoenaed to appear as a witness in a judicial procedure, not including arbitration arising out of the LVN's employment and in which the LVN is not a party) will receive the difference between jury pay or witness fees and straight-time earnings.

2. As a condition to jury pay, the LVN must notify the Nursing Office as soon as reasonable after he or she receives notice to report (normally within 24 hours), and the LVN must produce a receipt from the Jury Commissioner that he or she has been called or served, if such receipts are provided.

3. If a Day Shift employee is called and/or serves, and is released during the LVN's work time, the employee shall immediately notify the Nursing Office and shall report to work for the remainder of his or her shift if requested to do so.

4. If a PM employee is called and or serves, and is not released before 1:00 p.m., the LVN shall so notify the Nursing Office at the earliest opportunity, and shall not be required to report to work for the remainder of his or her shift, except where a serious need exists.

5. If a night LVN is called and/or serves, and is not released by noon, the LVN shall so notify the Nursing Office at the earliest opportunity, and shall not be required to report to work for his or her shift unless a serious need exists.

Section E   Leaves of Absence.

1. *Types and Maximum Duration of Unpaid Leaves.*
(a) Physical disability leave: An LVN is entitled to a maximum of one hundred and twenty (120) calendar days unpaid leave of absence for the LVN's own disability or illness; provided, however, that the LVN's total absence due to disability or illness (paid time off and unpaid leave) shall not exceed six (6) months.
(b) Military service:
(c) Personal leaves: An unpaid leave of absence for personal reasons may be requested by an LVN, and the granting or denial of any such leave, including but not limited to determining the length of any leave granted, shall be within the sole discretion of the Hospital.

2. *Eligibility for Leave.* With the sole exception of Workers' Compensation leaves of absence, no LVN will be eligble for a leave of absence prior to the completion of one year of employment. Regular full-time and part-time LVNs shall be eligible for leaves of absence in accordance with this Section E.

3. *Leave Procedures.*
(a) Request for leave: Except in an emergency, requests for leaves of absence shall be submitted by the LVN to the Nursing Office at least thirty (30) days in

advance of the requested time off. Written approval or denial of the requested leave of absence will be given within ten (10) calendar days after submission of the request.

(b) Emergency leaves: In case of an emergency, the Nursing Office shall be notified immediately of the emergency and the reasons which require a leave, and the Nursing Office will approve or deny the leave. If approved, and as soon as is possible thereafter, the LVN shall complete any necessary leave of absence application. Emergency leaves will be granted only for the reasons set forth in Section 1 above, and the granting of approval will not affect the Hospital's right to subsequently request verification of the reasons given when the leave was requested.

4. *Verification.* As a condition to authorizing, continuing or extending a leave of absence, the Hospital may require verification of the reasons given by the LVN who is requesting the leave. In addition, the Hospital may periodically request an update on the continued existence of reasons requiring a leave.

5. *Return from Leave.* An LVN who returns from a leave of absence on the approved due date will be returned to the same position if the leave is for thirty (30) calendar days or less. If the leave of absence is for more than thirty (30) calendar days, then an LVN who returns from a leave of absence on the approved due date will be returned to the same position if it is occupied by a Per Diem LVN or a Temporary LVN who has not become permanent; otherwise, the LVN will be assigned a position as similar as is possible to the one occupied prior to the leave of absences, and if no LVN vacancies exist as of the due date, then the LVN will be placed on the Per Diem List until such time as the LVN applies for, is offered, and accepts a Regular LVN position posted in accordance with Article 12, Section C.

6. *Failure To Return from Leave.* Any LVN who does not return to work on the due date will be terminated as of that date, unless a leave of absence extension has been requested in writing by the LVN and granted in writing by the Hospital prior to the return due date. If the Hospital denies an extension, the LVN must return to work as of the original date authorized.

7. *Performing Work While on Leave.* Performing work for another employer during an authorized leave of absence constitutes just cause for dismissal. However, an LVN on an authorized medical leave of absence shall not be prohibited from performing non-LVN work with the permission of the LVN's physician, subject to the Hospital's right to require periodic consultation by a Hospital-designated physician.

8. *Adjustment of Anniversary Date.* If a leave of absence is in excess of thirty (30) calendar days, the LVN's anniversary date will be adjusted forward for the full period of the leave. The LVN will retain previously accumulated fringe benefits, but no such benefits will accrue during the period of any leave.

Section F　Funeral Leave.

Three (3) days paid funeral leave shall be granted to LVNs in the event of death in the LVN's immediate family. The LVN may also request two additional days off with pay to be deducted, at the LVN's designation, from the LVN's accumulated sick leave, holidays or vacation time. If the LVN has no remaining sick leave, holidays or vacation time, then the LVN may request two additional days off without pay. The "immediate family" is defined as the LVN's spouse, mother, father, child, sister or brother.

Section G　Education Leave.

1. *Request from LVNs.* The Hospital will consider requests for paid educational leave where the LVN submits a description of the program, including a copy of the announcement and/or other brochure, and where the Director of Nursing believes (a) that the program directly relates to the LVN's assignment, and (b) the program would benefit the Hospital. The granting of education leave rests within the discretion of the Director of Nurses, and neither the granting nor the denial of any such leave shall be subject to the Grievance Procedure.

2. *Required Programs.* In the event the Hospital requires LVNs to attend an educational event outside the Hospital, time spent in such classes shall be considered time worked, and the Hospital will pay for any enrollment fees.

3. *Unpaid Time Off.* An LVN may request unpaid time off for education purposes, up to a maximum of five (5) days per year, but all such requests shall be subject to scheduling needs. Requests for educational purposes in excess of five (5) days shall be governed by the provisions in Section E above, Leaves of Absence.

Section H　Health and Welfare Program.

1. LVNs will be covered by the same hospitalization, accidental death and dismemberment, major medical insurance and dental program applicable to other Hospital employees. Coverage for Regular full-time and part-time LVNs will be paid in full by the Hospital. LVNs who wish to cover their spouses or dependents may do so, at their expense, and subject to the carrier's requirements and procedures.

2. An LVN granted an approved leave of absence under Section E above may continue health insurance coverage at the LVN's expense. An LVN who desires to continue such coverage shall provide written notification to the Hospital at the time of requesting a leave of absence and submit full payment of the premium to the Hospital on or before the tenth of each month. The honoring of LVN requests for

continued health coverage is subject to the eligibility requirements, limitations, and other provisions of requirements, of the Hospital's health insurance carrier.

Section I   Retirement.

LVNs shall continue to be covered by the Hospital's current pension program, and in the event improvements, changes, or other modifications are made to said retirement program during the term of this Agreement, the same provisions shall automatically apply to LVNs. The Hospital shall provide each LVN covered by said pension plan with a booklet describing benefits of the plan.

ARTICLE 9

Scheduling

1. *Posting of Schedules.* A schedule of days to be worked and days to be off shall be posted at least two (2) weeks in advance of the four (4) week period covered by the schedule.

2. *Changes in Schedule.* Once posted, the schedule will not be arbitrarily changed. LVNs may change days off with other nursing personnel, so long as the change is approved in advance by the Nursing Office in its discretion.

3. *Weekend Work.* The Hospital will use its best efforts to schedule Regular LVNs off on every other weekend, unless an LVN submits a written request for weekdays off or for a scheduling pattern which requires more frequent weekend work.

ARTICLE 10

Performance Evaluations

LVNs shall receive a performance evaluation, in writing, at the completion of their probationary period, at the completion of twelve (12) months' employment, and annually thereafter on their anniversary date of employment. Such evaluations shall be completed within two (2) weeks of their due date. The evaluation shall be discussed with the LVN, and the LVN shall sign the evaluation to indicate that it has been reviewed with the LVN; such signature, however, shall not be construed to indicate the LVN's agreement with the evaluation. The LVN may submit written comments concerning the evaluation, and is encouraged to do so. Any such written response shall be attached to the evaluation, and placed in the LVN's personnel file along with the evaluation. A copy of the evaluation shall be given to the LVN.

ARTICLE 11

Discipline and Discharge

Section A   Probationary Period.

Newly employed Regular LVNs shall serve a probationary period during the first ninety (90) calendar days of employment. Per Diem LVNs shall serve a probationary period during the first 520 hours of work following employment. During the probationary period disciplinary action may be taken for any reason without recourse by the LVN or Association to the Grievance and Arbitration Procedure, Article 13.

Section B   Just Cause.

Upon completion of the probationary period, disciplinary action concerning Regular and Per Diem LVNs (written warnings, unpaid suspensions, discharges) shall be for just cause. The foregoing does not preclude the Hospital from placing an LVN on suspension pending investigation to determine whether disciplinary action is in fact warranted.

Section C   Temporary LVNs.

Temporary LVNs shall commence the probationary period as of the date of reclassification, if any, to Regular full-time or part-time status, and in that event, the provisions of Section A above shall apply. Prior to such reclassification, grievances may be filed on behalf of Temporary LVNs alleging violations of applicable contract provisions, with the exception that disciplinary action shall not constitute a contract violation or be subject to the Grievance and Arbitration Procedure, Article 13.

Section D

Copies of written warnings or unpaid suspensions shall be sent to the Association within seventy-two (72) hours of issuance.

ARTICLE 12

Seniority

Section A

Seniority of Regular LVNs shall be defined as the length of employment as a Regular full-time or part-time LVN. Seniority among Per Diem LVNs shall be based upon hours worked as a Per Diem LVN, including credit for any time spent as a full- or part-time LVN at the rate of 173 hours for each month of such Regular status. If seniority between Regular and Per Diem LVNs needs to be determined, then a Regular LVN shall be credited with 173 hours for each month of Regular full-time status; and for each month of Regular part-time status, the LVN shall be credited with hours worked, to a maximum of 173 hours per calendar month.*

Section B

1. *Application of Seniority.* The Hospital shall be the sole judge of an LVN's general skill and ability. When the general skill and ability of LVNs is approximately equal, then the principle of seniority shall govern in reduction of force and recall, providing that the remaining or recalled LVN has the skill and ability to perform the position, and the LVN will accept the hours, scheduling, and clinical area of the position.

2. *Permanent Layoffs.* A permanent layoff is a layoff anticipated by the Hospital to be for more than thirty (30) days. Unless a suddenly occurring unexpected event causes the layoff, LVNs being permanently laid off shall receive one (1) week advance notice of such layoff. The Association shall be given a copy of any written notification of layoff. Temporary and Per Diem LVNs shall be the first LVNs to be laid off, in that order, and among the Per Diems, seniority shall govern. The foregoing is subject to the provisions of Paragraph 1 above, and to the proviso that the Hospital shall not be precluded from using Per Diem LVNs during a layoff where the coverage needed is not of such regularity and/or quantity of hours as to constitute a regular position.

3. *Temporary Layoffs.* In the event the Hospital must reduce the number of LVNs temporarily, or the number of LVN hours, due to patient census or other operational reasons, the Hospital will first ask for volunteers, from among the LVNs assigned to that work area on that day and shift, to take a day off without pay. In the event there are no volunteers or an insufficient number of volunteers, the Hospital will assign a day off without pay on a rotating basis from among the LVNs assigned to that work area on that day and shift. The Hospital will attempt to notify affected LVNs of the need for a day off without pay at least two (2) hours in advance of the LVN's scheduled shift, and earlier if possible. The taking of such a day without pay shall have no effect on an LVN's seniority or accrual of benefits. LVNs taking a day off shall be permitted to use accumulated Holiday or Vacation time if they so choose.

---

*The provisions for credit based on hours worked shall be effective on and after January 1, 1981. For Regular part-time employment prior to January 1, 1981, the LVN shall be credited with 85 hours for each calendar month of such Regular part-time employment. For Per Diem employment prior to January 1, 1981, the LVN shall be credited with 75 hours of work for each calendar month of such Per Diem employment.

4. *Break in Service.* Six (6) calendar months on layoff status shall constitute a break in service and the LVN shall have no further job rights. If the LVN subsequently is rehired, it shall be as a new employee.

Section C   Permanent Vacancies.

1. *Posting of Vacancies.* All permanent vacancies for LVN positions covered by this Agreement shall be posted for at least five (5) calendar days. Interested LVNs shall apply to the Nursing Office within this five (5) day period.

2. *Filling Posted Vacancies.*

(a) The Nursing Office shall be the sole judge of an LVN's qualifications, and has the right to select the best qualified applicant from those applying.

(b) If two or more current LVNs are judged approximately equal in their qualifications to fill a vacant position, then the LVN with the greatest seniority (whether Regular or Per Diem) shall receive the vacancy.

(c) If no current LVNs apply for a position within the five (5) day posting period, or if none of the current LVNs applying are judged qualified for the position, the Hospital may fill the vacancy from any source.

3. *Determination of Vacancies.* The Hospital shall determine whether a permanent vacancy exists, and its judgment shall not be subject to the Grievance and Arbitration Procedure, Article 13. The Hospital retains the right to transfer or reassign LVNs as necessary, but no such action shall be taken for the purpose of avoiding its obligations under this Section.

ARTICLE 13

Grievance and Arbitration Procedure

Section A   Definition.

A grievance is defined as a dispute concerning the interpretation or application of any express provision of this Agreement.

Section B   Procedure.

Grievances shall be taken up and settled in the following manner:

Step 1: An LVN shall first discuss the matter informally with the LVN's immediate supervisor within ten (10) days of the Hospital's action or inaction which is alleged to violate the Agreement. The LVN's immediate supervisor shall provide an oral answer to the Step 1 grievance within five (5) days or after.

Step 2: By no later than twenty (20) days after the alleged violation, the Association must submit a written grievance to the Director of Nursing if it is not satisfied with the Step 1 answer given to the LVN. The Director of Nursing shall provide an answer, in writing, within five (5) days after receipt of the Step 2 written grievance.

Step 3: If the Association is not satisfied with the answer given in Step 2 above, the written grievance must be submitted to the Hospital Administrator by the Association within ten (10) days of the date of the Step 2 answer. If requested, the Administrator or designee shall meet with the LVN and an Association representative in an effort to resolve the grievance. The Administrator shall provide an answer, in writing, within five (5) days following the meeting.

Step 4: If the Administrator's answer in Step 3 is not satisfactory, the matter may be submitted to final and binding arbitration by a written request from the Association to the Hospital for arbitration. Such a request for arbitration must be received by the Hospital within ten (10) days after the date of the answer in Step 3 above. If the parties are unable to mutually agree on an arbitrator, the parties shall apply to the Federal Mediation and Conciliation Service for a list of nine (9) arbitrators. Each party shall strike one name from a list until only one name remains, who shall be the arbitrator, the first strike being determined by the flip of a coin.

Section C   Hospital Grievances.

1. Hospital grievances shall be submitted directly to the Association within ten (10) days of the Association's action or inaction which is alleged to violate the Agreement. If requested, an Association representative, an Administrator or his designee, shall meet in an effort to resolve the grievance. The Association shall provide an answer, in writing, within five (5) days following the meeting or within fifteen (15) days after the date of the Hospital's grievance if no meeting is requested.

2. If the Association's Step 3 answer is not satisfactory, the matter may be submitted to final and binding arbitration in accordance with Section B, Step 4 above, and Sections D, E and F below.

3. If the Hospital's grievance concerns the interpretation and application of Section G, the following modifications in the Grievance and Arbitration Procedure shall apply:

(a) The Hospital's written grievance may be submitted at Step 4 of the grievance procedure, simultaneously with the demand for arbitration.

(b) The grievance and/or demand for arbitration shall be forwarded to the Association no later than five (5) days after the date of the alleged violation.

(c) The Association and the Hospital shall attempt to select a mutually acceptable arbitrator within twenty-four (24) hours after receipt of the demand for arbitration, and to have the grievance heard immediately thereafter. If the parties cannot agree to an arbitrator within the twenty-four (24) hour period, the grievance shall be heard immediately by one of the following arbitrators: Gerald Marcus, Herman Levy, Donald Wollett, Robert Burns, Robert LeProhn. The arbitrator shall be selected by each party striking one name from the list until only one name remains, who shall be the arbitrator, the first strike being determined by the flip of a coin. The arbitrator shall issue a written bench decision at the conclusion of the hearing.

Section D   Authority of Arbitrator.

The Arbitrator shall render a decision which shall be final and binding upon all parties concerned. However, the Arbitrator's authority is limited to interpreting the express provisions of this Agreement, and the Arbitrator has no authority to add to, subtract from or change the Agreement in any way. If the issue presented to the Arbitrator concerns suspension or discharge, and if the Arbitrator finds that such specific disciplinary action taken was not arbitrary or capricious, the Arbitrator shall have no authority to set aside, modify, or otherwise change the specific disciplinary action taken.

Section E   Arbitration Expenses.

The expense of the arbitration shall be borne equally by both the Association and the Hospital, except that each party shall be responsible for presentation of its own case and witnesses.

Section F   Time Limits.

1. The term "days" shall be defined as calendar days.
2. The time limits specified in Section B of this Article may be waived or modified at any time by mutual written agreement of the parties, or by oral agreement with subsequent written confirmation. Unless waived or modified in accordance with the prior sentence, the time limits contained herein shall be strictly construed. No grievance shall be arbitrable unless all time limits have been met. If the Hospital fails to respond, or to timely respond, the Association may move the grievance to the next Step.

Section G   No Strike-No Lockout.

There shall be no stoppages, interruptions of work, strikes, sympathy strikes, other forms of concerted disruption or interference, or lockouts during the life of this Agreement.

Section H   Employee Personnel Files.

1. *Employee Access.* LVNs may inspect their own personnel files at reasonable times upon their request.

2. *Association Access.* With respect to a particular complaint or grievance of an LVN concerning the interpretation or application disagreement, and on the LVN's written authorization, the Association may inspect at reasonable times relevant material in the LVN's personnel file upon which the Hospital is or will be relying.

ARTICLE 14

LVN Representative

Section A   Appointment of Representative.

The Association may appoint a Regular LVN who has been employed by the Hospital for at least one (1) year to serve as the Association's official representative in the Hospital. The Association will notify the Hospital of the name of the LVN chosen to be LVN Representative.

Section B   Functions.

The function of the LVN representative shall be to inform LVNs regarding rights and responsibilities under this Agreement, to ascertain that the terms and conditions of the Agreement are observed, to investigate grievances, to assist in matters relating to employer-employee relations and to participate, when requested to do so, in the steps of the grievance procedure. The LVN representative shall perform these functions on nonworking time; the sole exception is where a Hospital schedules a disciplinary or grievance meeting during the LVN representative's scheduled work time.

ARTICLE 15

Association Visitation

Section A

A representative of the Association shall be permitted to visit the Hospital at reasonable times to ascertain that the provisions of this Agreement are being observed and to confer with LVNs covered by this Agreement during their nonwork time and in nonwork areas. Such visits shall not interfere with the operation of the Hospital or the performance of LVN duties, and the Association representative shall inform Hospital Administration of his/her visit either prior to or upon entering the Hospital premises.

Section B   Holding of Meetings.

The provisions of Section A shall not be construed as including or allowing the holding of Association meetings on Hospital premises, without regard to whether an Association representative does or does not attend. The only exceptions are that the Hospital will consider requests for use of meeting space for activities which are educational (related to LVN clinical practice) or professional (planning dinners for LVN students, etc.) in nature.

ARTICLE 16

Discounts

Section A   Discounts Provided.

The Hospital shall provide discounts of twenty (20) percent of charges incurred through the Hospital's pharmacy, outpatient departments, or when hospitalized at the Hospital, provided that the item or service has been ordered for the LVN or member of the LVN's immediate family by their personal physician or other treating physician.

Section B   Implementation of Discounts.

The manner in which discounts are implemented is as follows:

1. For inpatient hospitalization, the LVN's hospital bill is submitted in full to the insurance company. Then, after payment has been received from the insurance carrier, any balance remaining is discounted in an amount equal to twenty (20) percent of the original bill. This same method applies to pharmacy prescription received through the Emergency Room, or when hospitalized.

2. For over-the-counter pharmacy prescriptions which are paid by the LVN at the time of picking up the prescription, the bill is discounted twenty (20) percent at the time of payment.

ARTICLE 17

Bulletin Boards

The Association may use space on an existing Hospital bulletin board for the posting of meeting notices and similar materials, subject to the availability of space. Controversial materials shall not be posted, and materials for posting shall be submitted and approved by the Hospital prior to posting.

ARTICLE 18

Personnel Manual

The Hospital's personnel policies shall continue to apply to covered LVNs, unless this Agreement contains express and contrary provisions. Covered LVNs shall receive a copy of any revised employee handbook and of any individual written revisions to the handbook, and a copy also will be forwarded to the Association.

ARTICLE 19

LVN Practice Issues

Upon request, the Director of Nursing Service and/or the Hospital Administrator will meet with LVNs, individually or as a group, to discuss matters relating to patient care, the role of LVNs, and to consider recommendations the LVNs may wish to present on these matters. These meetings shall not be held more frequently than once a month, except by mutual agreement, and the scheduling of meetings shall be by mutual agreement. The only subject which shall be arbitrable under this Article is whether the Hospital has complied with its obligation to meet upon request.

ARTICLE 20

Operation of Agreement

Nothing in this Agreement or its execution shall operate to preclude the Hospital from exceeding the rates of pay, benefits, or working conditions contained in this Agreement. If the Hospital does so, this shall be a matter of individual arrangement between the Hospital and the affected LVN(s) and the Hospital shall not violate this Agreement or its bargaining obligations to the Association by modifying, terminating, or extending any such individual arrangements, or by refusing to extend any such arrangements, to any other LVNs.

ARTICLE 21

Full Agreement

The express provisions contained in this Agreement constitute the full and exclusive agreement between the Association and the Hospital. This Agreement is executed for the purpose of conclusively determining the Hospital's obligations during the term of this Agreement on any and all issues concerning wages, hours and other terms and conditions of employment, including issues which were raised, or which could have been raised, during the negotiations leading to this Agreement.

ARTICLE 22

Term of Agreement

Section A

This Agreement shall become effective as of August 1, 1983, except when another date is specifically provided elsewhere in this Agreement, and shall continue in effect until July 31, 1985, subject to the reopening provisions of Section B below. Beginning with August 1, 1985, this Agreement shall be automatically renewed and extended from year to year thereafter, unless either party serves notice in writing upon the other party, not less than ninety (90) calendar days prior to August 1, 1985, or prior to the end of the term then in existence, of its desire to terminate or amend this Agreement.

Section B

Upon service of written notice upon the Hospital at least ninety (90) calendar days prior to August 1, 1984, this Agreement may be opened by the Association for negotiations limited to the issues of (1) wages; (2) two other items, to be selected by the Association, whether or not such items are already covered by this Agreement. In the event of a dispute over the issues in such limited opening, the Grievance and Arbitration Procedure (Article 13) shall not be applicable, and as of August 1, 1984, either party may engage in a strike or lockout in connection with the issues in any such dispute.

IN WITNESS WHEREOF, the parties hereto have executed this Agreement on this ___ day of _____, 1983.

CALIFORNIA LICENSED
VOCATIONAL NURSES'   LAKESIDE COMMUNITY
ASSOCIATION, INC.   HOSPITAL

By: _____   By: _____

APPENDIX A

Salary Schedule

Effective August 1, 1983, the LVN Salary Schedule shall be as follows:

	Step 1	*Step 2*	*Step 3*	*Step 4*	*Step 5*	*Step 6*
LVN	$6.72	$7.06	$7.41	$7.78	$8.17	$8.58
LVN (IV)		$7.23	$7.60	$7.97	$8.37	$8.79

1. An LVN's movement through the salary schedule shall be in accordance with Article 7, Compensation and Hours of Work, Section C, Tenure Step Movement.

2. LVNs employed on or after April 21, 1981, shall be employed at Step 1, of the LVN schedule, unless the provisions of Article 7, Compensation and Hours of Work, Section B, Credit for Prior Experience, are applicable.

3. For the purposes of this Appendix, the term "authorized to administer IV therapy" shall mean that an LVN has a current certification from the State of California *and* has successfully completed the Hospital's IV orientation program administered by the Hospital's IV Control Nurse or such other person as has been designated by the Hospital for such purpose. The determination that an LVN is authorized to administer IV therapy shall not be subject to the grievance/arbitration provisions contained in Article 13 of the contract.

4. Whenever an LVN employed by the Hospital becomes authorized to administer IV therapy, the LVN shall, effective the next pay period following such authorization, move to the LVN (IV) schedule at the same step in the salary schedule, provided that no such movement shall occur until an LVN has been employed by the Hospital for at least one year, unless

(a) A newly-hired LVN has three (3) or more years of acute care Hospital experience within the last five (5) years prior to the date of employment at the Hospital; or

(b) The Hospital, in its sole discretion, decides to waive the one-year waiting period contained in this paragraph.

Chapter 5

Public Employment Labor Relations Laws

DISTINCTIVE CHARACTERISTICS OF PUBLIC EMPLOYMENT

Those of you in public employment—whether it be federal, state or local government—may already be aware that the ground rules for labor relations and employee matters are not identical to those in private employment. You also may be aware that no one law governs all public employment. To the contrary, so much variation exists from state to state and among public employers that this chapter could not hope to cover in detail all of the laws that might affect you.

For this reason, this chapter is designed simply to compare and contrast the major public employment models with the National Labor Relations Act (NLRA). Some of the more common features in public employment labor laws also are discussed.

Some of the variations between public and private sector labor laws result from actual differences between public and private employers. The public employer, with rare and insignificant exceptions, is not seeking to maximize profits or its bottom line by providing a better, more desirable, or more efficient product. Instead, most of its funds are provided by taxpayers, and it may obtain additional monies because of political considerations and the influence of pressure groups. The employer also may not be readily identifiable. Is it the public at large; the legislature that may set wages, hours, and other terms and conditions of employment by passing budgets or other statutory measures; the governor or other executive, etc.?

Yet some of the variations may stem from perceived differences that may or may not actually exist. For example, what is unique about public employees? In the health care field particularly, the work they perform often is identical to that in the private health care industry. As a result, no compelling argument exists that the services provided by public employees are necessarily more critical to the patients or community than those offered by private health care institutions. Because of the community service nature of health care, strikes by employees in either sector are equally potentially devastating.

FEDERAL EMPLOYMENT AND EXECUTIVE ORDERS

For many years, the right of federal employees to engage in organizational activities was severely restricted. If you had been a federal employee in 1902, you would have been subjected to an Executive order issued by President Theodore Roosevelt that forbade "federal employees on pain of dismissal to seek legislation in their behalf 'directly or indirectly or through associations'."[1] Not until 1963, when President Kennedy issued Executive Order 10988, were most federal employees given the right to organize and to join and assist an employee organization. Following pressure for even broader bargaining rights, President Nixon in 1969 issued Executive Order 11491, which was further amended by subsequent Executive orders. Then, in 1978 the Civil Service Reform Act of 1978 (the Act) was signed into law.[2] The Act incorporates the preceding Executive orders and constitutes the statement of labor relations policy for federal employees as of early 1984.

Overview

The underlying objective of the Act is to maintain efficient government operations while simultaneously preserving and protecting the rights of federal employees to organize, bargain collectively, and participate through labor organizations in decision making that affects their working conditions. If you work for the U.S. Public Health Service, Veterans Administration, etc., then the persons you supervise probably are covered by the Act since it applies to all employees and agencies in the executive branch except for supervisors and certain designated agencies such as the General Accounting Office, the Federal Bureau of Investigation, and the Central Intelligence Agency, to name a few.

Comparison with NLRA

Supervisory Status. The Act excludes supervisors although it allows recognition of bargaining units containing supervisors where such units were recognized as of the Act's 1979 effective date.[3] The definition of supervisors in the Act should sound very familiar to you:

"[S]upervisor" means an individual employed by an agency having authority in the interest of the agency to hire, direct, assign, promote, reward, transfer, furlough, layoff, recall, suspend, discipline, or remove employees, to adjust their grievances, or to effectively recommend such action, if the exercise of the authority is not merely routine or clerical in nature but requires the consistent exercise of independent judgment, except that, with respect to any unit which includes firefighters or nurses, the term "supervisor" includes only those individuals who devote a preponderance of their employment time to exercising such authority.[4]

Not only does that Act include a supervisory definition clearly modeled after the NLRA but it also incorporates a different supervisory standard for registered nurses, just as the NLRB has applied a different test for determining registered nurse supervisors.

Administrative Agency Responsibilities. The Act places the control of federal employee labor relations in the hands of the Federal Labor Relations Authority (FLRA), which is the public sector version of the NLRB. The FLRA has full-time members who are responsible for interpreting and administering the statute, deciding major policy issues, formulating regulations, and disseminating information. Like the NLRB, its specific duties include determining the appropriateness of bargaining units, supervising elections, and holding unfair labor practice proceedings.

Recognition of Exclusive Bargaining Representatives. Unlike the NLRA, this Act allows a labor organization to be recognized as the exclusive bargaining representative of a group of employees only if the entity wins a secret ballot election. Under the Act, recognition cannot be achieved by demanding voluntary employer recognition and it cannot result from bargaining orders designed to remedy flagrant unfair labor practices.

Right To Be Consulted. The Act, unlike the NLRA, allows a labor organization that is not the exclusive bargaining representative certain "consultation rights" if no other union has been recognized as the exclusive representative. This means that the organization is entitled to be consulted on proposed changes and conditions of employment and has an opportunity to comment on the changes. Such comments, of course, are not binding on the agency proposing the changes.

Bargaining Obligations. Both parties, the federal agency and the labor organization, have the same duty to bargain in good faith as do employers and labor organizations covered by the NLRA. Yet the issues subject to bargaining are considerably more limited than in the private sector. For example, the agency may elect to exempt or exclude from bargaining such topics as the number of employees; the numbers, types, and grades of positions; staffing patterns; job content; and the technology used to perform agency work.[5]

Unfair Labor Practices. The Act outlaws certain conduct by labor organizations and federal agencies as unfair labor practices. This list is largely based on the unfair labor practices detailed in the NLRA. Like the NLRB, the FLRA has a general counsel who is charged with the duty of prosecuting unfair labor practice complaints in the federal service. The FLRA is the "court" and the general counsel becomes the "prosecutor."

Resolving a Negotiating Impasse. If negotiations reach a stalemate or impasse, the Act uses methods of resolution substantially different from those of the NLRA. It does not recognize the right to strike, which the NLRA does. It permits either party to utilize the services of the Federal Mediation and Conciliation Service or request assistance from the Federal Services Impasse Panel. If the panel's advisory action does not settle the dispute, then it may hold a hearing and take further action that may be binding on the parties. In the event both parties decide not to use the panel's services, they can submit to binding arbitration, but only if approved by the panel.

Grievances. The Act covers grievance issues in great detail. It defines a grievance as any matter relating to employment with an agency and any claimed violation, misinterpretation, or misapplication of any law, rule, or regulation affecting conditions of employment. The Act requires the parties to a collective bargaining agreement to negotiate a procedure to use in resolving grievances.[6] The NLRA does not require such a contract provision; however, most private collective bargaining contracts do include grievance and arbitration procedures.

STATE LAWS

Coverage of State Laws[7]

As might be expected in a society as diverse as ours, there is considerable variation in the various states' approaches to public employee labor relations. For example:

- Pennsylvania has a relatively uniform and comprehensive system of public employment labor relations law. The Public Employee Relations Act (PERA) covers, with only a few exceptions, all those who work for the state and local governments, school districts, and even nonprofit organizations receiving government grants.
- California, by contrast, has at least five major statutes, each covering just one segment of public employment. Two statutes apply to state employees, one to municipal and local government agencies, a fourth to local and county school districts and community college districts, and the fifth to state universities, colleges, and similar institutions. To add even further confusion, the California statutes are not uniform in their approach or structure since they establish different ground rules and enforcement mechanisms for the various public employers.

The Right To Organize and Bargain Collectively

Public employees have a constitutional right to organize and join labor organizations.[8] This right can be a "Catch-22" situation, however. While there is a constitutional right to organize, a public employer has no constitutional obligation to recognize the employees' collective bargaining representative or to engage in negotiations, although many such employers have done so voluntarily. Even where a state statute imposes a "bargaining" obligation upon a public employer, it often grants little more to the union than the right to meet and confer, to petition, and to be heard.[9] The trend of state law, however, is moving away from such limited rights and toward granting a full right of bargaining similar to that in the private sector,[10] a trend that could affect those in public health care employment.

Topics for Bargaining

As noted, the scope of bargaining in public employment is generally more limited than in the private sector. Either the state statute itself or the state courts' interpretation of it may exclude many subjects of bargaining that are included in the private sector. The NLRA concept of "mandatory" and "permissive" subjects of bargaining also has not been transferred to the public sector in any real sense.

State statutes can be quite specific in delineating the subjects that can be discussed. The test frequently is whether the subject is one that can be discussed at all or whether it has been reserved by law as an issue that the government employer must decide. For example:

- In Alaska, the Public Employment Relations Act states that the phrase "terms and conditions of employment" excludes "the general policies describing the function and purposes of a public" employer, so the excluded subject is not a proper item for bargaining.[11]
- In Connecticut, the statute governing state employees provides that the obligation to bargain concerning "wages, hours and other conditions of employment" cannot be construed to reduce the authority of the state personnel boards and agencies that by law have been given specified responsibility for the merit and grading of applicants and the civil service system.[12]
- In New York, pensions are excluded from direct bargaining with local government employers.[13]

Management Rights Provisions

The decision as to what are proper subjects for bargaining in the public sector is complicated by the so-called "management rights provisions." Typically, state statutes use very broad and sometimes vague and ambiguous language in defining management rights.

For example, a statute might state that the public employer is not permitted to agree to any proposal that would interfere with its right "to maintain efficiency of government operations" or "to carry out the statutory mandate and goals of the agency."[14] The meaning of this language is difficult to ascertain. As another example, some state statutes permit the public employer to refuse to negotiate (or even meet) with a labor organization on matters of "inherent managerial policy."[15]

The net result of such vaguely worded statutes is that the negotiations and administration of public collective bargaining agreements often are clouded by uncertainty as to whether the subject is a proper one for bargaining and whether even an agreed-upon provision is enforceable.

Impact of Civil Service Laws

An additional problem is created by civil service laws and other legislation. Many states, for example, have laws that attempt to implement the "merit principle." These laws require public employees to be selected and promoted on the basis of their merit rather than because of political or other affiliations. Civil service laws often contain other provisions covering grievance procedures, employee tenure, and salary scales. The effect of collectively bargained contracts on these laws is a complex and still unresolved issue.

Exclusive Representation

The private sector labor union is the exclusive representative of all employees in the bargaining unit, whether or not they are members. This concept of an exclusive bargaining agent is not adhered to uniformly by all states. Some states, such as California and Nebraska, have laws granting exclusive representation rights for certain groups of employees but, for other groups of employees, the recognized union represents only its members with employees being allowed to represent themselves individually, if they so desire.[16] A number of other states, however, do follow the private sector NLRA rule of exclusive representation for an entire bargaining unit. The trend is clearly toward such exclusive representation based on a majority vote in a secret ballot election conducted by a state public employee relations board or its equivalent.

Achieving Employer Recognition

The NLRA procedures for achieving employer certification have generally been adopted in state statutes or administrative regulations. This may have resulted from the pressure exerted in the 1960s by a rash of recognition strikes against public employers.[17]

Most state provisions encompass two methods for employer recognition of a labor organization: (1) voluntary recognition by mutual agreement between the public employer and the union and (2) certification following a supervised secret ballot election.

The Michigan State Public Employment Relations Act is a fairly typical example of state law in this area.[18] This act provides that representatives selected by employees in an appropriate unit are the exclusive representatives of all public employees in such unit for the purposes of collective bargaining with respect to rates of pay, wages, hours of employment, and other conditions of employment, and must be recognized by the public employer. However, there is one exception, fairly typical in state law: an employee has the right as an individual to present a grievance without union intervention.[19]

The Michigan statute also reflects the same type of election procedure followed by the NLRB:

1. An employee group alleging 30 percent or more support within the appropriate unit may file a petition with the Michigan Employment Relations Commission.
2. The commission, if it decides the unit is appropriate, will direct an election unless a prior election was held in the same unit during the preceding 12-month period.
3. The commission determines who is eligible to vote and establishes rules governing the election.
4. The commission will direct that a runoff election be held if there are more than two choices on the ballot and one of them does not receive a majority of the votes actually cast.
5. The commission, if the labor organization wins the election, then certifies it as the exclusive representative of the employees in that unit.[20]

Union Security

Theoretically there are only four basic forms of union security, as noted in Chapter 3. The closed shop, illegal in both the private and public sectors, requires that a person, before becoming an employee, must join the union. Union shop provisions require that employees become union members (or pay dues) within a specified time after beginning employment and maintain membership. A pure maintenance-of-membership clause requires employees to maintain membership once they have joined the union but no employee is required to join. An agency shop compels employees who are not members of the union to pay the union their share of the costs of negotiating and administrating the collective bargaining agreement. Dues deduction or check-off provisions are merely a mechanism for the collection of dues and fees that permit employees to authorize their employer to make payroll deductions

The trend in public sector legislation is toward permitting union security clauses similar to those in the private sector but the states are by no means uniform in their approach. For example, only four states permit union shop provisions[21] and four allow maintenance of membership.[22] At least 17 states permit agency shop provisions in negotiated agreements. However, some negotiated union security clauses have been declared illegal unless specifically authorized by state statute.[23] Most states permit dues checkoff or payroll deduction but, again, a few outlaw such agreements unless expressly permitted by statute.[24]

Unfair Labor Practices

The right of public employees to organize and to join labor unions (or to not do so) is of little value unless it is backed up by statutes that outlaw employer and union unfair labor practices. Nearly all states have adopted codes of unfair labor practices, many of them obviously modeled on the NLRA. These may prohibit unfair labor practices by employers, by labor organizations, or by both.

The types of conduct prohibited as unfair labor practices vary among the states. Again, the NLRA has been used as a guideline. For example, jurisdictions that follow the NLRA model make it an unfair labor practice to: interfere with public employee union activities, encourage or discourage union membership by discrimination, dominate or assist a union, discriminate against an employee for filing charges or giving testimony concerning violations of the statute, and/or refuse to bargain in good faith with the recognized representative of its employees.

Impasse and Strikes

Because strikes by public employees, unlike their colleagues in the private sector, still are unlawful in most states, other methods of breaking a deadlock or impasse have been devised. The most common alternate procedures are mediation, arbitration, and factfinding:

- Mediation, as practiced in both public and private sectors, calls for the use of an outside agency to get the parties talking again. When it succeeds, it produces an agreement. If it fails, the parties still are deadlocked and another alternative must be used. Most state jurisdictions provide for mediation as a procedure to try to break an impasse.[25]

- Interest arbitration (arbitration of a negotiation impasse) is provided for in most states in one form or another.[26] If other methods of resolving the impasse have failed, then some states permit (others require) that it be submitted to arbitration.

• Factfinding has been adopted by many states as an alternative to public sector strikes.

The New York and California procedures provide typical illustrations of the uses of these methods.

New York

• The parties first must attempt mediation.
• A fact-finding board is appointed to make recommendations for resolution if mediation fails.
• The public agency, if the factfinder's recommendations do not result in breaking the deadlock, must submit the factfinder's report and the agency's recommendations for settlement to the relevant legislative body. The union also is permitted to submit recommendations.
• The legislative body as a whole, or one of its committees, then holds a hearing at which the parties present their positions.
• The legislative body "takes such action as it deems in the public interest, including the interest of the public employees involved." In effect, the relevant legislative body makes the final decision.[27]

California

Different fact-finding procedures apply to different types of state employees, as noted at the beginning of this section. There is no provision in the California Government Code for fact-finding or arbitration for local government or state civil service employees but there are fact-finding statutes for public school and public college employees.[28] The process is as follows:

• The mediator cannot find a solution and determines that fact-finding may be appropriate; either party then may request fact-finding within 15 days.
• Each party selects one member of the fact-finding panel within five days after receiving the request for fact-finding from the other party.
• The Public Employment Relations Board (PERB, similar to the NLRB) appoints the chairperson or third member of the panel but the parties may agree on a different chairperson, if they are willing to pay the costs of chairperson's services.
• The panel meets with the parties within ten days of its appointment.

- The panel makes its findings of fact and recommendations for settlement if the dispute is not settled within 30 days of the panel's appointment (longer, if the parties agree). The recommendations are made public 10 days after they are given to the parties. These are merely advisory recommendations and are not binding on the parties.

Legal and Practical Status of Strikes

With few exceptions,[29] strikes by employees in the public sector are uniformly and strictly forbidden. This prohibition is partly historical and partly the result of the distinctive relationship between public employees and employers. In any event, the state courts have held unanimously that a public employee does not have any constitutional or common-law right to strike. The penalties for unlawful strikes can be severe. If they violate a court injunction, the strikers, their leaders, and the union may be subject to prosecution for contempt of court, fines, suspension or dismissal from employment, loss of pay, and other penalties.

Courts, however, are reluctant to penalize strike leaders. Sometimes they may believe it is counterproductive to the overall aim of settling the dispute that caused the strike. The courts also recognize that if an illegal strike is then settled, the public employer may be reluctant to seek enforcement of penalties against illegal strikers and their leaders. As a result, the possibility of strike actions (or "sick-ins," or "blue flu," or other varieties of economic action), illegal though they may be, are real factors in many public sector negotiations and may induce a public employer to reach a settlement it would not otherwise consider.

Enforcement of Contracts, Grievance, Arbitration

As described in Chapter 4, private sector collective bargaining agreements frequently are enforced by grievance and arbitration procedures incorporated in the contract itself. If a party refuses to arbitrate an issue or to abide by an arbitrator's award, the other party may enforce the agreement in court. In the public sector, no such uniform approach to the enforcement of collective bargaining agreements prevails.

Two major reasons have been advanced for the uncertainty and lack of development in this area of public employee labor relations:

1. The disciplining or discharge of a public employee frequently is governed by civil service statutes, rules, and regulations, in contrast to the private sector where a grievance/arbitration procedure frequently is the union's (and employee's) exclusive remedy.
2. An arbitrator's award can call for the payment of back wages or impose other monetary liability upon the employer. In the public sector, these payments

must be drawn from funds that may be controlled by a legislative body that may be reluctant to (or refuse to) commit taxpayer dollars.

Despite these considerations, negotiated grievance and arbitration procedures for public employees increasingly are permitted by state and local governments. These provisions, however, are so varied as to not be susceptible to any generalized summary. Yet if these variations are set aside, it appears that a national policy for both public and private employment is evolving in favor of voluntarily negotiated grievance and arbitration provisions.

NOTES

1. KURT HANSLOWE, THE EMERGING LAW OF LABOR RELATIONS IN PUBLIC EMPLOYMENT, at 35 (1967).

2. 5 U.S.C. §§ 7101–7135.

3. *Id.* § 7135(a)(2).

4. *Id.* § 7103(a)(10).

5. *Id.* § 7106(b)(1).

6. *Id.* § 7121(a)(1) (1978).

7. Two excellent sources for a further review of state laws governing public employee labor relations are T.W. Kheel, Vols. 9, 10, *Business Organizations, LABOR LAW,* §§ 43.01–58.04 (1979) and [4 State Laws] LAB. REL. REP. (BNA) at 4A (1983). The Kheel volumes, in particular, are invaluable and served as a basis for many of the summaries and trends in state law referred to in this text.

8. Griswold v. Connecticut, 381 U.S. 479, 483 (1965); McLaughlin v. Tilendis, 398 F.2d 287, 288 (7th Cir. 1968).

9. *See, for example,* MO. ANN. STAT. § 105.520 (Vernon 1982).

10. T.W. Kheel, Vol. 10, *Business Organizations, LABOR LAW* § 43.04[1] (1979).

11. ALASKA STAT. § 23.40.250(1), (7) (Michie 1972).

12. CONN. GEN. STAT. § 5–272(c), (d) (West Supp. 1983).

13. N.Y. CIV. SERV. LAW §§ 201(4) (McKinney 1982).

14. *See, e.g.,* HAWAII REV. STAT. § 89–9(d) (Supp. 1983) and VT. STAT. ANN. tit. 3, § 905(b)(1) (1972).

15. *See, e.g.,* MINN. STAT. ANN. § 179.66(1) (West 1982).

16. *Compare* CAL. GOV'T CODE § 3528 (West 1980) (right of individual state employees to represent themselves) with CAL. GOV'T CODE § 3573 (West 1980) (exclusive representation rights under Higher Education Employer-Employee Relations Act); Neb. Rev. Stat. 79-1288 (1981).

17. Anderson, *Selection and Certification of Representatives in Public Employment,* 20 N.Y.U. CONFERENCE ON LAB. 277, 278 (1968).

18. MICH. COMP. LAWS ANN. §§ 423.1 et seq. (West 1978).

19. *Id.* 423.211

20. *Id.* 423.212; 423.214.

21. Alaska, Maine, Washington, and Oregon.

22. California, Maine, Pennsylvania, and Washington.

23. California, Minnesota, New Jersey, New York, and Pennsylvania.

24. Board of Sch. Directors of Milwaukee v. WERC, 42 Wis. 2d 637 (1969).

25. T.W. Kheel, in *181 Business Organizations*, LABOR LAW § 56.03 (1977).

26. *Id.*, § 56.05.

27. N.Y. CIV. SERV. LAW § 209(3) (McKinney 1982).

28. CAL. GOV'T CODE §§ 3548.1 (West Supp. 1984), 3591 (West 1980).

29. Edwards, *The Developing Labor Relations Law in the Public Sector*, 10 DUQ. L.R. 357, 376–378 (1972).

Chapter 6

Discrimination in Employment

FAIR EMPLOYMENT PRACTICES

Job discrimination is now outlawed by numerous federal and state statutes. As a supervisor, you should know that practically every aspect of personnel practices and employee supervision is subject to do's and don'ts established by these laws. Sometimes, compliance with all applicable laws may seem an impossible task, particularly since, in contrast with the National Labor Relations Act, no one law governs fair employment practices.

Instead, private employers may be subject to three or four different federal statutes, in addition to state and local statutes, laws, and regulations. The same is true of public employers, which are governed by federal and state constitutional bans on discrimination plus being subject to some of the same laws that apply to private employers and to additional statutes specifically designed for public employment. If your facility has a collective bargaining agreement, it may contain a nondiscrimination clause—still another source of regulation.

Your life is further complicated by the fact that these numerous federal and state statutes may speak to only one form of prohibited discrimination, with different standards for employee coverage and different enforcement procedures.

This chapter is designed to simplify matters by analyzing briefly the various laws that might apply to your facility. (This is summarized in Appendix 6-A.) Chapters 7 and 8 discuss in greater detail the primary federal laws that may involve your institution.

FEDERAL NONDISCRIMINATION REQUIREMENTS

Employers in General

Employment discrimination can be challenged by your employees on many different federal grounds. Some of those most commonly involved are:

- United States Constitution
- Title VII of the Civil Rights Act of 1964
- Section 1981 of the Civil Rights Act of 1866
- Section 1983 of the Civil Rights Act of 1871
- Equal Pay Act of 1963
- Age Discrimination in Employment Act of 1967
- Veterans Reemployment Act
- National Labor Relations Act (discussed in detail in Chapter 3).

If your facility is a federal contractor or receives federal financial assistance, then in addition to these laws you may be subject to the affirmative action or other specialized requirements imposed by legislation such as the Rehabilitation Act of 1973, various Executive orders, Title VI of the Civil Rights Act of 1964, etc. Each of these is now summarized.

The United States Constitution

The due process clause of the Fifth Amendment and the due process and equal protection clauses of the Fourteenth Amendment govern employment practices in two ways:

1. They will invalidate any state or federal law that requires, allows, or encourages racial discrimination in employment by either public or private employers.
2. They can be used to strike down discriminatory practices of two types of employers: (a) federal, state, or other public employers, and (b) private employers whose businesses are so intertwined with state contracts, loans, regulations, and functions that their actions are considered to be "state [or public] action" for Constitutional purposes.

Of significance to you is that the mere receipt of Medicare, government grants, or loans (such as the former Hill-Burton funds) by private employers generally will not result in a finding that "state action" exists.[1] This means that these Constitutional provisions probably will not successfully serve as a basis for private lawsuits against most private health care employers.

Title VII of the Civil Rights Act of 1964 (Title VII)

Title VII[2] forbids discrimination (1) in employment; (2) on the basis of race, color, religion, sex, or national origin; (3) by employers, employment agencies, unions, and joint labor-management apprenticeship or training committees. Your facility will be covered if it is a public or private employer in an industry affecting commerce and employs at least 15 workers during each working day in each of 20 or more calendar weeks in the current or prior year.[3]

Title VII originally covered only private employers but in 1972 it was amended to take in state and local governments (and most of their employees excluding, e.g., elected officials); special provisions requiring nondiscrimination in federal government also were added.[4] You should note, however, that the enforcement procedures for Title VII claims against the federal government vary from those against private employers.[5]

Civil Rights Act of 1866

The Civil Rights Act of 1866 in Section 1981[6] guarantees to all "persons" the same rights to make and enter into contracts, to participate in legal proceedings, and to otherwise enjoy the "full and equal benefit of all laws and proceedings for the security of persons and property as is enjoyed by white citizens. . . ."[7]

Important issues about this law are that:

- It applies to all private and public employers, not just to those with a certain number of employees. Thus, even if your facility is not covered by Title VII, this law still applies.
- It cannot be used to sue the federal government as an employer but can be used as the basis for employment discrimination actions against state and local government employers.[8]
- It prohibits employment discrimination since, even without a written contract, the "right to contract" includes employment arrangements.
- It permits white employees to sue since it prohibits employment discrimination based on race.[9]
- It still is not clear whether it bans only racial discrimination or includes that based on national origin.[10]
- It does not cover discrimination based on sex or on religion.[11]
- Its reference to "all persons" is not limited to citizens, so it also prohibits employment discrimination against aliens.[12]
- It permits an employee or applicant for employment to sue under this Act without first filing a charge with the Equal Employment Opportunity Commission (EEOC), since the law is not administered by the EEOC or any other federal agency.
- It provides remedies for violations of the statute that are broader than, and not limited to, those for Title VII violations.

Civil Rights Act of 1871

This statute[13] as amended provides a remedy for the deprivation of federally protected rights under cover of state law, usage, or custom. This means that (1) the law's protection extends beyond racial discrimination to include national origin, sex, etc.;[14] (2) state and local government employers are covered; (3) private employers are covered only if they are acting under "color of" law akin to "state action"; and (4) private employers' receipt of Medicare, federal financial assistance, or other governmental funding, by itself, generally is not sufficient to constitute state action.[15] Again, if your facility is covered by this statute, employees or applicants for employment can bring suit without first pursuing their claims with the EEOC.

Equal Pay Act of 1963

The Equal Pay Act (EPA)[16] actually is an amendment to the Fair Labor Standards Act (FLSA), a federal wage-hour statute discussed in Chapter 9. Its objective is to require that female and male employees be paid equal wages for equal work. As explained in Chapter 9, "equal work" means the jobs involve equal skill, effort, and responsibility; are performed under similar working conditions; and are for the same establishment. "Equal wages" means all remuneration (including fringe benefits), not just money paid for hours worked.

Private employers who are otherwise covered by the FLSA are subject to the Equal Pay Act. This means that since hospitals and other institutions providing residential care to the sick, infirm, and aged are covered by the FLSA without regard to the size of the employer, your facility also will be covered by the EPA.[17] If your facility is a public employer, then it probably is covered by the Equal Pay Act even though the question has not been decided conclusively by the United States Supreme Court.

As Chapter 9 discusses, the FLSA was amended to make state and local governments subject to its minimum wage and overtime requirements. The United States Supreme Court then struck this down[18] but since the Equal Pay Act's coverage of these same public employers was not before the Court, that issue was not addressed. Most lower courts and the Department of Labor's Wage-Hour Division have taken the position that public employers are covered by the Equal Pay Act[19] so the wisest course for state and local government health care facilities is to comply with the Act by ensuring equal pay for equal work, thereby avoiding any question of liability.

Age Discrimination in Employment Act of 1967 (ADEA)

The ADEA[20] protects employees and applicants who are between 40 and 70 years old from discrimination because of age. Private employers engaged in an industry affecting commerce are covered if 20 or more workers (as contrasted with 15 for Title VII) are employed during at least 20 weeks in the current or prior year. State and local government employers also are covered by this law and while the term "employer" does not include the federal government, the Act contains special provisions applicable to federal employees.[21] In 1979 the responsibility for enforcing the ADEA was transferred from the U.S. Department of Labor to the EEOC, the same agency that administers Title VII.

If an employer is covered, then all of its employees are protected by the ADEA, with several major exceptions:

- Employees are not covered if they are 65 years of age but less than 70, have been employed for at least two years preceding retirement in a "bona fide" executive or high policymaking position, and have an immediate and vested retirement benefit of at least $27,000.[22]
- Elected state and local government officials and members of their staff are excluded from the Act's protection.[23]

Veterans' Reemployment Rights

All private and public employers must comply with federal legislation providing reemployment and leave rights for members of the military services, including reservists who perform training duty.[24]

National Labor Relations Act (NLRA)

Although not normally viewed as a nondiscrimination law, the NLRA[25] imposes an obligation upon labor organizations to act fairly and impartially toward members and employees it represents or seeks to represent. This means that unfair labor practice charges, and the enforcement powers of the National Labor Relations Board, can be used where, for example, a union refuses to process a grievance because the employee is black or female. The Board also has invalidated representation elections where the union's election campaign is based on racial appeals. (Broader aspects of the NLRA are presented in Chapter 3.)

Private Employers Who Are Federal Contractors

If your facility has a contract with the federal government, you may be subject to still more laws in addition to those that apply to all private employers. Generally speaking, the receipt of Medicare and special federal grant or project funds are not considered federal contracts although the government may regard them as federal assistance (see the following discussion of "Private Employers Who Receive Federal Assistance").[26]

If, for example, you have a government contract to operate a clinic providing health services for federal employees, and if that contract exceeds a set dollar amount and you have a specified number of employees, then you may be covered by one or more laws or regulations described below. It must be emphasized that the ones discussed here are only some of the laws and regulations applicable to federal contractors and that a thorough review of all statutory and other requirements is necessary if your facility has a government contract.

Executive Order 11141 (1964)

This order bans federal contractor discrimination against employees or applicants because of their age "except upon the basis of a bona fide occupational qualification, retirement plan, or statutory requirement."[27] No upper age limit is specified and, unlike Executive Order 11246 and its accompanying Office of Federal Contract Compliance Programs (OFCCP) regulations, the contract under Executive Order 11141 is not required to have a minimum value or affirmative action obligations.

Executive Order 11246 (1965)

This Executive order prohibits job discrimination based on race, color, religion, sex, or national origin by contractors (and their subcontractors) doing business with the federal government and requires that they take certain affirmative action. The OFCCP administers this as well as other federal statutes and Executive orders applicable to federal contractors.

Under OFCCP regulations, government contracts and subcontracts for more than $10,000 must contain certain provisions set forth in these regulations and the Executive orders: for example, provisions binding the employer to nondiscrimination, requiring equal opportunity statements in advertisements, allowing government access to the employer's books and records for determining compliance, etc. In addition, if the contract is for nonconstruction work of $50,000 or more and 50 or more employees, a written affirmative action plan must be provided and other specialized requirements must be met.[28]

A federal contractor's noncompliance with these obligations can result in the government's withdrawal or termination of the contract and/or a refusal to enter into any future dealings with the employer. The OFCCP also could sue the contractor to require compliance with Executive Order 11246. In such an action, the OFCCP can seek appropriate relief on behalf of women and minorities, including back pay.[29]

Vietnam Era Veterans' Readjustment Assistance Act of 1974

Federal contractors with contracts for $10,000 or more are required by this law to engage in affirmative efforts to provide employment for qualified disabled veterans and for veterans of the Vietnam era.[30] Such affirmative action need not be as extensive as the formal plan a contractor must adopt under Executive Order 11246 but it must comply with regulations issued by the OFCCP.[31]

Section 503 of the Rehabilitation Act

Under Section 503,[32] employees with federal contracts in excess of $2,500 must avoid employment discrimination against qualified handicapped persons and take affirmative action to employ and advance such persons.

Private Employers Who Receive Federal Assistance

No listing would be complete without a mention of still other laws that apply to "recipients" of federal financial assistance. A few examples are discussed next.

Title VI of the Civil Rights Act of 1964 (Title VI)

Title VI[33] prohibits employment discrimination based on race, color, or national origin by recipients of federal financial assistance if the primary purpose of the funding is to provide employment.[34] While the federal government considers Medicare, Medicaid, and similar forms of governmental aid to be federal financial assistance,[35] these types of funds are not for the primary purpose of providing employment. As a result, and even if your facility receives such assistance, the impact of Title VI will be to prohibit discrimination toward beneficiaries of the funds (patients, other individuals receiving services, etc.), and it generally cannot be used to regulate your employment practices.

Section 504 of the Rehabilitation Act of 1973

Section 504,[36] which was modeled after Title VI of the Civil Rights Act, outlaws discrimination by recipients of federal financial assistance against qualified handicapped individuals. Again, Medicare Part A and Medicaid are considered to be federal financial assistance by the Department of Health and Human Services (and other agencies), and it has issued regulations governing handicap discrimination that the federal government may attempt to apply to your facility if it participates in these programs.[37] In contrast with Title VI, Section 504 can be used to regulate employment practices even if the federal financial assistance is not for the purpose of providing employment[38] but a question remains as to whether Medicare and Medicaid constitute "federal financial assistance."[39] Because of this, you should seek clarification before responding to any government inquiries concerning employment discrimination based on handicap.

Private Employers in Apprenticeship Programs[40]

The National Apprenticeship Act of 1937 authorizes the issuance of apprenticeship program standards by the Secretary of Labor. Subsequently, two sets of regulations were issued: "Labor Standards for the Registration of Apprenticeship

Program,"[41] and "Equal Employment Opportunity in Apprenticeship and Training."[42] These prohibit discrimination based on race, sex, national origin, color, or religion. If a program is to be registered for federal purposes such as funding assistance, exemptions, grants, contracts, etc., then both sets of regulations must be met. This includes the requirement that an affirmative action plan be adopted and implemented in accordance with the Department of Labor's regulations if a sponsor has five or more apprentices. The only exception to this requirement is if the sponsor already has an equal opportunity and affirmative action program approved under Title VII or Executive Order 11246.[43]

STATE LAWS

Fair Employment Practice

Most state governments, and many local ones, have enacted fair employment practice laws, though they may be called by different names. Generally speaking, you will be covered by such state laws in addition to federal statutes. For example:

- Employers must continue to comply with all state or local government nondiscrimination laws and regulations.

- Employers must comply with both the state law and the Title VII standard if a state imposes stricter requirements than does Title VII or other federal law (stricter in the sense of providing additional protection to employees or applicants).[44] Compliance with Title VII will not relieve you from liability for violating state law.

- Employers, by the same token, may have no obligation to comply with a state fair employment, antidiscrimination, or other law if it conflicts with Title VII or other federal discrimination statute. In fact, if you violate federal law because you have relied on conflicting state law, your employer still may be liable for action viewed as discriminatory from the federal standpoint.

A good example: various states had weight-lifting and other protective restrictions that applied only to females when Title VII was enacted. Many courts found that Title VII precluded an employer's reliance upon these state laws because Title VII prohibits discrimination based upon sex.[45]

To be more specific, where state laws forbade an employer from working women more than "x" hours in a week but placed no such restriction on men, or where state law restricted the amount of lifting women could do, with no similar restriction on men, these state laws conflicted with Title VII. Why? Because the restrictions were based on sex stereotypes rather than individual capabilities. Accordingly, employers who continued to rely on these state laws were violating Title VII. The EEOC has incorporated this concept into its regulations by providing, in its "Sex Discrimination Guidelines," that employers cannot raise protective state legislation as a defense to an otherwise unlawful employment practice.[46]

Scope and Coverage

State laws vary widely in the kinds of discrimination they prohibit, in their coverage of employers, and in their enforcement proceedings.[47] For example:

- States are free to extend their laws and regulations to all employers, not just larger ones affecting interstate commerce, as is the case with Title VII. Yet many states have declined to do this and have limited their coverage to specified kinds of employers or to those with a specified minimum number of employees. The Illinois Fair Employment Practices Act defines "employer" in the same terms as Title VII.[48] This means that Illinois employers with fewer than 15 employees are not subject to either Title VII or to state law. In contrast, California excludes religious nonprofit associations or corporations but covers other employers with five or more employees.[49] These examples point up the importance of noting who and what are covered by your state (and federal) laws before you respond to any government inquiry.
- Some states' standards are stricter than those in federal law. For example, the federal Age Discrimination in Employment Act protects employees and applicants between the ages of 40 to 70.[50] However, states such as California protect employees and applicants from ages 40 on up with no maximum age limit. This means that persons who are 75, 80, or even 90 years old generally cannot be discriminated against because of age under California state law even though they are not protected by federal law after reaching age 70.[51]
- Some states outlaw types of discrimination that are not prohibited by federal law:
  1. California bars discrimination based on race, color, religious creed, national origin, ancestry, sex, age, marital status, medical conditions (any health impairment related to a diagnosis of cancer, of which the person has been cured), or physical handicap.[52] In contrast, federal law does not prohibit discrimination on the basis of marital status (except as covered by bans on sex discrimination), and federal law barring discrimination based on medical condition or physical handicap applies only to particular employers such as federal contractors, the federal government, and recipients of federal financial assistance.
  2. The Michigan Civil Rights Act prohibits discrimination on the grounds of height, weight, and marital status in addition to the forms barred by Title VII.[53]

3. The District of Columbia Human Rights Law bans discriminatory acts based on personal appearance, matriculation, family responsibilities, and sexual orientation in addition to those prohibited by Title VII.[54]

A LOOK AHEAD

The next two chapters review the primary laws that may cover your facility and regulate your actions. Always remember that it is critical to check before responding to any government complaint or other legal challenge:

- whether your employer is covered by the particular statute, regulation, or other requirement
- whether your employer is covered by more than one statute, regulation, or requirement and, if so, which one is stricter and is there any conflict in the obligations imposed.

NOTES

1. *See* cases cited in n.15 *infra.*

2. 42 U.S.C. § 2000e.

3. Title VII provides that governmental agencies are industries "affecting commerce," as is any "activity or industry 'affecting commerce' within the meaning of the Labor-Management Reporting and Disclosure Act of 1959," 42 U.S.C. 2000–e(h). This means, as a practical matter, that all public health care employers (and any private ones covered by the NLRA) come under Title VII if they have employed the required number of workers for the specified period of time.

4. Pub. L. No. 92–261, amending § 701(a) and (b), and adding § 717, 42 U.S.C. 2000e(a),(b); 2000e–16.

5. 42 U.S.C. 2000e–16.

6. 42 U.S.C. § 1981.

7. *Id.*

8. Brown v. General Serv. Admin., 425 U.S. 820 (1976); Johnson v. City of Cincinnati, 450 F.2d 786 (6th Cir. 1971).

9. McDonald v. Sante Fe Trail Transp. Co., 427 U.S. 273 (1976).

10. Budinsky v. Corning Glass Works, 425 F. Supp. 786 (W.D. Pa. 1977) (national origin discrimination not covered); *but compare,* Manzaneres v. Safeway Stores, 593 F.2d 968 (10th Cir. 1979) (§ 1981 limited to race but term cannot be given overly technical meaning, and thus allegations by Mexican-American plaintiff were covered), and Bullard v. Omi Georgia, Inc., 25 Fair Empl. Prac. Cas. (BNA) 731 (5th Cir. 1981) (national origin discrimination prohibited only if closely related to racial discrimination claims).

11. Bobo v. ITT, Continental Baking Co., 27 Fair Empl. Prac. Cas. (BNA) 502 (5th Cir. 1981) (sex discrimination not covered); Shanks v. Harrington, 21 Fair Empl. Prac. Cas. (BNA) 590 (N.D. Ia.) (religious discrimination not covered).

160   THE HEALTH CARE SUPERVISOR'S LEGAL GUIDE

12. Guerra v. Manchester Terminal Corp., 498 F.2d 641 (5th Cir. 1974), *affirming*, 350 F. Supp. 533 (D. Tex. 1972).

13. 42 U.S.C. § 1983.

14. Sylvania Educ. Ass'n v. Bd. of Educ., 14 Fair Empl. Prac. Cas. (BNA) 577 (N.D. Ohio 1976) (sex); Ramirez v. San Mateo County D.A.'s Office, 639 F.2d 509 (9th Cir. 1981) (national origin).

15. *E.g.*, Wright v. Methodist Youth Serv., 511 F. Supp. 307 (N.D. Ill. 1981) (substantial state funding and state agency referrals insufficient); Milner v. Nat'l School of Health Technology, 409 F. Supp. 1389 (E.D Pa. 1976) (licensed by state regulation, state assistance through tuition grants and student loans, and provision of a public service, still insufficient for state action).

16. 29 U.S.C. § 206(d).

17. See Chapter 9, n.2.

18. National League of Cities v. Usery, 426 U.S. 833 (1976).

19. See Chapter 9, nn.7, 35.

20. 29 U.S.C. §§ 621–34.

21. 29 U.S.C. § 633(a).

22. 29 U.S.C. 631(c); see special provisions for calculating value of certain retirement benefits and programs.

23. 29 U.S.C. 630(f).

24. 38 U.S.C. §§ 2021–26.

25. 29 U.S.C. § 151.

26. *E.g.*, in the OFCCP Affirmative Action Regulations for Handicapped Workers, 41 C.F.R. Part 60–741, it states that the term "government contract does not include . . . federally-assisted contracts." 41 C.F.R. § 60–741.2. *See* nn.37–39.

27. 29 Fed. Reg. No. 2,477.

28. Exec. Order No. 11,246; 41 C.F.R. 60–1 (contract requirements in general); 41 C.F.R. 60–2 (affirmative action requirements). New OFCCP regulations were proposed in 1980, 45 Fed. Reg. 86,216, but deferred indefinitely, 46 Fed. Reg. 42,865 (1981). Meanwhile, substitute proposed regulations were issued in 1981, 46 Fed. Reg. 42,968, 46 Fed. Reg. 46,815. The OFCCP also has other existing, proposed, or deferred regulations dealing with other aspects of federal contractor status, including those applicable to particular forms of discrimination; e.g., sex, national origin.

29. 41 C.F.R. § 60–1.26(a)(2).

30. 38 U.S.C. § 2012.

31. 41 C.F.R. 60–250; proposed regulations are pending, 45 Fed. Reg. 86206.

32. 29 U.S.C. § 793(a).

33. 42 U.S.C. § 2000d.

34. 42 U.S.C. § 2000d–3.

35. 45 C.F.R. § 80.2, Appendix A.

36. 29 U.S.C. § 794.

37. 45 C.F.R. § 80.1–.13; § 80.2, Appendix A (regulations for Title VI of Civil Rights Act of 1964 in which Appendix A lists those programs considered to be federal assistance for HHS purposes); 45 C.F.R. § 84, Appendix A, Subpart A–1.

38. Trageser v. Libbie Rehabilitation Center, 462 F. Supp. 424, 426 (E.D. Va. 1977) *aff'd on other grounds*, 590 F.2d 87 (4th Cir. 1978), *cert. denied* 442 U.S. 947 (1979); *see generally*, Consolidated Rail Corp. v. Darrone, _____ U.S. _____, 79 L.Ed. 2d 568, 578, n.19 (1984) (employer did not

contest receipt of federal financial assistance since government paid more than fair market value for the bonds it purchased).

39. Consolidated Rail Corp. v. Darrone, _____ U.S. _____ 79 L.Ed. 2d 568.

40. 29 U.S.C. § 50; 29 C.F.R. Part 30.

41. 29 C.F.R. § 29.1–.13.

42. 29 C.F.R. § 30.1–.19.

43. 29 C.F.R. §§ 30.3(b),(e), 30.4.

44. An example of a deviation from this general principle can be found in Cal. Fed. Savings & Loan Assn v. FEHC, Docket No. 83–4927R (C.D. Cal. 1984) in which the court found that California's fair employment law requiring, e.g., a reasonable leave of up to four months for maternity, was preempted by Title VII of the Civil Rights Act of 1964.

45. *E.g.*, Rosenfeld v. Southern Pacific Co., 444 F.2d 1219 (9th Cir. 1971). While a Title VII violation occurred in Rosenfeld, the Court also found that the employer was relieved of any backpay liability since it had relied, in good faith, on the state law.

46. 29 C.F.R. § 1604.2(b)(1).

47. For an overview of all states, see 8A LAB. REL. REP. (BNA), *State Fair Employment Practices Law*.

48. Ill. Ann. Stat. Ch. 68 § 2–101(B) (Smith-Hurd Supp. 1983).

49. CAL. GOV'T CODE § 12925(c) (West 1980).

50. 29 U.S.C. §§ 621–34.

51. CAL. GOV'T CODE § 12941(a) (West Supp. 1984).

52 CAL. GOV'T CODE §§ 12940–41 (West Supp. 1984).

53. Mich. Comp. Laws Ann. §§ 37.2202 (West Supp. 1983).

54. D.C. CODE ENCYCL. § 6–2221 (West Supp. 1979).

Appendix 6-A

Cataloging Major Federal Antidiscrimination Laws

This is a summary of some of the federal legislation under which questions of prohibited discrimination most commonly arise. It is not all-inclusive, however, since a number of other federal laws also exist and requirements of your own state and/or local governments also must be ascertained.

Source of Regulation	Employer Coverage	Discrimination Prohibited	Enforcing Agency
I. Employers Generally			
United States Constitution	Public employers and private employers acting "under color of state law"	Race, religion, national origin; sex questionable	None specified
Title VII of the Civil Rights Act of 1964	Public and private employers with 15 or more employees for at least 20 weeks in the current or prior year	Race, color, religion, sex, or national origin	EEOC
Civil Rights Act of 1866 (§ 1981)	State and local governments and private persons	Race; perhaps national origin	None
Civil Rights Act of 1871 (§ 1983)	State and local governments and private persons acting "under color of state law"	Rights protected by federal Constitution and laws (e.g., race, national origin, sex)	None
Equal Pay Act of 1963	Private employers covered by FLSA, probably all public employers as well [a]	Unequal pay for equal work by males and females	EEOC

Source of Regulation	Employer Coverage	Discrimination Prohibited	Enforcing Agency
Age Discrimination in Employment Act of 1967 (ADEA)	All private employers with 20 or more employees for at least 20 weeks in the current or prior year; state and local governments	Age (40 to 70)	EEOC
Veterans Reemployment Act (1974)	All public and private employers	Returning veterans, employees on military leave, employees who leave to go into the military, reservists, etc.	DOL Office of Veterans' Reemployment Rights (OVRR)
Apprenticeship Act (1937)	Sponsors of apprenticeship programs	Race, color, religion, national origin, or sex[b]	Department of Labor

II. Federal Contractors

Source of Regulation	Employer Coverage	Discrimination Prohibited	Enforcing Agency
Executive Order 11141 (1964)	Employers who contract with federal government	Age	Federal agency entering into contract
Executive Order 11246 (1965)	Employers "contracting" with the federal government: (1) in excess of $10,000 per year (2) in excess of $50,000 per year plus 50 employees	If (1), then prohibits color, religion, sex, or national origin discrimination; if (2), employers also must adopt written affirmative action plan	OFCCP
Veterans Readjustment Assistance Act	Employers who are party to a "contract" with the federal government in excess of $10,000 per year	Disabled veterans; veterans of the Vietnam era	OFCCP
Section 503 of the Rehabilitation Act (1973)	Employers who are party to a "contract" with the federal government in excess of $2,500 per year	Handicap	OFCCP

Source of Regulation	Employer Coverage	Discrimination Prohibited	Enforcing Agency
III. Federally Assisted Programs			
Title VI of the Civil Rights Act of 1964	Employers with programs or activities receiving federal financial assistance	Discrimination against beneficiaries or programs/activities because of race, color, or national origin; regulates employment if primary objective of federal assistance is to provide employment	Federal department/ agencies providing assistance
Section 504 of the Rehabilitation Act of 1973	Same as Title VI	Handicap	*E.g.*, Office of Civil Rights[c]

[a]While the question of EPA coverage of state and local governments in the wake of National League of Cities v. Usery, 426 U.S. 833 (1976), is not determined conclusively, most case law is to the effect that such employers are covered. See Chapter 9, nn.7, 35.

[b]Sponsors of programs with more than five apprentices are obliged to adopt a formal written affirmative program similar to that required of employers subject to Executive Order 11246's affirmative action requirements.

[c]Each agency providing the federal financial assistance is responsible for ensuring compliance and beginning in 1980 the Attorney General has had the responsibility for coordinating the agencies' enforcement efforts. The Office of Civil Rights in HHS had a primary role in formulating Section 504 regulations and its requirements applicable to HHS assistance would be a common source of information for health care providers.

Chapter 7

Race, National Origin, Sex, and Religion

AN INTRODUCTION TO TITLE VII

Protected Classes and Prohibited Discrimination

As discussed in Chapter 6, Title VII of the Civil Rights Act of 1964 (Title VII) prohibits discrimination in employment based on race, color, religion, sex, or national origin. The Equal Employment Opportunity Commission (EEOC) is the federal agency given the administrative responsibility for enforcing and interpreting Title VII and several other federal nondiscrimination laws. Before Title VII is reviewed in greater detail, however, some definitions and examples are in order.

Protected Classes. An employee or applicant who falls into one of the categories protected by the Act is called a member of a "protected class" (i.e., a black person, a female, a Mexican-American).

Race Discrimination. Segregating a company's facilities (restrooms, lunchroom, etc.) by race clearly constitutes employment discrimination based on race. Yet other practices that do not seem to be discriminatory on the surface can, in their operation, represent unlawful discrimination on the basis of race. For example, one employer required that all applicants for employment possess high school diplomas even if they were applying for jobs as laborers. Because fewer black persons than whites possessed such degrees, the company hired blacks at a much lower rate. The Supreme Court held that the diploma requirement was unlawful in that it was not related to the successful performance of the jobs and caused a disproportionate number of black applicants to be rejected from employment.[1]

National Origin Discrimination. Title VII also prohibits employer practices, policies, or actions that discriminate against individuals on the basis of their national origin. For instance, the County of Los Angeles required that all its applicants for firefighter be at least 5'7" in height. This practice resulted in the automatic disqualification of 41 percent of otherwise eligible Mexican-Americans because persons of that national origin tend to be shorter, on the average, than Caucasians. The court found that a height of 5'7" was not related to success on the job so it held the practice to be discriminatory.[2]

Sex Discrimination. The purpose of Title VII's ban on sex discrimination is to eliminate stereotypical beliefs about the abilities of women in the work force and to require that employers judge them individually on their own merits. For example, women previously were not hired to work in the construction industry because employers viewed jobs in that field as "man's work."

Religious Discrimination. Religious discrimination is treated somewhat differently from other forms. An employer must practice nondiscrimination "plus" make "reasonable accommodation"—that is, adjustments in its work schedule— to both applicants' and employees' religious practices. However, there are several exceptions to these concepts:

- Reasonable accommodation need not be made if it causes an "undue hardship" on the employer's business.[3] While there is no hard-and-fast rule for deciding what is an undue hardship, and a determination must be based on the facts of each case, it has been held that reasonable accommodation does not require an employer to significantly increase costs, decrease efficiency and service, or unfairly impose upon other employees.[4]

- Title VII contains an exemption applicable "to a religious corporation, association, educational institution, or society with respect to the employment of individuals of a particular religion to perform work connected with the carrying on by such corporation, association, educational institution, or society of its activities."[5]

Equal Employment Opportunity Commission

The duty of the EEOC is to investigate, attempt to conciliate, and sometimes litigate charges of employment discrimination. The EEOC, headquartered in Washington, D.C., is composed of five members appointed by the President. In 1972, when the EEOC was given the power to initiate lawsuits in its own name, the Office of the General Counsel was created to exercise this power.

In many respects the structure of the EEOC is quite similar to that of the National Labor Relations Board. For example:

- The word "EEOC" can refer to the five-person Commission in Washington, to the agency itself, or to one of its local offices.

- The EEOC has district offices in major cities as well as a number of area offices within districts.

- The EEOC, when contacting you regarding a charge of employment discrimination, generally does so through a regional office, not the national office in Washington.

In other ways, the EEOC and Title VII are quite different from the NLRB and the NLRA:

- The EEOC has issued standard guidelines or regulations containing its interpretation of what constitutes discrimination. The NLRB has issued no similar regulations under the National Labor Relations Act.
- The EEOC's investigation may disclose that no reasonable basis exists for concluding that discrimination occurred, yet Title VII still permits the affected Charging Parties (employees or applicants for employment) to press their claims through a private lawsuit against the employer, union, or employment agency. By contrast, the NLRB is the only enforcement mechanism for the NLRA; it generally does not allow private lawsuits where the claim involves an unfair labor practice or a question concerning representation subject to the Board's jurisdiction.[6]

Requirements and Guidelines for Title VII Claims

The machinery of Title VII and the EEOC is started by filing a charge of unlawful employment discrimination. This may be filed by the person claiming to be aggrieved, by a person on the complainant's behalf, or by a member of the Commission.

Requirements for Filing a Charge

A charge of discrimination filed with the EEOC generally must meet the following:

- The charge must be a written, sworn statement alleging that a violation of Title VII has occurred. As Exhibit 7–1 shows, the form names the employer, labor organization, or employment agency that the Charging Party alleges has violated Title VII.
- The charge is filed either with the EEOC itself (generally at a district office) or with a state fair employment enforcement agency recognized by the EEOC for some or all complaints under Title VII.
- The charge contains a short statement of the Charging Party's reasons for believing discrimination has occurred (EEOC staff persons frequently help Charging Parties phrase their claims).

Exhibit 7–1 Form for Filing EEOC Complaint

APPROVED BY OMB 3046-0012 Expires 12/31/83	**CHARGE OF DISCRIMINATION** IMPORTANT: This form is affected by the Privacy Act of 1974, see Privacy Act Statement on reverse before completing it.	CHARGE NUMBER(S) (AGENCY USE ONLY)
		☐ STATE/LOCAL AGENCY
		☐ EEOC

Equal Employment Opportunity Commission and
(State or Local Agency)

NAME (Indicate Mr., Ms. or Mrs.)	HOME TELEPHONE NUMBER (Include area code)
STREET ADDRESS	
CITY, STATE, AND ZIP CODE	COUNTY

NAMED IS THE EMPLOYER, LABOR ORGANIZATION, EMPLOYMENT AGENCY, APPRENTICESHIP COMMITTEE, STATE OR LOCAL GOVERNMENT AGENCY WHO DISCRIMINATED AGAINST ME. (If more than one list below).

NAME	TELEPHONE NUMBER (Include area code)
STREET ADDRESS	CITY, STATE, AND ZIP CODE

NAME	TELEPHONE NUMBER (Include area code)
STREET ADDRESS	CITY, STATE, AND ZIP CODE

CAUSE OF DISCRIMINATION BASED ON MY (Check appropriate box(es))

☐ RACE   ☐ COLOR   ☐ SEX   ☐ RELIGION   ☐ NATIONAL ORIGIN   ☐ OTHER (Specify)

DATE MOST RECENT OR CONTINUING DISCRIMINATION TOOK
PLACE (Month, day, and year)

THE PARTICULARS ARE

I will advise the agencies if I change my address or telephone number and I will cooperate fully with them in the processing of my charge in accordance with their procedures.	NOTARY — (When necessary to meet State and Local Requirements) I swear or affirm that I have read the above charge and that it is true to the best of my knowledge, information and belief
	SIGNATURE OF COMPLAINANT
I declare under penalty of perjury that the foregoing is true and correct	SUBSCRIBED AND SWORN TO BEFORE ME THIS DATE (Day, month, and year)
DATE CHARGING PARTY (Signature)	

Exhibit 7–1 continued

NOTICE OF NON-RETALIATION REQUIREMENT

Section 704(a) of the Civil Rights Act of 1964, as amended, states:

It shall be an unlawful employment practice for an employer to discriminate against any of his employees or applicants for employment, for an employment agency to discriminate against any individual, or for a labor organization to discriminate against any member thereof or applicant for membership, because he has opposed any practice made an unlawful employment practice by this title, or because he has made a charge, testified, assisted, or participated in any manner in an investigation, proceeding, or hearing under this title.

Persons filing charges of employment discrimination are advised of this Non-Retaliation Requirement and are instructed to notify the Equal Employment Opportunity Commission if any attempt at retaliation is made.

PRIVACY ACT STATEMENT
(This form is covered by the Privacy Act of 1974, Public Law 93-579
Authority for requesting and uses of the personal data are given below.)

1.   FORM NUMBER/TITLE/DATE
     EEOC Form 5, Charge of Discrimination, May 77.

2.   AUTHORITY
     42 USC 2000e 5(b)

3.   PRINCIPAL PURPOSE(S)   The purpose of the charge, whether recorded
     initially on Form 5 or abstracted from a letter, is to invoke the
     Commission's jurisdiction.

4.   ROUTINE USES. This form is used to determine the existence of facts
     which substantiate the Commission's jurisdiction to investigate,
     determine, conciliate and litigate charges of unlawful employment
     practices. It is also used to record information sufficient to main-
     tain contact with the Charging Party and to direct the Commission's
     investigatory activity. A copy of the charge will be served upon the
     person against whom the charge is made.

5.   WHETHER DISCLOSURE IS MANDATORY OR VOLUNTARY AND EFFECT ON INDIVIDUAL
     FOR NOT PROVIDING INFORMATION. Charges must be in writing, under oath
     or affirmation, setting forth the facts which give rise to the charge
     of employment discrimination and be signed by or on behalf of a per-
     son claiming to be aggrieved. However, use of EEOC Form 5 is not
     mandatory. Technical defects or omissions may be cured by amendment.

Source: Equal Employment Opportunity Commission. Washington. D.C. 20507.

- The charge must be filed, generally speaking, within 180 days of the claimed discriminatory employment practice. For deferral states (those states with laws and administrative agencies comparable to Title VII), the applicable time limit generally is extended to 300 days, or 30 days after the termination of state proceedings, whichever is sooner.
- A copy of the charge or notice of the charge's filing must be sent to the employer or other charged party within 10 days of filing to put you on notice that an action has been instituted. It is not required that you be notified of the Charging Party's name, although this information generally will be included.[7]

Your Response

Once you receive any EEOC charge filed under Title VII (or under your state fair employment law), be sure to retain all pertinent records and documentation: not only those concerning the individual(s) filing the charge but any other applicable materials. For example, if a Charging Party (for example, a black male) alleges that you discriminated against him on account of his race by failing to give him a promotion, you should collect all the data you have regarding the job and its qualifications, the records of the person who got the promotion, and the records of other employees who also were considered but were rejected. Any records concerning other promotions or promotional statistics also should be retained.

These records enable you to show that (1) the reason you did not give the Charging Party the promotion was because he was not as qualified as the person selected, and (2) other employees of other races were treated the same as the Charging Party since they also were rejected on the basis of lack of qualifications. In addition to these practical reasons, the EEOC requires that your personnel records be kept for six months or until final action is taken on a charge, whichever is later.[8]

EEOC Investigation

Title VII requires the EEOC to investigate all charges it receives but this does not mean that the inquiry starts as soon as you receive a copy of the charge. To the contrary, because of the agency's staffing and budgetary problems it may take several months, six months, or a year between your receipt of the charge and the EEOC's notification that it is beginning its investigation.

An EEOC investigation, which is triggered when a charge of discrimination is filed, seeks to determine whether there are reasonable grounds for believing that Title VII has been violated. The EEOC has very wide powers of investigation. For example, it can investigate issues "related" to the charge under investigation and is not limited to only the specific incidents cited.[9] It also has the authority to issue subpoenaes, receive evidence, examine witnesses, and take similar measures designed to allow for a full investigation.[10]

The investigation may follow differing courses of action, depending upon the type of allegations in the charge and other factors.[11] For example:

- If the charge claims employer discrimination against one or several employees, but not a broader "class" employee group, that does not a warrant a full investigation (e.g., other meritorious charges have not been filed on the same or similar issues, the employer has not demonstrated recalcitrance, etc), then the charge may be assigned to the expedited track called the Rapid Charge Processing System, particularly if the legal standards affecting the case are fairly clear. A Rapid Charge Processing System investigation generally is less extensive, and more limited in scope, than one processed by the Extended Unit.

- If the charge potentially involves a "class" or large group of employees, or raises issues identified by the EEOC as priority ones for litigation, or if a collective bargaining agreement may be affected, thereby necessitating the involvement of a labor organization, then the charge may be identified for processing by the Extended Unit. When this occurs, a review at the employer's site is more likely, the investigation will be more extensive, and an EEOC attorney may be involved directly.

- If a charge is identified through the EEOC's Early Litigation Identification Program as a case appropriate for an expanded investigation, this action is designed to place the agency in a favorable position for litigation if conciliation should fail. Similarly, if the charge is filed by an EEOC commissioner, the Systemic Program mode of investigation, which also is more extensive, may be used.

The investigative approaches and requirements adopted by the EEOC have changed over time and the agency continues to consider further modifications that may affect the particular investigatory steps it uses if a charge is filed against your facility. For these reasons, and also because the EEOC's selection of a particular approach will reflect its initial determination as to the significance of the charge and its potential litigation value, the securing of knowledgeable advice before responding to a charge of discrimination may be a necessity, not a luxury.

EEOC investigatory steps frequently have included the following:

1. The EEOC normally will ask your employer, by letter or otherwise, to provide a written response to each of the Charging Party's contentions, to answer certain questions, and to provide certain documents.
2. The EEOC staff person assigned to investigate will interview the Charging Party about the information in your written response.
3. The EEOC staff person may ask to visit your facility's premises.
4. The EEOC has the power to issue a subpoena to compel the production of evidence if the employer refuses to cooperate with its investigation.

Fact-Finding Conferences

A fact-finding conference may be scheduled after your employer responds to the charge, particularly where the issue relates to an individual claiming "differential treatment" rather than to a systematic form of discrimination. The Charging Party and the employer attend and are encouraged to bring their attorneys with them as an aid to implementing any settlement reached. Witnesses also may attend. The EEOC staff person in charge of the conference does all the questioning of the parties and their witnesses, so the attorneys are limited to advisory roles.

In the EEOC's view, the conference provides an opportunity to settle the matter at an early stage. If no settlement occurs or appears likely, the EEOC may use the facts uncovered at the conference in reaching a decision on the charge. In addition, these facts frequently influence the EEOC in deciding how the case should proceed; namely, whether to expand the scope of the investigation, to ask for additional documents, etc.[12]

Conciliation and Settlement

The initial phase can lead to what are called predetermination settlements. Prior to the EEOC determining whether reasonable cause exists for believing that prohibited discrimination has occurred, the Charging Party and employer may reach a voluntary settlement even if the agency does not initiate such efforts.

While various considerations may affect your employer's decision as to whether to offer a settlement, two primary advantages to such a move are that a properly drafted agreement will (1) protect your employer from a subsequent lawsuit by the Charging Party, and (2) eliminate the time and expense that accompanies an EEOC investigation. Yet certain cautions also are in order if a settlement is to be executed. These are discussed below.

If this predetermination phase does not produce a settlement and the EEOC then decides there is a reasonable basis for believing that the employer has violated Title VII, the agency must attempt to resolve the case through the informal use of conference, conciliation, and persuasion.[13]

If a settlement is reached, the EEOC will insist on a written agreement signed by all parties so that the solution is enforceable. Such an agreement should provide for the withdrawal of the charge, which can be done only with the consent of both the EEOC and the Charging Party.[14]

If no settlement is reached, the case may be forwarded to the EEOC's General Counsel for a decision as to whether the agency itself will file a lawsuit based on the charge. The EEOC initiates suits infrequently, particularly where the charge relates to an individual claim and no industrywide or other practices affecting large numbers of employees are involved.

Caution must be exercised by employers who enter into settlement agreements. You should be aware that the standard EEOC settlement agreement forms do not protect an employer from future charges or lawsuits that the Charging Party could file under other laws. This is because the EEOC's standard settlement language generally is limited to the specific charge at issue under Title VII and does not extend to releasing your employer from other possible claims based on the same (or similar) facts.[15]

For example, even though the Charging Party signs an EEOC consent form settling an individual's claim that Title VII was violated because of race discrimination, the individual still may attempt to sue on the same basic claims under the Civil Rights Act of 1866 or under state law.

The question then is how you might proceed. Very often, your best course of action is to obtain two written settlements:

1. the EEOC settlement agreement, which is signed by the Charging Party, respondent, and the agency
2. a private, separate settlement agreement, signed by the employer and Charging Party (not by the EEOC), that refers to and incorporates by reference the EEOC settlement agreement; this separate agreement should state expressly that the parties' settlement is disposing of all claims, not just those under Title VII, that are related to the case, to the Charging Party's supporting facts and allegations, and to the particular circumstances that occasioned the charge (e.g., the Charging Party's failure to be promoted or termination).

Be aware, however, that even if two settlement agreements are drafted, and even if an EEOC district director agrees to the Charging Party's withdrawal of a charge, an EEOC commissioner still may seek to file a charge with "like or related" allegations, so the possibility of an EEOC investigation or litigation is not entirely precluded.[16]

Because of all these potential dangers, it is critical that you obtain the advice of counsel before you agree to any settlement offer or sign any documents presented by the EEOC on behalf of the Charging Party. Legal assistance in drafting any such settlement agreements also is wise.

The 'Right to Sue' Letter

After the EEOC has completed its processing of the charge, and if no settlement has been reached, it will send a determination letter to the Charging Party and to the employer stating whether the agency has concluded that there is "cause" or "no cause" for believing that the employer violated Title VII. In either case, Charging Parties will be advised that they have 90 days in which to file a private lawsuit under Title VII.[17] In fact, one of the main purposes of the letter is to inform the Charging Parties that a lawsuit must be brought within 90 days from receipt of the letter if they wish to pursue their claim under Title VII. If they do not meet this deadline, in most cases they will lose the right to sue.

The right of individuals to sue their employer (or potential employer) regardless of the EEOC's determination is a critical feature of Title VII. Do not conclude, however, that an EEOC "no-cause" determination is of no value. Value does exist; a "no-cause" finding may discourage a Charging Party from filing a frivolous lawsuit, may influence other employees at your facility to refrain from filing charges that have no merit, and may be admitted into evidence if the Charging Party files suit and the case goes to trial.[18]

When lawsuits are filed under Title VII, they proceed in much the same way as any other civil action. Some are limited to one or a few number of named individual plaintiffs. However, if a plaintiff contends the employer has engaged in, or is engaging in, employment practices that adversely affect a great number of employees or applicants, the complainant may file a class action lawsuit. In class actions the named plaintiff(s) may represent a large group or class of unnamed individuals whose identities may not even be known, and any possible monetary liability is expanded accordingly. Under Title VII there is a higher incidence of these class action suits.

What Constitutes Discrimination

Proving Discrimination—The Plaintiff's Case

A Charging Party who files a Title VII lawsuit is referred to thereafter as the plaintiff while the employer (or union, or employment agency) is the defendant. In all Title VII suits, and before your employer is called upon to present a defense, a plaintiff must prove a prima facie case of discrimination, meaning that the plaintiff must introduce facts that, if true, would establish unlawful employment discrimination.

In attempting to prove their case, plaintiffs frequently use one of two theories, or both:[19]

- **Theory #1:** This is called "disparate treatment"—that is, the plaintiffs attempt to show that they were treated differently from other employees or applicants because of their race, sex, national origin, or religion. They may attempt to prove this by showing that the employer's actions were openly discriminatory. For example, one of your employees may testify that her supervisor openly made derogatory remarks about her sex. Or a plaintiff may try to prove differing treatment by pointing to equally discriminatory, but more subtle, action. For example, a black applicant may show that he was the most qualified employee for a position but that your employer chose a lesser qualified nonblack for the job.

- **Theory #2:** Plaintiffs also may attempt to show discrimination by the theory of "disparate impact." They must show that, although the employer's practices may be "facially neutral" (that is, they seem totally non-discriminatory when examined), they in fact operate to the disadvantage of a protected class. These types of cases commonly involve the use of statistics to illustrate disparities in the work force. For example, a plaintiff may attempt to prove that the employer's practices resulted in race discrimination by introducing into evidence statistics showing that 98 percent of the administrative personnel in a hospital are white but the proportion of qualified black administrators in the labor market is much larger than 2 percent.

The particular elements required to prove unlawful discrimination under Title VII will vary, depending upon the types of violation alleged, the theories under which the action is pursued (e.g., disparate impact vs. disparate treatment), etc. To illustrate this concept, it is useful to review the Supreme Court's identification of the elements a plaintiff must prove to show different treatment because of a prohibited form of discrimination.[20] In this type of case, and if the plaintiffs were applicants for a position with your employer, they must show that:

1. they are members of a protected class (e.g., Asians)
2. they were qualified for a job that was vacant at the time they applied
3. they were not hired
4. the job remained open after they were rejected and the employer continued to accept applications from persons with the same qualifications (plaintiffs also will want to show that the person hired was not Asian).

Once these elements are established at trial, the plaintiffs will have proved a prima facie case; to avoid liability, your employer would have to present opposing evidence.

Disproving Discrimination—The Defense's Case

The fact that plaintiffs can submit evidence to support their case does not mean that a finding of employer liability will result automatically. Liability still can be avoided if an employer rebuts the plaintiff's case by submitting evidence establishing a defense.

Examples of successful defenses used in Title VII cases, depending upon the theory of discrimination used by plaintiffs and the facts, include the following:

- contradicting plaintiffs' evidence by showing that a neutral practice does not have a more adverse effect on them and other persons of their race, national origin, sex, etc.

- establishing sound business reasons for the actions that the plaintiffs complain about, and showing that the same results could not have been achieved by alternative employer measures having less or no adverse impact on a protected class
- establishing that national origin, religion, or sex was a bona fide occupational qualification (BFOQ): that is, to perform the job successfully, a person must be of a certain national origin, religion, or sex—for example, using a female to portray women's roles in a play; a BFOQ defense cannot be used in race discrimination cases and rarely is used for other forms of discrimination because the EEOC and courts have narrowly construed this defense and effectively limited its use to a few occupations
- rebutting plaintiffs' case by showing that their "facts" are not true and/or that your employer's actions were based on nondiscriminatory factors; for example, your employer may prove that an employee's termination was based on unsatisfactory conduct or performance and not on discriminatory considerations; you also may be able to establish that an applicant was rejected because a better-qualified person was hired.

Countering Your Defense

Plaintiffs are entitled to counter your defense by submitting additional evidence establishing that your policy is a pretext, a subterfuge to hide your actual discriminatory reasons for taking the action complained of.

For example, your employer has sound business reasons for terminating employees who steal and can use those reasons in defending a Title VII case arising from the termination of a black employee. Nevertheless, if the plaintiff can establish that white employees who stole were not terminated, this evidence will have established that your business reasons were a pretext for discrimination.

Case Studies

Several examples illustrate the generalities just discussed.

Termination for Absenteeism: Assume that you have terminated an employee for excessive unexcused absenteeism of 15 days in one year. The terminated employee then files an EEOC complaint claiming she was discharged because of race, with the following allegations:

1. She is black and thus is protected by Title VII from discrimination based on race.
2. Her absences were not excessive and she had legitimate reasons for them.
3. She was terminated.

4. White employees have been absent at least 15 days, if not more, without being terminated.

These facts provide what is called a prima facie case by the Charging Party; that is, these allegations, if true, would prove a violation of Title VII. This means that your employer, through you, other witnesses, and other evidence, must establish valid, nondiscriminatory business reasons for the employee's termination. You might do this by showing that, for example:

1. You have terminated other employees (including whites) for absences of 15 days (showing that plaintiff's allegation is not true and no differing treatment existed).
2. You reasonably believed that the employee's absences were not legitimate and that is why you terminated her.

English Fluency Requirements: You may have a policy that requires that operating room R.N.s be verbally fluent in English. Your hospital then refuses to employ a registered nurse applicant from a non-English-speaking country who recently became a United States citizen. The reason for rejecting the applicant was because, during several interview sessions, you experienced extreme difficulty in communicating with him, he did not understand your questions, and you in turn frequently could not understand his answers. When rejected for employment, the applicant files an EEOC charge and can prove that:

1. He is licensed as a registered nurse in your state.
2. He had prior satisfactory experience as an operating room nurse before coming to the United States.
3. Your hospital had a vacancy.
4. He was not hired.
5. The person your hospital hired was of a different national origin.

The applicant is able to show that your facially neutral practice of requiring English fluency has an adverse impact on persons of his national origin. Because individuals who learn English as a second language generally are not as fluent, your language requirement therefore eliminates a disproportionately higher number of persons who are of the applicant's national origin. In fact, in examining your records, you find that your applicant flow data (number who apply, are hired, etc., by race, national origin) show that a greater number of applicants of the plaintiff's national origin have been refused hire by your hospital.

Even under these facts, you should be able to defend successfully against the charge or lawsuit by proving that your policy is based on business necessity. Operating room R.N.s must be able to understand verbal instructions and a nurse's words must be understandable. In addition, communication errors can cause serious (even fatal) mistakes and your employer cannot find an acceptable alternative to this requirement. Your rejection of the applicant, therefore, was not based on unlawful discrimination because of his national origin.

Topics of Particular Significance

Access to EEOC Data

Title VII prohibits the EEOC from publicly disclosing information obtained in its investigation.[21] This does not mean that any information, records, or data you give the EEOC will remain confidential. To the contrary, the EEOC distinguishes between making facts public and disclosing them to the parties, their attorneys, or government agencies that can show a lawful interest in the charge. In addition, the EEOC will make its investigative file available to the employer only after the Charging Party has filed suit under Title VII.[22]

Title VII Remedies

The purpose of Title VII is to assure equality of employment opportunities and to eliminate discriminatory practices that operate to the disadvantage of those protected by the Act. Courts will fashion broad remedies for those found to be victims of unlawful discrimination in order to make them "whole." For example:

1. The court may order an employer to change its personnel policies and practices.
2. The court may award the reinstatement of a terminated employee, a promotion, or the hiring of a rejected applicant.
3. The court may make monetary awards that can include back pay (wages lost because of the employer's unlawful action) and front pay (such as wages to a plaintiff who should have received a promotion until the next opening occurs and the person actually is placed in the position).
4. Title VII provides that courts have the discretion to allow reasonable attorney fees to a prevailing party,[23] and a prevailing Charging Party generally receives such fees. In some circumstances, an employee or applicant who has filed a charge with a state administrative agency before initiating a Title VII action also may be entitled to attorney's fees for the administrative proceeding.[24] In contrast, if the employer prevails at trial, it can recover attorney's fees only if the court finds the plaintiff's claim was frivolous, unreasonable, or groundless,[25] circumstances that can be difficult to show.
5. The prevailing party, whether plaintiff or defendant, may recover the costs of bringing or defending against the action. This ordinarily includes fees for

filing, court reporter, and witnesses, and costs incident to the discovery process.

Sexual Preference

Although Title VII outlaws discrimination based on sex, this prohibition to date does not include sexual preference (i.e., whether an applicant or employee is a homosexual or heterosexual). However, continuing efforts are made to persuade Congress that the Act should be amended to prohibit discrimination in employment based upon a person's sexual preference. Furthermore, unlawful sexual harassment can occur even where both the employee and the accused employer representative or fellow employee are members of the same sex.[26]

Selection Procedures

Employment applications, tests, advertising, questions asked at job interviews, and other selection procedures used by employers may be examined closely by the EEOC when a charge of discrimination is filed. Selection procedures that adversely affect members of a protected class are unlawful under Title VII unless the employer can establish a business necessity defense; that is, that the procedures or practices are necessary for the successful performance of the job.[27]

As to employment applications, careful consideration must be given to all the questions on the form (or asked in an interview) to determine whether they are job related and whether they may have a discriminatory impact on women or minority jobseekers. Potentially unlawful questions include subjects that have no relationship to qualifications for employment but that could be used for impermissible discriminatory grounds, such as:

- requiring that an applicant identify a relative to notify in case of emergency
- asking about the applicant's financial status
- asking applicants to reveal arrest records, place of birth, marital status, number of dependents, etc.

As to advertisements, as a general rule, help wanted and similar recruitment notices and materials should not indicate any preference, limitation, or discrimination based on race, color, religion, sex, or national origin. The primary exception is that if sex, national origin, or religion (but not race) is a BFOQ, then advertisements requesting that requirement will not be unlawful.[28]

As employers have become more aware of their legal obligations, the more blatant forms of discriminatory advertisements have become less frequent. However, you should be cautious of the less obvious but equally unlawful forms such as those that use masculine or feminine terms in their descriptions of the job. For example, advertisements must not specify ''male'' or ''female,'' or be placed under newspaper columns headed "male" or "female." Similarly, adjectives that reflect a preference as to sex, race, national origin, or religion must be avoided: "aggressive high-powered Rocky-III type sought for sales position with expanding sports equipment manufacturer."[29]

Advertisements also are unlawful if they impose requirements that have an impermissible impact on minorities. As discussed later under "Arrests and Convictions," requiring an applicant to indicate an arrest history generally is unlawful; it is not surprising, therefore, that help wanted ads specifying that applicants be free of arrest records were found to be unlawful by the EEOC.[30]

Employment testing that has an adverse impact on a protected class must bear a demonstrable relationship to successful performance of the job for which it is used.[31] As a general proposition, this requirement seems quite straightforward but its apparent simplicity is deceiving. Why? Because under Title VII, as interpreted by the EEOC and courts, a "test" is only a type of employer selection procedure and the term "selection procedure" has been defined broadly in the "Uniform Guidelines on Employee Selection Procedures" to include:

> Any measure, combination of measures, or procedure used as a basis for any employment decision. Selection procedures include the full range of assessment techniques from traditional paper and pencil tests, performance tests, training programs, or probationary periods and physical, educational, and work experience requirements through informal or casual interviews and unscored application forms.[32]

If the selection procedure, as so defined, has an adverse impact on a protected class, then a complex set of guidelines and requirements must be met if the process or test is to be validated, for Title VII purposes, as having a demonstrable relationship to the job. The net result is that testing and employer selection procedures constitute one of the most complicated and technical EEOC issues that may arise. Testing issues also are the source of much controversy, with many experts in statistics, psychology, and education disagreeing with one another and with the positions and requirements in the "Uniform Guidelines." So be cautious: if your facility wants to use tests and to determine whether they are valid, it is strongly recommended that you seek legal guidance and, if it is deemed necessary, that you retain individuals knowledgeable in the development of tests that comply with the EEOC guidelines.

Educational Requirements

All health care employers have a common objective: to recruit well-prepared and competent personnel. Yet educational requirements are tests for Title VII purposes (see preceding discussion) that frequently have an adverse impact since they may exclude a higher proportion of minority applicants. As a result, you must guard against setting educational standards that are artificially high and that are not actually required for or relevant to successful performance of the job.

Numerous occasions will arise, however, where your insistence upon certain minimum education standards may be justified, particularly among technical and professional classifications. In one case, a court found that a medical center did not violate Title VII by insisting that a blood bank technician hold either a Bachelor of Science degree or a certification by the Américan Society of Clinical Pathologists.[33] The court saw a direct relationship between the required college degree or certification and the safe and satisfactory performance of functions affecting the public's health and safety.

Obviously, you must continue to require that both employees and applicants meet the minimum licensure, certification, or other standards established by state law. You also should satisfy yourself that all educational standards are directly related, and objectively documented as such, to the requirements for performing the job.

Language and Communication Skills

The ability to read and write English may be an essential and integral part of certain jobs. Occasionally, however, you may assume that fluency in English is necessary but in fact it has little relationship to performing the work satisfactorily. For example, a person generally does not need to possess a high level of English reading and verbal skills to be a competent housekeeper since the work frequently requires only the ability to understand and communicate basic verbal and written instructions. Under these circumstances, if you required fluency in English, it could be an employment practice with a discriminatory impact on protected national-origin groups.

Similar problems are presented by prohibitions against employees' using languages other than English at the workplace. Under the regulations:

- The EEOC will closely scrutinize English-only rules since they may result in a discriminatory work environment.
- The EEOC will presume that a rule requiring the use of English at all times at the workplace is discriminatory.
- The EEOC will require that where rules are limited to specified times at the workplace (e.g., during worktime excluding breaks, lunch periods, etc.), they still must be supported by a showing of business necessity and the employer must notify employees of the times when the rules apply and the consequences for violating them.[34]

For example, an employer who hired a bilingual salesman was justified in requiring him to speak only English in public areas during working hours.[35]

Foreign Training and Experience

When the demand for registered nurses[36] has exceeded the supply available to a particular employer, some health care institutions have responded by hiring nurses trained outside of the United States. In this regard, there are several points that you as a supervisor should note:

- The licensing of nurses and other health care professionals is a function of the state in which you reside. States usually provide some method by which a foreign-trained nurse can become licensed, typically by permitting the person to take the local examination if the foreign training is considered "equivalent" to local training.[37]
- The possession of a state license does not automatically entitle an R.N. to work in the United States since the individual also must have a valid visa issued by the federal Immigration and Naturalization Service (INS).

In the past, a practice developed whereby foreign nurses would obtain a temporary visa based on their foreign qualifications and their status as "professionals." They later would take the local state examination in the hope of passing it and obtaining a permanent visa. Because a high proportion of foreign-trained nurses failed state licensing examinations, the INS changed its regulations.[38] Now all unlicensed foreign nurses seeking temporary visas must pass an examination conducted by the Commission on Graduates of Foreign Nursing Schools before they are issued temporary visas and can seek employment. This examination, which takes place twice a year, is conducted both within and outside of the United States.

You also should take care that your hiring practices do not result in discrimination based upon the nurses' national origin. Any distinctions you make between the training received in different foreign countries should be based on valid job-related grounds and applied consistently. Otherwise, if you hire nurses who have received training from Country *A* and reject applicants from Country *B*, your action may be seen as discrimination based on national origin since nurses who receive training in a certain country frequently are natives of that country. For example, an employer who routinely hires nurses trained in England, West Germany, and Israel but who rejects those trained in South America without first making a justifiable assessment supporting this distinction, could be opening the door to charges of discrimination.

Hiring Family Members

You could encounter two different types of problems in this area: (1) giving preference to applicants who are friends or are members of current employees' families or (2) refusing to hire friends or family members, particularly spouses, and terminating those who marry their fellow employees.

An employer's policy of giving preference to applicants who have relatives or friends at the workplace is a good example of an apparently neutral employment policy that easily could result in Title VII charges and/or lawsuits. If the existing work force contains marked racial or ethnic imbalances when compared with the community as a whole, such a policy merely serves to perpetuate the discrepancy by giving preference to applicants from the racial and ethnic groups that already are overrepresented.[39]

Prohibitions against the employment or continued employment of spouses raise issues of sex discrimination. This is because females may be underrepresented in certain occupations or employment settings so these rules may affect a higher proportion of women. For example, a university had a rule against employing more than one member of the same family. Based on that rule, it granted tenure to a male professor but not to his wife, also a professor. A federal court concluded that the rule was used to discriminate against women and found the university liable.[40]

In most health care facilities, adverse impact may be difficult to establish because they employ a high proportion of women in a variety of classifications. Even if the policy does affect proportionately more women and thus must be justified, you still may be able to defend the policy successfully based on business considerations if it is limited to precluding the employment of spouses in the same work area or prohibiting one spouse from supervising another, etc.

Dress and Appearance Policies

Establishing and maintaining dress and appearance policies can create problems regarding race, national origin, sex, and religious discrimination. For example, health care employers commonly have dress codes for employees. If your facility has such a policy or code, generally it will not be unlawful to have different dress standards for females and males, such as requiring that males must wear ties with their uniforms.

The primary danger in dress codes arises when a greater burden (or benefit) is applied to employees of one sex. In one case, a bank required its female tellers to wear particular uniforms while male tellers could dress in customary business attire. The court held the practice to be discriminatory: either the bank should require all tellers to wear uniforms or it should allow women to wear customary business attire the same as the men.[41] Similarly, in a hospital setting, if you provide uniforms to a certain classification, then they must be provided to employees of both sexes. If the cost of laundering the uniforms is borne by your employer, it should be for both male and female employees.

In another case a private hospital required its nurses to wear white caps. The EEOC held that this policy was not so necessary to the operation of the hospital as to justify the effect that it had upon the employment opportunities of an older Catholic nurse whose faith required that her head be completely covered at all times. For many years while working in the nursery, she had worn a scarf under her scrub cap without an employer complaint. However, when she was transferred to the floor, she was not permitted to wear the scarf, either beneath or as a substitute for a required cap. This policy was viewed by the EEOC as violative of Title VII.[42]

Policies that forbid certain hairstyles, beards, or other facial hair can result in discrimination problems unless the employer can show a sound business reason for them.[43] Generally speaking, separate rules for males and females on hair length, and rules regarding men's wearing of facial hair, will not result in a finding of sex discrimination.[44] However, certain hairstyles (such as Afros or cornrows) have been adopted as cultural symbols by racial minorities and an employer who discharges an employee on that basis "may" violate the law.[45]

Affirmative Action Plans

In considering the development or maintenance of an affirmative action plan, you should be aware that these are required of many federal contractors but that Medicare or Medicaid have not been considered to be government contracts.[46] If your employer is not a federal contractor, then such a plan could incur the risk of reverse discrimination charges by employees or applicants not receiving preference under the plan unless it complies with very specific requirements adopted by the United States Supreme Court.

Any employer who has a contract or subcontract with the federal government for $50,000 or more, and who has 50 or more employees, must establish an affirmative action plan and update it yearly.[47] In the plan, the employer analyzes the number of minorities and women in its work force, determines their availability in the general labor force, and sets hiring goals and timetables for the jobs in which women and minorities are underrepresented. The Office of Federal Contract Compliance Programs (OFCCP) is the federal agency that monitors affirmative action programs.

Even if not required to do so, an employer may voluntarily adopt an affirmative action plan when it is reasonably clear that certain jobs in its work force traditionally have been segregated. To avoid claims of reverse discrimination, however, these voluntary plans should not impose stringent and inflexible hiring goals that would effectively bar advancement by white employees.

For example, in a case dealing with a white employee's claim of reverse discrimination, the Supreme Court identified the elements of the employer's voluntary affirmative action plan that made the program acceptable:

1. The plan was designed to eliminate old patterns of racial segregation in jobs and to open up employment opportunities for blacks in occupations that traditionally had been closed to them.
2. The plan did not unnecessarily damage the interests of white employees, which would have been the case if it had required the discharge of whites and their replacement with blacks, or if it had absolutely barred the advancement of white employees, which it did not.
3. The plan was a temporary measure only; once the number of black employees in the particular jobs approximated the percentage of blacks in the local work force, the employer would cease preferential selection.[48]

Arrests and Convictions

On a national basis there is no doubt that members of minority groups are arrested with greater frequency than others. In a 1970 case, the evidence showed that blacks, while comprising 11 percent of the nation's population, accounted for 27 percent of reported arrests and 45 percent of those reported as "suspicion arrests."[49] Yet an arrest that does not lead to a conviction proves absolutely nothing about a person's character or criminal propensities, so inquiries into arrest record or employment restrictions based on arrests are violative of Title VII.[50]

Convictions are handled differently from arrests even though a disproportionately higher percentage of minorities are convicted of crimes. While a blanket refusal to hire an applicant (or a decision to terminate a current employee) because of "any" conviction may violate Title VII, reliance upon conviction(s) as a selection factor or to support disciplinary acts will not violate the Act where a relationship exists between the conviction and the nature and responsibilities of the job in question.[51] However, since many states have enacted laws regarding the use of criminal records and the permissible questions that can be asked of applicants, you should review your own state's laws as to inquiries about convictions.

Employee Preferences

Many state protective laws prohibited women from performing certain types of work (e.g., lifting more than 25 pounds), and the perception of many employers was that women were not interested in certain jobs. Under Title VII, however, an employer may not prevent women from applying for or filling certain jobs on the basis of state protective laws or on the theory that it is "man's work."

Instead, jobs must be open to both men and women. The only exception is where there is reasonable cause to believe on a factual basis that all, or substantially all, women would be unable to perform the duties of the job involved safely and efficiently.[52] Since this is extremely difficult to prove, women should be allowed, on an individual basis, to decide whether or not they are interested in and capable of undertaking a particular job.

Although women may not be denied a job based on sexual stereotypes, some occasionally will indicate preferences that echo the protections state law once afforded. For example, in one case, a female warehouse employee invoked the state law forbidding the lifting of weights of more than 25 pounds by females and received a lighter assignment. Later, she protested that she was receiving a lower pay rate than that of male warehouse employees performing the heavier work; understandably, the court saw little value in her argument and dismissed her claim.[53]

Patient Preference

While Title VII provides an exception or defense for discrimination resulting from a bona fide occupational qualification (BFOQ), this is interpreted very narrowly. For example, the EEOC's Sex Discrimination Regulations provide that a refusal to hire an individual because of the preferences of coworkers or of the employer or clients or customers (such as patients) all are unlawful. The only exception to this antipreference rule is when the sex of an individual is necessary for the purpose of "authenticity of genuineness," such as an actor or actress.[54]

This restrictive interpretation of Title VII by the EEOC has not prevented the courts from considering client preferences in appropriate circumstances. One such case arose when a male nursing student applied for a position as a nurse's aide at a nursing home. He was informed that the home did not employ male nurse's aides; when his female friend called the home reciting the same qualifications, she was urged to fill out an application.

The home testified that 22 of its 30 guests were female, that they would not consent to having their personal needs attended to by a male, and that some guests would leave if there were male aides there. The home further contended that it could not, as a practical matter, hire a male nurse's aide and assign job duties and responsibilities selectively.

The court found that the attitudes of the guests at the nursing home, although they could be characterized as "customer preferences," were of the type that could be used to justify a job qualification based upon sex. The fact that the home had to provide 24-hour supervision and care of elderly guests, and that the aide's job encompassed intimate personal care such as dressing, bathing, toilet assistance, and catheter care justified the home's requirements. In sum, the court recognized personal privacy interests and that the home could not legally force the female guests to accept personal care from males.[55]

A similar result was reached by a court reviewing an acute care hospital's refusal to assign a male nurse to OB-GYN on the basis that most women patients would object to a male nurse's performing the required intimate duties. The hospital also contended that double-staffing would result if a male nurse was assigned since a female nurse would have to be readily available to perform certain of the duties.

Although the court recognized that nurses of either sex were equally competent to perform the job, it also agreed that because of the "intimate touching required in labor and delivery," the hospital appropriately assigned only female nurses to OB-GYN. Finally, and in response to the argument that many women have male physicians, the court noted that the patients could choose whether they wanted a male doctor while they had no similar freedom of choice with respect to the R.N.[56]

Thus, in the health care field, courts have recognized that patient preference, although undoubtedly attributable to their upbringing and to sexual stereotyping of the past, can constitute a BFOQ in certain circumstances. But the courts also have emphasized that the health care employer has the additional burden of proving it could not selectively assign job responsibilities so that a male could be hired without having to perform personal care services for nonconsenting females. This additional factor may limit the case to small institutions and to certain other relatively unique circumstances.

Pregnancy and Maternity

Even before the passage of the 1978 amendment, the Supreme Court ruled that a company policy requiring women taking pregnancy leave to forfeit accumulated job seniority violated Title VII since it imposed a burden on women that men were not obliged to bear.[57]

However, the 1978 amendment specifically required that disabilities resulting from pregnancy and childbirth be treated the same, for employment-related purposes, as other disabilities.[58] Title VII's provisions on discrimination because of "pregnancy, childbirth or related medical conditions" also provide, however, that an employer is not required to pay for health insurance benefits for abortion, "except where the life of the mother would be endangered if the fetus was carried to term, or where medical complications have arisen from an abortion. . . ."[59] As amended, Title VII does not require an employer to give "special treatment" to pregnant women; it simply requires that they be treated the same as other employees.

The EEOC also issued regulations under the pregnancy amendment, as well as "Questions and Answers on the Pregnancy Discrimination Law" that include the following official positions, among others:

1. The employer must hold jobs open for women temporarily on leave because of pregnancy or related conditions on the same basis as they are held open for men and must grant leaves under the same terms and conditions.
2. The employer cannot prohibit women from returning to work for a fixed time after childbirth.
3. The employer may apply to pregnancy-related conditions the same rules it uses to determine an employee's ability to work due to other physical conditions (medical verifications, etc.).
4. The employer cannot refuse to hire pregnant women who are able to perform the "major functions necessary to the job."
5. The employer must grant to women with pregnancy-related conditions the same opportunities for "light work" as are extended to employees with other types of disabilities.
6. The employer cannot limit disability benefits for pregnancy-related conditions to married employees.[60]

The pregnancy amendments to Title VII created major questions concerning health care coverage that subsequently were answered as follows:

1. If no spouse or dependent health coverage exists, the employer need not provide pregnancy coverage for employee spouses or dependents.
2. If female employees' spouses have health coverage, then pregnancy coverage must be included for the spouses of male employees.
3. If health coverage is offered to spouses, pregnancy-related coverage must be at the same level as the coverage for the spouses of female employees; for example, 80 percent coverage for both.
4. If the employer excludes pregnancy-related conditions of nonspouse dependents, that exclusion will be upheld if it applies to male and female employees equally.[61]

Comparable Worth Theory

The principle of comparable worth is a potentially far-reaching theory holding that whole classes of jobs traditionally are undervalued because they have been held by women and that this inequality, in the form of lower wages, amounts to prohibited sex discrimination. This theory is somewhat different from the Equal Pay Act, which mandates equal pay for equal work. To date, the theory of comparable worth has met only with mixed success in the courts.

In one of the first federal cases on this subject (in 1980), for example, the plaintiffs urged the court to find that nurses historically had been underpaid because their work had not been properly recognized and because they almost universally were women.[62] The plaintiffs declared that the defendants, the City and County of

Denver, when establishing wage rates for nurses should be required to look to nonnursing jobs of "comparable worth" instead of comparing their wage scales to other nursing jobs in the community. The court rejected this argument, finding that Title VII did not cover claims of "comparable worth."

The "comparable worth" theory was then addressed by the United States Supreme Court in *County of Washington v. Gunther* (1981). While the Court pointedly disavowed the comparable worth argument, it did hold that a claim of sex-based wage discrimination could be pursued under Title VII even if the alleged discrimination did not involve unequal pay for equal work as defined by the Equal Pay Act.[63]

In *Gunther*, the county set the pay scale for female prison guards, but not male guards, at a level lower than that warranted by its own survey of outside pay scales for such jobs. The Court held that if this disparity resulted from intentional sex discrimination, it would violate Title VII even though the male and female prison guard classifications were not equal in skill, effort, responsibility, etc.

The court carefully noted that it was not approving a Title VII action under the comparable worth theory; instead, it based its decision on traditional Title VII prohibitions against intentional sex discrimination. The Court stated that the standard defenses available under the Equal Pay Act—that the pay differential was based on (1) a seniority system, (2) a merit system, (3) quality or quantity of work done, or (4) factors other than sex—also would apply to this "new" Title VII action.[64]

Based on the *Gunther* decision and related cases,[65] it now appears that:

- Employers "may" be able to continue to rely upon surveys of salaries paid by other employers in setting wage rates even though these market figures are claimed to be inherently discriminatory.
- Employers whose pay differentials reflect deviations from their own internal pay classification (or job evaluation) system or from their survey of the external market should carefully justify and document these variances on the basis of business necessity, recruitment and retention problems, job responsibilities, and other job-related requirements under the Equal Pay Act.

The state of Title VII law concerning pay differentials based on intentional sex discrimination is expanding rapidly; for this reason, counsel should be sought before action is taken that could result in lower compensation for classifications or positions predominantly composed of female employees.

Sexual Harassment

Sexual harassment is one of the most sensitive and expanding areas of employment discrimination law, particularly after the EEOC published its 1980 regulations explicitly recognizing that sexual harassment was unlawful sexual discrimination under Title VII.[66] This EEOC position is accepted by the courts,[67] and may be supplemented by state law.[68]

Under these EEOC regulations, unwelcome sexual advances, requests for sexual favors, and other verbal or physical conduct of a sexual nature such as (1) visual forms of harassment (cartoons, drawings, etc.); (2) physical interference with normal work or movement (blocking, following, etc.); and (3) verbal harassment (jokes, slurs, derogatory comments, etc.) constitute sexual harassment when they are an:

- *Employment condition:* submission to such conduct is either explicitly or implicitly a term or condition of employment; or
- *Employment consequence:* submission to or rejection of such conduct is used as a basis for employment decisions affecting the employee; or
- *Offensive job interference:* the conduct has the purpose or effect of either unreasonably interfering with an employee's work performance, or creating an intimidating, hostile, or offensive working environment.[69]

While this definition is helpful in determining what constitutes unlawful sexual harassment, it is not all inclusive:

- The EEOC's review of sexual harassment charges will be based on the "record as a whole" and the "totality of the circumstances" present.[70]
- The Act's protection against sexual harassment extends to homosexuals.[71]
- The Act precludes the denial of benefits or employment opportunities to employees who would have received such benefits or opportunities "but for" the sexual favors granted by another employee.[72]

Significant differences in potential employer liability can depend upon whether the claimed sexual harassment is done by supervisors, coworkers, or non-employees.

An employer is strictly liable for the acts of supervisors and agents (1) whether or not the acts complained of are authorized (or even forbidden) by the employer, and (2) whether or not the employer knows or should know that the acts are occurring.[73] Thus, in one case, an employee stated a Title VII violation because of her termination for refusing sexual favors demanded by her supervisor, even though the employer's policy prohibited such harassment and even though the employer had an internal grievance procedure that the employee did not follow.[74] As an additional illustration, an employer can be liable for a supervisor's sexual harassment and creation of a hostile work environment even if the employee loses no benefits of employment.[75]

In contrast, an employer generally is liable for sexual harassment by nonsupervisory fellow employees or by nonemployees only if the employer knows or should know of the conduct and fails to take immediate and appropriate corrective action.[76] However, since an employer sometimes has less control over the actions of nonemployees, the EEOC also considers the extent of the "employer's control and any other legal responsibility which the employer had with respect to the conduct of such nonemployees."[77] For example, in a health care facility, questions may arise as to the degree of control that can be exerted over persons such as attending physicians, registry employees, outside sales persons, and so forth.

To avoid potential liability for claims of sexual harassment, preventive steps should be taken by your employer before any employee complaints are received, such as:

- developing and distributing a written policy prohibiting all forms of sexual harassment;
- initiating discussions of the subject to sensitize all employees to the issue, including management and supervisory employees;
- developing or reaffirming the existence of an internal grievance procedure, and an employee's right to use that procedure for sexual harassment complaints.[78]

Because of the substantial potential liability presented by sexual harassment claims, and because the EEOC's regulations emphasize the importance of corrective action by employers, all complaints of sexual harassment must be seriously and promptly investigated. At the same time, confidentiality must be maintained. The accused individuals have the right to be free from rumors or harassment based on charges, and thus caution must be exercised in any such investigations.

These considerations and the need for a neutral investigation (particularly since the claim may be against a supervisory employee) frequently mean that a member of the employer's personnel or administrative staff should be involved in, or in charge of, the investigation. Consultation with legal counsel also may be advisable. After the investigation is completed and it appears that sexual harassment may have occurred, prompt and effective steps should be taken to eliminate the harassment and to correct any prejudice to the employee. Such steps may include taking disciplinary action against employees engaging in sexual harassment, rescinding disciplinary action against an employee because the employee refused sexual favors, and granting a denied promotion.

In conclusion, you must keep in mind that the comments in this chapter are based upon federal law only. State laws may be more liberal than federal law and/or may impose additional or different requirements on your employer. Or your state may have adopted federal law in lieu of enacting its own separate anti-discrimination law. In any event, it is imperative that you review your state's laws and regulations before taking employment action of any kind.

NOTES

1. Griggs v. Duke Power Co., 401 U.S. 424 (1971).

2. Davis v. County of Los Angeles, 566 F.2d 1334 (9th Cir. 1977), *vacated on other grounds*, 440 U.S. 625 (1979).

3. 42 U.S.C. § 2000e(j).

4. Brener v. Diagnostic Center Hosp., 671 F.2d 141 (5th Cir. 1982).

5. 42 U.S.C. § 2000e-1.

6. Examples of exceptions are that (1) private suits alleging breaches of the union's duty to represent its members fairly may be brought by individuals; (2) an employer may bring an action for breach of contract or for damages resulting from a union's secondary strike activity or its breach of a no-strike clause even though the union's conduct also violates the NLRA.

7. 29 C.F.R. §§ 1601.6–.14, as amended by 49 C.F.R. § 13873 (April 9, 1984).

8. 29 C.F.R. § 1602.14.

9. Sanchez v. Standard Brands, Inc., 431 F.2d 455 (5th Cir. 1970).

10. 42 U.S.C. § 2000e-9; 29 C.F.R. 1601.15–.18.

11. EEOC COMPL. MAN. (BNA) N:3071 (Resolution Modifying Rapid Charge Processing System); Compliance Procedures § 12 (Early Litigation Identification), §§ 16, 17 (Processing Systemic Cases, Requests for Systemic Investigation), §§ 20, 21 (Backlog Charges).

12. 29 C.F.R. § 1601.15(c); EEOC COMPL. MAN. (CCH) ¶¶ 523–39.

13. 42 U.S.C. § 2000e-5(b).

14. 29 C.F.R. § 1601.10, .24(a), as amended 49 C.F.R. § 13873 (April 9, 1984).

15. The EEOC has sample form agreements and standard provisions to be used in negotiated settlements reached before a cause determination is made, and after a cause determination has been issued. EEOC COMPL. MAN. (CCH) ¶¶ 541–548 ¶¶ 1221–1308.

16. EEOC COMPL. MAN. (BNA) § 7.9.

17. 42 U.S.C. § 2000e-5(f)(1); 29 C.F.R. § 13873 (April 9, 1984).

18. Georator Corp. v. EEOC, 592 F.2d 765 (4th Cir. 1979).

19. For a discussion of the discrimination theories of disparate treatment and disparate (adverse) impact, from the EEOC's perspective, see EEOC COMPL. MAN. (CCH) ¶¶ 2075–2084.

20. McDonnell Douglas Corp. v. Green, 411 U.S. 792 (1973).

21. 42 U.S.C. § 2000e-8(e).

22. EEOC COMPL. MAN. (CCH) ¶ 1785, *see generally* ¶¶ 1781–1791.

23. 42 U.S.C. § 2000e-5(k).

24. New York Gaslight Club v. Carey, 447 U.S. 54 (1980).

25. Christianburg Garment Co. v. EEOC, 434 U.S. 412 (1978).

26. Williams v. Saxbe, 413 F. Supp. 654, 659 n.6. (D.D.C. 1976), *vacated on other grounds*, 587 F.2d 1240 (D.C. Cir. 1978).

27. The EEOC, U.S. Civil Service Commission, Justice Department, and OFCCP adopted "Uniform Guidelines on Employee Selection Procedures" in 1978, 29 C.F.R. Part 1607. These establish stringent standards for the use and validation of employee selection procedures where those procedures have an adverse impact on protected classes.

28. 29 C.F.R. § 1604.5; EEOC COMPL. MAN. (CCH) ¶ 5401–02.

29. *Id.*

30. Discharge of Black guard for arrest record was race bias, *see* EEOC Dec. No. 74–90 (1974).

31. Albemarle Paper Co. v. Moody, 422 U.S. 405 (1975); Griggs v. Duke Power Co., 401 U.S. 424 (1971).

32. 29 C.F.R. § 1607.16Q.

33. Townsend v. Nassau County Medical Center, 558 F.2d 117 (2d Cir. 1977).

34. 29 C.F.R. § 1606.7.

35. Garcia v. Gloor, 618 F.2d 264 (5th Cir. 1980).

36. While the text discusses this subject in terms of R.N. recruitment, many of the same potential problems and suggested guidelines are pertinent to the hiring of other personnel, e.g., physical therapists.

37. *E.g.,* CALIF. BUS. & PROF. CODE § 2736 (West Supp. 1984).

38. 8 C.F.R. § 214.2(h)(2)(IV).

39. Lea v. Cone Mills Corp., 301 F. Supp. 97, 100 (M.D.D.C. 169), *aff'd in part, rev'd in part*, 438 F.2d 86 (4th Cir. 1977).

40. Sanbonmatsu v. Boyer, 357 N.Y.2d 245 (1974); *but see*, Yuhas v. Libbey-Owens Ford Co., 16 FAIR EMPL. PRAC. CAS. (BNA) 891 (7th Cir. 1977), *cert. denied*, 17 FAIR EMPL. PRAC. CAS. (BNA) 87 (1978) (ban on employment of spouses did not violate Title VII).

41. Carroll v. Talman Fed. Sav. & Loan Ass'n, 604 F.2d 1028 (7th Cir. 1979).

42. Dress regulation results in religious discrimination, *see* EEOC Dec. No. 71–779 (1970).

43. *E.g.,* EEOC v. Trailways, Inc., 530 F. Supp. 54 (D.C. Colo. 1981); *but see* EEOC v. Greyhound Lines, 635 F.2d 188 (3d Cir. 1980).

44. Fountain v. Safeway Stores, Inc., 555 F.2d 753 (9th Cir. 1977); Longs v. Carlisle De Coppet & Co., 537 F.2d 685 (2d Cir. 1976) *(per curiam)*.

45. *See* Jenkins v. Blue Cross Mut. Hosp. Ins., 538 F.2d 164 (7th Cir. 1976); *contra,* Rogers v. American Airlines, Inc., 527 F. Supp. 229 (S.D.N.Y. 1981) (braids); EEOC COMPL. MAN. (CCH) ¶¶ 3500–3507 (grooming standards).

46. See Chapter 6, n.26.

47. 41 C.F.R. Part 60–2.

48. United Steelworkers of America v. Weber, 443 U.S. 193 (1979); *see also* EEOC Regulations on Voluntary Plans, 29 C.F.R. Part 1608.

49. Gregory v. Litton Sys., Inc., 316 F. Supp. 401, 403 (C.D. Cal. 1970), *aff'd*, 472 F.2d 631 (9th Cir. 1972).

50. *Id.*

51. Richardson v. Hotel Corp. of Am., 3 FAIR EMPL. PRAC. CAS. (BNA) 1031 (E.D. La. 1971), *aff'd*, 468 F.2d 951 (5th Cir. 1972) (termination of black bellman who had access to guest rooms and who was convicted of theft did not violate Title VII).

52. Weeks v. Southern Bell Tel. & Tel. Co., 408 F.2d 228 (5th Cir. 1969); EEOC Sex Discrimination Guidelines, 29 C.F.R. § 1604.2(b)(1).

53. Erickson v. Lustra Lighting Div. of IT&T, 9 EPD ¶ 9892 (N.D. Cal. 1974).

54. 29 C.F.R. § 1604.2(a)(1)(iii),(2).

55. Fesel v. Masonic Home, 447 F. Supp. 1346 (D. Del. 1978).

56. Backus v. Baptist Medical Center, 510 F. Supp. 1191 (E.D. Ark. 1981), *vacated on other grounds*, 671 F.2d 1100 (8th Cir. 1982); *see also* Brooks v. ACF Indus., Inc., 537 F. Supp. 1122 (S.D. W. Va. 1982) (female lawfully denied job cleaning male bath house).

57. Nashville Gas Co. v Satty, 434 U.S. 136 (1977)

58. 42 U.S.C. § 2000e(k).

59. *Id.*

60. 29 C.F.R. § 1604.10 and Appendix thereto (Questions and Answers 21, 22).

61. Newport News Shipbuilding and Dry Dock Co. v. EEOC, 51 U.S.L.W. 4837, 32 FAIR EMPL. PRAC. CAS (BNA) 1; ____ U.S. ____, 77 L. Ed. 2d 89, 103 S. Ct; 32 EPD ¶ 33,673 (1983); 29 C.F.R. § 1604, Appendix (Questions and Answers 21, 22).

62. Lemons v. City and County of Denver, 620 F.2d 228 (10th Cir. 1980); *but see* I.U.E. v. Westinghouse, 631 F.2d 1094 (3d Cir. 1980).

63. County of Washington v. Gunther, 452 U.S. 161 (1981); *also see,* American Fed. of State, County, & Mun. Employees v. State of Washington, ____ F.S. ____ 32 FAIR EMPL. PRAC. CAS. (BNA) 808 (W.D. Wa., 1983).

64. 33 FAIR EMPL. PRAC. CAS. (BNA) at 816.

65. *See e.g.,* Kouba v. Allstate Ins. Co., 691 F.2d 873 (9th Cir. 1982); Briggs v. City of Madison, 28 FAIR EMPL. PRAC. CAS. (BNA) 739 (W.D. Wisc. 1982). *But see,* EEOC COMPL. MAN. (BNA), N:3021 ("Ninety-Day Notice on County of Washington v. Gunther," the EEOC's Interpretive Memorandum that indicates that job-rating systems, and reliance on market factors, are not immune from Title VII claims alleging sex-based or "comparable worth" issues).

66. 29 C.F.R. § 1604.11.

67. Bundy v. Jackson, 641 F.2d 934 (D.C. Cir. 1981); Heelan v. Johns-Manville Corporation, 451 F. Supp. 1382 (D.C. Col. 1978); Henson v. City of Dundee, 682 F.2d 897 (11th Cir. 1982).

68. *See, e.g.,* CAL. GOVT. CODE § 12940 (West 1980).

69. 29 C.F.R. § 1604.11(a).

70 . 29 C.F.R. § 1604.11(b).

71. Wright v. Methodist Youth Services, 511 F. Supp. 307 (N.D. Ill. 1981). (Overt homosexual advances by a male supervisor is unlawful sexual harassment even though discrimination on the basis of sexual preference is not prohibited by Title VII.)

72. 29 C.F.R. § 1604.11(g).

73. 29 C.F.R. § 1604.11(c).

74. Miller v. Bank Of America, 600 F.2d 211 (9th Cir. 1979).

75. Bundy v. Jackson, 641 F.2d 934 (D.C. Cir. 1981) (Title VII is violated by repeated sexual advances and subjective comments from male supervisors where the employee still received satisfactory performance evaluations and several promotions); *but see,* Davis v. Western-Southern Life Insurance Company, ____ F. Supp. ____ (N.D. Ohio 1984), 34 FAIR EMPL. PRAC. CAS. (BNA) 97 (N.D. Ohio 1984). (Strict liability for supervisorial conduct is not appropriate for hostile environment cases where employee retains benefits of employment, particularly if the employer takes prompt remedial action.)

76. 29 C.F.R. § 1604.11(c), (e).

77. 29 C.F.R. § 1604.11(e).

78. 29 C.F.R. § 1604.11(f).

Chapter 8

Age, Handicap, and Veterans

AGE

Federal Age Discrimination in Employment Act

Discrimination against older citizens attracted the attention of Congress in 1967 and resulted in the Age Discrimination in Employment Act (ADEA) of 1967.[1] As the name suggests, this Act is limited to discrimination in employment.

- Covered employers are those in industries affecting commerce that have 20 or more employees for 20 or more weeks in the current or preceding year. The term "industry affecting commerce" again is defined so as to include employers subject to the NLRA.[2]
- Labor organizations also are covered if they have a hiring hall or 25 members and they, as certified by the NLRB, represent employees in an industry affecting commerce or meet other specified requirements.[3]
- Employment agencies are subject to the Act and are defined simply as "any person regularly undertaking with or without compensation to procure employees for an employer and include an agent of such a person. . . ."[4]

Public employees originally were not covered but in 1974 the Act was amended to include most employees of states and their political subdivisions. A separate section was added to prohibit age discrimination in federal employment,[5] subject to special procedures for the processing of claims.

Protected Age Groups

Originally, the protected group consisted of employees or applicants for employment who were at least 40 years old but less than 65. In 1978, however, amid some controversy, Congress extended the upper age limit to 70. Those amendments also removed the upper age limit of 70 for mandatory retirement of federal workers. Thus, since January 1, 1979, the ADEA has prohibited discrimination by private employers because of age against applicants or employees who are at least 40 years old but less than 70.[6]

The ADEA also prohibits discrimination because of age between two or more employees within the protected group.[7] For example, 50-year-old employees will have a remedy if they are able to show that your employer discriminated against them in favor of 45-year-old persons. You could not successfully use as a defense that the employees who "benefited" from the discrimination also were members of the protected age group.

Jurisdiction, Requirements, and Procedures

Administration of the ADEA follows the Fair Labor Standards Act (FLSA) scheme and was assigned originally to the Wage and Hour Division of the Department of Labor (DOL) but since 1979 enforcement has been transferred to the Equal Employment Opportunity Commission (EEOC). The EEOC, as discussed earlier, is the federal agency that handles employment discrimination claims under Title VII.

If one of your employees (or applicants for employment) files an age discrimination claim, you should be aware that pursuit of the claim follows two distinct phases:

1. The EEOC or state agency investigates the charge and, under the Act, is required to attempt to resolve the case through "conciliation, conference and persuasion"[8] in an effort to reach a voluntary settlement.
2. The settlement effort may fail, in which case either the individual claiming discrimination (often termed the Charging Party), or the EEOC (or the corresponding state agency, if there is one in your state) may bring a lawsuit against your employer.

If the appropriate agency decides to bring suit "in the name of" the Charging Party, then the employees or applicants lose their right to proceed on their own.[9] Whoever brings the suit, however, the court has the power to order an appropriate remedy, including employment (if the Charging Party has been denied employment), reinstatement (if the employee has been discharged), promotion, and back pay, etc. Other damages (called liquidated damages, since a certain amount or formula is set in advance) also may be awarded in an amount equal to the employee's actual damages, if the employer willfully violates the ADEA. An individual also may recover attorney fees.[10]

The law says that before the Charging Party actually can file a lawsuit, certain preliminary steps must be taken.[11] First, the Charging Party must file a charge with the EEOC within 180 days of the alleged act of discrimination. The claimant then must wait a further 60 days before filing suit. This requirement is designed to allow the government agency an opportunity to settle the claim before litigation is begun.

Again, be aware that many states have their own age discrimination statutes and agencies to enforce them. If you are located in a ''deferral'' state (the EEOC must defer to the state's process), then (1) the Charging Party must use the state procedures, and (2) a charge with the EEOC also must be filed within 300 days after the alleged act of discrimination or within 30 days after being notified that the state's proceedings were terminated, whichever is earlier.[12] In addition, the EEOC and state agency frequently agree to divide their responsibilities to avoid duplicate investigations. Your becoming aware of the nature of the agreement between the EEOC and your state agency will help you understand why one is actively pursuing a claim while the other simply stands by.

If a lawsuit is to be brought, the Charging Party must file it in the proper court within two years of the alleged unlawful act; if the employer's action is ''willfull,'' and not merely negligent, the claimant has three years in which to file suit.[13] There is an exception to this in that these filing periods are ''stayed'' (interrupted), for a maxiumum of one year while the EEOC attempts conciliation of the dispute.[14] What this means is that the maximum possible period for filing the suit is four years from the date of the allegedly unlawful act.

What Constitutes Age Discrimination

The same types of theories discussed with regard to Title VII (Chapter 7) are generally applicable to age discrimination claims. This should be particularly true now that the EEOC is enforcing the ADEA.

Yet one additional theory to remember is that, as discussed earlier in this chapter, the ADEA protects older workers even where the ''beneficiary'' of the discrimination is within the protected group of 40 to 70. The simple rule is that there must be no discrimination against employees because of their age if they are within the protected group.

For example, if you have two applicants for a position, one age 45 and one 55, you cannot allow age to be a factor in the hiring of either since both are within the protected group. On the other hand, you are free to show a preference for older workers as a class. For example, you could advertise a preference for employees ''40 or over''; however, it would be unlawful if the advertisement referred to ''over 40 but less than 50'' since that would discriminate against the 50-70 group, just as a requirement of ''70 and over'' unlawfully excludes all members of the protected class. The best policy, therefore, is simply to avoid using age as a factor in your employment decisions.[15]

As is true of any lawsuit, a person alleging unlawful discrimination ''because of'' age must present what lawyers call a ''prima facie'' case. That is, the plaintiffs must prove a number of key elements to establish their claim before the defendant-employer even has an obligation to put forward its defense. The key elements of an age discrimination case are similar to those of a Title VII discrimination case and, as a reminder, two indispensable parts of a plaintiff's employment discrimination case are to prove that:

1. the employee or applicant for employment is a member of the protected age group (at least 40 but less than 70)
2. the plaintiff has been "adversely affected" by the employer's action (for example, being forced to retire, discharged from employment, not hired, etc.), and "adverse effect" can be shown by either a direct act against the particular plaintiff or by an act having an adverse differential impact on protected employees as a group.

If the employee or applicant does establish a prima facie case of age discrimination, it is the employer's turn to offer a clear and reasonably specific explanation for its action.[16] Failure to produce any evidence at this stage would result in the plaintiff's winning the case.

Among the possible defenses used by employers, the first might be that age played no part in your decision or action; in other words, that you acted on the basis of factors other than age.

For example, the original Department of Labor regulations specifically recognized the validity of physical fitness requirements that are reasonably necessary for the specific work to be performed if they are applied uniformly and equally to all applicants for the job, regardless of age. The substitute EEOC regulations omit any similar language but do acknowledge that a defense based on "factors other than age" can be proved by demonstrating business necessity for any employer practice that has an adverse impact on protected older employees.[17] Thus, while the terminology has changed, physical fitness requirements still should be a permissible factor "other than age" where:

- the physical fitness requirements are directly related to the actual physical requirements of the particular job and are reasonably necessary for the performance of that work.
- no alternative measures with a lesser adverse impact are reasonably available
- the fitness requirements, including any accompanying physical examination, are applicable to all employees or applicants for the position.

Another defense in the "age is not a factor" category is where an employee is terminated, or other adverse action is taken, for "good cause."[18] The statutory reference to "good cause" has been interpreted to mean for a cause other than age. As a result, and unless the employer's reasons are so flimsy or arbitrary that they appear to be a pretext for its true discriminatory intent, courts generally will not independently evaluate whether the nondiscriminatory explanations are satisfactory from the courts' perspective.[19] However, since you must be prepared to demonstrate nondiscriminatory reasons, your adherence to standard supervisory principles and proper documentation as to the grounds for disciplinary action is critical in defending against claims based on age, just as they are for claims based on Title VII, the NLRA, etc.

As in Title VII cases, an employer is permitted to argue that while it did use age to discriminate between employees, its actions were lawful since age is a "bona fide occupational qualification" (BFOQ) for that job.[20] This defense will be construed narrowly (as it is under Title VII). The EEOC has indicated that the employer must show:

- that the age limit is reasonably necessary to the essence of the business, and either

- that all or substantially all individuals excluded from the job involved are in fact disqualified, or

- that some of the individuals so excluded possess a disqualifying trait that cannot be ascertained except by reference to age.

The employer whose objective in securing a BFOQ is public safety must prove that the challenged practice does indeed effectuate that goal and that there is no acceptable alternative that would better or equally advance it with less discriminatory impact.[21]

While the courts have used varying standards to determine the existence of a BFOQ, examples of those recognized to date include limitations clearly imposed for the safety and convenience of others, most notably the public, such as upper age limits for airline pilots and bus drivers.[22] If, on the other hand, the age limit is imposed because of the employer's concerns for the employee's own safety (where the safety of others is not affected) or because of the employer's perception or assumptions of abilities based on age, then successful use of the BFOQ defense is unlikely.[23]

The ADEA also provides, as an employer defense, that it is not unlawful to observe

> "the terms of a bona fide seniority system," but such a system cannot be used as a pretext for age discrimination, it cannot excuse the discriminatory failure to hire an individual based on age, and it cannot require or permit the mandatory retirement of protected individuals.[24]

Most seniority systems operate, in practice, to protect older employees by rewarding length of service and thus may be a primary reason why Congress recognized this employer defense to ADEA claims. In any event, under the EEOC's regulations, your seniority system must comply with the following guidelines in order to constitute a bona fide seniority system:

1. The system must be based on length of service as the primary factor in determining rights of employees, although merit and ability considerations also may be incorporated.
2. The system must give greater rights to those with longer service unless the employer can demonstrate that the granting of lesser rights is not a subterfuge for avoiding ADEA obligations.
3. The system must be communicated to affected employees and applied consistently.
4. The system should not include any practices violative of Title VII.[25]

State Age Discrimination Laws

A large majority of the states have enacted laws aimed at preventing employer discrimination on the basis of age although some 15 still lack such legislation. As might be expected, there is little uniformity among those states banning age discrimination in either the type of employer covered or the age group protected:[26]

- A few states have created statutes outlawing employment discrimination on account of age but covering only public employers.
- Two states, California and Indiana, have excluded from coverage employers that are religious nonprofit corporations or organizations.
- Most states have a size limitation and cover only employers with a minimum number of employees, such as five or ten.

The greatest variety probably involves which age groups are protected, an area in which it is difficult to make any broad generalizations:

- Several states simply outlaw discrimination based on age without fixing any maximum or minimum.
- Others follow the lead of the federal government and protect employees in the 40-to-70 age group.
- Still others have retained the earlier federal model of protecting only employees who are at least 40 and less than 65.
- Some states have fixed a maximum age (e.g., 60) but no minimum.
- Other states have created a minimum age but no maximum; in these cases, the burden tends to pass to the employees, after a certain age, to show that they still are capable of performing the work.

• One state simply declares that it is state policy not to deny the right to work on account of age but goes no further and does not expressly outlaw such discrimination.

Just because your state has a law prohibiting age discrimination does not necessarily mean that the state itself will take any active steps to ensure compliance. Some states do have an active and functioning state agency (frequently termed a commission), similar to the federal EEOC, that investigates, attempts to conciliate, and litigates claims of age discrimination. Other states, while legislating against age discrimination in employment, have no agency or have one that performs only limited functions.

You should become familiar with the scope of your state age discrimination law and find out whether there is a state agency that polices it. With a working knowledge of the law and the mechanics of its enforcement, you will be better equipped to head off claims before they can arise and to handle them when they do.

Topics of Particular Significance

Age Discrimination and Employment Benefits

This is perhaps the most hazardous area for employers because discrimination, or what the government interprets as discrimination, is not always obvious and the "rules" become complex. Nevertheless, your benefit plans (pensions, disabilities, health and life insurance, etc.) must be reexamined constantly to ensure they do not have discriminatory provisions.

Initially, you should know that there are certain circumstances when you are permitted to treat older employees differently under a "bona fide employee benefit plan" (so long as it is not a device to get around the principles of the ADEA). However, the presence of an employee benefit plan, no matter what form it takes, never can excuse the failure to hire any person based on impermissible considerations of age.[27]

Furthermore, in the past an employer could insist that employees retire at the "normal" retirement age stipulated in its retirement or pension plan. Under current federal law, however, mandatory retirement cannot be imposed on employees who are less than 70 years old. The sole exception affects higher paid executives: an employer may retain mandatory retirement for employees at 65 if, for at least two years prior to retirement, they were employed in a "bona fide executive or a high policy position" and if they are entitled to an immediate nonforfeitable pension of at least $27,000 a year.[28]

The EEOC has developed guidelines on its interpretation of the ADEA exemption for employer actions under a bona fide employer benefit plan. While the design, structure, and legal permissibility of benefit plans and their provisions are beyond the scope of this manual, the following summary of the EEOC's position does highlight the considerations to be evaluated in determining whether the exemption is available.

1. The term "benefit plan" does not include benefits whose costs do not vary significantly with age, such as paid vacations, uninsured sick leave, and jury and funeral leave.
2. Fringe benefits in the form of cash compensation that are akin to wages (such as shift differentials) are not benefit plans for purposes of the exemption.
3. Life insurance benefits, the cost of which does vary with age, may be reduced for older workers so long as their cost for older workers is equal to that for younger workers. For example, if it costs $5 a month to provide $10,000 in term life insurance for a 21-year-old employee while $5 a month buys only $4,000 of the same insurance for the 69-year-old, then providing $10,000 and $4,000 coverage respectively to the two employees would be acceptable.
4. A bona fide employee benefit plan must describe its provisions accurately in writing to all employees, it must provide benefits consistent with that description, and employees must be informed of any changes. These requirements generally will be met by employers' following the reporting and disclosure requirements of ERISA (see Chapter 10).
5. Plans paid solely by employees, by employees and employer, and totally by the employer all are subject to the EEOC's guidelines and some specialized rules and prohibitions are applicable, depending upon the form of financing.
6. The employer's actions must be required by the plan and may not be an optional provision or simply the employer's interpretation of a plan that has no express provision requiring the action taken.
7. The cost data projections used to determine the necessary benefit must be reliable, valid, and reasonable.
8. Adjustments can be on a benefit-by-benefit basis or on a package basis; different rules apply to the two approaches.
9. Additional requirements are applicable to retirement plans with a differentiation made between defined benefit and defined contribution programs.[29]

As a result of the 1982 Tax Equity and Fiscal Responsibility Act (TEFRA) amendments to the ADEA, it no longer is permissible to offer employees different health benefits based on age or to offer Medicare "carve-out" coverage in which the private health plan is a secondary payer for services covered by Medicare.

Employees aged 65 through 70 must be given the right to elect between Medicare coverage and any health plan offered by the employer. Both the EEOC and the Health Care Financing Administration have issued regulations concerning these health insurance prohibitions and they should be reviewed when revising or developing plans.[30]

This is an area in which you and your employer should not act without the benefit of expert advise. The rules governing age and benefit plans are extremely intricate and a variety of laws may be applicable. Just one example is that both ADEA and ERISA (see Chapter 10) may apply and their requirements may not be totally consistent. Furthermore, your various benefit plans may be very different, in ways that are not readily apparent, from the types generally discussed in the EEOC regulations and in other materials. Simply be aware of the fact that benefit plans can produce age discrimination problems, of the types of issues that exist, and of how essential it is to ask for help when it is needed.

Help Wanted Ads and Employment Agencies

The EEOC's interpretations of ADEA are very restrictive as to what can and cannot be said in help-wanted ads. In its view, phrases and words such as "age 25 to 35," "recent college graduate," "college student," or "young" are discriminatory against persons within the protected age group and thus violate ADEA unless one of the defenses exists. The same is true of references to "retired person," "over 65," etc., since they discriminate among members of the protected class. By contrast, the EEOC indicates that while the phrase "state age," by itself, is not violative of the ADEA, such references will be scrutinized closely since they may deter older applicants.[31]

The courts, on the other hand, have not been quite so rigid in the few cases that have considered the use of particular advertisements. To avoid liability however, the safest rule of thumb still is the following: words and phrases that indicate or even imply you have a preference based on age are, almost without an exception, unlawful. Also, be aware that you cannot use as a defense the fact that you relied on an employment agency to recruit for you and that it was the entity that discriminated. The point is that liability is created by discriminating practices, and your employer is no less liable because it or you used an outside recruiter.

The phrasing of advertisements is an obvious area where discrimination against older workers can occur yet this can be avoided easily by a little thought and careful wording. As a matter of policy, it also is appropriate to have help wanted advertisements double-checked by someone familiar with the potential problems.

Applications and Preemployment Inquiries

Charges of unlawful discrimination can easily be avoided by deleting any reference to age on employment applications, requests for resumes, interview checklists, etc. Applications should not ask a person's age and all personnel handling applications or conducting interviews, including receptionists and the like, must be warned to stay away from the subject. Reasons for asking a person's age on such applications are so closely scrutinized, and so rarely can have any practical value, that the practice should be abandoned in all but the few cases where it can be justified.

Indirect references to age also should be avoided. For example, if you ask the year an applicant graduated from high school you are indirectly asking, or eliciting, information that will disclose the person's age. These types of questions therefore should be avoided.

However, if a request for dates can be justified by business reasons (for example, needing to know when an applicant graduated from a professional program so that you can verify the information), then be sure the application also states why the question is asked, that the information will be used only for such purposes, and that the form also contains a statement such as, "The Age Discrimination in Employment Act prohibits age discrimination against persons at least 40 but less than 70 years of age."[32]

Improper Classification

Any limiting, segregating, or classifying of employees according to age will be closely inspected and is virtually an invitation to discrimination claims For example, in a system where employees' wages are based on how much they produce, paying all older workers at a different rate is unlawful even if the employer can show that older persons, as a class, are less productive than the younger ones. Such wage distinctions are unlawful because older employees may be just as productive as (sometimes even more than) their young coworkers. Lumping all older workers together in a class means you could be punishing the more productive older ones simply because of their age.

Aptitude Tests

Chapter 7 already will have alerted you to the potential dangers involved in the use of tests for job applicants as hiring and promotion barriers. Just as with race and other protected groups, these tests are invalid if they adversely impact a protected group unless they meet certain standards.

In the case of older employees, there is an added danger you should note. The Department of Labor stated, in ADEA regulations issued during the period of its enforcement responsibility for the Act, that older workers had less familiarity with modern aptitude tests and, as a result, were more disadvantaged by the use of such tests. The department's theory was that younger workers, through more recent exposure at school and college, tend to be more familiar with modern testing methods and have developed greater skills in this area.

Although this theory has not been incorporated within the EEOC's regulations, if it were agreed to and accepted by the EEOC or the courts, then the use of certain types of tests as a sole means of selection could result in improper discrimination against older workers.

Use of Statistics

While individual plaintiffs in age discrimination cases must prove their case by relevant evidence, the courts will accept evidence of a general pattern of such discrimination. The courts have come to rely on statistical proof of employment discrimination to establish a pattern because direct evidence seldom is available.[33] In other words, where employers have an improper motive in discharging someone, they rarely will document the reason, nor is it easy for a plaintiff to come by other evidence of an illegal motive.

For example, statistical evidence has increased rapidly in recent years and, since both sides frequently use it, a complex and sophisticated separate area of litigation has developed:

- The plaintiff in an age discrimination case might compare the proportion of older employees in your employer's work force with the proportion of older workers in a relevant (regional, local, industry) population pool. If such a comparison shows a significant discrepancy, the plaintiff could use this to establish a prima facie case of disparate treatment. This could happen where the plaintiff shows that only 10 percent of those in the employers' work force are between 40 and 70 while the figure is 50 percent for the relevant overall labor force pool.

- Your employer might respond with its own statistical data. Continuing the same example, it might show that in recent months its proportion of new hires who are older "protected" employees equals or exceeds the proportion in the relevant population pool. As an alternative, your employer might counter by attacking the whole basis of the plaintiff's statistical calculations or by showing that it has made substantial and vigorous, but unsuccessful, efforts to hire older employees.

Deciding what is the relevant population pool against which to measure the employer's work force often is the critical issue in a discrimination trial.

As a further example, age discrimination cases show that plaintiffs are presenting statistical data similar to those used in Title VII claims. In one case, a 58-year-old manager was fired after completing one year of employment. During that period he had performed more than adequately. He was able to show that, following an 18-month period of wholesale changes in the managerial group, the average age of managers had declined from 53 to 41. The court found that this statistical evidence, along with other inferences, proved a violation of the ADEA.[34]

Physical Examinations

As an employer, you must make sure that any physical examination has a job-related reason and is reasonably necessary for the specific work to be performed. What you must particularly guard against is the use of physicals to eliminate older applicants by testing factors not really necessary to perform the job. Where physicals are necessary, they should be required of all employees (regardless of age) and adequate records must be kept documenting the examinations and showing how they are linked to the specific job sought by an applicant or occupied by an existing employee.

Advancement from Within

Of course, unlawful discrimination can involve your existing employees as well as applicants. To guard against this, you must constantly ensure that older employees are given the same opportunities for advancement and promotion as all others. For example, your training programs must not exclude older employees where promotion, higher salaries, or other benefits can result.

Supervising the Older Employee

You will be aware by now that it is relatively easy to slip into practices that, while innocently intended, have the effect of discriminating against protected groups, including older employees. Avoiding future problems requires constant vigilance to ensure that inadvertent discriminatory practices have not crept into your personnel policies and practices.

Your most difficult task will be to detect and control discrimination that results inadvertently from your own personal beliefs. A supervisor who believes that older employees are less capable may pass them over for promotion, merit raises, or other advancement. The same adverse consequences can result if training opportunities, assistance from you through performance evaluations, etc., are extended to younger employees but not to those you perceive as "approaching" retirement age. The best remedy is be aware of the law and its potentially serious consequences. But that is not enough; there also must be regular checks to ensure that no discriminatory patterns are emerging.

THE HANDICAPPED

Rehabilitation Act of 1973

The Rehabilitation Act can be viewed as a series of laws designed to assist handicapped persons:

- Section 501 applies only to the federal government and requires affirmative action to employ qualified handicapped individuals.
- Section 502 provides that handicapped individuals have free access to federal and federally financed buildings constructed after 1968.
- Section 503 covers federal contractors and imposes an affirmative action obligation to employ qualified handicapped individuals.
- Section 504 covers recipients of federal financial assistance and provides that qualified handicapped individuals must not be denied the benefits of or participation in such programs.[35]

Of most relevance to the health care industry is section 504, primarily because the federal government has taken the position that Medicare and Medicaid, programs in which most health care institutions participate, are federal financial assistance. For this reason, most of this subchapter discusses the obligations imposed by section 504.

Section 504 and Federal Financial Assistance

Modeled after Title VI of the 1964 Civil Rights Act, section 504 provides that no handicapped person can be denied the benefits of any program or activity receiving federal financial assistance. In regulations published May 4, 1977, by the Department of Health, Education, and Welfare (now Health and Human Services), the department took the position that two forms were prohibited: (1) discrimination against handicapped beneficiaries of the services provided (e.g., Medicare patients), and (2) employment discrimination against employees and applicants for jobs.

The department has listed, in its regulations issued under Title VI, 200 or more programs it viewed as "federal financial assistance"; included among these are at least 20 that are of direct relevance to health care providers. For example, your institution may participate in one or more of the following programs;[36] if so, the department's position is that your facility must comply with section 504:

- project grants and contracts for research and demonstration relating to new or improved health facilities and services
- grants for construction or modernization of emergency departments of general hospitals
- grants for construction and initial staffing of facilities for prevention and treatment of alcoholism
- grants for construction and initial staffing of facilities for mental health of children
- teaching facilities for nurse training

- teaching facilities for allied health professions personnel
- general research support
- immunization programs
- health research training projects and fellowship grants
- advanced professional nurse traineeships
- grants to institutions for traineeships for professional public health personnel
- grants for graduate or specialized training in public health
- improvement grants to centers for allied health professions
- traineeships for advanced training of allied health professions personnel
- contracts to encourage full utilization of nursing educational talent
- research projects relating to maternal and child health and crippled children's services
- health research facilities
- teaching facilities for health professions personnel
- supplementary medical insurance benefits for the aged (Medicare)
- project development grants for rehabilitation facilities
- continuing assistance to state-administered programs, including grants to states for old age assistance; aid to families with dependent children; child welfare services; aid to the blind; aid to the permanently and totally disabled; aid to the aged, blind, or disabled; medical assistance (Medicaid).

Although the department listed these as federal financial assistance, its regulations and its attempts to regulate employment practices were challenged. As a result, in 1984 the United States Supreme Court determined that an employer's employment practices, as well as its provision of services to program beneficiaries, can be regulated under section 504 if that program receives federal financial assistance. However, the question of whether Medicare or Medicaid actually constitutes "federal financial assistance" still is unresolved.[37]

Therefore, an appropriate caution is that HHS may not have jurisdiction to regulate your facility under section 504, you should not automatically assume that this jurisdiction exists, and assistance should be sought if a handicap discrimination claim is filed.

The Role of HHS

Since section 504 is applicable to all programs receiving federal financial assistance, Congress created a potential enforcement nightmare: dozens of federal agencies administer these programs and if each followed its own interpretation of the Act, conflicts and inconsistencies inevitably would emerge.

To avoid such a situation, HEW initially was given overall responsibility for coordinating the activities of the various agencies. Although this responsibility now rests with the Department of Justice, HEW's (now HHS's) standards for determining who are handicapped individuals, the practices considered to be discriminatory, and the obligations of a recipient toward the handicapped continue in effect and form the basis for the following discussion.[38] In addition, since any federal funds received by health care facilities typically come from HHS, that department's own enforcement procedures and interpretations are of primary importance.

Within HHS, the Office of Civil Rights (OCR) has the specific task of ensuring recipients' compliance with section 504. Through its regional field offices, the OCR receives complaints, conducts investigations, and initially attempts to obtain compliance with the Act by conciliation or settlement of claims. If the OCR is not successful at this stage, it can start proceedings to withhold federal assistance (e.g., for terminating your facility's participation in Medicare) or it may refer the matter to the Department of Justice. The Attorney General's office may then decide to bring a lawsuit against the alleged defaulter if such a course is necessary to obtain compliance with the Act.[39]

For claimed violations of section 504, it also is possible that charging parties may bring their own private lawsuit against your employer.[40]

What Constitutes Discrimination

As a general rule, your initial understanding of handicap discrimination should commence with an understanding of the definition of "qualified handicapped person" and of the types of individuals it encompasses. Once you know who is in this protected group, you can apply the rules prohibiting employment discrimination against such individuals.

The Act defines a handicapped person as anyone who:

- "has a physical or mental impairment which substantially limits one or more major life activities,
- "has a record of such impairment, or
- "is regarded as having such an impairment."[41]

Section 504 also states that "physical and mental impairment" include "emotional or mental illness."[42] Similarly, a person "regarded as having an impairment" is one who:

- has a physical or mental impairment that does not limit major life activities, but is treated by the recipient as constituting a limitation
- has such activities limited as a result of the attitudes of others

- has none of the impairments as defined but is treated by recipient as such a condition.

You should note further that "physical and mental impairment" includes drug addiction and alcoholism, if the individual is not precluded, because of current usage, from performing the job and their employment is not a direct threat to property or other persons.[43]

Who is a qualified handicapped person? In this area, your most difficult problem as a supervisor will be to identify the persons protected by the Act. You will have noted that section 504 does not cover all handicapped persons; it only protects "otherwise qualified handicapped" individuals. The regulations then describe a "qualified handicapped person," with respect to employment, as one who "with reasonable accommodation, can perform the essential functions of the job in question."[44] In summary, then, an "otherwise qualified handicapped person" protected by section 504 is an individual who:

- is, was, or is thought to be, handicapped, and
- with "reasonable accommodation" to this handicap, can still perform the "essential functions of the job."

This type of definition means that an individual might be an "otherwise qualified handicapped person" for some positions but not for others, depending upon the handicap, the position, and the type of accommodations required.

What is reasonable accommodation? Examination of the section 504 regulations makes clear that "reasonable accommodations" is the linchpin of the entire regulatory scheme. But what does it consist of and how far does an employer have to go to meet the requirement? The department, in Appendix A analyzing its regulations, includes an interesting and cautionary explanation and example:

Paragraph (k) of § 84.3 defines the term "qualified handicapped person." Throughout the regulation, this term is used instead of the statutory term "otherwise qualified handicapped person." The Department believes that the omission of the word "otherwise" is necessary in order to comport with the intent of the statute because, read literally, "otherwise" qualified persons include persons who are qualified except for their handicap, rather than in spite of their handicap. Under such a literal reading, a blind person possessing all the qualifications for driving a bus except sight could be said to be "otherwise qualified" for the job of driving. Clearly, such a result was not intended by Congress. In all other respects, the terms "qualified" and "otherwise qualified" are intended to be interchangeable.[45]

Therefore, according to HHS, you are not obligated to accept every handicapped person into your program or facility. On the other hand, you cannot deny employment or benefits to a handicapped person simply because the handicap precludes the individual's participation. Instead, recipients of federal financial assistance must reasonably modify or adapt their programs or facilities to meet the needs of the handicapped.

The regulations provide practical guidelines for recipients, starting with this general principle: even if you deny benefits or participation to a handicapped person, you still will comply with the law if you can show that accommodating such an individual would result in undue hardship on the operation of your program.[46] Factors taken into consideration in deciding whether an accommodation would impose an "undue hardship" include:

1. the overall size of your program
2. the type of operation you are engaged in
3. the nature and cost of the accommodation.[47]

The regulations explain that reasonable accommodation in employment practices may include:

1. making the facilities used by your employees readily accessible and usable by handicapped employees and
2. restructuring jobs, providing part-time or modified work schedules, acquiring or modifying equipment or devices, providing readers or interpreters, and other similar actions.[48]

Finally, the validity of requiring any significant form of affirmative action by private employers has been brought into question by a decision of the United States Supreme Court.[49] The Court noted that section 504 is limited to requiring nondiscrimination and that it was not the intention of Congress to impose affirmative action obligations on recipients. Regulations requiring "substantial adjustments" in existing programs beyond those necessary to eliminate discrimination were viewed as creating duties never intended by the statute.[50] At the same time, the Court cautioned there is a fine line between a lawful refusal to extend affirmative action and illegal discrimination. Thus, there will be times, even in the Supreme Court's view, when refusal to modify a program will be considered unreasonable, discriminatory, and in violation of section 504.

Under the regulations, employers covered by the Act must avoid discrimination against a "qualified handicapped person" in all aspects of employment decisions. Specifically, you may not limit, segregate, or classify employees or applicants because of their handicap if this has an adverse effect on them.[51] On the other hand, you would be entitled and often obliged to single out handicapped persons for more favorable treatment as long as this does not result in discrimination against other protected groups.

The regulations have isolated a number of specific activities you should note as resulting in prohibited discrimination:[52]

1. Recruitment, advertising, and the processing of applications for employment;
2. Hiring, upgrading, promotion, award of tenure, demotion, transfer, layoff, termination, right of return from layoff and rehiring;
3. Rates of pay or any other form of compensation and changes in compensation;
4. Job assignments, job classifications, organizational structures, position descriptions, lines of progression, and seniority lists;
5. Leaves of absence, sick leave, or any other leaves;
6. Fringe benefits available by virtue of employment, whether or not administered by the recipient;
7. Selection and financial support for training, including apprenticeship, professional meetings, conferences and other related activities, and selection for leaves of absence to pursue training;
8. Employer sponsored activities, including social or recreational programs;
9. Any other term, condition, or privilege of employment.

Another object of section 504 is to assure that persons are not denied the benefits of federally assisted programs because of their handicap. An obvious, almost symbolic, example is wheelchair access to buildings, public transportation, and other facilities. But the concept of program accessibility is considerably wider than that and includes making programs available to persons with disabilities not "traditionally" considered to be handicapped.[53] To this end, HHS regulations describe what constitutes program accessibility.

As a general principle, programs and activities should be operated in such a way that, viewed in their entirety, they are readily accessible to and usable by handicapped persons.[54] Yet this does not mean, says HHS, that every part of a facility must be accessible and usable.

The regulations suggest some steps that can be taken to increase program accessibility: redesign of equipment, reassignment of classes or services to more accessible buildings, assignment of aides, home visits, delivery of services at alternate sites, and, more substantially, structural alterations of existing facilities and/or construction of new ones with accessibility as a feature.[55] The regulations also prescribe the methods by which buildings can be constructed or altered in order to comply.

The burden is much lighter on small enterprises (defined as those with 15 or fewer employees). If you are such an enterprise, you can satisfy your obligations under the Act by consulting with the handicapped person in question and referring the individual to an alternate source of the particular service sought. This exception is applicable where accommodating the handicapped person would require a significant alteration of your existing facilities.[56]

As is evident, program accessibility can become a complex, multifaceted question involving your facility in enormous upheaval and costs. Any but the most minor changes should not be attempted without careful planning and outside consultation.

State Protection of the Handicapped

Interplay between State and Federal Law

Many states, counties, and cities have local legislation that limits handicap discrimination to some degree. Since the federal government has not made the field its exclusive domain, you should make yourself aware of whatever local laws and regulations are applicable to your institution. While the Rehabilitation Act limits its coverage of private employers to those receiving federal financial assistance or holding federal contracts, local legislation may be broader. Just because you avoid coverage under the Rehabilitation Act does not mean that you are permitted to ignore state and local laws on handicap discrimination. Furthermore:

- You cannot use state legislation as a shield to avoid claims of handicap discrimination under the Rehabilitation Act. If, for example, a local law imposes some prohibition on employment of the handicapped or restricts the provision of services to such persons, you cannot use that law as a defense if your activity violates the Rehabilitation Act.[57]
- You must apply whichever is the strictest standard if your facility is covered by a local law, a state law, and the Rehabilitation Act since compliance with one will not necessarily mean compliance with the others.
- You cannot avoid your statutory obligations by showing that you complied with the terms of a collective bargaining agreement.[58]

Coverage and Scope of State Laws

Some forty states have enacted laws banning discrimination in employment against handicapped persons. As is the case in age discrimination coverage, the states have not adopted a consistent approach to either the type of employer covered or the person protected:

- A few states limit their coverage to state, county, and other public employers, excluding all private employers.[59]
- Others, obviously following the example set by the Rehabilitation Act, limit coverage to public employers and to employment supported in whole or in part by public funds.[60]
- State acts that do cover private employers generally exclude small firms, typically those with five or fewer employees or some such similiar number.
- California and Indiana exlude religious nonprofit employers, as they do in age discrimination.

There is a similarly varied approach to the definition of "handicapped person." Generally speaking, state legislation does not define the term as broadly as the Rehabilitation Act. Thus, for example,

- Colorado protects persons who traditionally have been regarded as handicapped: the blind, visually handicapped, deaf and hearing impaired, and other physically disabled persons.[61] This excludes emotionally and mentally disabled persons from coverage.
- States where emotionally and mentally disabled persons are protected frequently require that the disability be demonstrated by medically accepted clinical or laboratory diagnostic techniques.[62]
- States such as California have specifically narrowed the definition of "physical handicap" to exclude persons suffering from alcoholism or drug addiction. (Persons covered by section 504.)[63]
- All states recognize, in one form or another, the principle of reasonable accommodation so that you, as an employer, are not obliged to hire every handicapped person no matter what the extent of their disability. New York, for example, would not protect the right of a handicapped person to obtain employment unless the individual can perform the job in a "reasonable manner."[64]
- Other states follow the federal model and require employers to make reasonable accommodation unless it would result in undue hardship. The Colorado statute goes even further and does not require accommodation to an employee's handicap if it would result in "additional expense."

Procedurally, the states tend to follow the federal pattern by establishing a Human Rights Commission or similarly titled agency for processing all discrimination claims, including those involving the handicapped.

Topics of Particular Significance

Section 501 and Federal Employment

If you are employed by the federal government your agency is covered by the Act. Section 501 obligates all federal departments, agencies, and instrumentalities to draw up and implement affirmative action plans for the hiring, placement, and advancement in employment of handicapped individuals. The plans must be kept current and must provide sufficient assurances that there is adequate hiring and advancement of handicapped persons.

In addition, an interagency committee was created that provides a focus for the employment of handicapped persons, both within and outside the federal government's sphere. This committee periodically reviews the adequacy of employment practices as they affect the handicapped.

Section 503 and Federal Contractors

As noted in Chapters 6 and 7, various federal laws and executive orders require affirmative action in the employment policies of federal contractors. That affirmative action is aimed at remedying the present effect of past discrimination. These concepts are seen again in section 503 of the Rehabilitation Act: if your facility has a federal contract in excess of $2,500, the document must contain a provision requiring your employer to take affirmative action to employ, and advance in employment, qualified handicapped individuals.

Handicapped persons who believe an employer is in breach of its contractual obligations may file a complaint with the Office of Federal Contract Compliance Programs (OFCCP), the agency charged with enforcement of section 503 rights. So far, the courts have held that individual handicapped persons do not have the right to sue the employer directly under section 503 but instead must rely on the OFCCP.[65]

An important question to virtually every health care provider is whether Medicare and/or Medicaid is a "government contract." Department of Labor regulations to enforce section 503 define "government contracts" without clarifying whether Medicare or Medicaid fall within the definition. On the other hand, HHS has taken the position, in the section 504 regulations, that Medicaid and Medicare Part A are "federal financial assistance."[66] If this HHS position is correct, then Medicaid and Medicare Part A should not be federal contracts. In any event, you still may be employed by a hospital or other health care institution that has a "contract" with the government quite apart from its receipt of Medicare or Medicaid reimbursements. In such a situation, section 503 and its regulations may apply to your operations.

Preemployment Medical Inquiries

Preemployment inquiries are treated in the same manner as testing and selection devices. You can ask questions concerning a person's handicap or insist on a medical examination before you extend an offer of employment only if you have a job-related reason.[67] The exceptions to this rule arise where you are taking affirmative action by deliberately singling out handicapped persons for more favorable treatment or where the information is necessary to determine whether "reasonable accommodation to an individual's handicap" is possible. Under such circumstances, you are permitted to inquire into a person's medical condition if:

- your questions clearly reveal why you are seeking the information
- you adequately reassure the applicant that the questions are voluntary, that the answers will be treated confidentially, and that refusal to answer will not result in any adverse treatment.[68]

Health Examinations

Hospitals and other health care institutions have a direct and legitimate interest in the health of their employees and applicants. Many hospitals, for example, require applicants to undergo preemployment medical examinations, consistent with the requirements of the Joint Commission on the Accreditation of Hospitals. The section 504 regulations do not prohibit such examinations and you are permitted to condition employment on the results of an examination, provided that:

- all employees undergo such examinations
- the results are not used to discriminate against the handicapped, which means that if a physical or mental impairment is detected you can exclude the applicant only if the problem is job-related and you cannot reasonably accommodate the handicap.[69]

Confidentiality of Data

Once you have obtained information on a person's handicap, you must be careful to treat it confidentially. This means separating the information from an employee's general personnel file, perhaps retaining it in an employee health file, and releasing it only to those who can show a proper interest, specifically:

- First aid and safety personnel generally are included as individuals with a proper interest.
- Supervisors and managers should not automatically be given full access. If, for example, an employee is placed on restricted duties or in some other way

needs accommodating, then the affected supervisors need to know the nature of the accommodation required and to be alerted to any adverse health signs; however, medical examination data, diagnoses, etc., should not be disclosed to them.

- Government officers investigating compliance with the Act may be entitled to examine such records but since compliance questions often raise complex legal problems, you should check with legal counsel before submitting any such records to any agency.[70]

Tests

Again, the use of tests or other selection criteria is a particularly vulnerable area. You cannot use such tests or other selection devices if they tend to screen out handicapped persons unless the instruments are shown to be job-related. Just as with older employees, you should not test an applicant's general physical or mental aptitude and you should limit testing to the specific skills required for the particular job.[71]

Drug and Drinking Problems

You should be aware that HHS includes drug addicts and alcoholics in the term "handicapped person" and there may be occasions when such persons are covered by the Act. Clearly, this is a controversial topic and HHS, in analyzing its own regulations, went to considerable length to explain and justify its position.[72]

The Act itself provides some protection to you as an employer of alcoholics and drug addicts. Thus, section 706 states that the term "handicapped individual" does not include alcoholics or drug abusers whose current use of such substances prevents their performing their job duties or whose employment would constitute a direct threat to property or the safety of others.[73]

The special treatment given to alcoholics and drug addicts is reflected by the HHS regulations. In summary, these regulations state that:

- You are not obliged to ignore alcoholism or drug addiction in determining whether a person is qualified for a position or to participate in a program.
- You are entitled to hold a drug addict or alcoholic to the same standard as other employees or participants.
- You may justify termination of such individuals for their failure to meet the same standard used for other employees, even if the failure is caused by the alcoholism or addiction.
- You can take into account any manifestations of the illnesses such as absenteeism; disruptive, abusive, or dangerous behavior; violations of rules; and unsatisfactory work performance.

- You may have rules prohibiting the possession and use of alcohol or drugs in the workplace, and you are entitled to apply these rules to alcoholics or drug addicts provided such persons are not singled out and the rules are applied evenly to all employees.

Unlawful discrimination against drug addicts and alcoholics occurs when you deny them program participation or employment solely because of their problem. Thus, the regulations specifically prohibit hospitals and outpatient clinics from refusing services to such individuals simply because of their substance abuse.[74] However, if their condition substantially interferes with the operation of the program, then a decision to deny access may be warranted.

VETERANS' RIGHTS

Veterans Readjustment Act

Scope and Coverage

The Vietnam Era Veterans Readjustment Act of 1974[75] prohibits federal agencies and government contractors from discriminating against two classes of veterans, the disabled and those of the Vietnam War Era. Private employers are covered by this Act only if they hold contracts of $10,000 or more with any federal agency or department or any federally owned corporation (and remember, participation in Medicare is not construed as a federal contract). If your employer has such a contract, however, you must promise to take affirmative action to employ, and advance in employment, qualified disabled veterans and veterans of the Vietnam Era.

Protected Veterans

Unlike many other areas of employment discrimination, this protected class is defined with some precision. Thus, a "disabled veteran" is one who (1) is entitled to a disability compensation under laws administered by the Veterans Administration for a disability rated at 30 percent or more, or (2) was discharged from the armed forces for a disability incurred or aggravated in the line of duty.[76]

A "veteran of the Vietnam Era" is one who served on active duty for 180 days or more, any part of which occurred during the Vietnam Era.[77] This means a veteran need not have served in Vietnam itself to gain protection but the Vietnam veteran remains protected for only a limited period and coverage ceases four years after the individual's discharge. The Act, therefore, is designed to provide Vietnam veterans with carryover protection for a specified time period to facilitate their reentry into civilian life, not for lifelong protection.

Enforcement Procedures

As is true of other federal contractor laws, OFCCP has been delegated the task of enforcing the nondiscriminatory and affirmative action obligations of federal contractors. Under OFCCP procedures:

- A protected veteran must file a complaint within 180 days from the date of an alleged violation unless an extension is granted for good cause.[78]
- A complaint against a federal contractor that has an internal review procedure must be referred for processing under that procedure.
- A federal contractor that has no internal review procedure (or following processing by the federal contractor) will have the complaint investigated by the OFCCP.
- The OFCCP, if the evidence indicates that the contractor has not been in compliance with its affirmative action obligations, will concentrate its initial efforts on obtaining compliance through conciliation and persuasion.[79]

As is the case under section 503 of the Rehabilitation Act and Executive Order 11,246, there are numerous remedies for noncompliance. These include withholding progress payments on an existing contract, termination of an existing contract, and barring a contractor from future government contracts, and at each of these steps, a court injunction against the prohibited activity also may be obtained. The federal contractor is entitled to a formal administrative hearing to present its defense.[80]

Veterans' Reemployment Rights

General Rights

The Veterans Reemployment Act[81] covers all private employers. There are no limitations based on size, receipt of federal financial assistance, federal contractor status, etc. Furthermore, the veteran need not have served during the Vietnam Era nor have any disability in order to have the protection of the Act. This means, very simply, that your facility is covered.

Basically, a person who leaves employment to complete a period of military training or service is entitled to be restored to a position of like seniority, status, and pay if:

- a certificate evidencing satisfactory service is received
- the individual makes application to the preservice employer within 90 days after being released from such training or service, or from hospitalization continuing not more than one year after such discharge
- the individual still is qualified to perform the duties of the job.

In addition to reemployment rights, a returning veteran, once employed, may not be discharged without cause for one year.[82]

Reservists

A reservist or national guardsman ordered to active duty for training of not less than three months is treated as a returning veteran and must apply for reemployment. But unlike a veteran completing military training or service, the reservist or national guardsman must apply for reemployment within 31, not 90, days of release.[83]

Reservists called for less than three months' active duty or training—most typically weekend camps or annual training—are permitted to return to their position without application for reemployment. However, they must report for work immediately upon their release from training (or from a hospital, if hospitalized during training), unless circumstances beyond their control prevent them from doing so.[84]

Seniority and Fringe Benefits

The seniority and other fringe benefits to which the returning veteran is entitled is an important and somewhat complex subject. The Act guarantees reemployment without loss of seniority but does not define "seniority."[85] In deciding how to measure seniority, the courts have used various sources, including collective bargaining agreements,[86] practices and customs in the industry,[87] and the employer's policies.[88]

The controlling general principle, however, is that the returning veteran must be restored, as near as possible, to the status that would have been enjoyed if the individual had continued in employment for the military service period. If, for example, during the absence the individual would have received two salary increases based on length of service, then the returning employee must be reinstated at the higher pay level.

The extent to which the returning veteran is entitled to other benefits depends upon the nature of the benefit and the way it is earned. The main principles are the following:

- The returning veteran is to be given the same benefits that would have been received if not for the absence unless they are based strictly upon actual presence on the job.
- The returning veteran clearly is entitled to be credited with the period of absence in the armed services if the amount of the benefit is computed solely on the employee's length of service or seniority.

- The returning veteran cannot, on the other hand, claim an "accelerated" entitlement based on the period of service if the benefit is computed on the basis of actual compensated service.[89]

For example, if the amount of annual vacation entitlement increases automatically, such as three weeks of vacation after ten years' service, then the veteran's period of service will be counted in establishing employee entitlement or rate of vacation time accrual upon return. Why? Because earning vacation at a higher rate clearly is an attribute of seniority. On the other hand, a year-end bonus based on the actual sales of each employee during the year obviously has no relationship to seniority and the employer can ignore the veteran's period of absence in calculating the bonus.

In determining whether fringe benefit credit is applicable to a returning veteran, and the amount of the benefit to which the person is entitled, you should adopt a cautious approach. The courts have analyzed many benefits that, employers say, are based on an employee's actual presence or compensated service with the employer, and have found them to be based on seniority. Once such a finding is made, the returning veteran is entitled to full credit for the military service and the employer has no defense to the claim.

NOTES

1. 29 U.S.C. § 621–34.
2. 29 U.S.C. § 630(b),(h). The term "industry affecting commerce" is defined to include "any activity in business 'affecting commerce' within the meaning of the Labor-Management Reporting and Disclosure Act of 1959," 29 U.S.C. § 630(h); see Chapter 6, n.3. It also should be noted that one court has ruled that the ADEA may be inapplicable to religious institutions. Ritter v. Mount St. Mary's College, 495 F. Supp. 724 (D. Md. 1980), *relying on* NLRB v. Catholic Bishop of Chicago, 440 U.S. 490 (1979); *but see*, Usery v. Manchester East Catholic School Bd., 430 F. Supp. 188 (D.N.H. 1977).
3. 29 U.S.C. § 630(e).
4. 29 U.S.C. § 630(c).
5. 29 U.S.C. §§ 630(b), 634.
6. 29 U.S.C. §§ 631(a),(b).
7. 29 U.S.C. § 623(a); 29 C.F.R. § 860.91. The EEOC's published interpretation of the ADEA reflects a similar prohibition although it would allow preference to older persons within the protected age group under certain circumstances. 29 C.F.R. §§ 1625.1–.13.
8. 29 U.S.C. §§ 626(d); 29 C.F.R. §§ 1626.1–.19 (EEOC PROCEDURES UNDER ADEA).
9. 29 U.S.C. § 626(c)(1).
10. 29 U.S.C. § 216(b); 29 U.S.C. § 626(b).
11. 29 U.S.C. § 626(d).
12. 29 U.S.C. §§ 626(d), 633(b).
13. 29 U.S.C. § 626(e)(1).

14. 29 U.S.C. § 626(e)(2).

15. It should be noted, however, that the EEOC's published interpretation of the ADEA regulations takes the position that the "extension of additional benefits, such as increased severance pay, to older employees within the protected age bracket may be lawful if an employer has a reasonable basis to conclude that those benefits will counteract problems related to age discrimination." 29 C.F.R. § 1625.2.

16. Texas Dept. of Community Affairs v. Burdine, 450 U.S. 248 (1981).

17. 29 C.F.R. § 1625.7(d).

18. 29 U.S.C. § 623(f)(3).

19. Brennan v. Reynolds & Co., 367 F. Supp. 440 (N.D. Ill. 1973); Simmons v. McGuffey Nursing Home, 619 F.2d 369 (5th Cir. 1980) (unsatisfactory performance and strained personal relationships with nursing home's stockholders [three of whom were former relatives] constituted good cause).

20. 29 U.S.C. § 623(f)(1).

21. 29 C.F.R. § 1625.6(b).

22. *E.g.*, Murnane v. American Airlines, 482 F. Supp. 135 (D.D.C. 1979), *reh'g denied*, 482 F. Supp. 151 (D.D.C. 1979), *aff'd*, 26 FAIR EMPL. PRAC. CAS. (BNA) 1537 (D.C. Cir. 1981), *cert. denied*, 28 FAIR EMPL. PRAC. CAS. (BNA) 712 (1982) (upheld practice of requiring that applicants for employment as airline pilots be under 30), *but compare*, Smallwood v. United Airlines, Inc., 26 FAIR EMPL. PRAC. CAS. (BNA) 1655 (4th Cir. 1981), *cert. denied*, 28 FAIR EMPL. PRAC. CAS. (BNA) 1656 (1982) (rejected employer's requirement that applicant be younger than 35); Hodgson v. Greyhound Lines, Inc., 499 F.2d 859 (7th Cir. 1974), *cert. denied*, 419 U.S. 1122 (1975) (upheld requirement that bus driver applicant be no older than 35).

23. *See generally*, Dothard v. Rawlinson, 433 U.S. 321, 332–33 (1977) (Title VII case concerning sex as BFOQ in which Court stated that "In the usual case, the argument that a particular job is too dangerous for a woman may appropriately be met by the rejoinder that it is the purpose of Title VII to allow the individual woman to make that choice for herself."); Weeks v. Southern Bell Tel. & Tel. Co., 408 F.2d 228 (5th Cir. 1969) (Title VII BFOQ defense to sex discrimination rejected where employer relied on assumptions as to weight-lifting ability of women).

24. 29 U.S.C. § 623(f)(2).

25. 29 C.F.R. § 1625.8.

26. To review the various state provisions, refer to *State Fair Employment Practice Law*. 8A LAB. REL. REP. (BNA) (1983).

27. 29 U.S.C. § 623(f)(2).

28. 29 U.S.C. § 631(c)(1).

29. 29 C.F.R. § 860.120.

30. 29 U.S.C. § 623(g) (Tax Equity and Fiscal Responsibility Act of 1982, TEFRA, amending ADEA, 29 U.S.C. § 623 by adding subsection (g), and amending Medicare, 42 U.S.C. § 1395y(b) by adding (3)(A),(B)); 29 C.F.R. § 1625.20 (EEOC Regulations); 42 C.F.R. § 405.340–.344 (Health Care Financing Administration Regulations). Also note that the EEOC's regulations refer to employees aged 65 through 69, which is consistent with the provisions of TEFRA, while the regulations issued by Health Care Financing Administration apply the first day of the month in which individuals turn 65 through the last day of the month they attain age 70, 42 C.F.R. 405.34.(b)(3).

31. 29 C.F.R. § 1625.4.

32. 29 C.F.R. § 1625.5.

33. Marquez v. Omaha Dist. Sales Office, Ford Div., 440 F.2d 1157 (8th Cir. 1971).

34. Schulz v. Hickok Mfg. Co., 358 F. Supp. 1208 (N.D. Ga. 1973).

35. 29 U.S.C. §§ 791–94.

36. 45 C.F.R. Part 80, app. A, pts. 1 and 2; 45 C.F.R. Part 84, app. A, subpt. A, 1–2 (Medicaid as financial assistance).

37. Trageser v. Libbie Rehabilitation Center, Inc., 462 F. Supp. 424 (E.D. Va. 1977) (Medicaid is payment for services rendered, not federal financial assistance), *aff'd on other grounds*, 590 F.2d 87 (4th Cir. 1978), *cert. denied*, 99 S. Ct. 2895 (1979); *see also* Consolidated Rail Corp. v. Darrone, ___ U.S. ___, 79 L.Ed. 2d 568, 578, n.19 (1984) (suggestion by court that federal financial assistance requires payments by government in excess of value received).

38. Exec. Order No. 12,250, 45 Fed. Reg. 72,995 (1980) (responsibility for coordinating implementation by federal agencies given to Department of Justice); 46 Fed. Reg. 440686 (Departmernt of Justice adopts HHS guidelines).

39. 45 C.F.R. § 84.61 (Title VI HHS procedures apply to Section 504); 45 C.F.R. §§ 80.6–.10.

40. Consolidated Rail Corp. v. Darrone, ___ U.S. ___ 79 L.Ed. 565 (1984).

41. 29 U.S.C. § 706(7)(B).

42. 45 C.F.R. § 84.3(j)(2)(i).

43. 29 U.S.C. 706(7)(B); 45 C.F.R. pt. 84, app. A, subpt. A, 4; (see also discussion in the section on drinking, drugs, and employees in Chapter 13).

44. 45 C.F.R. § 84.3(k)(1).

45. 45 C.F.R. pt. 84, app. A, subpt. A, 5.

46. 29 U.S.C. § 706(7)(B); 45 C.F.R. pt. 84, app. A, subpt. A–4.

47. 45 C.F.R. § 84.12(c).

48. 45 C.F.R. § 84.12(b).

49. Southeastern Community College v. Davis, 442 U.S. 397 (1979).

50. *Id.* at 410.

51. 45 C.F.R. § 84.11(a).

52. 45 C.F.R. § 84.11(b).

53. 45 C.F.R. pt. 84, app. A.

54. 45 C.F.R. § 84.22.

55. 45 C.F.R. § 84.22(b).

56. 45 C.F.R. § 84.22(c).

57. 45 C.F.R. § 84.10(a).

58. 45 C.F.R. § 84.11(a)(4).

59. Arkansas, Mississippi, Texas.

60. COLORADO REV. STAT. § 24–34–801 (1982).

61. *Id.*

62. NEW YORK EXEC. LAW § 292.21 (McKinney 1982).

63. CAL. ADMIN. CODE tit. II, div. 4 § 7293.6(a)(4).

64. N.Y. EXEC. LAW § 292.21 (McKinney 1982).

65. *E.g.*, Simpson v. Reynolds Metals Co., 629 F.2d 1226 (7th Cir. 1980); Fisher v. City of Tucson, 663 F.2d 861 (9th Cir. 1981).

66. 45 C.F.R. pt. 84, app. A, subpt. A, 1; see also, Chapter 6, n. 26.

67. 29 C.F.R. § 84.14(a).

68. 45 C.F.R. § 84.14(b).

69. 45 C.F.R. § 84.14(c).
70. 45 C.F.R. § 84.14(d).
71. 45 C.F.R. § 84.13(a).
72. 45 C.F.R. pt. 84, app. A, subpt. A, 4.
73. 29 U.S.C. § 706(7)(B).
74. 45 C.F.R. § 84.53.
75. 38 U.S.C. § 2012.
76. 38 U.S.C. § 2011.
77. *Id.*
78. 41 C.F.R. § 60–250.26(a).
79. 41 C.F.R. § 60–250.23(g)(2).
80. 41 C.F.R. § 60–250.29(a).
81. 38 U.S.C. § 2021–26.
82. 38 U.S.C. § 2021(b)(1).
83. 38 U.S.C. § 2024(c).
84. 38 U.S.C. § 2024(d).
85. 38 U.S.C. § 2021(b)(1).
86. Aeronautical Industr. Dist. Lodge v. Campbell, 337 U.S. 521 (1949).
87. McKinney v. Missouri-Kansas-Texas R.R. Co., 357 U.S. 265 (1958).
88. Burke v. Boston Edison Co., 279 F. Supp. 853 (D. Mass. 1968).
89. Accardi v. Penn. R.R. Co., 383 U.S. 225 (1966)

Chapter 9

Wage And Hour Requirements

FEDERAL AND STATE LAWS

A body of federal and state laws and regulations, collectively called "wage-hour" law, establishes the minimum standards you must meet for the wages, hours, and other working conditions of your employees. In the federal sphere, the Fair Labor Standards Act (FLSA)[1] is by far the most important law and is emphasized in this chapter. You also should be aware, however, that:

- Wage-hour laws supplementing, and sometimes exceeding, the FLSA exist in almost every state.
- Health care institutions generally must comply with both the FLSA and state laws in states that have established their own requirements.
- The FLSA may be applicable even if your facility is a public employer.
- Institutions that sell goods or services to the government under certain circumstances may come under additional wage-hour, prevailing wage, or other specialized requirements.[2]
- Wage-hour law applies even if your facility has no collective bargaining agreements.
- If the employees you supervise are covered by such agreements, however, you must comply with whichever is the stricter standard: the provisions of the contract or of the law.

FAIR LABOR STANDARDS ACT (FLSA)

The FLSA, expressed in its simplest terms, has two principal wage-hour objectives: namely, employees covered by that law:

225

1. must be paid the current minimum wage
2. must be paid at one and a half times their regular rate when they work more than 40 hours in a week.

As simple as they sound, these straightforward concepts frequently create complex problems when you start applying them. Most of the complexity involves two major questions that have spawned intricate rules and even more intricate exceptions:

1. What is the employee's "regular rate" on which to base the overtime rate of time and one-half?
2. When is an employee considered to be "at work"?

The issues raised by these questions are too numerous and detailed to be covered comprehensively and accurately in this one chapter. Instead, the focus here is on the basic concepts you will encounter most frequently. Some recurring issues are discussed in greater detail in this chapter's Topics of Particular Significance. Beyond that, you should seek specialized guidance (from your personnel department, consultant, legal counsel, etc.) when you actually encounter specific wage-hour problems with employees you supervise.

Scope and Coverage

Private Hospitals and Nursing Homes

Your hospital or other "institution primarily engaged in the care of the sick, the aged, the mentally ill or defective who reside on the premises of such institution" is covered by the FLSA if it employs two or more employees who "handle" products (food, supplies, equipment, etc.) manufactured or produced out of state. Once this happens your entire hospital is covered.[3]

Note that in determining coverage, it does not matter how much business your hospital or nursing home does.[4] This means, practically speaking, that all private hospitals and nursing homes, and many other health care facilities, must comply with the FLSA regardless of size or type of ownership.

Public Hospitals

If you are employed by a federally operated hospital, your facility also is covered by the FLSA, as are most federal employees.[5] By contrast, and after the 1974 amendments extended coverage to the states, their political subdivisions, and most of their employees as well, a United States Supreme Court decision held that the FLSA's minimum wage and overtime provisions could not be extended to many nonfederal public employers. In particular, the Court found that these requirements could not be constitutionally applied to the integral operations of the states and their political subdivisions (e.g., counties, districts, municipalities) in areas of traditional governmental functions.[6] Some of the issues to note if your facility is a nonfederal public employer, therefore, are that:

- The Court held inapplicable only the FLSA's minimum wage and overtime provisions.
- The Age Discrimination Act, the FLSA prohibitions against discrimination for participating or assisting in FLSA enforcement proceedings, and probably the Equal Pay Act, continue to apply.[7]
- The Secretary of Labor has interpreted "areas of traditional governmental functions" as including, among others, hospitals and public health.[8]
- The facility must also establish that it is in a state or political subdivision before it can be exempted from the FLSA's minimum wage and overtime provisions.[9]

Enforcement

The FLSA is administered by the Wage and Hour Division (the Division) of the U.S. Department of Labor. The Division has offices in most major cities, each responsible for enforcing the Act in its own region.

Possible Enforcement Mechanisms

As an employer you could be faced with at least four types of actions if violations of the FLSA occur:

1. a suit in the name of the Secretary of Labor to collect unpaid minimum wages and overtime pay due employees and possibly an equal amount as liquidated damages
2. a suit by the Secretary on behalf of a group of employees for an injunction to force compliance with the law
3. a criminal prosecution instituted by the Justice Department against employers who "deliberately" violate the FLSA, with a fine of up to $10,000, imprisonment up to six months, or both
4. suits by individual employees for back wages, liquidated damages, and attorneys' fees and costs.[10]

Wage-Hour Claims and Investigations

Enforcement of a wage-hour claim generally begins with an investigation of your facility by a local office of the Wage-Hour Division. Such an investigation may be triggered by:

- an individual employee's complaint to the Division
- the Division's own decision to follow up on a previous investigation or audit
- a random spot check.

The Division is charged with investigating compliance with the FLSA through meetings with employers, reviewing their records, interviewing employees, and similar activities. The Division also can obtain subpoenaes to ensure access to an employer's records.

The Division normally begins its investigation with a conference in which records are requested, perhaps for just one particular work area. A representative of your facility may be asked to help by explaining the records. Private interviews may take place. A follow-up conference generally is held to let you know of the Division's findings. If back wages are claimed and asserted to be owing, the employer will be asked to work out how much is due and pay it.

If a claim is not settled during or after the investigation, then any suit to collect minimum wages, overtime pay, or liquidated damages generally must be brought within two years. In the case of a willful violation by the employer, however, a three-year period is allowed.

The Division normally phones or writes you in advance of its investigation but sometimes you will get very little advance notice. If the Division makes no advance contact, but the government employee simply appears at your facility without a subpoena and demands immediate cooperation with an investigation, your best course of action may be to ask for a brief opportunity to consult with legal counsel prior to allowing access to your records or the opportunity to interview personnel. Why? Because even though the Division has broad investigatory powers, they are not unlimited and can be challenged under appropriate circumstances. Therefore, time may be needed to consider whether the Division's request is valid, what it wants to investigate, and what records should be made available.

If the Division's agent refuses your request for an opportunity to consult with counsel and demands immediate entry, then whether or not the person has a subpoena, an appropriate response might be to allow access under protest and still call your attorney immediately. In such circumstances, the Division agent should be told that you are complying under protest only because the person is claiming the authority and right to conduct an onsite investigation.

Employees, Volunteers, Trainees, Independent Contractors

The FLSA does not come into play unless there is an employer-employee relationship and the status of a particular individual may be questionable. Is the individual an employee, a volunteer donating personal time for charitable reasons, a student-trainee learning a profession at your facility, or a contractor who is self-employed?

In reviewing the criteria discussed in this chapter to decide whether someone is an "employee," remember that, where there is doubt, the FLSA often is interpreted to favor an employer-employee relationship.

Volunteers

The first factor involving volunteers is the nature of the services performed. People who make a gift of their services by performing activities of a humanitarian, public service, or religious nature, or by serving in the area they can best help a health care facility, generally are not considered employees covered by the Act. In a hospital context, volunteer services involving ministering to the comfort of patients, such as providing reading material, reading to or playing with them in pediatric wards, and similar activities directly related to their comfort, relaxation, or entertainment generally would fall within this category.

Where employees wish to volunteer their services outside their normal duties, however, the donated time must be confined to ministering to the comfort of patients and similar activities. The exemption probably does not cover such deeds as folding bandages or acting as a receptionist.

Once "volunteers" are covered by the FLSA they have become "employees," and must be paid the minimum wage and receive the statutory overtime, if earned, etc.

These concepts were applied to a physician's wife who volunteered a few hours each week as a nurse, to a housewife who served as a secretary, and to a hospital office employee who volunteered her services to minister to the comfort of patients outside her regular working hours. All three individuals were considered to be performing services outside of the ambit of the Act; hence, they were not "employees."[11]

Another vital factor is the expectation of pay. If you want to make sure the individual remains a volunteer, the person must donate services without expecting any pay. For example, a conscientious objector, without expecting to be paid, volunteered his services to a nursing home for six months to fulfill military obligations. At the end of six months, he agreed to stay on at the home and work for only "nominal wages." The Wage-Hour Administrator said that the six-month period was exempt but the second period, since it contemplated some payment of wages, changed the volunteer into an employee.[12] The nursing home had to pay the "volunteer" the minimum wage and, of course, the overtime and equal pay provisions of the FLSA were applicable.

Members of religious orders, nuns, priests, lay brothers, ministers, deacons, and others whose religious duties require them to serve in hospitals operated by their church or order are not "employees." You should note that the exemption may fall away if the nun, etc., serves in a religious institution operated by another religious group.[13]

Trainees

Students in the health care field often receive on-the-job training in medical facilities as part of their education. These arrangements vary greatly and sometimes, even without your being aware of it, the student may begin to function very much like an "employee." If so, the FLSA may require the medical facility to treat the individual as an employee and to comply with the minimum wage, overtime, and other wage-hour requirements.

To aid in distinguishing between nonemployee and employee students, the factors used by the Department of Labor in enforcing the distinctions are guides. A person is not considered an employee if:

1. the training, even though it includes the actual operation of the employer's facilities, is similar to that given in a vocational school
2. the training benefits the trainees or the students
3. the students are not displacing regular employees but work under close observation
4. the employer gets no immediate advantage from the students' activities and on occasion the students actually are a burden
5. the students are not automatically assured of a job when they finish training
6. the employer and the students understand that the students are not entitled to wages for the time spent in training.[14]

However, a state wage-hour law may impose additional and more stringent criteria that also must be met to avoid a finding that the student is an employee. Moreover, a student may be a "student" for some purposes and an "employee" for others. For example, the student may not be an "employee" under state or federal wage-hour law for the payment of minimum wages yet be an "employee" or otherwise fall within a different statutory definition for purposes of determining entitlement to unemployment compensation and/or workers' compensation.[15]

These considerations mean that training programs require careful thought to make sure the applicable wage-hour criteria for establishing student status are met. The need for malpractice or other liability insurance, the students' exclusion from coverage by employee benefits and other terms and conditions, and similar factors also must be addressed when training is provided. In addition, assistance from the participating school may be critical: it is helpful to develop written standards for training within a department and to obtain the school's agreement to them and to the defined division of rights and obligations between the school and the hospital.

Independent Contractors

A medical facility offers and requires a multitude of varying services. Some of these are supplied by your facility directly (with your own employees) but others may be provided by a third party with its own employees, the so-called independent contractor. However, the third party's status as an independent employer may be challenged and, if this is successful, your employer may end up being obligated to pay minimum wage and overtime to the supposedly independent contractor and/ or to its employees.

This risk exists because your wage-hour obligations are not limited to the individuals you call employees. Instead, under FLSA as well as other legislation, employees are those who, as a matter of "economic reality," are dependent upon the business to which they render their services. Specific criteria have been developed to test this "economic reality," and one or more "no" answers to the following questions should alert you that further consideration may need to be given to determining whether your independent contractor actually is an employee for wage-hour purposes:

- Can the "contractor" decide how the services are to be provided?
- Does the individual (or the business entity) have a substantial investment in tools or equipment necessary for performing the job?
- Does the individual (or the business entity) undertake a substantial cost, such as employing and paying other employees?
- Is there an opportunity for the individual to profit or risk a loss, depending upon the third party's exercise of management skill?
- Are special or independent skills and judgments required to provide the service?
- Does the individual (or the business entity) provide services that normally are not an integral part of the medical facility's business?
- Does the individual (or the business entity) have a formally organized business that seeks work from facilities or businesses other than your own?[16]

For example, a third party that provides a linen service using its own fleet of trucks and its own employees is an independent contractor. A part-time employee of the medical facility who contracts to mend linen or repair hospital equipment by the individual's own labor on the individual's own time is not an independent contractor and must be paid the minimum wage and required overtime for such work. However, the question is a factual one and the whole relationship between the employer and employee must be examined. This means that the presence of some or all of the listed criteria may not decide the question conclusively.

Minimum Wage Requirements

The federal minimum wage for employees covered by the FLSA was increased to $3.35 an hour as of January 1, 1981.[17] This requirement looks quite simple but, as they say, appearances can be deceiving. In reality, it often is difficult to decide whether you are, in fact, paying the minimum wage:

- For example, if an employee is paid $x per week you can't simply divide $x by the scheduled hours to ascertain whether that rate is at least the minimum wage. Why not? Because you cannot determine compliance with the minimum wage obligation until you first compute the number of hours actually worked in accordance with the FLSA's definition of worktime.

- The situation of hourly paid employees sometimes (but not always) is simpler: if they are paid solely on an hourly rate basis, their rate may not fall below the law's minimum requirement. Yet even here, if you have not counted the hours that the FLSA considers to be worktime (for example, restricted on-call time), you could be paying less than the minimum wage and be committing other violations (such as not paying time and a half for overtime).

The danger in that second point is illustrated by the following example:

Suppose that a licensed practical nurse is paid $3.50 an hour for five eight-hour day shifts. For one night a week, you require the employee to sleep over at your facility from 11 p.m. to the start of the shift, without pay, to be available for immediate relief coverage. All of this "sleepover" time is "hours worked" for minimum wage and overtime purposes. As a result, the FLSA would say that the employee "worked" 48 hours but received only $2.92 an hour ($3.50 × 40 hours, or $140 pay divided by 48 hours of FLSA worktime), which is less than the minimum wage.

This example illustrates the danger of assuming that your facility is complying with its minimum wage obligations simply because the stated hourly pay equals or exceeds the minimum wage.

Permissible Deductions

As a general rule, wages must be paid in cash or in a "negotiable instrument payable at par," such as a check. As a major exception to this rule, an employer is allowed to deduct the reasonable cost of "board, lodging or other facilities," if these customarily are furnished to the employees.[18] The Division has ruled that "other facilities" means deductions for benefits that by their nature are like board or lodging: meals furnished by the employer, housing, general merchandise, fuel, electricity, water and gas, and transportation (if the travel time involves commuting to and from work and does not count as time worked under the FLSA).

The value of these deductions may be counted toward your minimum wage obligation if it is the custom to supply them. There is some uncertainty on this issue because the Wage and Hour Division and the courts disagree as to whether employees not only must receive the benefit of the facilities for which they are charged but also must be able to choose whether they want to accept them.[19]

In calculating whether you have paid the minimum wage, you cannot include credits for discounts you have allowed employees. The Division takes the view that in giving employees such favors, you simply are making the job more attractive by accommodating your work force.

Hours Worked

Under the FLSA, "work" has been interpreted very broadly to include physical or mental work, controlled or required by the employer, and pursued necessarily and primarily for the purpose of the employer and its business.[20] The Wage and Hour Division has expanded even further upon the definition (emphasis added):

> Work not requested but *suffered* or *permitted* is worktime. For example, an employee may voluntarily continue to work at the end of a shift. He may be a pieceworker, he may desire to finish an assigned task or he may wish to correct errors, paste work tickets, prepare time reports or other records. The reason is immaterial. *The employer knows or has reason to believe that he is continuing to work and the time is working time.*[21]

Notwithstanding the breadth of the worktime definition, however, there are exclusions; e.g., under certain circumstances employee activities performed prior to or after the "work" (called preliminary or postliminary activities) and time that employees are relieved of duty and can use primarily for their own purposes (uncontrolled standby) is nonworktime. These and a number of other specific worktime and nonworktime issues common to the health care industry are discussed in Topics of Particular Significance.

Overtime Provisions

In health care facilities, the federal overtime pay requirement is based on a 40-hour workweek, or on an 80-hour biweekly pay period, and an 8-hour day.

One of the major features of the FLSA is the basic workweek of 40 hours. Work in excess of 40 hours in any workweek must be paid for at one and a half times the employee's regular rate of pay.[22] The exception to this rule is the "8 and 80" option that is available to hospitals and to other facilities primarily engaged in caring for the sick, infirm, aged, or mentally retarded who reside on the premises:[23]

- The 8 and 80 option requires that overtime be paid for the greater of the number of hours of work in excess of 80 hours in a biweekly pay period of

14 calendar days (rather than in excess of 40 hours) or the number of work hours in excess of 8 in a day.[24]

- The 8 and 80 must be the result of an agreement or understanding between the employee (or the employee's representative) and the employer entered into prior to the performance of work.[25]

- This requirement of an understanding or agreement is satisfied where an employee accepts payment of wages without objection after there is a bulletin board notice or payroll insert stating that overtime will be figured on a 14-day period in accordance with the FLSA.[26] Any such notice provided through these or other methods, however, should set out the system in detail and refer to the specific provisions of the FLSA.

There also are a number of things that the FLSA does not require. For example:

- The FLSA does *not* require overtime after a minimum number of hours in a day, if you are using the 40-hour workweek as the basis for overtime pay.
- The FLSA does not require any overtime to be paid at a double-time rate.
- The FLSA does not require any overtime premium for work performed on the sixth or seventh day of a workweek, holidays, Saturdays, or Sundays, unless such work causes the total weekly hours to exceed 40 (or 80, under the 8 and 80 option).

What Is a Workweek and Workday?

An employee's workweek is any fixed and regularly recurring period of 168 hours—seven consecutive 24-hour periods. It need not be Monday through Sunday but may begin on any day and at any hour of the day. Once established, however, it remains fixed and may be altered only if the change is permanent and is not an attempt to evade the FLSA's overtime provisions.[27] Similarly, under the 8 and 80 option, a 14-day (or biweekly) pay period consists of 14 consecutive 24-hour workdays (or two workweeks), and the first workday starts when the 14-day period begins, and ends 24 hours later.[28]

What Is the Regular Rate?

Overtime pay must be at the rate of one-and-a-half times an employee's "regular rate." This regular rate is an hourly rate but it is not the same as the stated hourly rate of pay for that classification. Instead, the FLSA effectively divides all employee wages or other compensation into three categories:

1. Amounts that must be included (or added to any employee's stated wage rate) to determine the regular rate of pay upon which overtime must be paid

include "all remuneration for employment" except for certain exclusions set forth in the FLSA itself.[29] Examples of amounts included are wages, salaries, commissions, bonuses, incentives, and differentials (e.g., shift differentials, etc.).

2. Amounts that are excluded from an employee's regular rate of pay calculation but that cannot be credited toward overtime compensation are, for example, monies paid as gifts or discretionary bonuses; payments for vacations, sick leave, holidays, and other "occasional periods when no work is performed"; employer contributions for fringe benefits such as health insurance and pensions; and certain profit-sharing, thrift, or savings plans.[30]

3. Amounts that can be excluded from an employee's regular rate of pay calculation but that can be credited toward overtime compensation include: premium rates for hours of work in excess of eight in a day or 40 in a week (or in excess of normal or regular working hours); time and a half premium rates for work on Saturdays, Sundays, holidays, the sixth or seventh day in a week, or regular day of rest; and time and a half rates for work outside an established normal workday or workweek.[31]

Calculating an employee's regular rate for a particular week or pay period can be an intricate exercise and almost every rule has an exception or a qualification. So, again, it must be emphasized that specific knowledge of FLSA requirements and the explanatory guidelines and regulations of the Wage and Hour Division is essential. Moreover, an employee's regular rate of pay for overtime purposes can vary from week to week (or pay period to pay period), depending on hours worked and other includable forms of compensation the person receives.

Thus, the moral is: be aware that (1) overtime is paid at one and a half times the employee's regular rate of pay (not just the employee's stated hourly rate), and (2) unless you are skilled in this area, do not attempt to make the calculations yourself.

Exemptions from Minimum Wage and Overtime

There are three so-called "white collar" exemptions from the minimum wage and overtime requirements of the FLSA: executive, professional, and administrative. The exemption analysis in Appendix 9–A can aid in determining whether individuals are exempt employees.

However, whether or not they are exempt (not covered by FLSA's minimum wage and overtime requirements), remember: there are no exemptions from the equal pay provisions of the Act, which require that all employees, without regard to sex, be paid the same for equal work. Thus, even if an employee is exempt under the professional, administrative, or executive category, your facility still must ensure that the individual receives equal pay for equal work, regardless of sex, and regardless of the position.

Also remember that the Wage and Hour Division does not give blanket exemptions to any group or class of employees since the factual determination of exempt status requires an individual evaluation. Nevertheless, the Division has given some guidance for determining whether an employee may be exempt as a professional, provided the individual meets the other requirements. The educational and advanced knowledge requirements are satisfied in the professions of medicine, registered nursing, accounting, engineering, pharmacy, teaching, and various physical, chemical, and biological sciences such as medical technology.

Thus, even though the mandatory course of study has become shortened, nurses who are registered by the appropriate state examining board are recognized as professionals under the regulations.[32] The Division's regulations provide further examples of the kinds of activities engaged in by individuals qualifying for administrative, executive, or professional exempt status, and the definitions for terms used in Appendix 9–A.[33]

EQUAL PAY ACT

Scope and Coverage

In 1963, the FLSA was amended to include what has become known as the Equal Pay Act. Congress stated the purpose very simply: "The bill would add one additional fair labor standard to the Act; namely, that employees doing equal work should be paid equal wages, regardless of sex."[34]

As a result of this Act, it is unlawful for an employer to pay wages "at a rate less than the rate at which it pays wages to employees of the opposite sex in such establishment for equal work on jobs, the performance of which requires equal skill, effort, and responsibility, and which are performed under similar working conditions."[35] Key issues in the Equal Pay Act are:

- "Skill," "effort," "responsibility," and "working conditions" are the critical words. Where these are substantially equal, the rate of pay also must be equal. .
- No employee is exempt from the Equal Pay Act. The professional, executive, and administrative exemptions from the FLSA apply only to its minimum wage and overtime requirements. This means that employers must reward equal work with equal pay at all levels.
- The FLSA minimum wage and overtime provisions, as noted in the earlier discussion of FLSA coverage, do not apply to most health care facilities operated by the states and their political subdivisions. The Wage and Hour

Division and most federal courts, however, continue to take the position that the Equal Pay Act still is applicable to such employers.[36]

• The administrative enforcement of the Equal Pay Act was transferred in 1979 to the Equal Employment Opportunity Commission (EEOC).

What is Equal Work?

In deciding whether male or female employees are doing equal work, you should examine the jobs' "skill, effort, and responsibility" and the similarity of the working conditions. You must scrutinize a job as a whole and ignore insignificant differences. For example:

• *Equal Skill* involves the experience, training, education, and ability needed to do the job; by contrast, the efficiency of the individual employee's performance is not, by itself, considered relevant.[37]

• *Equal Effort* measures the physical or mental exertion needed to do the job. Differences limited to the way the job is performed are not enough to justify variances in wage rates. If an employer argues that one job is different from another because it requires more effort, the additional effort must be significant.[38] To illustrate: a hospital in New Orleans paid its female aides less than the male orderlies. It successfully defended its action by arguing that its different pay rates were not based on sex since they were not paid for equal work. Specifically, the employer established that: (1) extra effort was required of the male orderlies, (2) the extra duties represented a significant proportion of the worktime of the employees receiving the additional pay (i.e., the extra effort was not limited to some of the employees receiving the additional pay), and (3) the extra tasks had a dollar value in keeping with the wage differential received.[39]

• *Responsibility* is concerned with the degree of accountability required in the performance of the job. Sometimes the responsibility is only potential or temporary. For example, two employees may have similar responsibilities but one of the jobs may require that the employee also relieve the regular supervisor during that person's normal absences (days off, vacations, attendance at meetings and outside functions, etc.). Payment of a differential to a male relief supervisor in these circumstances would not violate the Act.[40] Of course, however, the differential would have to be paid to both males and females who occupied such a position.

Even if it can be established that jobs are of equal skill, effort, and responsibility, they still must be performed under "similar working conditions" and in the same establishment before Equal Pay Act questions arise.

- *Similar working conditions* is a practical question: Are the differences in working conditions the kind you normally would take into consideration in setting wage levels? Thus, jobs in different departments may have the "similar" working conditions. Some factors might be: inside vs. outside work, exposure to heat, cold, wetness, humidity, noise, vibration, hazards (risk of bodily injury), fumes, odors, toxic conditions, dust, and poor ventilation.[41]

- *Same establishment* arises because the same employer may have different establishments. Generally speaking, an "establishment" for these purposes is a physically distinct place of business; this means that different plants in separate locations operated by a single employer generally would be different establishments.[42]

STATE WAGE-HOUR LAWS

Scope and Coverage

You must constantly be aware of any relevant state wage-hour provisions applicable to your facility since they often differ from the federal requirements and compliance with one will not excuse noncompliance with the other. Instead, as noted earlier, the law most favorable to the employee will apply.

The states have wide variations in how they regulate minimum wages, maximum hours, and the manner in which wages are paid. For example, some states, such as California, Connecticut, and New York, have rules governing many employer-employee issues covering a variety of different industries. At the other end of the scale, Mississippi has no minimum wage law and, except for factory employees, no maximum hour or overtime provisions for adult workers.

Between these two extremes is a patchwork of state wage and hour laws, sometimes covering employees ignored by federal regulation, sometimes covering areas where federal law is silent, and sometimes simply duplicating or falling short of the federal requirements.

Determining what your facility's obligations are under state law often is difficult. This is because state wage and hour laws frequently are scattered among various statutes, wage orders, regulations, and interpretative memoranda. Moreover, only a few states, such as Washington, Oregon, and Wisconsin, have minimum wage orders applicable to employees in all industries; most other states regulating minimum wage do so on an industry-by-industry basis.

The FLSA specifically provides that where a state law or municipal ordinance establishes a higher minimum wage or a shorter maximum workweek, the more stringent state requirements apply.[43] This is reflection of the general rule that where your facility is covered by more than one law, you normally must conform to the one most favorable to the employee.

Daily Overtime

As noted earlier, the FLSA simply provides that work in excess of 40 hours must receive an overtime premium. Federal law has no maximum hours of work in a day unless an 8 and 80 is in effect, when overtime must be paid after eight hours.

Even if your facility does not use the 8 and 80, check whether your state's wage and hour law has a daily overtime provision. Most states follow the FLSA and simply provide for overtime after 40 hours in one week. However, some states, such as California, require that work in excess of eight hours in any one day receive premium compensation at one and a half times the regular rate of pay whether or not an 8 and 80 is in effect. And some states, again such as California, require that double time be paid after 12 (or other specified number of hours) in a single workday.

Payment of Wages Due

Almost every state regulates the way wages are paid. Such laws typically provide that:

- Wages must be paid at stated intervals (usually semimonthly).
- Wages may be sent by mail or paid at the employees' normal place of employment during normal work hours.
- All wages earned must be paid within a specified period from the date of termination.
- Wages must be paid in United States currency or with a check or similar instrument drawn on an account within the state.
- Unpaid wages may be recovered by the state labor commissioner or similar state official on behalf of employees.
- Deductions cannot be made from an employee's paycheck for purchases from the employer or other prohibited purposes.
- Kickbacks to an employer are illegal.

TOPICS OF PARTICULAR SIGNIFICANCE

What Are 'Hours Worked'?

Knowing whether a certain activity is or is not FLSA "hours worked" is critical for two reasons. First, if it is not hours worked, then you can choose to pay or not pay without fear of violating the Act. For example, if one of your employees works uncontrolled standby (see below), then the person need be paid no additional compensation, half time, "*x*" dollars, or any other appropriate arrangement.

Second, if it is work hours, then it must be compensated but you also must include these hours when calculating overtime. For example, assume the employee works 40 hours a week and once a week is on controlled standby from 7 p.m. to 7 a.m. These additional 12 hours would be worktime, and since the employee now has "worked" 52 hours in that week, 12 hours must be paid for as overtime at one and a half times the employee's regular rate.

Hours worked issues that arise frequently in a health care setting are discussed next.

Waiting Time. The general principle holds that when an employee is "engaged to wait," it is worktime and must be paid for as such; if the employee is simply "waiting to be engaged," however, then these are not work hours. The Division's regulations[44] indicate that this bureaucratic jargon generally means the following:

Waiting can be an integral part of a job. For example, the x-ray technician who waits 15 minutes for the next patient to come in, the operating room nurse who waits for a room to become available so the next procedure can start, the medical transcriber who has to wait for dictation to be returned, etc., generally are still "on duty." While they may not have duties to perform at that time, their instances of inactivity are unpredictable and they have been "engaged to wait" under those circumstances.

Employees are "waiting to be engaged" when they have been relieved of duty or simply are waiting to start work at a specified hour and have sufficient time to use it effectively for their own purposes. That time is not compensable as work hours unless the employer has contractually obliged itself to pay for it. For example, an ambulance driver is sent to another town to pick up a patient, leaves at 8 a.m., returns with the patient at noon, is relieved of all duty until 4 p.m., when the patient will be returned to the other town. The four hours between noon and 4 p.m. generally should not be worktime. By contrast, if the driver arrives back at 4 p.m., as scheduled, and has to wait for an hour while the patient is being prepared for the return trip, the hour between 4 and 5 o'clock is worktime (i.e., the employee has been "engaged to wait").

The factual circumstances surrounding the activity that must be evaluated to determine whether the time is worktime include:

- how long a time the employee is relieved of duty
- whether the time effectively can be used for the employee's own purposes
- whether waiting is an integral part of the job and the nature of the job
- whether there are any understandings, agreements, or arrangements between the employer and employee or employee representative, and what they require
- whether employees have been told they are relieved of duty and when they are to report back for work

- whether employees may leave the employer's premises or the jobsite if the activity is performed away from such premises.

Standby Time. Standby time and whether it is controlled (worktime, and thus compensable) or uncontrolled (not worktime and compensation not statutorily required) involve issues similar to those just discussed. The key issue here, however, is whether employees are free to use the time for their own purposes.

- If the employee is required to remain on call on your premises, or so close to your premises that the time cannot really be used for the person's own purposes, then the employee is "working" while "on call," and the on-call hours must be counted as hours worked. This is called "controlled standby."
- If the employee, on the other hand, can leave the premises and simply has to leave a telephone number where the individual can be reached, this generally is uncontrolled standby, not hours worked.[45]

Essentially, time spent on call will not be considered hours worked where the procedure for contacting the employees, the required response time, and the frequency of calls allow them to engage in other activities of their own choosing.

In an early case, a rural hospital required an employee on standby to stay within 20 minutes' traveling time of the facility. Because of the nature of the rural locale, the employee was considered able to go freely about his own business and the time was uncontrolled standby, not hours worked. Yet because each case must be considered separately, the potential exists that in other circumstances the same requirement could be considered too restrictive, thereby requiring that the standby time be counted as hours of work.[46]

Rest Period. Short rest periods of 5 minutes to 20 minutes make an employee more efficient, according to the Wage and Hour Division, and where an employer provides them, they must be paid for as hours worked.[47] The FLSA does not require that there be rest periods, only that if they are given, they be counted as time worked. Here again, however, your state law may have specific rules. For example, some states require employers to give rest periods of 10 minutes, or "*x*" minutes, during every half shift, or on some other basis. So if your state laws, or your facility's personnel policies, do require rest periods, then federal law will insist that they be compensated for as worktime.

Meals. Bona fide meal periods are not hours worked; however, they do not include coffee breaks, time for snacks, or even a short break called a meal period, since all of those are considered rest periods. Instead, and to qualify as a meal period:

1. The employee must be completely relieved from duty for the purpose of eating a regular meal; this means that when a night shift nurse is required to

eat at the nurse's station and watch for call lights, etc., the entire period is counted as hours worked.

2. The meal period ordinarily must last 30 minutes or more.
3. Employees must be free to leave their work station; however, they can be confined to your facility's premises if the remaining requirements just described are met.[48]

The issue of meal periods (and rest breaks) is extensively regulated by state wage-hour laws so check these requirements as well as do not assume that they are identical to the FLSA's standards.

Residing on Employer's Premises. Employees who reside at your premises are not "working" all of the time they are on the premises if they can use some of the time for their own purposes (eating, sleeping, personal activities of their own choosing, etc.) and if they can leave for personal reasons. While any reasonable agreement of the parties will be accepted,[49] practical and legal difficulties can arise when it becomes necessary to interpret your agreement. Therefore, make sure that any such arrangement between your facility and an employee clearly states when the person is at work and, more importantly, what constitutes the employee's own time.

Preparatory and Concluding Activities. The general rule is: time spent at the beginning or end of the workday (on the facility's premises or at the worksite) in putting on or changing clothes or similar activity is hours worked if it is really part of the employee's principal activity—e.g., putting on sterile garments for work in a sterile environment. Of course, as usually is the case, there is an exception: even where these are part of your employee's principal activity, a specific term, custom, or practice under a collective bargaining agreement can convert these activities back into nonworktime.

Furthermore, these activities are not worktime if they are performed simply for the employee's convenience and are not directly related to the individual's principal activity. Then again, these same activities may become worktime if a collective bargaining agreement, custom, or practice under such an agreement views it as worktime.[50]

Travel Time. Time traveling to and from work generally is not hours worked. This is because the Portal-to-Portal Act (amending the FLSA) specifically provides that time spent in walking, riding, or traveling to and from the actual place of performing the employee's principal activity is not compensable as hours worked unless required by an existing collective bargaining contract, custom, or practice. Yet time spent traveling during the course of the workday as a part of the employee's principal activity will be considered hours worked.[51]

Beyond these simple statements, the situation becomes more complex—for example, employees who must travel out of town on emergency callbacks, etc. While resolving these issues is beyond the scope of this manual, care should be taken, if you actually come across such situations, to make sure that an advance determination is made as to whether or not they constitute worktime.

Lectures, Meetings, and Training Programs. These types of programs are not worktime if all four of the following conditions exist:

1. Attendance is outside the employee's regular working hours.
2. Attendance is voluntary, and this really means voluntary: any understanding that failure to attend will be considered adversely by your employer destroys the voluntary aspect.
3. The course is not related directly to the employee's present job. Training is directly related to the job if it is designed to make the employee more efficient. By contrast, a training course designed to equip the employee for a higher level job is not "directly related," even though it incidentally improves the individual's skills in doing the present work. Of course, if employees, on their own initiative, decide to take courses after hours at some outside institution, this will not be hours worked even though the training is directly related to their work.
4. The employees perform no productive work for your facility during their attendance.[52]

The Wage-Hour Division also has indicated that special situations may exist where training programs will not be worktime even though all of those factors are not present:

> As an example, an employer may establish for the benefit of his employees a program of instruction which corresponds to courses offered by independent bona fide institutions of learning. Voluntary attendance by an employee at such courses outside of working hours would not be hours worked even if they are directly related to his job, or paid for by the employer.[53]

Adjusting Grievances. Time spent in adjusting grievances during the hours when employees are required to be on the premises is hours worked. On the other hand, if a union is involved, this question will depend on the collective bargaining agreement or customs or practices under the contract.[54]

Medical Attention. As phrased by the Division, this involves: "Time spent by an employee in waiting for and receiving medical attention on the premises or at the direction of the employer during the employee's normal working hours on days when he is working constitutes hours worked."[55] This means, for example, that if you ask employees to report to employee health during their shift to see a physician for an injury, etc., that will be paid worktime.

Reporting Time Pay. The FLSA does not require that an employee receive some or any minimum payment for reporting to work when no work is available. However, state wage-hour provisions frequently do require such pay, and you may have a collective bargaining agreement that covers this issue.

Sleeping Time. It is not unusual, in a health care setting, for an employee to be "on duty" for prolonged periods during which there is sleeping time, so the question arises, "is this worktime?" For an answer, first check whether the employee is on duty for less than 24 consecutive hours.

If the employee is required to be on duty less than 24 consecutive hours, the sleeping time always must be counted as hours worked. An example given by the Division is the telephone operator who must be on duty through the night but is allowed to sleep when not answering calls. Even if you provide a place to sleep, the entire period is worktime.[56]

If, on the other hand, the employee is on duty for more than 24 hours, there may be a different conclusion:

1. You and your employee may agree in advance (which should be properly documented) to exclude a properly scheduled sleeping period of not more than eight hours.
2. The entire eight hours may be excluded from the employee's hours worked as long as you provide a proper place to sleep and the individual, in fact, usually has an uninterrupted sleep.
3. The maximum you may exclude is eight hours even if you allow the employee more than eight hours of sleeping time.
4. An interruption in the employee's sleep by a call to duty must be counted as hours worked, although the rest of the eight hours still can be excluded.
5. The entire period must be counted as hours worked if the period of sleep is interrupted so continuously and frequently that the employee cannot be guaranteed a "reasonable night's sleep."[57]

Compensatory Time Off

Federal law has no specific provisions for compensatory time off (CTO). This does not mean that CTO is illegal but it does mean that it must be taken within the same pay period (a seven-day or 14-day pay period under an 8 and 80 hour option, whichever is applicable) as the overtime worked.

For example, suppose you are on the 8 and 80 option and your employee works 44 hours the first week of the pay period (three 8-hour days and two 10-hour days), then works only 34 hours the second week and is paid for 80 hours. Although the employee has "earned" four hours' overtime for the two 10-hour days, no overtime need be paid. Why? Because the employee received, in fact, six CTO hours the second week in compensation for the four hours of daily overtime worked the preceding week. Thus, the employee was compensated at a rate that exceeded time and a half and it was within the same pay period as the one during which the overtime hours were worked.

Recordkeeping

This is an area where you, as a supervisor in the health care industry, have an important, continuing responsibility:

While the FLSA does not dictate that records be kept in any particular manner, or that time clocks or timecards be used, the records must be accurate. It is difficult to overemphasize the importance of keeping clear, accurate, and presentable records in compliance with the wage-hour laws. There are at least three good reasons why:

1. Failure to maintain accurate records is a violation of law.
2. Accurate records are vital to protect against an employee's claims that the Act was violated.
3. The maintenance of records known to be false could render your facility liable to prosecution under the False Information Act, which contains penalties even heavier than those under the FLSA.[58]

Information To Be Kept

The Wage and Hour Division requires that the employer's records contain the following for each employee covered by the minimum wage and overtime provisions of the Act:

1. the employee's name (the same name as is used for Social Security) and any identifying symbol or number used in lieu of the employee's name on any time, work, or payroll record—all on the same document
2. the employee's home address, including ZIP code; date of birth, if under 19; sex, which may be shown by use of a prefix such as Mr., Mrs., Miss or Ms.); and occupation
3. the time of day and day of week in which the employee's workweek begins (if your employer has established one workweek, e.g., Monday through Sunday, for all employees, some simple note to that effect is sufficient but if different workweeks exist for individuals or groups of employees, a separate notation must be kept for each person or group)
4. the regular hourly rate of pay, the basis on which wages are paid, and the amount and nature of each payment excluded from the regular rate (section 7(e) of the Act lists exclusions from the regular rate, such as gifts, time-and-a-half premium pay for Saturday, Sunday, and holiday work, vacation time, etc.)

5. the hours worked each workday and total hours worked each workweek
6. the total daily or weekly straight-time earnings
7. the total weekly premium pay for overtime
8. the total additions to or deductions from wages paid each pay period (employers also must maintain individual employee accounts showing the dates, amounts, and nature of the additions and deductions)
9. the total wages paid each pay period
10. the date of payment and the pay period it covers
11. a copy of the agreement or understanding if the 8 and 80 option is in effect and, if the agreement is not in writing, a memorandum summarizing its terms and showing the date it was entered into and the period for which it remains in effect.[59]

The Division's regulations also provide that:

1. The first three categories of information listed above are to be kept for exempt employees (professional, executive, administrative, or combination).[60]
2. Sufficient information must be kept concerning exempt employee compensation to permit making a determination of the employee's total compensation (salary and benefits) for each pay period.[61]
3. Notices prescribed by the Division are to be posted by employers of nonexempt employees.[62]
4. Records must be kept for three or two years, depending on their nature.[63]

Failure To Keep Accurate Records

Aside from the requirements of the FLSA, clear and accurate records are of immense value to an employer in defending wage claims. No less an authority than the United States Supreme Court has warned employers who fail to keep proper and accurate records that employees will not be denied recovery simply because they cannot show exactly how much worktime was not properly compensated. Instead, courts will allow employees to "prove" the amount and extent of their work without much difficulty so the burden then shifts to the employer to contradict this evidence.[64]

The message is clear. To avoid being placed in such an embarrassing and vulnerable position, you must ensure that accurate and presentable records are kept, covering at least the items specified in the regulations.

Lastly, and as always, be aware of any independent state recordkeeping laws that apply to your facility. As noted earlier, these state laws often go further than the FLSA so compliance with federal law may not be enough.

Uniforms

The term "uniform" generally is defined as wearing apparel and accessories of a distinctive design, color, or quality. Under this definition, therefore:

If you simply insist that employees wear a common form of dress, e.g., light shirt and dark pants or skirt, this normally is not viewed as requiring that they provide their own uniforms. Similarly, a nurse's white uniform, because it is so common and interchangeable, may not be a uniform for wage-hour purposes although a "pastel shade only" requirement might be.[65]

Under federal law, a hospital or other health care facility can require its employees to wear a specified type of uniform at the employees' own expense. But where you impose such a requirement, and employees must provide actual uniforms, the main wage-hour problem is that you must ensure that the uniform's cost and the time and expense of maintaining them do not reduce the employees' wages below the statutory minimum. If that occurs, the following guidelines[66] would apply:

- If employees purchase the uniforms themselves, you must reimburse them the next payday to the extent that the cost reduces their income below the minimum wage. You cannot reimburse the employees over a series of pay periods.
- If you supply the uniforms, you may deduct from the employees' next paycheck the portion of the costs that would not reduce their wage below the statutory minimum.

For example, assume that the minimum wage applicable to a certain employee for a 40-hour workweek is $134, and that the employee actually is paid $150 a week. If the cost of the uniform is $40 and the employee is paid weekly, the employer would be permitted to deduct no more than $16 a week since a larger amount would reduce the wage below the $134 that is the statutory minimum. It also is permissible, however, to prorate the total cost of $40 over a series of pay periods provided that in each period the employee receives at least the minimum wage. In this example, the employer could deduct, say, $10 a week for four weeks without violating the minimum wage.

The same basic principles are applicable to laundry costs. You can insist that employees pay for their own laundry as long as these costs do not reduce their wage below the minimum. If they do, your employer must reimburse the employees for the difference. Where there is no agreement between your facility and employees as to the value of such laundry costs, the Wage and Hour Division would accept $3.35 a week or 67 cents daily (one hour a week at the minimum wage) as reasonable laundry costs for maintaining a uniform. If either party can show clearly that the actual costs are higher or lower, then the actual cost—not the Division's opinion—may apply.[67]

These are simplified examples; in a real situation, other facts may require different considerations or conclusions. This is particularly true since the area of uniforms frequently is the topic of a state law that may or may not prohibit employers from requiring employees to provide them. Your state's law must be checked before any such requirement is imposed.

Employee Waiver of FLSA Rights

If you have paid less than the minimum wage or otherwise violate the FLSA, you cannot say that the employee agreed to your actions and use that as a defense. Both the Division and the courts agree that public interest and an employer's stronger bargaining position prohibit any such waiver of rights.

This means, for example, that if employees ask for an extra day off a month from now and in exchange want to work overtime today without pay, you cannot agree. And if you do agree, the employees—if they subsequently claimed overtime pay—would be entitled to such pay for the actual overtime hours.

Alternative Hours of Work Arrangements

Since the FLSA does not require daily overtime after eight hours of work (unless your facility is on an 8 and 80 option), it is possible to structure a variety of alternative workweeks calling for more work hours per day, but fewer workdays a week, so long as overtime is paid after 40 hours. Again, however, state law may limit or regulate these variations. As an example, California permits an employer to agree with employees on a regularly scheduled week of four 10-hour days (the 4-10 workweek) with daily overtime payable for the 11th and subsequent hours in a day.[68]

Alternative workweeks often are attractive (at least initially) to employees, but take care: any such options must be carefully slotted into the FLSA. You may find that the 8 and 80 are incompatible with a state option or with wage-hour requirements and that one or the other will have to be dropped.

NOTES

1. 29 U.S.C. §§ 201–219.

2. For example, facilities contracting with the federal government to provide services in excess of $2,500 "through the use of service employees," a definition that excludes persons meeting the FLSA definitions of administrative, executive, or professional employees, generally are subject to prevailing wage, prevailing fringe benefit, safety, health, and other requirements imposed by the Service Contract Act of 1965, 41 U.S.C. §§ 351–58. Other federal legislation includes, among others, the Walsh-Healey Public Contracts Act, 41 U.S.C. §§ 35–45 (applicable to federal government contracts for the

manufacture or supply of articles where the cost exceeds $10,000), and the Davis-Bacon Act, 40 U.S.C. §§ 276a–a5 (applicable to mechanics or laborers engaged in public construction or public works in excess of $2,000). In addition, state legislation may be pertinent to state contracts, grants, etc. Thus, consultation with counsel is highly recommended whenever contracts with or the sale or provision of goods or services to any governmental entity is involved.

3. 29 U.S.C. §§ 203(s), 206–07.

4. 29 U.S.C. § 203(s)(1), (5).

5. 29 U.S.C. § 203(d), (e)(1) and (2).

6. National League of Cities v. Usery, 426 U.S. 833 (1976).

7. Wage-Hour Interpretive Bulletin, 29 C.F.R. § 775.2(e) and the cites contained therein; *see infra* note 35.

8. 29 C.F.R. § 775.2(a).

9. Richland County Ass'n for Retarded Citizens v. Marshall, 660 F.2d 388 (9th Cir. 1981), *vacated,* 454 U.S. 389 (1982) (vacated because appellate court lacked jurisdiction).

10. 29 U.S.C. § 216.

11. Wage-Hour Opinion Letter, No. 626, LAB. L. REP. (CCH) ¶ 30616 (June 28, 1967).

12. Wage-Hour Opinion Letter, No. 1240, LAB. L. REP. (CCH) ¶ 30,826 (Dec. 27, 1972).

13. *Id.*

14. Field Operations Handbook of the Wage and Hour Division, § 10611(b) (1980).

15. *E.g.*, Einstein Med. Center v. Labor Bd., 87 L.R.R.M. (BNA) 2778 (1974).

16. *See, e.g.*, Wage-Hour Opinion Letter, No. 476, LAB. REL. REP. (BNA) WHM 91:463 (October 19, 1978).

17. 29 U.S.C. § 206(a)(1).

18. 29 U.S.C. § 203(m); 29 C.F.R. Part 531.

19. Davis Brothers, Inc. v. Donovan, 700 F.2d 1368 (11th Cir. 1983); *contra,* 29 C.F.R. §531.30 (essential that the employee give voluntary and uncoerced agreement).

20. Tennessee Coal, Iron & Railroad Co. v. Muscoda Local No. 123, 321 U.S. 590 (1944).

21. 29 C.F.R. § 785.11.

22. 29 U.S.C. § 207(a).

23. 29 U.S.C. § 207(j).

24. *Id.*

25. 29 C.F.R. § 778.601.

26. Wage-Hour Opinion Letter, No. 663, LAB. L. REP. (CCH) ¶ 30,656 (September 22, 1967), and No. 597, LAB. L. REP. (CCH) ¶ 30,586 (April 21, 1967).

27. 29 C.F.R. § 778.105.

28. 29 C.F.R. § 778.601(d).

29. 29 U.S.C. § 207(e).

30. 29 U.S.C. § 207(e),(h); 29 C.F.R. § 778.108, §§ 778.201–.224.

31. *Id.*

32. 29 C.F.R. § 541.302(e)(1).

33. 29 C.F.R. §§ 541.99–.119 (executive); 29 C.F.R. § 541.201–.215 (administrative); and 29 C.F.R. § 541.301–.315 (professional).

34. 1963 U.S. CODE CONG. AND AD. NEWS (88 Star.) 688 (1963).

35. 29 U.S.C. § 206(d)(1).

36. *See, e.g.*, Usery v. Alleghany County Instit. Dist., 544 F.2d 148 (3d Cir. 1976); *cert. denied*, 430 U.S. 946 (1977); Pearce v. Wichita County, 590 F.2d 128 (5th Cir. 1979) (finding state hospital subject to EPA); 29 C.F.R. § 775.2(a).

37. 29 C.F.R. § 800.125.

38. 29 C.F.R. § 800.127.

39. Hodgson v. Brookhaven Gen. Hosp., 486 F.2d 719 (5th Cir. 1970).

40. 29 C.F.R. § 800.129, .130.

41. 29 C.F.R. §§ 800.131, .132.

42. 29 C.F.R. § 800.108.

43. 29 U.S.C. § 218.

44. 29 C.F.R. §§ 785.14–.16.

45. 29 C.F.R. § 785.17; *see also*, Walter Allen v. United States, 96 Lab. Cas. (CCH) ¶ 34,324 (Ct. Cl., 1983) (uncontrolled standby: stay within range of beeper, maintain log of calls, remain sober); Wage-Hour Opinion Letter, No. 995, LAB. L. REP. (CCH) ¶ 30,542 (May 28, 1969) (uncontrolled standby: carrying bellboy device).

46. Wage-Hour Opinion Letter, No. 856, LAB. L. REP. (CCH) ¶ 30,862 (August 14, 1968).

47. 29 C.F.R. § 785.18.

48. 29 C.F.R. § 785.19.

49. 29 C.F.R. § 785.23.

50. 29 U.S.C. §§ 203(o), 254; 29 C.F.R. §§ 785.9, 785.24–.26.

51. 29 U.S.C. § 254; 29 C.F.R. §§ 758.33–.41.

52. 29 C.F.R. §§ 785.27–.32.

53. 29 C.F.R. § 785.31.

54. 29 C.F.R. § 785.42.

55. 29 C.F.R. § 785.43.

56. 29 C.F.R. § 785.21.

57. 29 C.F.R. § 785.22.

58. 18 U.S.C. § 1001; *see* U.S. v. Moore, 185 F.2d 921 (5th Cir. 1950).

59. 29 C.F.R. §§ 516.1–516.2.

60. 29 C.F.R. § 516.3.

61. *Id.*

62. 29 C.F.R. § 516.4.

63. 29 C.F.R. §§ 516.5–516.6.

64. Anderson v. Mt. Clemens Pottery Co., 328 U.S. 680, 687 (1946).

65. *E.g.*, California Industrial Welfare Commission, Order No. 5–80.

66. Wage-Hour Opinion Letter, No. 392 LAB. L. REP. (BNA) WHM 95:142 (1976); Wage-Hour Opinion Letter, No. 422, LAB. L. REP. (BNA) WHM 95:143 (July 1, 1977); *see generally*, 29 C.F.R. § 531.3(d).

67. Wage-Hour Opinion Letter, No. 1326, LAB. L. REP. (CCH) ¶ 30,932 (May 7, 1974); Wage-Hour Opinion Letter, No. 508, LAB. L. REP. (BNA) WHM 95:146 (1981) (no uniform maintenance required for minimum wage or overtime purposes if wash and wear uniform).

68. California Industrial Welfare Commission, Order No. 5–80.

Appendix 9–A

Guidelines to FLSA Administrative, Executive, and Professional Exemptions from Minimum Wage and Overtime Requirements

Employee _____

Position/Title _____

Department _____

Job Code _____

PURPOSE

This Fair Labor Standards Act exemption analysis record is designed to assist in determining the exempt or nonexempt status of a particular employee for purposes of minimum wage and overtime requirements. Any employee employed in a bona fide executive, administrative, professional, or combination capacity, as illustrated by these guidelines, is exempt from the minimum wage and the overtime pay provisions of the Act, but not the Equal Pay provisions.

EXPLANATORY NOTES

In determining an employee's exempt status, and in answering questions in these guidelines, it must be remembered that:

1. "Primary duty" means more than half the employee's time is taken up with its exercise.
2. The words "salary" and "salary basis" are used throughout this analysis.
   a. In calculating the amount of salary, the value of any board, lodging, or similar benefit must be ignored.

Source: Based on the streamlined tests and other guidelines in 29 C.F.R. §§ 541.0–541.315; *see also* 29 C.F.R. § 541.600 (rules on combination exemptions, *e.g.*, employee performing professional and executive duties); Lab. L. Rep. (BNA), WHM 92:501–811.

b. Employees are paid on a "salary basis" if they regularly receive each pay period a predetermined amount not subject to reduction because of variation in the continuity or quality of work performed.

c. An hourly employee cannot be exempt.

d. Exempt employees must receive their full salary for any week in which they perform any work, and regardless of the number of hours worked, except that:

  (1) An exempt employee need not be paid a salary for any week in which no work is performed.

  (2) Deductions may be made for absences of a day or more in the week for personal reasons other than sickness or accident.

  (3) Deductions may be made for absences of a day or more in the week because of sickness or disability if the employer has a plan, policy, or practice of providing compensation for loss of salary caused by sickness or disability. The employer need not pay the employee for days of absence (i.e., a waiting period) before the employee becomes qualified for compensation under such plan, etc., or after the employee has exhausted any allowance under the plan, etc.

  (4) Deductions for absence may be made without defeating the exemption if the absence is caused by sickness or disability for which benefits are provided under state sickness and disability law.

  (5) Deductions for absence because of industrial accidents may be made if the employee is compensated for loss of salary in accordance with a workers' compensation law.

  (6) No deduction from an employee's salary may be made for absence of less than a workweek for jury duty, attendance as a court witness, or temporary military leave. However, the employer may set off against the salary due for the week in which the absence occurs any jury fees, witness fees, or military pay the employee receives for that week.

  (7) Deductions for absences of less than a day normally may not be made. If they are made, the exemption will be defeated.

3. Two main types of guidelines are used to determine FLSA professional, executive, or administrative minimum wage and overtime exemptions:

a. If the employee earns $250 a week or more a "streamlined test" composed of only a few factors can be used.

b. If the employee earns less than $250 a week but at least $155 a week, additional standards must be met before the employee is exempt for minimum wage and overtime purposes.

c. Since many exempt employees earn at least $250 a week, the "streamlined tests" are the basis for these guidelines. These guidelines should not be used to determine exempt status unless the employee earns at least $250 a week.

EXEMPTION CHECKLISTS

Answer "YES" or "NO" and insert factual answers to the questions asked.

Questions for All Three Exemptions

Employee Earnings: To be answered for all three exemptions.

1. Is the employee on a salary basis of at least $250 per week ($1,083.33 per month)? (If no, these guidelines cannot be used and the employee's exempt status must be determined by an analysis of additional factors found at 29 C.F.R. § 541.1 (Executive), § 541.2 (Administrative) and § 541.3 (Professional).)   Yes:_____ No:_____
2. If yes:
   a. What, briefly, are the permissible deductions (if any) from the employee's salary for absence from work?

A. Executive Employee Exemption

Employees are exempt as executive employees *only if* their duties and responsibilities meet *all* of the following qualifying tests:

1. Is the employee's *primary duty* the managing of an enterprise, a customarily recognized department, or subdivision of a department?   Yes:_____ No:_____
   If yes:
   a. What, briefly, are the employee's duties and which ones are considered to be managerial?
   b. What portion of the employee's time, approximately, is taken up with duties of a managerial nature?
   c. What department or subdivision is supervised?
2. Does the employee customarily and regularly direct the work of at least two full-time employees, or one full-time and two part-time employees, or four part-time employees?   Yes:_____ No:_____
   a. How many full-time employees does the employee regularly supervise?

b. How many part-time employees does the employee regularly supervise?

c. What kind of authority does the employee have with regard to the supervised employees (e.g., directing the work, authority to hire, fire, promote)?

B. Administrative Employee Exemption

Employees are exempt as administrative employees *only* *if* their duties and responsibilities meet *all* of the following qualifying tests:

1. Is the employee's *primary duty* the performance of office or nonmanual work directly related to management policies or general business operation of the employer?   Yes:____   No:____
   If yes:
   a. What are the employee's duties and which ones are considered office or nonmanual work directly related to management policies or general business operations of the employer?
   b. Can all of the following be answered with a "yes" and with pertinent examples?
      (1) Does the employee's work affect policy or does the employee carry out policies set by top management? Example: _____
      _____   Yes:____   No:____
      (2) Are the employee's duties of an administrative nature rather than "producing" certain services or products? Example: _____
      _____   Yes:____   No:____
      (3) Is the employee generally not required to perform routine clerical duties? Example: _
      _____   Yes:____   No:____
      (4) Do the employee's duties contribute significantly toward managing or operating the facility? Example: _____
      _____   Yes:____   No:____
   c. What portion of the employee's time is engaged in the office or nonmanual work described above? Example: _____

2. Does the employee customarily and regularly exercise discretion and independent judgment regarding matters that generally are not decided by clerical personnel?   Yes:____   No:____
   If yes:
   a. What, briefly, are the employee's duties and how does the employee exercise discretion and independent judgment with regard to matters of some significance?
   b. How frequently does the employee exercise discretion and independent judgment in carrying out the above-described duties?

C. Professional Employee Exemption

Employees are exempt as professional employees *only* *if* their duties and responsibilities meet qualifying tests 1 and 4, or 2 and 4 below:

1. What is the employee's primary duty?
   a. Does it require knowledge of an advanced type in a field of science or learning?   Yes:____   No:____
   b. Does it require the consistent exercise of discretion and judgement?   Yes:____   No:____
   c. Briefly describe those duties requiring knowledge of an advanced type in a field of science or learning. _____
      _____

   d. How is the advanced knowledge generally acquired (college, other education that is not on-the-job, length of education or training, etc.)?
      _____
      _____

   e. What, briefly, are the duties that require the consistent exercise of judgment and discretion?
      _____
      _____

   f. What portion of the employee's time is engaged in duties requiring the described advanced knowledge and the exercise of judgment and discretion? _____
      _____

2. Is the employee's *primary duty* the performance of
work in a recognized field of artistic endeavor
where the work requires invention, imagination, or
talent?   Yes:____ No:____
   a. What, briefly, are the duties that require imag-
      ination, talent, or invention?
   b. What is the field of artistic endeavor?
   _____
   c. What portion of the employee's time is engaged
      in the described work?
3. An employee engaged in teaching or the practice of
law or medicine *and* earning less than the $250, still
will be exempt if:
   a. *Teacher*
      (1) Is the employee licensed or recognized as a
          teacher by the facility? and   Yes:____ No:____
      (2) Does the employee teach, tutor, instruct, or
          lecture for the purposes of imparting knowl-
          edge?   Yes:____ No:____
   b. *Law*
      (1) Is the employee licensed as an attorney? and   Yes:____ No:____
      (2) Is the employee engaged in the practice of
          law?   Yes:____ No:____
   c. *Medicine*
      (1) Is the employee licensed as a physician? and   Yes:____ No:____
      (2) Is the employee engaged in the practice of
          medicine? or   Yes:____ No:____
      (3) Does the employee possess the degree
          required for the practice of medicine? and   Yes:____ No:____
      (4) Is the employee an intern or resident?   Yes:____ No:____

Signed _____   Reviewed and
Date _____   Verified by _____
            Employee   Date _____
                                Dept. Head or Admin. Officer

_____

FLSA Exemption Status   **Exemption Classification**
__Nonexempt   __Exempt   __Executive   __Administrative
                                   __Professional __Combination

                                   Approved _____
                                   Date _____

Chapter 10

Regulation of Employer-Employee Relationships

DISABILITY PROGRAMS

Disability programs are a form of insurance that provide benefits when employees are unable to work because of sickness or injury. These programs may be self-insured, employer- and/or employee-financed, or publicly funded, and should be distinguished from workers' compensation benefits that are paid only if the illness or injury is work-related. Because disability programs are established to benefit your employees, you should be familiar with what they provide and help those individuals by referring them to appropriate sources (such as your personnel office) for obtaining additional information or assistance.

In the public sphere, the federal government and a few states have established disability insurance programs with compulsory employer contributions. The principal federal legislation is the 1935 Social Security Act,[1] which provides that:

- Qualified individuals who become completely disabled are entitled to monthly retirement benefits.

- Individuals over 31 must be "fully insured," that is, they must have worked in Social Security employment for at least 20 quarters during the last ten years if they are to receive benefits.

- Persons between 24 and 31 years of age qualify only if they have worked in half of the quarters between age 21 and the date of disability.

- Persons under 24 qualify only if they have worked six quarters of the last 12.

- Individuals are not entitled to federal benefits until five months after the disability and only if they provide satisfactory proof that the disability has lasted or is expected to last at least 12 months.

State disability insurance programs are not offered by all states, but those that exist generally are designed to provide limited short-term benefits to individuals who are unable to work because of sickness and injury unrelated to the job.[2]

In common with many other employers, those in the health care field frequently offer their employees private disability insurance programs with temporary or long-term disability benefits. In addition, collective bargaining agreements may require benefits financed by the employer alone or by both employer and employee for covered personnel. In either case, the coverage and extent of the benefits will be determined by the particular employer policy, collective bargaining agreement, or insurance policy, and the benefits may or may not be supplementary to state and federal payments.

Many states have laws providing compensation for loss resulting from the injury, disablement, or death of an employee through a job-related injury. Be aware that this compensation does not depend on your employer's being at fault. For example, even if employees' work-related accidents are caused by their own negligence, they still will be entitled to compensation. This does not mean, however, that there is no advantage to showing that your employer is free of blame. To the contrary, a definite advantage can exist since, if your employer is at fault, the employee may have a separate legal action or may be entitled to extra damages under the workers' compensation statute—and if it is the employee who is at fault, the employer should have a solid defense against any such action.

Claims, Procedures, and Employer Responses

Disability claims under federal or state programs are relatively straightforward and generally do not require any participation by you or your employer. Under the Social Security Act, the disabled employee simply makes application on a standard form to the local district office of the Social Security Administration. At the same time, adequate proof must be submitted that the employee is either totally disabled or expects to be disabled for at least 12 months. While applicants do not lose their rights if they delay filing their application, retroactivity limited to one year.[3]

For example, an employee who files a claim 18 months after the disability occurs loses six months of benefits. A waiting period of five months also must elapse before the claim is processed. Once the claim actually has been filed, a determination will be made, generally by a state agency under an agreement with the Department of Health and Human Services,[4] that the applicant is or is not disabled and entitled to benefits.

By contrast, your employer's involvement in workers' compensation claims is far more active. For example, many state statutes insist that the worker notify the employer within a specified period that the injury has occurred. This notification requirement is in addition to any obligation to file a formal claim for compensation. Notifying the employer is an essential step and employees who fail to do so may be prevented from taking their claims further.

While an employer, or its insurance carrier, usually can settle a workers' compensation claim with an injured employee, many state statutes require the formal approval of the state commission (or its equivalent) before such a settlement is valid. So be careful: if your state does require such approval and you do not obtain it, then any settlement you reach might not protect your facility from further liability under the workers' compensation law. This may be true even if you actually paid the claimant a significant sum of money in accordance with your settlement.

If the claim is not settled, it is investigated and a hearing is held before the compensation commission or its equivalent, after which the commission makes a decision. If the commission reaches a finding favorable to the injured worker, it makes an award based on the extent of the employee's injury or disability. You should note that in some states, however, the claim itself is filed in a regular court and is processed like any other lawsuit through the courts.

Employee Status of Disabled Workers

Many states make it unlawful to discharge or retaliate in any way against an employee who files a workers' compensation claim or receives a disability rating.[5] Generally speaking, this may not prevent you from discharging an employee if a permanent disability prevents the person from ever performing the job in the future. It also might not preclude you from filling the position during a worker's extended absence and conditioning the employee's return upon the availability of an opening.[6]

Again, caution is required since your specific obligations are governed by the law of your own state as well as any applicable collective bargaining agreement.

UNEMPLOYMENT INSURANCE

The federal government and various states have established a coordinated compulsory unemployment insurance program with the object of shifting at least a part of a person's unemployment burden from the individual to the taxpaying community as a whole.[7] With the exception of three states,[8] the program is financed entirely by two separate employer-paid taxes.

The federal tax is imposed under the Federal Unemployment Tax Act[9] on all but the smallest of employers and the money is used to finance the costs of administering the program itself. The various state taxes (for the most part, only employers who have employees for less than 20 weeks in any year are excluded) are used to fund payment of the actual benefits.

The federal tax theoretically is determined by multiplying the employer's total wages by the statutory maximum rate (3.5 percent in 1984, 6.2 percent in 1985, and thereafter). Because of two possible tax credits, however, most employers pay considerably less than that: (1) one credit is given to your employer in an amount equal to that paid into the state unemployment insurance fund and (2) the amount due may be reduced further if your employer has a favorable unemployment experience record. As a result of these credits, an employer's federal unemployment tax may be as low as eight-tenths of one percent.[10]

State unemployment tax rates vary among the states. All, however, generally reflect the same principle: namely, a new employer starts at a fixed rate that will vary thereafter depending upon actual claims experience. In other words, if your employer has a high number of valid unemployment insurance claims, it will be penalized by an increase in its state tax rate. This explains why you may want to contest any untrue or misleading reasons given by a former employee to the unemployment agency in filing a claim. If you do not contest invalid claims, or do not challenge claims filed by former employees who are not entitled to unemployment benefits, then increased tax liability can result.

You should note that a claimant's entitlement to benefits has nothing to do with the employee's particular needs but is based solely on a formula in the various state acts. Tremendous variation exists in the states' minimum and maximum weekly amounts—for example, Louisiana's minimum is $60, and maximum weekly benefits for the applicant range from $84 in Puerto Rico to $206 in the District of Columbia.[11] These figures exclude any dependent allowances that also may be payable.

Claims, Procedures, and Employer Responsibilities

While the steps to be followed and the requirements to be met may vary among the states, the typical sequence is as follows:

- A claimant must file a timely claim under the appropriate state statute to obtain unemployment benefits.
- The claimants will be asked to supply information on a number of subjects including their qualifications and experience, the reason why they left their last job, the details of any strike at that facility, and other relevant information.
- The employer generally will receive a notice of the claim and, if you are to respond, do so very quickly because most states give you only a limited time to contest a claim—and if you fail to do so, the claim will be paid. For example, suppose you are in one of the states where benefits are not payable if an employee is discharged for misconduct and your former employee says he was fired for no reason; however, in fact, he was fired for a violation of your

policies (fighting) and you can prove it. Under such circumstances, the employee's claim may be denied provided you give your version in a timely fashion.

- The state agency itself initially decides whether your former employee should receive unemployment benefits.
- The employer and the claimant both can appeal the agency's decision to an administrative body, which holds a hearing.
- A claimant who appeals must show eligibility for benefits but you must show that the employee is disqualified for one of the reasons in the statute, e.g., misconduct, voluntary quit, refusal to accept other work. This means that if you do not produce any evidence, then the claimants, once eligibility is shown, will succeed automatically.[12]
- A party unhappy with the decision on appeal has the right to seek review thereafter in the courts.

Use by Striking Employees

Many of the state acts limit benefits or disqualify claimants entirely if their unemployment is the result of a labor dispute. Part of the justification for this denial is because it is unfair to force an employer to finance a strike against its own business by its own employees and also because the employees are without work voluntarily.

Although this general principle is reasonably clear, a number of subsidiary questions are not as easily answered.

Sympathy Strikers. As long as the underlying cause is the type of labor dispute covered by the state statute, no distinction generally is made between "primary" strikers and "sympathy" strikers.[13]

Strike during Layoff. If you have a strike at a time when some of your employees already are on layoff status, these laid-off employees may continue to receive benefits unless you offer them work that has become available but they still stay out.[14]

Lockouts. Unless your state has a specific exemption, lockouts by an employer may be treated the same way as other labor disputes and, if so, the affected union employees would not be entitled to unemployment benefits.[15] If your employer engages in an offensive lockout, however, your employees may be eligible for benefits. As with other unemployment issues, however, this general rule is subject to differing state provisions and interpretations, particularly when there are events such as offensive lockouts by employers or lockouts by those engaged in multi-employer bargaining who are responding to selective strikes.[16] For this reason, the impact of particular employer actions or reactions on employee unemployment benefit eligibility should be determined and considered before acting.

Temporary Unemployment. A striking employee who finds a temporary job, then loses that job, still cannot claim unemployment benefits. If the employee accepts a permanent job, however, the labor dispute becomes irrelevant. This means that if the employee loses the second permanent job, unemployment benefits can be claimed.

Nonparticipation. A strike sometimes forces an employer to reduce operations and lay off uninvolved employees. For example, if a strike requires you to close down a whole department, you might have to lay off nonunion clericals. Generally speaking, if you lay off employees because of reduced census or other strike-related reasons, these individuals can claim unemployment benefits. Why? Because they are not "on strike," or honoring a strike, and their inability to work is not of their own choice.

Partial Employment or Underemployment

People can claim unemployment benefits only if they make themselves available for work. This means a claimant must continue to look for work and accept it whenever offered. Yet an employee does not have to accept any job offered but may refuse "unsuitable" work. Even here, however, the employee cannot refuse work simply because it is not appealing; there must be some worthwhile reason, such as the employee's qualifications, health, physical fitness and training, experience, prior earnings, length of unemployment, and distance from home.

Similarly, simply because a part-time or temporary job is offered does not mean that the claimant can turn it down automatically. To the contrary, the claimant should accept a part-time job as long as it is otherwise suitable. This means, in other words, that a secretary previously working in a full-time job should take a mornings only secretarial job offered at the same wage rate and under the same type of working conditions. But there is an exception: a temporary job offer may be turned down if the employee can show that its acceptance would make it more difficult to find a permanent job.

Remember that this discussion is only a summary of typical state procedures and requirements. Variations do exist and you should be sure to verify the rules used by your own state before you make any decisions, or take any action, on unemployment issues. And, as always, get expert advice.

ERISA

The last 30 years have seen a big increase in the number and size of private employer benefit plans, primarily in the areas of pensions and health insurance. This rapid growth was accompanied by an increase in the number of allegations that pension funds were being misused and plans mismanaged. These claims produced pressure on the federal government to increase regulation of benefit plans and eventually, after several unsuccessful attempts, Congress passed a pension reform law called the Employee Retirement Income Security Act of 1974 (ERISA or the Act).[17] Its main purpose is to make sure that employees covered by these plans receive benefits that are due to them and to set up strict standards for those who administer these programs.

ERISA does not require that you set up benefit plans for your employees; it simply says that if you do have such plans and they are covered by ERISA, they must comply with certain minimum standards. ERISA affects two different types of employee benefit plans: (1) pension plans providing retirement benefits and (2) welfare plans providing health, accident, death, etc., benefits.

The Act addresses six basic topics:

1. *Reporting and disclosure provisions.* Once a plan is covered by the Act, reports must be filed with as many as three different federal agencies (the Department of Labor, the Internal Revenue Service, and the Pension Benefit Guarantee Corporation). Some (but not all) of the information in these reports also must be disclosed to participants and beneficiaries in a summarized fashion.

2. *Fiduciary standards.* The Act does not require that the funds be invested in any specific security or investment. It does require that the person exercising control over the plan use the care, skill, prudence, and diligence that a cautious person would use in conducting a similar enterprise.

3. *Participation and vesting.* The Act makes sure that employees do not have to satisfy unreasonable age and length-of-service requirements before becoming eligible to participate in a benefit plan. In addition, employees who work for a specified minimum period under a pension plan must be vested in that plan (meaning, for example, that if they move on to another job, they will retain their rights to the pension benefits they have earned), thereby being assured of at least some pension on achieving retirement age.

4. *Pension plan termination.* The Act attempts to protect employee rights to benefits should the plan be terminated.

5. *Tax matters.* The Act tries to apply the tax laws governing pensions more fairly. Persons who set up their own pension programs in IRA and Keogh plans, for example, are given some tax advantages. (An IRA is an Individual Retirement Account and a Keogh plan is a pension investment program for self-employed persons.)

6. *Funding.* The Act seeks to assure that an employee pension benefit plan meets certain minimum funding obligations to ensure that enough cash will be available to make payments to beneficiaries when they become due.

The participation, vesting, funding, and plan termination insurance provisions apply only to pension plans; the reporting, disclosure, and fiduciary requirements are applicable to both pension and welfare plans.

TERMINABLE-AT-WILL CONTRACTS

For years it was accepted that employers had an absolute right to discharge employees unless the termination violated a written contract of employment, a collective bargaining agreement, or a state or federal statute that protected specified classes of workers. This concept, known as the "terminable-at-will" doctrine, recently and quite dramatically has shown signs of wear. Furthermore, the degree to which the doctrine still exists varies tremendously among the states.

It is no exaggeration to say that this decade may well see an explosion of claims by employees, all arguing that their termination was invalid on one or more theories still being developed by the courts. Yet several distinct rationales appear to be emerging as the basis for limiting your employer's ability to terminate employees "at will": (1) public policy limitations, (2) contractual constraints, either express or implied, and (3) implied promises of good faith and fair dealing.

Public Policy Limitations

If you discharge an employee as retaliation for engaging in some protected activity or for refusing to do something unlawful, the person may be able to sue you and your employer for wrongful dismissal. Examples of the kinds of activities protected by public policy considerations include belonging to or participating in a union, serving on a jury, filing a workers' compensation claim, reporting violations of consumer protection laws, or refusing to take part in an illegal scheme to fix prices.[18] Discharges for engaging in these activities have been found to be against public policy and a breach of the employment contract.

The main point to remember from these newer cases is this: if you discharge individuals in retaliation for engaging in some activity affirmatively protected by the law, especially if they could claim they were carrying out a public duty in some way, your act may be considered suspect by the courts. If so, both you and your employer may be exposed to a claim for damages for unjustified dismissal.

Contractual Constraints

The second group of cases restricting the terminable-at-will doctrine consists of an employer's personnel policies or manuals, verbal representations, or other statements or conduct that have created a contractual relationship between the employer and employee. The ease with which such a contract can be implied, and then serve as the basis for a lawsuit contesting the employee's termination, is illustrated by a leading Michigan case:

> No pre-employment negotiations need take place and the parties' minds need not meet on the subject; nor does it matter that the employee knows

nothing of the particulars of the employer's policies and practices or that the employer may change them unilaterally. It is enough that the employer chooses, presumably in its own interest, to create an environment in which the employee believes that, whatever the policies and practices, they are established and official at any given time, purport to be fair, and are applied consistently and uniformly to each employee. The employer has then created a situation 'instinct with an obligation.'[19]

While this doctrine is not universally accepted,[20] its existence and potential use underscore the necessity for ensuring that personnel manuals, handbooks, and other written materials do not contain employment commitments that the employer is unable, or unwilling, to fulfill. This potential liability also emphasizes the importance of adhering to the employer's policies and procedures without creating additional promises on its behalf through written or verbal statements to employees or applicants for employment.

Promise of Good Faith and Fair Dealing

Some state courts, as is illustrated by Massachusetts and California, have found that an implied covenant of good faith and fair dealing may exist in employment relationships.[21] This covenant or promise is breached by an employer who terminates an employee arbitrarily or unfairly, or in violation of the employer's own practices or unilateral policies. Again, the development of this doctrine, and the resulting increase in potential liability, reinforce the need for consistent adherence to an employer's policies and procedures, and the following of basic supervisory principles prior to implementing any employee terminations.

BLACKLISTING AND STRIKEBREAKING

Blacklisting, as originally defined, occurred when employers circulated the names of union members to other employers to make sure that union activists would not find work. Blacklists have the obvious goal of discouraging union membership so it is hardly surprising that federal labor law prohibits this practice. As one court said back in 1940, "long experience ha[s] shown that one of the most provocative and effective means by which employers sought to impede the organization of workers was the blacklisting of union men, thereby denying them opportunities for employment."[22] Aside from isolated and inconsequential instances, it is hoped that this practice now is of historical interest only.

Strikebreaking is another example of antiunion activity that calls to mind an earlier period in the history of labor relations. While strikebreaking has been the object of preventive legislation, that word never has included legitimate employer responses aimed at ending strikes or operating at maximum capacity during a strike. In other words, while a union has the right to strike, under a 1938 decision that still stands, an employer also has the right to continue its business during a strike, even if it means hiring permanent or temporary replacements (depending on the nature of the strike).[23]

Today the word strikebreaking generally is used to describe the hiring of certain outside individuals to replace strikers. Both federal and state legislatures have regulated and, in some cases, restricted strikebreaking as so defined. Thus, if an employer imports strike replacements from out of state, it may be in violation of a federal statute called the Byrnes Act.[24]

In some states, you cannot offer jobs where a strike is in progress unless the applicant is told about the existence of the labor dispute. Still other states try to limit the use of so-called professional strikebreakers, that is, the use of individuals who make a practice of working where a strike is in progress. While some of these state acts may be preempted by federal labor law, you should investigate the provisions and impact of state law if you ever anticipate that a work stoppage may occur.

LICENSURE LAWS

A hundred years ago, only physicians were licensed and even then, licensing generally was left to the control of private medical societies. Today, by contrast, a multitude of health care professions and occupations are licensed by state authorities under a variety of statutes.

Licensing usually is controlled and enforced by a state administrative agency. In broad outline, the state enforcement machinery usually contains one or more of the following features:

- The state sets up a new administrative board, or recognizes an already existing one, for each profession or occupation and the board then has the task of administering the licensing law.
- A state statute frequently defines, sometimes specifically but often in more general terms, what constitutes "practice" of the licensed occupation.
- The statute or the licensing body establishes the procedure for obtaining a license, which may include an examination and/or recognition of qualifications or diplomas from colleges or vocational schools.
- State statutes often set out penalties for unlawful practice and provide for suspension or expulsion following a decision that the licenseholder has engaged in "unprofessional activities."

EMPLOYMENT REFERENCES

In some states,[25] you commit a crime when an employee you discharged cannot obtain employment because you misrepresented the reason for the firing. On the other hand, a truthful statement concerning the reason why the individual no longer is employed is not a violation of the law. Aside from possible criminal prosecution, however, adverse employment references may result in a civil suit if your ex-worker is not hired by a second employer. This potential exposure to suit exists even if the adverse reference is totally accurate since the correctness of your reference serves only as a defense.

Because of these risks, each facility should have a uniform policy on how it will respond to reference requests. Your facility may have decided to respond to specific requests by giving, as you consider appropriate, a simple, truthful, and objectively provable statement of the reasons for termination. Or, remembering that no law requires you to provide a reference, your facility may limit responses to a simple verification of the dates of employment and position(s) held. This latter course is particularly attractive in circumstances where there are risks of distortion, inaccuracy, or missing facts.

ACCESS TO EMPLOYER FILES

For a number of reasons, employers today often amass considerable documentation on individual employees. Good supervision usually requires good documentation and if you fail to record and document the significant aspects of an employee's work performance and conduct you may find it difficult to justify subsequent employment-related decisions. In addition, as noted earlier, a number of statutes regulating the employer-employee relationship require you to maintain various types of personnel records.

Inevitably, pressure has mounted on employers to open their personnel files to employees who insist on seeing them. Indeed, at least 13 states have legislation governing employee access to personnel files. Some of these states such as Connecticut, Maine, and California have gone even further, however, by creating a general right of employee access.[26] If your state has such a law, you need to be very familiar with the extent of employees' rights, what documents they are allowed to see, whether only they can look at the file or whether attorneys and other representatives can inspect the documents on their behalf, etc.

Other states have granted very specific rights of access that may be in addition to or instead of a general right of access to personnel files. For example, in California, if you discharge an employee because of a report by an outside investigator, the employee is entitled to a copy of that report.[27] Similarly, a federal law insists that if you use an investigative consumer or credit report to check on an employee or applicant, you must give that person written notice that you have asked for the report and give the individual a written copy once you have obtained it.[28]

Just as employees may have a right to see their personnel file, they also have a right to have the contents kept confidential—an aspect of the law of privacy. You should note that publication of "private facts" (talking about, writing about) a person can be an invasion of these privacy rights. Therefore, allow persons to inspect the personnel files only if they have a genuine and proper reason for doing so. Put another way, uncontrolled and indiscriminate release of materials is a dangerous practice and all such data, indeed all of your supervisory information, should be treated confidentially.

DETENTION AND SEARCH OF EMPLOYEES

A health care institution frequently is placed in a difficult dilemma with regard to detention and searches of employees. While its right to stop and search employees is limited, it must at the same time consider the safety and security of its other employees, patients, and visitors.

Since each state has developed its own laws in this area, it is important to seek expert advice and then develop and maintain a uniform policy and procedure. In this process, the following summary of common problem areas and restrictions illustrates the competing and overlapping concerns that must be accommodated in the development of such a policy:

- The use of physical force to stop persons, such as temporarily blocking their exit (not allowing them to leave, or permitting them to go only if they leave behind certain personal possessions), may lead to your being sued for false imprisonment. Nevertheless, in certain circumstances, the law allows you to use force to stop and detain someone, as illustrated by a reasonable and objective belief (not just an unsubstantiated suspicion) that the individual has committed a major crime.

- The use of force to stop someone also may be regarded as an "assault," with potential criminal and civil liability. Again, certain actions that the law normally would consider an assault may be privileged (excused) under special circumstances. Because these rights and risks vary greatly from state to state and because of the magnitude of the risk, you definitely should seek legal advice, where practical, before detaining any employee.

- The Constitution gives everyone the right to be free from unreasonable searches by the government. This right does not cover searches conducted by private employers unless it is possible to argue that the employer is carrying out some state purpose.

- The Constitution does not prevent private employers from searching employees or their property but this does not mean you can do so without repercussions, since search in itself may be an assault or a false imprisonment if you physically have to stop and hold the employee in order to do so. Furthermore, if the employee challenges your disciplinary action through the grievance and arbitration provision of a union contract, you may find that an arbitrator will refuse to allow evidence that is found in an improper search. In other words, if you discharge an employee for theft, and the stolen property is recovered by searching the employee in an inappropriate manner, an arbitrator may decide that you cannot use the evidence or may insist that you justify the discharge with other facts.

These cautions should not cause you to forget that you usually will be protected if you act reasonably and with moderation. For example, you generally are free to ask an employee to submit to a search where you suspect, on reasonable grounds (such as an obvious bulge in the clothing similar to a missing object) that the person has committed theft. You also may warn such employees that if they do not submit to a search, you will take disciplinary action for their refusal. If, despite this warning, employees still refuse a search of themselves or their possessions (purses, bags, etc.), then do not conduct a search by force but take appropriate disciplinary action.

If your facility is experiencing a rash of pilfering or other unlawful activity, or simply as a preventive measure, you would be wise to post or otherwise distribute a very clear and explicit notice to employees that searches may be required (periodically as indicated, or upon leaving and entering the facility). The policy also should state that you will take disciplinary action against those who will not submit to a reasonable search. Under those circumstances, you will be on even stronger grounds if subsequently you discipline or terminate an employee for refusing to allow a search.

Again, as always, your best course in this area is to develop a clear policy and procedure after consultation with counsel familiar with local (state) law. Once you have developed a policy and procedure, this should be widely publicized and attention drawn to it regularly.

NOTES

1. 42 U.S.C. §§ 301–1397.
2. *See, e.g.,* Cal. Unemp. Ins. Code § 100 (Deering 1971).
3. 42 U.S.C. § 423(b).
4. 42 U.S.C. § 421(a).
5. *See, e.g.,* Cal. Lab. Code § 132a (West Supp. 1984).
6. Judson Steel Corp. v. Workers' Compensation Appeal Bd., 22 Cal. 3d 658 (1978).

7. For a review of state unemployment provisions and interpretations, *see generally*, UNEMPL. INS REP. (CCH).

8. Alabama, Alaska, and New Jersey.

9. 26 U.S.C. §§ 3301–3311.

10. 26 U.S.C. §§ 3301, 3302; *also see*, UNEMPL. INS. REP. 1B (CCH). ¶¶ 1101–1170.

11. UNEMPL. INS. REP. 1B (CCH), ¶ 300 (Coverage and Benefit Provisions of State Unemployment Insurance Law).

12. Cal. Dept. of Human Resources Dev. v. Java, 402 U.S. 121, 134 (1971).

13. *E.g.*, Butcher v. Florida Indus. Comm'n, 231 So. 2d 47 (Fla. Dist. Ct. App. 1970), *cert. denied*, 400 U.S. 992 (1970).

14. Clapp v. Unemployment Compensation Comm'n, 325 Mich. 212, 38 N.W.2d 325 (1949).

15. UNEMPL. INS. REP. 1B (CCH), (1976) ¶ 1980; *contra*, Holland Motor Express v. ESC, 42 Mich. App. 10, 201 N.W.2d 299 (1972).

16. *E.g.*, McKinley v. Cal. Employment Stabilization Comm'n, 34 Cal. 2d 239 (1949) (a strike against one employer a strike against all, and employees still are ineligible for benefits).

17. 29 U.S.C. §§ 1001–1461.

18. *E.g.*, Tameny v. Atlantic Richfield, 27 Cal. 3d 167 (1980); Frompton v. Central Ind. Gas Co., 297 N.E.2d 425 (Ind. Sup. Ct. 1973); see Annot., 12 A.L.R. 4th 544 (1982).

19. Toussaint v. Blue Cross & Blue Shield of Michigan, 882 (Mich. Sup. Ct. 1980), 292 N.W.2d 880; Weiner v. McGraw-Hill, Inc., _____(New York Court of Appeals, 1983) (course of dealing between employer and employee can create a contract requiring just cause for termination); Walker v. Northern San Diego County Hospital District, 135 Cal. App. 3d 896 (1982) (probationary period policy may serve as contractual restriction on employer's right to discharge employee after completing probation).

20. *E.g.*, Johnson v. National Beef Packing Co., 551 P.2d 779 (Kan. Sup. Ct. 1976) (benefits conferred by manual were gratuitous and did not establish contractual relationship); Jackson v. Minidoka Irrigation District, 563 P.2d 54 (Idaho Sup. Ct. 1977).

21. Fortune v. National Cash Register, 364 N.E.2d 1251 (Mass. Sup. Jud. Ct. 1977); Cleary v. American Air Lines, Inc., 111 Cal. App. 3d 443 (1980); Pugh v. See's Candies, Inc., 116 Cal. App. 3d 311 (1981).

22. NLRB v. Waumbec Mills, 114 F.2d 225, 232 (1st Cir., 1940).

23. NLRB v. Mackay Radio & Tel. Co., 304 U.S. 333 (1938).

24. 18 U.S.C. § 1231.

25. *See, e.g.*, CAL. LAB. CODE §§ 1050–1056.

26. California, Connecticut, District of Columbia, Maine, Michigan, New Hampshire, Oregon, Pennsylvania, South Dakota, Tennessee, Utah, Vermont, and Wisconsin, LAB. RELS. RPTR. 4 (BNA) (State Labor Laws).

27. CAL. LAB. CODE § 2930.

28. 15 U.S.C. § 1681d.

Part III

Working at Supervision

Chapter 11

A Suggested Methodology for Supervision

THE 3 AREAS OF SUPERVISION

Chapter 2 emphasized that competent supervision requires the development of knowledge and skills in three major areas:

1. You must possess a working knowledge of the legal framework that governs an employer's relationship toward its employees.
2. You must be knowledgeable as to the variety of functions you should perform as a supervisor.
3. You must know how to apply your knowledge of supervisory functions and of the applicable legal framework in your day-to-day performance.

The first area, the legal framework, was discussed extensively in Part II. The basic legal standards, or do's and don'ts, presented in those chapters should be kept in mind as you proceed now to the second and third major areas, which are the subject of Part III.

Specifically, this chapter:

- outlines the functions most typically performed as a part of supervision
- discusses a suggested methodology for approaching the task of how you apply the legal principles in your daily supervisory performance.

Chapter 12 explains the procedural or notice requirements you must comply with before taking action; Chapter 13 discusses types of substantive issues you will face: poor performance, misconduct (fighting, sleeping on the job, etc.) and how you can prove them; and Chapter 14 lets you apply the suggested methodology and your skills and knowledge by analyzing six case studies.

WHAT IS SUPERVISION?

If you attempted to develop a full appreciation of the many functions and responsibilities included in the term "supervision" by turning to your standard reference source, the dictionary, you would find it of little assistance. One definition states that supervision is "the action, process, or occupation of supervising; [especially as in] a critical watching and directing (as of activities or a course of action)."[1] For the term "supervise," it simply says "superintend, oversee"[2] and that a supervisor is "one that supervises; esp.: an administrative officer in charge of a business, government, or school unit or operation."[3] This exercise in circuitous explanation thus provides little substance as to what, if anything, you should do as a supervisor.

The next step in the quest for a workable definition, or fuller explanation of what it means to supervise, might be to review the vast amount of literature and research. While such a review would be helpful and is recommended, the diversity of approach and sheer volume of such materials precludes reliance upon them as a workable tool for summarizing, in a comprehensive yet comprehensible way, what you should do as a supervisor.

Therefore, out of necessity, and without any pretense that it includes every conceivable supervisory function you may perform, Exhibit 11–1 is presented as a checklist or outline of the major functions performed by supervisors.

Even a brief glance at this checklist illustrates that the dictionary definition of supervision is misleadingly simple. Supervision is not composed of just one self-inclusive function. Instead, it includes a whole spectrum of activities that relate to the responsibility for directing a work force (whether one employee or many) toward a goal set by the employing institution.

When viewed in this fashion, supervision becomes a method for ensuring (or attempting to ensure) that the persons employed to perform a particular activity (your supervised employees) know what they are to do, whether they are doing it satisfactorily, how to do it better, and how their activity contributes to the overall goals of the institution. Conversely, it is a method for ensuring (and, again, or attempting to ensure, depending on how you perform your functions) that competent individuals are employed, that incompetent ones no longer work there, that the institution receives the benefit of input by all employees, and that the work activity does in fact contribute to the facility's overall mission by performing its appointed role in a satisfactory manner.

A more extensive review of Exhibit 11–1 demonstrates that many subfunctions or different tasks might be required in the performance of any one supervisory activity. For example, if you are to ensure that employees comply with your employer's existing policies and procedures, then you must:

- review those policies and procedures with new employees (whether they be new in employment or transferred into your work area)

Exhibit 11–1 Outline of Supervisory Functions

A. Hiring Employees
1. Determining minimum and preferred qualifications for the position.
2. Reviewing applications, resumes, etc.
3. Selecting applicants for interviews.
4. Interviewing applicants.
5. Checking references and verifying other employment information.
6. Extending an offer of employment.
7. Notifying unsuccessful applicants.
8. Orienting and training new employees.

B. Assigning Employees and Setting Standards
1. Determining job content and specific duties.
2. Setting performance standards.
3. Evaluating each employee's individual capability to perform assignments.
4. Assigning employees to particular positions or duties.
5. Changing performance standards or employee assignments as necessary.

C. Evaluating Employees
1. Completing written evaluations (at stated intervals and on an as-needed basis).
2. Providing continuing verbal evaluation to employees.
3. Meeting with employees to discuss evaluations and employee perspective.
4. Following up with employees on any problems indicated by the evaluations (deficient areas of performance or conduct) to ensure that corrective action has been taken.
5. Ensuring that good (as well as poor) performance is noted and discussed with employees.

D. Improving Employee Performance
1. Counseling employees.
2. Demonstrating proper performance.
3. Seeking employee input or suggestions as to performance of work, functioning of the work area, etc.
4. Suggesting or providing in-house or outside educational assistance.
5. Following up with problem areas.
6. Distinguishing between employees who cannot and those who will not perform satisfactorily.

E. Ensuring Compliance with Policies and Procedures
1. Reviewing policies and procedures with employees.
2. Updating employee awareness of policies and procedures at stated intervals.
3. Explaining the purpose of policies and procedures to encourage voluntary compliance.
4. Ensuring that supervisory actions comply with employer's policies and procedures (for example, adherence to policies and procedures governing scheduling of employees; approval of time off, overtime, and requests for leaves of absence; eligibility for and accrual of paid benefits; etc.).
5. Enforcing policies and procedures by notifying employees of noncompliance.
6. Notifying employees of consequences of noncompliance.
7. Initiating management's consideration of appropriate changes in policies and procedures (including those suggested by employees).

Exhibit 11–1 continued

F. Taking Disciplinary Action
1. Conducting predisciplinary investigations (such as talking to witnesses, reviewing employer's policies and procedures, reviewing legal standards, talking with employees, etc.).
2. Determining whether disciplinary action is appropriate.
3. Preparing documentation of disciplinary investigation and action to be taken.
4. Issuing disciplinary action, such as oral reprimands, written warnings, unpaid suspensions, and terminations.
5. Informing employee(s) of disciplinary action taken, and of consequences if there is a repetition.
6. Following up to ensure that there is no repetition of the conduct or performance that led to disciplinary action.

G. Completing the Communication Cycle
1. Relaying communication between supervised employees and other administrative personnel (such as other departments, administration, etc.).
2. Initiating communication or discussions with employees concerning the institution's actions on their suggestions or concerns and ensuring that those suggestions or concerns receive consideration and timely responses.
3. Discussing the institution's rules and objectives as well as new actions or changes in direction with employees for their information and input.
4. Contributing your own suggestions, information, or advice.

- provide notice to your employees of any modified or new policies
- comply with those policies yourself
- help employees to comply by providing any additional explanation, teaching, or access to internal or external resources that may be necessary
- notify (or counsel) employees individually or as a group concerning any failure to comply with your (and the employer's) policies and the potential consequences of noncompliance
- take disciplinary action, as necessary, if employees violate the policy on one or more occasions, depending upon the seriousness of the issue involved.

When all of these functions or steps necessary to complete a particular supervisory activity are recognized, you can see why supervision takes time and why it may be helpful to yourself to have a method for analyzing:

- whether supervisory action is warranted
- what that action should be
- what defects may exist in any intended decision or recommendation

- whether your proposed action can be defended successfully (or the probability that it can be, since guarantees are not possible) if challenged by employees or applicants for employment.

A METHODOLOGY FOR DECISION-MAKING

The Deliberate Approach

Supervisory functions must be handled, generally speaking, in a deliberate and analytical fashion. However, this will not occur if you act hastily when you are still caught up in the emotion of events. Thus, the major precept of any approach to supervision must be to emphasize that you must give yourself the time (or take the time) to:

- think through the nature of the problem you are facing
- investigate the facts
- check your own employer's policies and procedures to determine which ones apply and how
- review legal standards
- analyze whether the action you want to take is warranted or whether a modified supervisory response would be more appropriate and, in a related vein, whether the action can be defended successfully if challenged.

Admittedly, there will be some occasions when speed is essential—for example, if you see two employees fighting in the cafeteria, you must take some action quickly and you do not have the luxury of freezing events until you can decide what to do. Even under these types of circumstances, however, it is possible to take immediate appropriate action. For example, you can send the employees off duty with instructions to come in later for an interview as to the possibility of disciplinary action; in the interim, you can use the time you have given yourself to consider, in a deliberate way, what your final supervisory action should be.

Applying Self-Analysis to Supervisory Actions

Once you have the time to approach a supervisory problem the same way you would go at any other type of situation—in a calm fashion—then you must have some systematic method for determining what to do. In other words, how do you decide, in the time available, what supervisory action (if any) you should take?

The advocated method for this decision-making process emphasizes developing your own ability to analyze your proposed action against the procedural and substantive requirements imposed on employers:

1. *Procedural* simply means that you must consider whether all of the notice or due process preconditions to supervisory action have been met. Has there been:

   - notice to employees of your employer's policies, standards, and expectations?
   - notice of your dissatisfaction with an employee's performance or conduct?
   - notice of the employment consequences should the unsatisfactory performance or conduct continue?
   - a fair and sufficient investigation into the facts, including your speaking directly with the employee?

2. *Substantive* means whether you and your employer can prove that the employee did (or did not do) whatever you claim to be the case. This often means you also must determine whether any of your employer's policies and procedures or any external standards or legal requirements are applicable.

The various types of procedural and substantive issues you should consider when making supervisory decisions are summarized in Appendix 11–A, which is designed as a checklist to compare against the specific action you propose to take or recommend. Although many of the issues in that list have special significance for disciplinary decisions, they also are pertinent to your nondisciplinary supervisory decisions.

For example, in assigning an employee, have you determined:

1. Procedurally, whether the person was given appropriate and timely notice of the assignment or of changes or modifications in the job or functions, etc.?

2. Substantively, whether the employee has the capability to perform the assignment and whether you can prove that the assignment was not completed or was refused by the employee, and that the noncompletion of the assignment was not caused by factors beyond the individual's control, etc.?

The specific issues in Appendix 11–A are discussed further in Chapters 12 and 13 but before then, an example of how you apply the suggested methodology to a disciplinary problem may be helpful.

A good example of supervisory decision making can be found by referring back to the situation where you discovered two employees fighting in the cafeteria (see section on "Deliberate Approach" earlier in this chapter, and Chapter 14, Case Study #1). Your first reaction might be to terminate both employees. After all, what is there to investigate or consider when you actually saw them fighting?

The answer is, you still have a substantial amount of work to do and issues to consider before you implement that first reaction. For example, assume that you do restrain yourself and simply send the employees off duty with the instruction to contact you the next day concerning possible disciplinary action. Thereafter, your next steps would be as follows:

1. Procedurally, you must:
   - Talk to any other employees or individuals who were present when the fight started to determine what they heard or saw; you should ask: Was there any yelling or talking between the employees before the fight, and if so, what was said? Who threw the first punch? Did either employee attempt to withdraw from the fight, etc.?
   - Check your employer's policies and how any similar incidents have been handled in the past: Has your employer terminated other employees for fighting on the premises? Is there a written policy on the subject? If termination was not used previously for the same conduct, what action was taken and is there any reason to deviate from that prior practice in this instance?
   - Talk to both employees (individually) to determine their version of the event, and if those vary from what other eyewitnesses say, is there any way to reconcile the stories and, if not, which one appears more credible?

2. Substantively, and after completing your investigation, you must consider:
   - What conduct constitutes fighting?
   - What defenses or mitigation might be present?
   - Are the elements of fighting present, as a factual matter? Does a defense exist? Has another form of misconduct occurred?

In this case, suppose that you talked to three other employees who were present during the fight. All three eyewitnesses say that Employee #1 was yelling and using profanities and racial slurs toward Employee #2, who tried to ignore the comments. They assert that Employee #2 did not respond in any fashion until the first employee threw a surprise punch, that Employee #2 then responded by hitting Employee #1, and that both continued to fight without either making any attempt to withdraw from the altercation.

Subsequently you talk separately to both protagonists and while Employee #2 admits that the facts were essentially as given by eyewitnesses, Employee #1 claims the contrary in the case, stating that he was provoked into throwing the first punch. You also consult your employer's written policies and find the following statement: "Fighting is such serious misconduct that termination is to occur, regardless of the employee's length of service or past record, and lesser disciplinary action can be taken only where the employee did not initiate the confrontation, in which case a disciplinary suspension may be used.'' Further inquiries also disclose that your employer's policy on fighting has been followed consistently in all past occurrences. Every employee who has initiated a fight has been terminated, while employees who were provoked into a physical response were suspended.

Under these circumstances, you should conclude that your first impulse was incorrect and that termination is not the appropriate employer response for both employees:

1. With regard to Employee #1, you have a variation between his version and that given by four other employees. Assuming that no reason exists for all four other employees to conspire to present a false story, you could reasonably accept their version as reflecting the probable facts. Based on these facts, and your employer's policy, you then could conclude that Employee #1 did engage in fighting and that no mitigating circumstances, as recognized by the institution's policy, were present.

2. With regard to Employee #2, however, your investigation has disclosed that the individual was provoked, that he did not initiate the fight, and that your employer's policy (as written and enforced) recognizes that termination need not occur where an employee did not initiate the confrontation.

Thus, the ultimate conclusion you reach may be to terminate Employee #1 and to suspend Employee #2, an action that reflects a legitimate employer policy that fighting, regardless of the circumstances, should not occur but that also recognizes that some limited form of progressive discipline may be used where mitigating factors are present.

This example also illustrates the dangers of acting in haste and on your first impression. Assume that you had followed your first reaction by immediately terminating both employees for fighting. Then assume that Employee #2 files a grievance under a collective bargaining agreement and that it is submitted to arbitration and/or that he files an EEOC charge claiming discriminatory treatment, stating that he was provoked by racial slurs and that the employer had used suspensions but not terminations for employees who engaged in prior incidents of fighting under similar circumstances, and that these suspended employees were Caucasian. Under these assumptions, how would you and your employer have fared?

While it is impossible to predict the ultimate outcome with 100 percent accuracy, it can be stated that you would run a substantial risk of losing the arbitration case. Why? Because you may be required to prove ''just cause'' for Employee #2's termination. In determining whether just cause is present, arbitrators will consider whether the employee was provoked, whether both employees were equally at fault, whether the employer has a consistently enforced disciplinary policy concerning fighting, whether it was followed in this instance, etc.

In other words, arbitrators will evaluate the same issues that are listed in Appendix 11–A and that were just discussed as supporting a suspension (not a termination) for Employee #2 as the more appropriate disciplinary action.

Moreover, if Employee #2 filed a discrimination charge in addition to or in lieu of a union grievance, the EEOC could take a dim view of your action, for two primary reasons:

1. The use of racial slurs is prohibited discrimination under Title VII, and your taking equal disciplinary action against both Employee #1 and #2, even though you knew that Employee #2 responded only after he was provoked by the slurs, could be viewed as condoning discriminatory remarks by employees.
2. The EEOC also will note that Employee #2 was subjected to disparate treatment since he was terminated while your employer had merely suspended Caucasian employees who were provoked into fighting under similar circumstances.

Thus, if you had followed your first impulse and terminated both employees, your employer would have incurred a significant (but unnecessary) risk of future financial liability to the employee as well as the possibility of future reinstatement. This risk was contained, however, when, instead, you followed a deliberate analytical approach to your decision making. Such an approach allowed you to discover for yourself the defects in your initial response, and as a result, your final decision was to reject a termination for Employee #2.

While the suggested methodology does not assure you that no challenge will be filed by Employee #2, since he is free to protest a suspension through a union grievance, an EEOC charge, etc., your use of the advocated approach has dramatically increased the probability that you will be able to defend your final decision successfully.

This discussion is designed to illustrate the necessity for using a methodical approach to supervisory decision making by analyzing your proposed action from both a procedural and substantive perspective. The checklist in Appendix 11–A provides a thumbnail sketch of the specific issues pertinent to each perspective, and you may wish to refer to that outline as you proceed to Chapters 12 and 13. Since the following chapters do discuss procedural and substantive considerations in detail, you also may find it helpful to annotate this Appendix with supplementary notes as to additional issues or factors to be considered as you analyze your own future supervisory actions.

NOTES

1. WEBSTER'S NEW COLLEGIATE DICTIONARY 1170 (8th ed., 1975).
2. *Id.*
3. *Id.*

Appendix 11–A

Checklist of Issues for Supervisory Decision Making

A. Procedural Issues To Consider
1. Did employee have notice of:
   ___ The applicable policy, procedure, or other requirement of your employer?
   ___ The work-related expectations you may have concerning the person's job performance, conduct, or attendance?
   ___ The dissatisfaction you have with an employee's conduct, performance, or attendance, and of the corrective action the individual must take?
   ___ The consequences, including the possibility of disciplinary action, if the unsatisfactory conduct, performance, or attendance continues?
   ___ The relevant changes in your employer's policies, procedures, or other requirements?
2. Did you investigate the facts before taking disciplinary action?
   ___ Did you interview witnesses, obtain their statements or your own investigatory notes of what they knew, saw, or heard, and did you verify or discount any conflicting "facts" that arose?
   ___ Did you review all the documentation for discrepancies, missing facts, omitted dates or signatures, etc.?
   ___ Did you review the employee's prior record?
   ___ Did you speak to the employee to determine that person's version of the events or problem?
   ___ Did you review your documents or double-check with your witnesses or other individuals with firsthand knowledge if any inconsistency emerged between the employee's version and that of other witnesses (or your own understanding of the facts) to determine whether the differences could be resolved?

_____ Did you evaluate the facts (outlining your facts can be extremely helpful in this regard) so as to discard irrelevant ones and those that could not be proved or did not appear credible?

3. Have your employer's policies, procedures, or requirements been enforced consistently and evenly?

_____ What type of disciplinary action has been taken for past infractions?

_____ Have you considered the possibility of deferring disciplinary action in this case, if enforcement has not been consistent, in favor of informing all employees that the policy, etc., will be enforced in the future (group notice), and proceeding with disciplinary action only for future infractions?

_____ Are there any aggravating factors that support disciplinary action if there has not been consistent enforcement and, if so, can you still comply with other applicable notice requirements?

4. Have you obtained advice, direction, or approval as required by your employer's own procedures or requirements, e.g., from personnel, your superior, legal counsel, etc.?

5. Was the employee notified of the right to union representation for the investigatory interview, if applicable, and was the union given notice of the disciplinary action, if applicable?

6. Have you prepared an appropriate written notice of your final disciplinary action, discussed it with the employee, asked the person to sign the notice to acknowledge receipt of a copy, and provided a copy for the worker's personnel file? Remember, if your disciplinary action is to terminate an employee, then double-check your own internal procedures since they may not require a meeting or that a copy be provided to the employee.

7. Have you followed progressive discipline, if it is appropriate (for example, is the infraction not so serious that termination for a first-time offense is warranted) and is your intended disciplinary action the next appropriate step to take?

B. Substantive Issues To Consider

1. What is the general nature of the problem you are facing: unsatisfactory performance, misconduct, or absenteeism/attendance?

2. Can you determine, if the issue is unsatisfactory performance:

_____ How the employee's performance is unsatisfactory?

_____ What the employee must do to correct the performance?

_____ Whether the employee appears to be unable or unwilling to perform (since your plan of action may be influenced by this distinction)?

_____ Whether the employee's performance fluctuates between satisfactory (or even excellent) to poor, indicating the ability to do the work but a lack of concern or consistency (again, this distinction may influence your decision)?

_____ Whether your expectations are consistent with how other employees perform the job (if not, you may need to establish revised standards or give notice to all employees that existing ones will be enforced before you proceed to any disciplinary action)?

_____ Whether the employee has received any assistance from you or others and whether any such aid (or external sources of help), such as written materials, continuing education programs, seminars, etc., would be helpful?

3. Can you identify, if the issue is misconduct:

_____ What type of misconduct is involved, such as theft, sleeping on duty, under the influence of alcohol or drugs, insubordination, unauthorized absences, destruction of property, fighting, etc. (remember, there may be more than one type of misconduct)?

_____ What requirements you must meet to prove that type of misconduct and whether your facts establish each such activity (for example, sleeping on duty requires sleeping, not merely closing one's eyes, and on duty time, excluding rest breaks, meal periods, etc.)?

4. Have you considered, if dependability (absenteeism or tardiness) is the problem:

_____ Whether the primary problem is extensive absences (long absences because of health problems), one- or two-day absences (may be health but the employee may have personal problems or is deliberately using up sick leave as it accumulates), or tardiness (the easiest to deal with from a disciplinary standpoint)?

_____ Whether you are contesting, or conceding, that the absences are health-related?

_____ Whether there is any factual basis for contesting the legitimacy of any claims that the absences are health-related?

_____ Whether your facts support a conclusion that the employee is engaging in a deliberate pattern of absenteeism/attendance akin to misconduct (such as not calling in sufficiently in advance of an absence, not returning to work at the end of an approved leave, being absent on days adjacent to days off, holidays, etc.)?

_____ Whether any medical verification or information is necessary, whether it has been obtained, and whether your policies allow mandatory referral to employee health or to an employer-selected physician?

_____ Whether any of the absences were the result of workers' compensation illness or injuries?

5. Have you identified whether any legal do's and don'ts apply to your problem and, if so, will your intended action comply with those legal standards?

6. Do any of your employer's policies or procedures speak to the problem you are facing; if so, is your intended action consistent with those policies?

7. What has been your employer's response to past occurrences of the same type of problem at issue here and is your intended action consistent with those responses?

8. Have you checked and double-checked:

   • any relevant employer policies, rules, or procedures, as enforced and as communicated to employees

   • any applicable outside standards (such as those of the Joint Commission on Accreditation of Hospitals, etc.)

   • any pertinent union contract provisions

   • your employer's own past practices, etc.?

9. Has supervisory action been taken for this incident (whether disciplinary, a performance review detailing deficient areas of performance, or counseling, etc.); if so, is a follow-up appropriate and, again, if so, have you flagged a follow-up date to ensure that it will occur?

Chapter 12

Procedure: Notice, Notice, and More Notice

A REVIEW

Chapter 11 advocated that your supervisory decision-making process emphasize developing your own ability to analyze a proposed action against the procedural and substantive requirements imposed on employers. Procedure and substance then were defined in the following terms:

- procedural means that you must consider whether all of the notice or due process preconditions to supervisory action have been met.
- substance involves whether you and your employer can prove that the employee did (or did not do) whatever you claim to be the case. (Substance is the subject of Chapter 13.)

Within that framework, this chapter discusses in greater detail some of the more common procedural requirements that affect not only the validity of your decision or recommendation but also the probability that it will be upheld if it is challenged internally or by the employee. Again, it may be helpful if you annotate the Appendix 11-A checklist of procedural issues as you review the following material.

PROCEDURE EQUALS NOTICE

Procedural requirements, regardless of the specific form taken (such as progressive discipline, communicating with employees, performance evaluations, investigatory steps prior to discipline, documentation, etc.) generally have one common denominator: they represent an attempt to provide employees with notice.

Time and time again, arbitrators have refused to uphold the decisions of employers who have not provided an employee with adequate and timely notice, in whatever form appropriate for the particular problem. Other decision makers (EEOC, judges, juries, NLRB, etc.) also rely on, or may be influenced by, the presence of notice (with its appearance of fairness) or by its absence (with its appearance of arbitrary, pretextual, or hasty action). Therefore, providing employees with due process or notice is not a mere technicality; it is critical to the validity of any intended supervisory response.

PURPOSE OF NOTICE

The necessity for ensuring that disciplinary or other employee action is not tainted by insufficient notice or by a failure to meet other procedural requirements is particularly critical now (and absence potentially more costly) because of erosions in an employer's right to terminate employees at will. Similarly, proof that you have complied with all of these requirements, as has been noted, is one of the best ways to protect your employer against employees' being able to claim successfully that they were terminated "because of" their race or religion, union activity, or any other protected grounds.

If you still are not persuaded that an ounce of prevention is worth all the trouble of complying with the procedural demands imposed on your employer, remember that these requirements have two other purposes: (1) fairness to your employees, and (2) an opportunity for corrective action.

Fairness to Your Employees

Telling employees very directly what you expect of them not only is good preventive supervision, it also is the right thing to do. Employees are entitled to know what you want and where they stand in relation to your expectations. They also are entitled to know these things before adverse action is taken. So remember:

- It is important for you, as a supervisor, to ensure that your corrective actions not only are fair and reasonable but that they are seen and perceived as such by other employees.

- Employees' morale is directly affected by actions that appear to them to be arbitrary and unfair.

- Your actions will be seen as unfair, and in a real sense they will be unfair, if you ignore basic principles of notice and procedural due process.

Supervisors do employees no favor by phrasing constructive criticism or corrective supervisory actions in such soft language that the message, "You must improve now!" becomes garbled. Your standards can be strict and your expectations high and your actions still will be fair, in perception and in reality, if you communicate forthrightly, with no hidden messages and no hidden meaning.

Opportunity for Corrective Action

A primary goal of effective supervision is to ensure that your employees maintain satisfactory performance. Yet it is difficult for them to do this if you fail to give adequate and timely notice of your expectations and how they measure up; in other words, they generally cannot correct the problem if they are not told that it exists. Thus, providing an employee with appropriate notice is a means of encouraging voluntary improvement and of requiring improvement through corrective disciplinary action where voluntary efforts are unsuccessful.

There is again that one important exception to this. Conduct can be so clearly wrong that everyone knows without being told that it will not be tolerated. If this happens, the need to provide employees with the opportunity to mend their ways become irrelevant. For example, you do not have to prove that your employees were told or otherwise notified that they should not steal, physically abuse patients, or permit other equally serious offenses. If they do engage in such conduct, they do not have to be given (and generally should not be given) a second opportunity, assuming that prior instances of similar conduct have resulted in consistent responses from your employer.

TYPES OF NOTICE

Group vs. Individual Notice

In determining the best way to provide your employees with notice, distinguish group notice from individual notice:

- Group notice, as the name suggests, is the type directed to the work force as a whole, or to departments, or to other groups of employees. Examples are written policies, employee handbooks, orientation sessions, meetings, postings, etc.
- Individual notice, by contrast, focuses on a particular employee and is directed toward correcting that specific person's work habits or behavior patterns. The more common examples of this type are performance evaluations, nondisciplinary counseling sessions, and progressive discipline.

Group Notice—How It Is Given

Your employer's policies, procedures, and practices can be made known to your employees in a variety of ways. Most frequently, you should use a variety of methods, depending upon what works best for you and your employer, and how your facility handles employee communications (e.g., whether printed employee handbooks exist, bulletin boards are accessible, etc.).

In deciding which method(s) you believe the most effective, consider also whether you can prove in any subsequent arbitration, lawsuit, or other claim that the notice was given. In other words, if you know that you discussed a particular revision to a policy at an employee meeting but you have no record of the meeting, you will experience great frustration (to say the least) if your version is disputed subsequently, under oath, by the employees and you have no written document supporting your recollection.

Group Meetings

This is a very effective means of communicating with your employees since the possibility for question-and-answer sessions can clear up misunderstandings quickly. The personal contact between the speaker and the group avoids the coldness of a bulletin board and permits you to explain the reasons for your actions. However, group meetings are not without their defects:

- It will be found that their effectiveness often diminishes as the size of the group grows.

- It can be relatively difficult to prove that notice was given if the record of what was said at the meeting is poor, particularly since it often will be disputed by participants.

- It can be difficult to prove that an individual employee was present unless an accurate register such as a sign-in sheet is taken and kept. The fact that the employee should have been there will not prove that the person actually was present.

To avoid these difficulties, while still retaining the plus aspects of using meetings for communicating with your employees simultaneously, consider these steps:

- Have all employees sign in at the meeting (no initials—they can be very difficult to decipher later).

- Prepare a brief written summary of the meeting. It need not be long or elaborate; it need only state clearly the essential points discussed. Then distribute the minutes to all employees, and have them sign the document to indicate that they have read it.

- Check your distributed minutes periodically to be sure that all employees have in fact signed them and, if not, distribute them to those whose names are missing.
- Keep a copy of all signed minutes; do not throw them away after a year or two even if you are forced to store them under your desk. Too often for comfort, the document you have discarded turns out to be exactly the piece of paper you desperately need later.

Posted Notices

Because they generally are brief and can be reproduced easily, many employers post notices on bulletin boards as a method for communicating with employees. It is all too well known, however, that few employees actually read them, or read them with any care; as a result, they tend to be a relatively poor means of providing notice. Moreover, you never can be certain, and therefore prove, that a particular employee read the minutes or that the individual was even at work during the time they were posted.

Some, but not all, of these problems can be avoided by having, as one of your rules (in the employees' handbook or elsewhere) the requirement that employees must check the bulletin board every week (or other stated interval), and if they fail to do so they still are responsible for knowing the contents of all posted notices. Even with this procedure, however, problems can develop, so never rely on this as your sole form of group notice.

Communication Journals or Logs

This method of communication is used frequently with some degree of success within particular work areas, departments, or nursing units. Properly used, a communication book (whether a notebook binder, a steno pad, etc.) is a way to encourage daily communication and to disseminate information among employees on various shifts or work schedules as to changes in policies or procedures, actions that need to be taken, areas that need correction, and related topics.

Again, however, problems can develop if you ever need to demonstrate through use of the journal that particular employees knew, or should have known, what you expected of them. So, to avoid these potential difficulties:

- All employees should be informed that they must review the journal's most recent entries on a daily basis (or other stated period).
- All employees also should be told that they are responsible for knowing the contents of the journal and that any future defense in which they say "I didn't read it" will not be acceptable.

- These points should be communicated in a provable fasion, e.g., in a group meeting followed by distributed and signed minutes, an orientation with similar documentation, etc.

Policies and Procedures Manuals

Policies and procedures manuals can take several forms. Sometimes, an employer's personnel policies and procedures are presented in a manual (updated periodically) in addition to, or in lieu of, an employee handbook. Just as frequently, particular work areas or departments will have manuals containing policies and procedures pertaining to that function (e.g., one manual for nursing, another for pharmacy, etc.).

Both types tend to be comprehensive so they can be a good way of communicating with employees; of notifying them as to your policies, standards, expectations, and how certain things should be done (or not done); and, as discussed next, of providing subsequently what your policies actually are.

To benefit from these advantages, however, you also have to avoid some of the common pitfalls they can present:

- The manuals must be reviewed periodically to be sure that they actually represent your current policies and practices. If they do not, then the employer must determine whether they still represent what your practices and policies should be, in which case all employees would need to be informed that, effective prospectively, the policies will be enforced as written. By contrast, if your actual practices (not the written policies) are preferable as is or with some modification, then the written policies should be revised and notice of the changes provided to all affected employees.
- Revisions to the manual should be distributed to all affected employees or some other form of documented employee review should be provided before or when they are placed in the manual.
- The manual must be kept in an accessible location and, again, periodic review should be documented by employee sign-ups or some similar method of written acknowledgment.
- Employees should be required to review the entire manual (not just revisions or recent entries) at stated time intervals to refresh their recollection and, again, to ensure that the manual is a form of communication and not just a depository for storing policies and procedures.
- Supervisors—you—must be familiar with any manuals and you never should take disciplinary action without reviewing the applicable provisions.
- The manual obviously will be revised or amended from time to time. When that is done, take care that a copy of the prior policy and procedure is retained, with its effective date. This is essential when you need to counter later

allegations as to the contents of your policies and procedures manual at any given time.

Employee Handbooks

Easy to carry and to read, employee handbooks are popular with many employers. But you can suffer disastrous consequences later unless a great deal of care and attention is given to their preparation. A few of the points to remember are that:

- Employee handbooks must conform to your written policies. For example, if your handbook summarizes, in one paragraph, the procedures employees must follow in requesting leaves of absence, the summary must not be inconsistent with the procedures, requirements, and limitations in your three-page written official policy document on that topic.
- Handbooks must be updated periodically so they will continue to conform to your current standards, policies, and procedures.
- Handbooks must be given to all employees, who must sign a receipt to be retained by your employer.
- The receipt should state that the employees have received copies and that they must review its contents within one week (or other time period) and that it is their responsibility to inquire of you or someone else if they have any questions.
- The receipt should not have the employees acknowledge that they have read and understood the handbook; since they sign the receipt at the time they are given a copy, this type of statement, while common, is a factual impossibility.

Orientation Sessions

Orientation sessions are a valuable method for introducing new employees to your institution. They can be equally helpful in communicating information and in documenting that material if several basic guidelines are observed:

- A standard checklist, outline, or text of the material to be covered should be used by all individuals responsible for conducting the sessions to ensure a consistency of approach and that the same material is covered in all classes.
- Logs or registers should be signed (not initialled) by all employees attending the sessions.
- A checklist or outline of the essential points covered should be signed by the attending employees.
- All documents should be retained; after all, they will be of very little value to you if they are discarded soon after the session.

Current and new employees assigned to your area should be oriented as to the particular policies, procedures, rules, and expectations that pertain to your service. For example:

- Has your area made any modifications in personnel rules and procedures such as different reporting time requirements because of different starting times for shifts, etc.?
- Are there any specialized procedures or requirements employees need to be aware of and where are they kept if they are in writing (as they should be)?
- Do you use (and require that they review) communication logs, etc.?

These are just a few of the points to be covered. Again, you need to ensure through checklists, etc., that the same information is imparted to everyone in a documented fashion.

Enforcement of Rules

An excellent method for letting your employees know that the rules will be enforced is to actually do so consistently and constantly. This serves as notice to all employees that the rules exist and will be followed.

By contrast, inconsistent or irregular enforcement may be interpreted as notice to employees that you no longer regard a particular rule as pertinent or one that they need to follow. In this regard, you probably are familiar with the temptation—common to some supervisors—to identify "special cases" that justify equally special (which usually means more lenient) treatment. This temptation must be resisted and limited to very exceptional circumstances that can be demonstrated objectively as supporting the deviation. Why the need for this caution? Because creating unnecessary exceptions to a rule inevitably results in undermining the rule itself; similarly, these exceptions in effect tell your employees that the rule may or may not be enforced, depending upon your inclinations at the moment.

Union Contracts

In one sense, union contracts are another form of notice to your employees. No union contract can include all of the policies, procedures, requirements, expectations, etc., that apply to your employees. While the contracts should not be viewed as a method for you to communicate with such individuals, they frequently do contain provisions governing employees' performance, seniority, standards for discipline, etc. For this reason, and because the contract language will govern even if the employees failed to read the document, you should always review these provisions to determine what they tell your employees before you take disciplinary or other supervisory action.

Individual Notice—How It Is Given

Individual notice is directed toward a particular employee. You as a supervisor are saying to an individual: you should—or must—change your ways. You are telling the employee this through one of the following means.

Counseling Sessions

Counseling is not and should not be regarded as a disciplinary action. Instead, it is an opportunity, and an excellent means, for:

- discussing with an employee your perceptions of the individual's performance and of any areas that need to be improved
- reviewing written policies, procedures, or other expectations that pertain to any areas of unsatisfactory performance or even satisfactory areas but where you believe the employee could perform even better
- hearing directly from the individuals what their perceptions are of your expectations and requirements and any areas where they believe they are having difficulties or could use assistance, etc.
- asking an employee to give an explanation or version of a particular problem that might clear up the matter by revealing facts not previously known to you
- allowing you to reinforce how something should be done, how an employee is doing it incorrectly, and why you expect improved performance.

In summary, counseling is still another method of giving notice to individual employees of what your standards and expectations are and of providing them with an opportunity to improve, knowing the standards against which they will be measured. This opportunity can be lost, however, if you forget that counseling must be separated very clearly from disciplinary action. While disciplinary action might result later if the employee does not improve (whether the problem be performance, conduct, or absenteeism/tardiness), any such future discipline would be taken because of an incident subsequent to a counseling session. The notice of your expectations, as provided through counseling, may be relevant to establishing employee awareness of your standard, but it is not the basis for any subsequent disciplinary action.

If employees ever question whether counseling is disciplinary, inform them clearly that this is not the case; if you fail to do so, then your employees might reasonably perceive the sessions as potentially disciplinary in nature and request a union representative be present (see *Weingarten* rule, Chapter 4). Once this happens, the mutual advantages of having a supervisor and an employee sitting down to discuss problems in a nonadversarial environment may be lost.

For the same reason, counseling sessions should not be documented on any forms that you use for written warnings, suspensions, or other disciplinary action. Instead, a summary of the topics covered, with as much detail as is called for under the circumstances, should be prepared soon afterward and a copy given to the employee. One way in which such a memo can be written is illustrated in Exhibit 12–1.

Performance Evaluations

Regular, accurate, and comprehensive performance evaluations are seen as one of the least attractive aspects of a supervisor's duties. This is unfortunate, because (1) they are vital to sustaining subsequent disciplinary action for poor performance; (2) they are an effective way (if done properly) to develop and maintain a competent work force; and (3) they can undercut the validity of any future disciplinary action if they are done improperly.

Exhibit 12–1 Documenting a Counseling Session

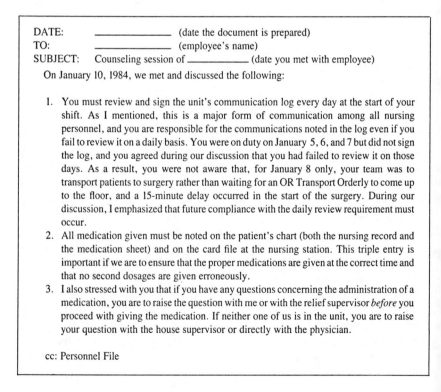

DATE: _____ (date the document is prepared)
TO: _____ (employee's name)
SUBJECT: Counseling session of _____ (date you met with employee)

On January 10, 1984, we met and discussed the following:

1. You must review and sign the unit's communication log every day at the start of your shift. As I mentioned, this is a major form of communication among all nursing personnel, and you are responsible for the communications noted in the log even if you fail to review it on a daily basis. You were on duty on January 5, 6, and 7 but did not sign the log, and you agreed during our discussion that you had failed to review it on those days. As a result, you were not aware that, for January 8 only, your team was to transport patients to surgery rather than waiting for an OR Transport Orderly to come up to the floor, and a 15-minute delay occurred in the start of the surgery. During our discussion, I emphasized that future compliance with the daily review requirement must occur.

2. All medication given must be noted on the patient's chart (both the nursing record and the medication sheet) and on the card file at the nursing station. This triple entry is important if we are to ensure that the proper medications are given at the correct time and that no second dosages are given erroneously.

3. I also stressed with you that if you have any questions concerning the administration of a medication, you are to raise the question with me or with the relief supervisor *before* you proceed with giving the medication. If neither one of us is in the unit, you are to raise your question with the house supervisor or directly with the physician.

cc: Personnel File

Performance evaluations have two primary purposes:

1. They increase the overall efficiency and competence of your employees by highlighting their good points, drawing attention to unacceptable work performance or habits, and suggesting areas that need or require improvement.
2. They serve as a documented form of notice to the individual employee of unsatisfactory performance and of areas that must be improved.

Many different types of performance evaluation forms exist. Some are quite simple and are limited to listing a group of factors (such as quality of work, quantity of work, dependability, leadership, etc.). You as the supervisor then are asked, for each factor, to rate whether the employee has been "very unsatisfactory, unsatisfactory, satisfactory, good, or excellent" during the period under evaluation. Other systems are quite elaborate and require participation by both you and the employee. Furthermore, the form may vary from department to department or classification to classification.

One example of an evaluation format is presented in Appendix 12-A at the end of this chapter. This is the form used by the Santa Rosa (Cal.) Memorial Hospital. Under the Santa Rosa system, the evaluation form actually incorporates the employee's job description, with each expectation in that description given a weight to reflect its importance. This approach encourages a consistency between the factors you assess and the actual functions of the position and helps encourage the evaluation of all employees against the same criteria.

Regardless of the specific form used by your facility or work area, there are a variety of procedural steps and requirements that you should follow in performing an evaluation:

Be Objective. Be sure to rate the employee separately on each factor. In other words, avoid the halo effect (whereby a good employee's superb technical skills cause you to forget that the person never is on time); and equally important, avoid the reverse halo effect (where the poor aspects of an employee's interpersonal skills blind you to the fact that the individual always volunteers to help when a crisis occurs).

Include Supporting Comments. Even if you have to make space on the form or add a page or two, be sure that you take the time to comment on each factor you are rating. For example, if you mark the employee as "unsatisfactory" on attendance, insert a notation that supports this conclusion (e.g., the employee was absent 10 days during the year under evaluation, all of them single days off). These comments serve two purposes: they allow you to remember later why you came to that conclusion and they demonstrate to the employee that the rating has an objective basis.

Discuss It with Your Employee. After you have completed the evaluation, you must review it with the employee, point by point, because evaluations serve little purpose and provide no notice to anyone if they are simply completed and put in a file without ever being communicated fully to the employee.

Respond to Employee Disagreement. If an employee disagrees with your rating or opinion, or with any of your comments or conclusions, take the time to double-check your own ratings and conclusions even if this means you have to investigate further whether the individual's comments are correct or incorrect.

Change Your Ratings. If you have double-checked your initial ratings after discussing the preliminary evaluation with the employee and you come to the conclusion that you should change the evaluation, do not be afraid to do so. Changing the rating will not diminish its validity. To the contrary, it will increase its accuracy, enhance your credibility, and serve notice to employees that their participation is worthwhile and can have an impact. By contrast, if you still believe that your initial rating should not be changed, then simply enter a brief note as to what the employee's comment was and why you stand by your rating.

Sign and Date the Evaluation. When the final evaluation is ready, and again after it has been discussed with the employee, make sure that the person signs the form to acknowledge that it was reviewed. Also be sure that you date the evaluation when the final copy was prepared and that employees date it when they sign it. Time and time again, undated evaluations have surfaced; if they become pertinent to a challenged supervisory action, you might find yourself spending numerous hours reviewing personnel records, etc., in an attempt to determine when the evaluation was given.

Cope with Employee's Refusal to Sign. If an employee refuses to sign the evaluation, there is no need to force the issue. You should simply explain that signing does not indicate the employee's agreement with its contents; it simply is an acknowledgment that the person saw it, reviewed it, and received a copy. If the employee continues to refuse to sign, simply note the facts of refusal and that the evaluation was reviewed with the individual on a particular date. It also may be wise to have another supervisor sign as a witness to the fact that the evaluation was reviewed with the employee (if applicable) and a copy given to the individual.

Review All Evaluations. Periodically, whether every six months or whenever, you should review all evaluations completed during that time period to determine whether any common problems appear to be surfacing. For example, all employees—or a significant number of them—may have been rated unsatisfactory on reporting in by x time if they are sick, or on the completion of their nursing care plans. When this occurs, it is a signal to you that additional group notice or review of your policies, standards, and expectations may be necessary before further enforcement attempts are made through disciplinary action.

Next you should be sure to follow up on the evaluations. Where an assessment discloses unsatisfactory areas of performance, conduct, or absenteeism/tardiness, you must identify for the employee what has to be done to correct the problem and a date by when the employee should do it. You also may wish to identify resources that may be of help to the employee.

For example, if you have identified that a registered nurse's charting is unsatisfactory, you should also be specific as to:

- How it is unsatisfactory; e.g., whether it is incomplete (such as consistently failing to state the time a particular treatment was given), is illegible, etc.
- What the employee must do to correct this deficiency. To continue this same example, it might be as simple as explaining that the person must always include the time the treatment was given or must slow down handwriting so that it can be read—or print, if that should be necessary.
- When the improvement must occur. With these examples, immediate improvement can be expected. In other areas, particularly where the employee might benefit from additional inservice or needs an opportunity to brush up any rusty skills, you may wish to give 30 days (or another time span) to improve to a satisfactory level.

Once these factors have been identified, thus providing notice of what the employee must do, then the responsibility shifts to you to ensure that appropriate follow-up action takes place if the improvement does not occur. For example, if you gave the employee 30 days to improve a particular area but you never check during the following year, all of the work you put into the evaluation is for naught. Why? Because the purpose of the evaluation was to improve the employee's performance, even if this objective requires subsequent disciplinary action if progress has not occurred. This is not possible if you never double-check to determine, at the end of 30 days, what the employee has done. Instead, all that happens is that one year after the first evaluation, you again may be writing an assessment that describes the same weakness in performance and wondering to yourself why the employee has not improved.

You also should follow up to determine whether employees have met the goals they themselves identified or whether they have taken any steps toward those objectives. It is very popular to have employees identify their personal work goals for the coming year. Frequently, you will see evaluations in which employees, in their own writing, have stated that they "will be developing [their] own professional skills and knowledge by increasing attendance at educational programs and that [they] recognize [they] must develop more tact in working with coworkers."

However, in the follow-up evaluations a year later, they list these same goals, which surface again and again in following evaluations. Yet no checking is ever done to determine whether in fact these employees did anything toward these goals. When this breakdown occurs, the employees soon realize that their identification and statement of personal goals is simply a game that has no significance and that they will not be held accountable in any way. This undermines the effectiveness of the evaluation process and any hopes you may have had for using that process to obtain demonstrated improvement in performance.

Progressive Discipline

The use of progressive discipline has long been recognized as a necessary ingredient of supervisory responses to problems of unsatisfactory performance, conduct, or absenteeism/tardiness. What progressive discipline is, and is not, and when it is required, is described in Exhibit 12–2. You frequently will hear it be said that progressive discipline requires that you follow four increasingly severe steps when taking action:

1. oral reprimands
2. written warnings
3. suspensions (time off without pay)
4. termination.

Each of these steps is discussed in Exhibit 12–2.

Oral Reprimands. An oral reprimand simply means that you tell the employee, verbally, that a certain aspect of performance, conduct, or dependability is unsatisfactory, reminding the person that if no improvement occurs, or if it happens again, further disciplinary action may need to be taken. While this definition is quite simple, the use of oral reprimands and their role in progressive discipline have caused confusion.

An oral reprimand can be documented briefly in your own anecdotal notes but it should not be written up in full and given to the employee. Why not? Because if you do that, what is the distinction between an oral reprimand and a written warning? The answer is: "none, as a practical matter," so it can only result in confusing the employee or others as to what disciplinary action you actually took.

An oral reprimand can be difficult to distinguish from nondisciplinary counseling since, in both instances, you may be verbally reviewing areas of performance and how you want the employee to do something differently. As a result, your employees may be unclear as to whether you are taking disciplinary action (and even whether they may have a *Weingarten* right to union representation, see Chapter 4) or whether it is simply a nondisciplinary discussion.

For these reasons, and if your facility or your work area relies on counseling sessions to any great extent, you may not need to use oral reprimands as part of your progressive disciplinary process. Remember, oral reprimands are simply one

Exhibit 12–2 Checklist for Progressive Discipline and Documentation

First: Always make sure that you already have provided your employees with group or other pertinent notice describing the rule, policy, procedure, or standard, as appropriate.

Then:

1. *Oral Reprimand* (if used by your facility)
   ___ Do privately (not in the presence of other employees or supervisors).
   ___ Reexplain rule/policy/procedure/standard and the need for compliance by the employee.
   ___ Limit your documentation to a brief notation in your notes: include the date, location, problem, what you told the employee, and retain any pertinent written materials.
   ___ Conduct subsequent follow-up if required (e.g., to determine whether the employee has taken corrective action, to ascertain whether further disciplinary action is necessary, etc.), and document.
   ___ Remember, an oral reprimand is not a written warning.

2. *Written Warning*
   ___ Check prior disciplinary action, performance evaluations, etc., before you issue a written warning to ascertain whether these same problems have been discussed with the employee previously.
   ___ Investigate before you decide to issue warning.
   ___ Be prepared to defer, modify, or abandon the warning if you write it before asking the employee's version and the facts that emerge warrant such a step. Remember, it is better to change your mind when new facts are disclosed than to proceed with an inaccurate and unwarranted disciplinary action.
   ___ Include the following in the warning:
   ___ (1) The facts leading to the warning: who, what, when, where, applicable employer policy, etc.
   ___ (2) The corrective action you expect from the employee and a restatement of the standard, if appropriate.
   ___ (3) The consequences to the employee if corrective action is not taken or if another incident occurs.
   ___ (4) References to prior counseling sessions, verbal reprimands, or other disciplinary action or discussions on the same issue (e.g., "Last week I told you that you must be at your duty station ready for work at 9 a.m.").
   ___ (5) Signatures of yourself and the employee (or a witness, if the employee refuses to sign) and the date.
   ___ (6) A copy for the employee.

3. *Disciplinary Suspension* (time off without pay)
   ___ Investigate before you tentatively decide a suspension would be appropriate (this includes determining whether the employee had prior related written warnings if progressive discipline is appropriate, etc.).
   ___ Talk to the employee before you make a final decision and double-check the individual's version, as appropriate.
   ___ Make your decision, document it, notify the employee, and discuss decision with the person.
   ___ Keep your documentation (or written notice of suspension) similar to the written warning except that you will:

Exhibit 12–2 continued

_____ (1) Confirm the suspension (where you already have given the employee verbal notice of your decision, e.g., by telephone) but still include all points in (1) to (6) above for written warnings.

_____ (2) Specify the workdays covered by the suspension and the date, day of the week, and shift of the employee's return to work.

_____ (3) Notify employee that termination is the next probable step if there is a reoccurrence or no improvement.

4. *Termination*

_____ Check and doublecheck: has progressive discipline been followed? If not, does an exception exist and is termination warranted by the seriousness of the conduct?

_____ DO ALL INVESTIGATION PRIOR TO MAKING DECISION, INCLUDING TALKING TO EMPLOYEE AND VERIFYING/DISPROVING THAT PERSON'S VERSION, OBTAINING WRITTEN (IF POSSIBLE) WITNESS STATEMENTS FROM EMPLOYEES, PATIENTS, VISITORS, ETC. (Note: Your documentation of a termination will vary from that used for other disciplinary actions, depending on the circumstances.)

_____ (1) Complete all investigatory documentation before the termination notice is prepared (but do not attach to termination paper; generally, you are not required to give—and should not give—this underlying documentation to the employee).

_____ (2) Present statement of reasons; EXERCISE EXTREME CAUTION since the reasons you give are the reasons you must prove.

_____ (3) Make sure the final paycheck is ready to give to the employee with the termination notice.

_____ (4) Obtain any and all necessary approvals of your intended decision before it is communicated to the employee.

form of notice to an employee. If you already have provided such notice through group meetings, policies, and procedures, comments to employees, etc., or through documented counseling sessions to provide a greater opportunity for full discussion of problem areas (in contrast to oral reprimands), then eliminating the use of oral reprimands should have no adverse consequences for your future disciplinary action.

Written Warnings. These are an essential component of progressive discipline: you are telling an employee what was unsatisfactory, when it was done, what you expect the individual to do in the future or how you expect it to be done, by what date, and what will happen if it is not done. Thus, it serves as notice that the employee is entering the disciplinary stage and that more severe action will result if there is no improvement or if the misconduct is repeated.

Suspension. A disciplinary suspension says that the employee is one step short of being terminated and you are attempting to make clear the seriousness of the situation by depriving the person of pay, with the length of the suspension to be dependent upon the incident itself and how your employer has responded previously (or says it will respond) to such situations.

As Exhibit 12–2 indicates, documentation of a suspension is very similar to that used for a written warning. Again, you are presenting the "who, what, when, where" facts, that you expect of the employee, and what will happen if it does not occur.

Suspension as a form of discipline must be distinguished from a suspension pending investigation:

- A disciplinary suspension is your final supervisory decision. You already have investigated the facts and have determined that such a suspension is appropriate.

- A suspension pending investigation is not disciplinary action and no decision to take such action has been made. Instead, it is a procedure used for serious circumstances where, if the allegations are true, some risk to the employee, to patients, to your employer, or to others could result if there were a repetition. In such circumstances, you may decide to use a suspension pending investigation to allow yourself the opportunity to investigate whether disciplinary action is necessary, knowing that you must compensate the employee for worktime lost if you ultimately conclude that no disciplinary action (or action short of a suspension) is warranted.

Because this distinction exists, you also should be clear in your communications with an employee as to whether you are suspending the individual or simply having the person report off-duty during your investigation (suspension pending investigation). If it is the latter, the employee should be told that worktime lost will be paid for if the resulting disciplinary action is less severe than a suspension covering the period of absence. If you do not do this, numerous practical difficulties can arise; for example, the employee (or union) may conclude that you already have taken disciplinary action and attempt to grieve a nonexisting employer disciplinary response.

Termination. This is the final step of progressive discipline, and since the consequences for the employee—and for you and your employer—are extremely severe, no termination should occur unless:

- You have evaluated your facts and the sequence of progressive discipline and/ or other notices to the employee, if applicable, against the procedural and substantive checklist in Appendix 12–A.

- You have fully investigated the current incident and have spoken to the employee to verify your version of the events or to cross-check the employee's version before taking action.

- You have double-checked your own policies and procedures and complied with any internal requirements that terminations be approved by a designated individual.
- You have prepared appropriate documentation.
- You have exercised caution in preparing the termination notice and in phrasing the reasons. Remember, as noted, the reasons you give for the termination are the reasons you subsequently may have to prove.

Exceptions to Progressive Discipline

Your policies and procedures should never state that you must follow progressive discipline in all instances or imply that the absence of progressive discipline will void the disciplinary action you take. This suggestion is supported by two very important considerations:

1. A recognized exception to progressive discipline, as discussed previously, is that employees are expected to know that certain of their actions may lead to immediate termination.
2. Progressive discipline "may" have been appropriate but the absence of a particular step does not automatically invalidate disciplinary action (or lead to a conclusion that disciplinary action cannot be taken) if you've provided other forms of timely notice to the employee, before this incident, of your expectations, what the person must do, and what will happen if it is not done.

In other words, remember again that progressive discipline is simply one form of giving notice to employees, and alternate forms may be substituted under appropriate circumstances.

Performance Appraisal and Development Form

POSITION DESCRIPTION

EMPLOYEE: _____ Last Review Date: _____ This Review Date: _____
JOB TITLE: _____ SUPERVISOR: _____

Job Code: _____

Position Summary: Is directly responsible to Charge Nurse for nursing care given within the 8-hour shift; administers all aspects of nursing care and performs appropriate duties as assigned to promote optimal functioning of unit. Full, part-time or relief position.

Education/Experience Requirements: Must be a graduate of an accredited School of Nursing and currently licensed as an R.N. in the State of California. Staff Nurse I has less than one year's experience in an acute care hospital. Staff Nurse II must have one year's experience in the last five years in an acute care hospital as a Staff Nurse where knowledge, skills, and leadership ability have been demonstrated in that specific area.

Duties, Responsibilities and Specific Objectives	5 - Distinguished 4 - Commendable 3 - Competent 2 - Needs Improvement 1 - Unsatisfactory	*Performance Rating* For Each Standard 1–5	*Weight* Importance Of Each Standard 1–10	*Total Points* For Each Standard (Rating × Weight)
I. **Patient Care**		10		
A. Demonstrates technical skills in nursing care.		____	____	____

Source: Reprinted with permission of Santa Rosa Memorial Hospital, Santa Rosa, Cal.

Duties, Responsibilities and Specific Objectives	5 - Distinguished 4 - Commendable 3 - Competent 2 - Needs Improvement 1 - Unsatisfactory	Performance Rating For Each Standard 1–5	Weight Importance Of Each Standard 1–10	Total Points For Each Standard (Rating Weight)
B. Demonstrates application of theory based on scientific principles to nursing procedure.		——	——	——
C. Demonstrates understanding of policies and procedures of other departments.		——	——	——
D. Ability to organize, execute care plans as prescribed by physician.		——	——	——
E. Ability to initiate, organize, execute and evaluate nursing care plans.		——	——	——
F. Sets priorities according to patient needs.		——	——	——
II. **Psychosocial Aspects**			8	
A. Identify patients' psychosocial needs (psychological, social, spiritual, etc.).		——	——	——
B. Initiate appropriate intervention (i.e., social services, spiritual care, family, etc.).		——	——	——
III. **Communications**			10	
A. Gives accurate, objective, and comprehensive oral reports to oncoming shift and/or charge nurse.		——	——	——
B. Maintains continuous effective communication among staff members.		——	——	——
C. Works actively to maintain a climate conducive to open communication with the patient.		——	——	——

Duties, Responsibilities and Specific Objectives	5 - Distinguished 4 - Commendable 3 - Competent 2 - Needs Improvement 1 - Unsatisfactory	*Performance Rating* For Each Standard 1–5	*Weight* Importance Of Each Standard 1–10	*Total Points* For Each Standard (Rating Weight)
D. Communicates with patient's family as appropriate, i.e., emotional support, answering questions.		____	____	____
E. Maintains continuous effective communication with physicians regarding patients.		____	____	____
F. Maintains continuous effective communication with other departments (i.e., Lab, X-Ray, Nuclear Medicine).		____	____	____
G. Charts in a manner that is appropriate, legible, concise, accurate, and informative and documents treatment and procedures:				
1. Nursing notes		____	____	____
2. Med rands and Medication cards		____	____	____
3. Graphics, Intake & Output Sheets		____	____	____
4. Requisitions		____	____	____
5. Incident reports, consents, releases		____	____	____
H. Utilizes NCP as a tool of communication.		____	____	____
IV. Technical Skills		10		
A. *I.V. Therapy:*				
1. Initiates I.V. Therapy in a manner prescribed by SRMH policy. Minimum requirement: Butterflys and Longdwells.		____	____	____
2. Maintains I.V.s and Hep-lock as prescribed by				

Duties, Responsibilities and Specific Objectives	5 - Distinguished 4 - Commendable 3 - Competent 2 - Needs Improvement 1 - Unsatisfactory	Performance Rating For Each Standard 1–5	Weight Importance Of Each Standard 1–10	Total Points For Each Standard (Rating Weight)
SRMH policy (site care, tubing changes, rate calculations, etc.).		____	____	____
3. Administers I.V. meds safely and as prescribed by SRMH policy.		____	____	____
4. Administers blood and blood components safely and as prescribed by SRMH policy.		____	____	____
B. *Medication:*				
1. Administers all medications according to SRMH policy.		____	____	____
2. Demonstrates working knowledge of all medications including incompatibilities and utilizes proper resources.		____	____	____
3. Assesses patient condition with regard to medications administered (injection site, side effects, vital signs, effect of medication, etc.).		____	____	____
4. Assumes responsibility for maintaining adequate pharmaceutical supplies.		____	____	____
C. *Equipment:*				
1. Demonstrates ability to set up and maintain the following equipment:				
Blood warmer		____	____	____
Stryker Turning Frame, Circoelectric Bed		____	____	____

Duties, Responsibilities and Specific Objectives	5 - Distinguished 4 - Commendable 3 - Competent 2 - Needs Improvement 1 - Unsatisfactory	*Performance Rating* For Each Standard 1–5	*Weight* Importance Of Each Standard 1–10	*Total Points* For Each Standard (Rating Weight)
McGaw Pump		——	——	——
Hypothermia—Lipidus Mattress		——	——	——
K-Pads—Bed Scales		——	——	——
Suction & Drainage—Tracheal & Gastric		——	——	——
Wound Suction		——	——	——
O_2—Triflow		——	——	——
Closed Chest Drainage System		——	——	——
Traction—Pelvic, cervical		——	——	——
Crash Cart and Life Pak		——	——	——
2. Demonstrates knowledge of other equipment pertinent to area.		——	——	——
D. *Treatment and Procedures:*				
1. Demonstrates ability to perform treatment according to Nursing Procedure Manual.		——	——	——
2. Takes appropriate nursing action in emergency situations.		——	——	——
3. Maintains CPR certification.		——	——	——
4. Assists physician with procedures appropriate to working area:				
Cut-Down		——	——	——
Lumbar Puncture, Biopsies		——	——	——
Chest Tube Insertion		——	——	——
Pelvic Exam		——	——	——
CVP Subclavian		——	——	——

Duties, Responsibilities and Specific Objectives	5 - Distinguished 4 - Commendable 3 - Competent 2 - Needs Improvement 1 - Unsatisfactory	Performance Rating For Each Standard 1–5	Weight Importance Of Each Standard 1–10	Total Points For Each Standard (Rating Weight)
Sigmoidoscopy		‾‾	‾‾	‾‾
Paracentesis		‾‾	‾‾	‾‾
Thoracentesis		‾‾	‾‾	‾‾
5. Initiates and maintains isolation technique according to hospital guidelines and under direction of Nurse Epidemiologist.		‾‾	‾‾	‾‾
6. Physical Assessment and Observation:				
a. Systematically assesses cardiovascular, respiratory, renal and neurological condition of patient.		‾‾	‾‾	‾‾
b. Formulates a nursing diagnosis and takes appropriate action based on this diagnosis.		‾‾	‾‾	‾‾
V. **Legal/Safety**			10	
A. Insures patient safety (siderail policy, safety vests, infection control, etc.).		‾‾	‾‾	‾‾
B. Maintains safe hospital environment by disposal of contaminents, by evaluation and maintenance of equipment, and by housekeeping.		‾‾	‾‾	‾‾
C. Demonstrates knowledge of action plan for safety drills.		‾‾	‾‾	‾‾
D. Makes complete Incident Report for any unusual occurrence.		‾‾	‾‾	‾‾

Duties, Responsibilities and Specific Objectives	5 - Distinguished 4 - Commendable 3 - Competent 2 - Needs Improvement 1 - Unsatisfactory	*Performance Rating* For Each Standard 1–5	*Weight* Importance Of Each Standard 1–10	*Total Points* For Each Standard (Rating Weight)
E. Demonstrates awareness of legal aspect of documentation on patient record.		___	___	___
F. Receives and records physician orders according to hospital policy.		___	___	___
VI. Professionalism				
A. Demonstrates reliability for attendance and performance.		___	___	___
B. Functions as effective role model for staff and patient through professional behavior and appearance.		___	___	___
C. Demonstrates self-motivation in personal and professional growth.		___	___	___
D. Protects rights of patient.		___	___	___
E. Maintains confidentiality of all hospital-related matters.		___	___	___
VII. Leadership				
A. Makes assignments and delegates duties based on staff qualifications and patient needs; promotes teamwork.		___	___	___
B. Functions as resource person for other staff members.		___	___	___
C. Orients new personnel.		___	___	___
D. Utilizes time and resources efficiently to problem solve.		___	___	___
E. Gives and accepts constructive criticism.		___	___	___
F. Demonstrates organizational abilities.		___	___	___
G. Staff Nurse II will assume position of Charge Nurse when necessary.		___	___	___

Duties, Responsibilities and Specific Objectives	5 - Distinguished 4 - Commendable 3 - Competent 2 - Needs Improvement 1 - Unsatisfactory	Performance Rating For Each Standard 1–5	Weight Importance Of Each Standard 1–10	Total Points For Each Standard (Rating Weight)
VIII. Teaching			8	
A. Staff—motivates and instructs other staff members.		____	____	____
B. Patient & Patient Family—functions as health resource and teacher for patient and family.		____	____	____

Overall Performance Rating (Circle One)

This rating is computed by dividing total points by total weights.

Distinguished	- 4.21 - 5.00
Commendable	- 3.41 - 4.20
Competent	- 2.61 - 3.40
Needs Improvement	- 1.81 - 2.60
Unsatisfactory	- 1.00 - 1.80

Exceptional Accomplishments

Employee Development & Performance Improvement Plan

List specific objectives (measurable, if possible) on which the employee will be rated in the next review. Give a weight (1–10) to show the importance of this area as a new standard.

Weight

Present Job Step _____

RECOMMEND _____

NEXT REVIEW DATE _____

****

Rating Supervisor ———————————————   Date ———————————

Department Manager ——————————————   Date ———————————

Employee ———————————————————   Date ———————————

Distribution of Copies:
  White—Personnel   Yellow—Originating Dept.   Pink—Employee

Chapter 13

Substance: Proving Your Case

TYPES OF ISSUES

Now that you have become familiar with the various types of procedural and notice requirements you should consider before taking supervisory action, it is time to analyze your decision-making process from another perspective, one that focuses on substantive issues and requirements such as:

- What is the general nature of the problem you are facing: performance, misconduct, or attendance/tardiness issues?
- What is the specific type of problem you are attempting to resolve?
  1. If performance is at issue, does it concern an employee's unwillingness to perform satisfactorily, an inability to do so, etc.?
  2. If an employee's conduct is at issue, are you dealing with fighting or theft or insubordination, etc.?
  3. If absenteeism or tardiness is involved, are you concerned about excessive absences resulting from genuine health difficulties, or sick leave absences of doubtful validity, or chronic tardiness, etc.?
- Can you identify (and meet) all of the elements that are required to establish the appropriateness of your intended supervisory response for that specific type of problem?
- Have you taken into account (and complied with) any applicable employer policies, union contract provisions, or legal standards?

The major substantive issues you must consider were presented in the Appendix 11–A checklist (again, it may be helpful if you annotate that list for future reference). This chapter provides further assistance by describing in detail the particular considerations applicable to a wide variety of issues raised by an employee's performance, conduct, and lack of dependability.

Identifying the Problem

Substantive requirements vary tremendously, depending on the nature of the problem facing you. Therefore, each inquiry must begin by identifying and classifying the general category into which the problem falls. In other words, are you concerned about an employee's performance, conduct, or dependability?

Conduct vs. Performance

Simply stated, an employee who has acted improperly should be classified as a conduct problem while one whose work product is below standard presents a performance problem. This straight-forward distinction, however, has many important consequences for your decision-making process:

- Performance problems generally must be handled by giving the employee adequate notice of what is required and by following progressive discipline. This means that discharge usually is not considered unless and until the employee proves unable or unwilling to improve the performance to a satisfactory level. On the other hand, you can—and should—respond to serious misconduct with more immediate and more severe disciplinary action, including possible discharge. But remember, every generality has an exception: Any performance problem that does present an identifiable danger, hazard, or unacceptable risk to patients, employees or others, *is* that exception.
- Some performance problems will result in nondisciplinary action. For example, if an employee's health deteriorates to the extent that the person cannot perform the job, termination may be necessary (but only after also evaluating such an action against legal standards such as handicap laws). Yet the resulting termination is not disciplinary in nature so your action may be judged by a lower standard. In other words, you may be required to show only that the termination was not arbitrary or capricious, a much easier task than showing just cause. By contrast, your responses to employee misconduct inevitably will be disciplinary, so your justification should comply with just cause standards. If the misconduct concerns criminal activity or immorality, you may be required to meet an even higher standard of proof since it may be claimed that a discharge for such reasons can leave a stigma on the employee.
- Poor performance reflecting incompetency or a lack of qualifications may be handled appropriately by a transfer or demotion to a position within the employee's competence (assuming that the individual is qualified for the new position and you are not transferring the person just to get rid of a problem). However, transfer or demotion is not an appropriate response to employee misconduct.

- Misconduct frequently occurs because of the employee's intentional or negligent disregard of your employer's policies or of generally accepted standards of behavior. Performance problems, by contrast, generally occur not because an employee deliberately breaks the rules but because the person is unable or unwilling to do the work satisfactorily. Again, however, the exception might be illustrated by employees whose performance is full of errors because they are deliberately careless.

How To Classify Poor Attitudes

When your analysis reveals that the employee's problem does not result from an inability to perform but from attitude to the job, to coworkers, and to the employer, do not simply inform the person that the poor attitude must be corrected (or, worse yet, by imposing discipline for this "offense"). Why not? Because this is a very subjective determination, difficult to prove, and leads easily to a conclusion that the real problem is simply a personality conflict between the employee and yourself.

This advice does not mean that poor attitudes do not exist or that you cannot take corrective action. To the contrary, it just means you should proceed in an alternate fashion by focusing on job-related concerns and whether the attitude has any impact on the employee's performance, conduct, or dependability. Once this determination has been made, you should phrase (and analyze) your response in terms appropriate for that impact.

In other words, if the impact is that an employee is careless in completing work, you generally will approach the situation as one involving unsatisfactory performance, and corrective action should consist of progressive discipline with clear warnings to the individual. If, on the other hand, the impact is that the employee is verbally abusive to patients or other employees or brusque to the point of rudeness, or abrupt and incomplete in communications with others, the situation frequently can be handled as a conduct problem, with a more immediate and severe response.

If no impact appears to exist, you should recognize that you may not like the employee's carriage, tone of voice, or a variety of other personal characteristics. If this is the case, remember that you are not required to like all of your coworkers, supervised employees, or superiors. Your only obligation is to identify your own personal problems and predilections, distinguish them from your legitimate job-related concerns on behalf of your employer, and continue to work effectively with those individuals regardless of your reactions to their style.

If you are concerned with how frequently or how much an employee misses work or is tardy, then you are confronted by a dependability problem. While absenteeism and tardiness share many common features with conduct issues (in the sense that lateness may result from intentional disregard for your legitimate expectations that an employee will be at work on time) or with performance issues (since an employee may be unable to report consistently because of genuine health problems), they also have distinct substantive requirements. As a result, you should classify these problems separately and respond to them as if they presented different types of issues.

Once you have identified the general nature of the problem, then focus on the specific kind of complaint. Again, the purpose of continuing your analysis is to answer the question, "What supervisory response would be appropriate?" This answer depends on accurately determining the precise nature of the deficiency.

DEALING WITH PERFORMANCE PROBLEMS

Identifying the Nature of the Deficiency

You must focus first on the actual deficiency that is the subject of the complaint: inconsistency, consistently poor performance, errors of judgment, low output, failure to follow internal procedures, and so on. What is it that the employee is doing incorrectly or unsatisfactorily? Unless you isolate your specific concern in this fashion, you will not be able to eliminate irrelevant considerations, to tell the employee what must be done to correct the performance, to identify any pertinent policies or statements of procedure, etc.

Distinguishing Won't from Can't

Your next inquiry should be, "Why is this employee failing?" Here, you distinguish between those who are able to do the job but will not from those who cannot perform satisfactorily even though they are attempting to do so. Ask yourself:

- Has the employee performed competently in the recent past? If the answer is yes, the person probably is able to do so now but will not.
- Is the employee's performance erratic? If so, you may again have a "will not" or careless employee.
- Is the employee anxious, frequently asking for your advice or approval? If so, you may have a "cannot."
- Have you demonstrated correct performance but the employee still has difficulty in performing satisfactorily even when you are present? If so, you again may have an employee who "cannot" perform to your expectations.

The Employee Who Can't. If you are satisfied that the problem is one of incompetency or inability to perform, then you should try to identify the reason. Is the employee simply unqualified for the job? Is it the type of problem that can be remedied by inservice training, by working with another employee on a buddy system, or by other affordable and reasonable training or assistance (offering to enroll such persons in a baccalaureate program is neither)? Or is the demonstrated lack of knowledge and skill so fundamental that the employee would lack the ability to handle the job even with assistance from the employer? Similarly, does the employee understand what you expect? Is the person aware of any statements of procedure, standard protocol, listing of job duties (and how to do them), etc.?

How these and other questions are answered will determine your appropriate response. As examples:

- If a lack of qualifications has been identified that can be corrected in a reasonable length of time, this should be pointed out to the employee and a suggested plan of action developed. In such circumstances, disciplinary action may be inappropriate unless the employee refuses (or is unable) to take corrective action and the performance remains unsatisfactory.
- If unfamiliarity with your expectations, statements of procedures, etc., appears to be the cause of the problem, you should review with the employee the areas of deficiency, the applicable policies and expectations, and the corrective action you are requiring the person to take.

However, never assume that the employee will be unable to improve. When you are faced with a performance problem, as noted, you must always let the employee know that you are unhappy with the work, what must be done to correct the performance, and what will happen if there is no improvement. Generally, the individual also should be given a reasonable opportunity to improve.[1]

The Employee Who Won't. If your investigation leads you to conclude that the employee could perform satisfactorily now (the person has performed satisfactorily in the past, and/or has the required knowledge and skills, etc.), then exercise caution. Why? Because these types of facts can lead you to assume that employees have personal problems that could be corrected if they only discussed it with you, the supervisor, or that the temporary lapse in job performance should be ignored while they work out the problems, etc. More likely than not, these kinds of supervisory responses do not result in correcting the performance problem or in providing any assistance to the employee.

A few suggestions on typical problems to avoid when dealing with an employee who won't:

- Do not invade personal privacy by forcing the employee to discuss personal matters with you.
- Avoid placing too much emphasis on "saving" the employee if that would be overly intrusive on the individual's rights or if it sacrifices your legitimate expectations that the person will perform satisfactorily.

- Continue to expect (and require) satisfactory performance, notwithstanding any personal problems the employee may have.
- Remember that the employee may simply be an inconsistent worker. If so, do not empathize or sympathize; instead, require that the employee take immediate corrective action and maintain a consistent level of performance at the risk of future disciplinary action.

A careful and considered analysis of the problem often will suggest what response may be appropriate for the employee who can but will not. Whatever your response, timely follow-up is essential to ensure that the employee is maintaining satisfactory performance.

Distinguishing Group Performance Problems

Your supervisory response frequently must be structured differently if you are dealing with a similar problem among several, or all, of your employees. These are called group performance problems, as opposed to those limited to one individual.

To identify these problems, you must be alert to a recurring pattern of performance difficulties, or to similar deficiencies in different performance evaluations, or to persistent and related complaints from other departments, patients, etc. Then, if it appears that several, many, or all of your employees are having the same difficulty, you would be well advised to defer any disciplinary action until after you have communicated and reinforced with all of these persons what they should be doing and how they should be doing it. Why? Because if many employees are having the same problem, and you single out certain individuals as examples for disciplinary action, this typically results in accusations of discriminatory, arbitrary, and inconsistent treatment. Equally important, it can cause resentment among your employees and a belief—which would have some merit—that you are acting unfairly.

Thus, the importance of identifying a group problem is to ensure that you recognize situations where many employees are having a common difficulty and where notice or reminder (or assistance) to all those in the group concerning your expectations is appropriate. Thereafter, if individuals still fail or refuse to comply, your follow-up would be directed toward them through corrective disciplinary action.

Standards That Apply to Performance Problems

After you have tentatively identified a performance problem and its nature, ask yourself, "What is the standard against which I am measuring this employee?" Is it statutory? A requirement by the Joint Commission on Accreditation of Hospitals? A rule, policy, or practice established by your hospital? Or, has the employee simply fallen short of the standard you would expect from anyone who is reasonably proficient and concerned? Whichever one applies, good supervisorial practice requires you to identify the applicable standard clearly and to be in a position to explain where and how the employee does not measure up.

Your written internal policies or external legal standards will not be relevant to every performance problem. Nevertheless, you should always check to see whether there are any applicable policies or standards before you develop your response. To do this, you should review the most common sources for such standards, such as:

- state licensing requirements for health care facilities
- state licensure requirements for various professions that also govern the conduct and permissible area of practice of all individuals possessing such licenses
- state regulations establishing occupational standards in the health care industry (for example, some states prescribe minimum qualifications for directors of nursing)[2]
- criteria established by voluntary professional associations (however, these criteria may be higher or lower than those of your own state or employer and thus they generally are only a resource for you and are not controlling)
- federal and state laws regulating certain aspects of a health care employer's operations, such as the use of narcotics and other controlled substances, disposal of radioactive materials, storage and preparation of foods, etc.
- standards required of institutions participating in state or federal health programs (e.g., Medicare)
- the duty of care imposed on health care employers and employees by the courts through medical malpractice and related claims
- standards and criteria to be met by your institution for accreditation by the JCAH
- union contract standards, expectations, or limitations on job responsibility
- requirements under employment laws such as the Occupational Safety and Health Act safety standards and/or state law
- the standard of care and level of knowledge and skills that could be expected of all employees possessing the training and/or education required for the position held by the individual at issue.

Finally, your own employer's standard job descriptions must be totally familiar to you and to all of your employees since (1) they frequently exceed the minimum qualifications and standards imposed by the state, by the JCAH, and other regulatory bodies; and, (2) the mere fact that a license allows an employee to perform certain functions under state law does not mean that your employer has included all such functions in the individual's realm of responsibility.

Now that the importance of identifying pertinent standards has been emphasized, a word of caution is in order. Many legitimate expectations of employees are incorporated in written materials such as policies and procedures manuals, nursing department policies, job descriptions, etc., but some are not. Why? Because the rule of conduct may be so universally observed and enforced that it can be expected of employees without being written into any document and because it is not possible to cover every eventuality in your standards.

The fact that your expectations, or satisfactory performance by the employee, has not been reduced to writing does not preclude you from taking action or from requiring that the person correct that performance. It only means that you may need to take greater care in reviewing the standard with the employee, and in documenting that review, before you proceed with corrective action.

Correcting Problems with the Employee

Once again, you must communicate the problem to the employee; Chapter 12 pointed out the key word: notice. When you have identified a problem, you achieve nothing by keeping it from the employee. As soon as possible, and using one of the means discussed in Chapter 12, you must tell the employee clearly and precisely what is being done wrong (it may be wise to document this discussion, with a copy to the employee).

You then must specify the applicable standards. Here is the opportunity to reemphasize what the standards are, how the employee has fallen short and what the person should be doing. By your actions you are giving notice not only to that individual but to all other affected employees.

The next step is identifying the corrective action required. The appropriate action will depend upon a number of factors:

- Does this call for disciplinary or nondisciplinary action?
- Is this an employee who can, but won't, or an employee who cannot and who may benefit from additional assistance?
- What is the seriousness of the performance deficiency?
- Do other employees consistently meet the standard, expectation, or policy?
- Has this employee (and others) been given notice (if appropriate) of the standard expectation or policy before this incident?
- How has the standard, expectation, or policy been enforced in the past?
- Is some form of progressive discipline applicable (it generally will be)?
- Have there been prior adequate warnings?

- What is the employee's work record?
- How long has the employee been employed?

A major problem can be whether you should provide or offer assistance. Sometimes the investigation and analysis will lead you to believe that the problem is correctable and that you and your institution should provide the employee with aid and assistance. While this is a praiseworthy approach, some words of caution:

- Do not discriminate; be sure that you are willing to offer the same help to all employees with similar problems.
- Be especially cautious about offering professional psychological help and avoid conditioning continued employment on submission to psychiatric assistance except in very unusual circumstances (and even then you would be well advised to do so only after you have sought legal and/or medical assistance to verify that this appraisal is correct).
- Confine offers of help to occasions when you think it will achieve something; in other words, do not use the help as a device to put off making hard decisions.
- Continue to expect that the employee must be an active participant in improving the performance; otherwise, the person may contend that the performance did not improve because you did not fulfill the promise of support.

Next you must address the possible consequences if the problem is not corrected. You rarely will deal with a problem that is confined to just one employee so your failure to act may well limit your ability to respond to similar problems with others in the future. Therefore, your actions must be appropriate to the identified problem. If you allow yourself to treat this employee in a special way because you are sympathetic to the personal problems, or because the individual is liked by everyone, etc., then you may be establishing a precedent you may not wish to remember, or to be bound by, on future occasions with less sympathetic employees.

You also should analyze whether your standards or expectations should be changed in any way. Sometimes you will conclude that the employee may have fallen short of your expectations but that the standards are unrealistically high. In such cases, the appropriate corrective action should be a recommendation to your own superiors to modify the standards to conform with reasonable expectations and to notify all employees of any such changes. In the absence of such modifications, it would be difficult for you to defend corrective action that requires superhuman qualities from your employees.

Supervisory follow-up is extremely important. Consistent and regular enforcement of standards demands that problems be followed up in an appropriate and timely fashion. Once you have identified performance deficiencies, and spoken to the employee, and identified the required corrective action and the consequences if it does not occur, then you must follow up with the individual to assure yourself that satisfactory performance has been achieved. If it has not, you should proceed with disciplinary action.

The lack of follow-up once some action has been taken is a typical lapse in supervisory responses and when this occurs it undercuts the effectiveness of your earlier steps. It also may seriously limit your ability to handle recurrences by the same employee (and even recurrences of similar problems with other employees). It is important to remember that supervisory follow-up is a form of notice and a failure to follow up can serve as notice to all employees that the standard or expectation will not be enforced.

HANDLING CONDUCT PROBLEMS

Employee misconduct can involve a variety of issues, so your first task is to identify the specific type you are concerned about: Is it insubordination, or intentional destruction of property, or reporting under the influence of alcohol or drugs, etc.? While you may be able to quickly identify the type of misconduct you are dealing with, you also must convince yourself that the employee actually committed the misconduct, which may be a much more difficult and time-consuming task.

After identifying the problem, review the elements of the case to make sure that all essential elements are present. For example, if one of your employees is accused of insubordination, you must make sure the person (1) received an order, (2) was aware that disciplinary action would be taken if it were disobeyed, and (3) actually refused to carry it out.

Absence of one of these elements may require you to investigate further, drop the charge, or consider alternatives. If there was no insubordination, for example, consider whether the employee failed to perform the tasks satisfactorily, which should be labelled as a performance problem and handled through progressive discipline.

Thus, there is a necessity for ensuring that your facts fit the claimed offense. This leads to some of the more common misconduct issues you may encounter.

Insubordination

Elements of the Offense

To prove a claim of insubordination, you generally must show that all of the following were present:

1. Direct Order. This is a common source of problems in insubordination cases. In your investigation, make sure that there was a clear and direct order. A request generally is not sufficient, nor can you rely on a belief that the employee ought to have known what was expected.

2. Notice of Consequences If Employee Refuses. Although your case will be much stronger if the employee is specifically warned at the time of the refusal that nonaction will result in disciplinary action, the presence of such a specific warning is not universally required. The reason is that the nature of the order, the employer's prior handling of disobedience, and other factors sometimes can be used to show that the employee knew that the refusal opened the way for disciplinary action. However, there is no reason to take a chance, so telling the employee of the consequences of disobeying the order is always wise.

3. Refusal by Employee. First, is the action actually a refusal? A clear and unambiguous refusal presents no problem. But what about the employee who develops a practice of arguing over work assignments and who then resumes work at a deliberately slow pace? While this type of action (or inaction) does complicate matters, do not despair. You still may be able to prove, from the surrounding circumstances, that the employee is deliberately attempting to undermine the supervisor's authority by refusing to comply fully with the order or to comply in a timely manner.

A second point is whether the refusal has been withdrawn. Do not react too quickly to refusals to work. Instead, when feasible, allow the employee a reasonable opportunity to withdraw the refusal. An employee can signify a change of mind either by letting you know that the person no longer is refusing the order or by announcing a refusal to comply but immediately proceeding to complete the assignment. In addition, learn to distinguish the occasions when the employee withdraws a refusal after the time for completing the task has passed; that clearly is insubordination. Indeed, even if an employee refuses initially but almost immediately withdraws the refusal, you must follow up by reaffirming that on future occasions, a refusal—even if retracted—may result in disciplinary action.

There are two reasons why you should exercise caution: (1) if given an opportunity to reflect, the employee might in fact withdraw the refusal; and, (2) if this does not occur, your case of insubordination will be much stronger since there can be no mistaking that the employee actually refused to carry out your order. Of course, in the health care field there will be occasions when a refusal to perform an assigned task has such serious and immediate consequences that you will not have the luxury of giving the employee an additional opportunity to think better of the action. In such a case, the absence of a second chance should be justified.

4. Distinguishing Failure to Perform. Failure to perform an assigned task is not insubordination unless the employee was directly ordered to do it and refused, by actions or words. Continued failure to perform assigned tasks where there is no order can justify progressive disciplinary action but generally will not support the more immediate and serious type of employer response, such as a suspension or termination, that attaches to insubordination. For this reason, be careful and do not categorize an employee's failure to perform, which is a type of performance problem, as insubordination.

Obey Now—Grieve Later Rule

Even if an employee believes that your order is incorrect, outside the job description, or wrong for other reasons, the person generally must carry out the assigned task first, then file a grievance. As a result, arbitrators rarely will assist employees who try to use self-help by claiming that they were entitled to refuse because they had a legitimate grievance or because they were right (an exception to this rule is dealt with next). Put another way, you are not expected to resolve complaints or get an employee to agree with how you want the job done before the person performs the work assignment.[3]

Because this rule has widespread acceptance from arbitrators (and should be pertinent to any challenges filed with the EEOC, civil lawsuits, etc.), it is a good practice to tell the unhappy employee to use your grievance process to voice the complaint but that the immediate duty is to obey the order. Proof that you gave the employee this advice will strengthen the justification for your disciplinary action.

Exceptions for Health And Safety

Genuine fears that your order presents imminent danger to health and safety are legitimate grounds for employee refusal to obey an order. However, employees generally cannot use this defense if the risks are a normal part of the work and are no greater than the risks presented to all other employees. Nevertheless, in handling insubordination problems, be sure to investigate thoroughly any question of health or safety before taking disciplinary action.

Professional Disputes As Insubordination

In addition to the previous exception, you cannot require an employee to perform an illegal act or one that violates a specific statute. If you attempt to do so by discharge or other adverse employment action, you may be exposing your employer to lawsuits or other claims for back pay or other damages. Similarly, an order that would cause a health care professional to violate established and recognized rules of practice may be improper and, if so, the employee might defend the refusal on those grounds.

However, where the issue is one of judgment, then even a professional or licensed employee normally is not entitled to refuse and if the person does, disciplinary action may be appropriate. Authority structures are just as essential to the operation of health care institutions as they are to other employers, and health care employees should not be permitted to refuse orders simply because they believe them to be errors of judgment. Therefore, it is appropriate to establish a procedure to handle preimplementation inquiries as to the accuracy of the judgment through increasingly higher supervisory levels, to the medical director of the unit, etc., for use in such situations.

Sleeping on Duty

Elements of the Offense

When faced with a claim that one of your employees has been sleeping on duty, examine the facts carefully to ensure that the offense actually occurred. Although it may sound obvious, remember that the employee must actually have been asleep; it is necessary to distinguish instances where the facts could be interpreted as simply dozing or resting with closed eyes. Sometimes, whether or not the employee has made preparations for sleeping (e.g., using a bed in an empty patient room) may help you in making this distinction. However, it is not required that the employee deliberately intended to fall asleep or take a nap; instead, the offense is committed if the employee "positions herself so as to invite sleep in obvious disregard of the duty to remain alert and watchful."[4]

In your inquiry, make sure that the offense took place on work time, not during a lunch period or a rest break when employees are free to do as they please (with some obvious exceptions, of course). Similarly, because sleeping while on duty is "the" essential element of this offense, disciplinary action generally will not be upheld if an employee is found asleep after the shift has ended, no matter how strong the probability that sleep commenced during working hours.

Mere inattentiveness to duty is a distinctly different type of problem and should not be categorized as "sleeping on duty." Generally, inattentiveness will be treated as a problem of performance, not of misconduct, and your focus will be on improving the employee's work performance. Failure to categorize the offense correctly may lead to your disciplinary action's being overturned since sleeping on the job generally is regarded as a more serious offense and any arbitrator or other decision maker hearing the case may assume that you would have imposed a less severe penalty if you had categorized the problem correctly.

Consequences If Proved

The seriousness of the offense will influence the type of discipline you impose. All instances of sleeping on duty are subject to discipline but obviously some are more serious than others. For example, a stationary engineer in sole charge of a hospital's boilers has a far greater responsibility to stay awake—and a greater potential for harm to others if the person does not—than a clerk in medical records.

So, in reviewing the case, be sure to determine whether your employer has a policy of disciplining all employees equally for this offense (a permissible approach) or whether discipline reflects the actual and potential risks created by the person's action (also permissible but the distinctions among employee classifications may be difficult to observe in practice). If your employer uses the latter approach, however, pay attention to the employee's degree of responsibility and to the chances of detection since, under such circumstances, these factors may be pertinent to the appropriateness of your final disciplinary action.

Drinking or Drugs

Drinking or Under the Influence of Alcohol

When you are presented with a complaint involving the use of alcohol, you must distinguish between drinking on the premises and being under the influence of alcohol while on duty.

One type of case involves drinking on the premises. The elements of this offense obviously are that the employee is drinking and is on the employer's premises. This sounds straightforward but several cautionary notes are in order: (1) it is not required that an employee actually be under the influence of alcohol; (2) your employer may (and should) define what constitutes the employer's premises, including parking areas, etc.; and (3) the offense may occur even if the employee is off duty, so long as the drinking occurs on the premises and your employer has prohibited this conduct.

By contrast, being under the influence does require that the employee actually be in that condition while on duty. This is where supervisors frequently run into problems. Why?

First, because some supervisors confuse the term "drunk" with "being under the influence"—and you should not use the word "drunk" (which may be construed as a certain level of alcohol that may not be present or provable) to characterize the employee. Second, because the term "under the influence" may be used, based on your opinion or that of another eyewitness observer, without noting the aspects of the employee's behavior that lead you to this conclusion. Since this opinion evidence (that the employee was "under the influence") may not be admissible or credited, your investigation and documentation must indicate whether the individual was exhibiting any of the following characteristics:

- breath—any smell of alcohol?
- gait—staggering, uncertain?
- eyes—bloodshot, dilated?

- speech—slurred, incoherent, stumbling?
- thought processes—confused, rambling, contradictory?
- demeanor—belligerent, unnaturally elated, morose?
- fine motor movements—clumsy, awkward?
- pallor—flushed, pale?
- blood alcohol—alcohol-urine, alcohol-breath test.

Unless you are able to show objectively that several of these signs are present, your opinion testimony generally will be worthless. On the other hand, neither you nor other witnesses need to have any medical training or prior experience in detecting alcohol abuse if you can offer clear testimony as to the physical aspects of the employee's behavior and can compare the person's normal behavior with the conduct under examination.[5]

Another type of case involves off-duty conduct. As a general rule, you have no right to control an employee's drinking habits away from work unless it impairs performance or results in the individual's arriving intoxicated. If the person does not arrive at work under the influence and does not drink on your employer's premises but has frequent absenteeism or other difficulties caused by off-duty drinking, then concentrate your efforts and your supervisory decision making on the work-related problem; that is, focus on the lack of dependability and not on your assumptions (even if they are correct) as to the reasons for the employee's difficulties.

You should be aware, however, that there is one exception to the rule that off-duty drinking habits generally are no concern of the employer's. If the employee has had prior work-related problems resulting from use of alcohol, and you have conditioned continued employment on the employee's agreement to participate in an alcohol rehabilitation program, under such circumstances a failure to stay on the wagon may be used as the basis for disciplinary action.

Use of Drugs

The problem of drug abuse, or the personal use of illegal drugs or other controlled substances by health care employees, has become of increasing concern from at least three standpoints:

1. Employees who come to work under the influence of drugs present many of the same dangers as (if not more than) are caused by persons whose functioning is impaired by alcohol.
2. Employees' temptation to supply their own needs by obtaining drugs improperly from their own work setting may be increased by their dependency and the accessibility of drugs in a health care facility.
3. Employees will find that the effects of drug usage can be devastating.

When faced with the possibility that your own employees are drug users or abusers, you should keep several issues in mind:

- Employers' "proof" of whether an employee is under the influence of drugs should be based on objective analysis of the person's physical or mental characteristics. For this reason, the examples of behavioral characteristics listed in the preceding section on drinking may be equally useful when dealing with employees who are drug abusers.
- Employee assistance programs (your own or others in the community) may be an option.
- Employee users who steal drugs generally should not be handled any differently from nonuser employees who engage in similar misconduct.
- Drug enforcement authorities may need to be called in where theft or loss of drugs is occurring; this should be done without regard to whether the suspected employee may be a drug user.
- Employers should focus on the impact of drug use on the employee's functioning (and not the fact of drug use) in any inquiry and in determining whether disciplinary or other action would be appropriate.

A common theme running throughout these listings of issues may be obvious, namely, that employees who report for work under the influence of drugs or alcohol present many similarities so you can use similar approaches in dealing with them. This similarity should be kept in mind in studying the later sections on "Blood, Breath, Urine, and Other Tests" and "Rehabilitation Act and Rehabilitation Programs."

It is essential to remember that the use of alcohol is not a crime in and of itself while the use of some drugs is a crime. This distinction can be of significance when investigating or determining your appropriate response; therefore, the advice of legal counsel is warranted when you are dealing with drug-related issues.

Sale vs. Possession of Drugs

The unlawful sale of drugs is a serious offense with far-reaching consequences. It is even more so in the health care industry, with its greater access to dangerous drugs. As a result, you are entitled to take sterner action against employees who violate these laws. You still must be prepared to prove your charge, however, and thus you should carefully distinguish instances where an employee is "merely" in possession of drugs from cases where the person sells or attempts to sell them.

Possessing illegal drugs or controlled substances on your employer's premises is a form of misconduct that can be the subject of legitimate prohibition and disciplinary action. The essential elements are that you can prove:

- That the employee had possession of the substances or that they were physically on the employee's body or in the individual's exclusive control. This means that possession could not be proved if illegal drugs were found on the top shelf of a storeroom accessible to all the employees in that department (absent other proof) but could be proved (under normal circumstances and absent other explanations) if the drugs were in the employee's pocket or purse or in a locked file cabinet accessible only to that person.
- That the substances are illegal drugs or controlled substances. This generally requires the physical testing of an actual specimen. Moreover, the employer also must consider the possibility that the drugs are legitimately in the employee's possession, i.e., that they were prescribed by a physician and that a physician's order exists for them.

If it becomes clear that you are dealing with a sale issue, then distinguish between off-duty and on-duty or on-premises sales. Decision makers tend to view the last two as more serious to your employer's interests, thereby justifying more extreme measures and responses. However, drug sales off the premises and off duty have been used to support disciplinary action.[6] If you face such a problem, refer to the guidelines listed later for handling off-duty misconduct.

Incidents of potential drug sales, because of their consequences, frequently produce outright denials from the challenged employee. Such situations present some of the more difficult issues you will ever face. Furthermore, in the absence of physical evidence, such as a marijuana cigarette, proving the sale of marijuana or other drugs or controlled substances is difficult. While listing the individual manifestations of the large variety of dangerous drugs obviously is beyond the scope of this manual, suggestions for resolving the inevitable credibility problems include the following:

- Was there a sale (or attempted sale), i.e., can you prove that the employee was offering drugs for sale and that this offer was communicated to another individual or that an actual sale occurred?
- Is your witness familiar with marijuana or whatever drug is involved?
- How close was your witness to the incident when it occurred?
- Did more than one witness observe the individual on this or other occasions?
- Can you discard the possibility that the item in the employee's possession was not a drug (or was not a drug for which the person had a prescription)?
- Was a sample retrieved and did subsequent testing prove the type of substance?

One last note: Offenses involving the sale of drugs are regarded seriously by the authorities and should be reported promptly. When this happens you will lose control of the investigation to some degree. Do not let this stop you from attempting to conduct your own inquiry and/or reaching your own conclusions based on your employer's standards of acceptable conduct and irrespective of the eventual disposition of any criminal charges.

Whatever you do, do not condition disciplinary action on the ultimate outcome of any criminal charges since they can be dismissed or result in a plea bargain or otherwise leave you holding the bag.

Careless Handling of Drugs

When reviewing facts that could represent incidents of drug theft, possession, or sale, you also should analyze whether you really are dealing simply with incompetent handling of drugs. If you are, you generally are facing a performance problem, not a question of misconduct.

The incompetency may be caused by an employee's genuine misunderstanding of the mandatory procedures to be followed in accounting for the facility's drugs, or a lack of knowledge or training, or a simple inability to do the job. If so, careful future supervision or inservice retraining may correct some of these problems. If not, in all but exceptional cases, the employee still should be given an opportunity to come up to standards unless retaining the person in the same position presents a real danger.

Blood, Breath, Urine and Other Tests

Modern blood, urine, and breath tests are extremely accurate indicators of the alcohol level in the bloodstream and hence the alcohol level in the brain. Where you have such evidence and it exceeds the level for drunk driving in your state, you can accept it as conclusive proof of intoxication or being under the influence.[7]

While many drugs can be detected in the blood or urine through tests similar to those for alcohol, there apparently is no reliable test for marijuana in the human body.[8] However, some researchers have developed techniques for detecting the presence of marijuana in the mouth and on the fingers of a recent smoker.[9]

In considering the possible use of tests, remember that you cannot force an employee to undergo one even though refusal to submit to a blood, breath, or urine test may be sufficient, by itself, to warrant disciplinary action, up to and including discharge.[10] You also must have some evidence of drinking or drug usage before you can reasonably request that the employee submit to such a test and before you take disciplinary action if the person refuses to do so.

In addition, if your employer is to perform the test, then (1) give your employee the choice between the available tests if there are more than one type and (2) check any medical privacy or confidentiality restrictions applicable in your state that may affect how or whether your employee can agree to disclosure of the test results to supervisory personnel.

Assistance from Drug Enforcement Authorities

Where you are presented with facts that indicate that a serious drug offense has occurred on your premises, the following guidelines are important:

- Do not attempt to handle these problems on your own; report the incident to the authorities and let them conduct their own investigation.
- Make it clear to the employee (assuming that the person is aware of the investigation or claimed misconduct) that you will be conducting your own investigation and that your future decision as to whether disciplinary action is warranted will be based on your own employer's standards of conduct; it will not be determined by the results of the police or other official investigation.
- Ask the local police or prosecutor's office to assist you with copies of reports and results of chemical/blood tests, etc.; however, laws in some states forbid release of these files.

Drug enforcement is a complex program and authorities often choose, for policy reasons, not to prosecute, to drop charges, or to plea bargain even when they have overwhelming proof the offense has been committed. For this reason, it must be reemphasized that you generally must avoid committing yourself to be bound by the results of a criminal investigation.

If you do bind your employer to the results of such investigations or proceedings, you will not be able to take action where charges are dropped, etc., even though you have access to proof that misconduct occurred and that disciplinary or other action is appropriate.

Rehabilitation Act and Rehabilitation Programs

As noted in Chapter 8, the Rehabilitation Act of 1973 precludes discrimination because of handicap by recipients of federal financial assistance or federal contractors, among others.[11] While drug addiction and alcoholism qualify as handicaps under the Act, a 1978 amendment clarified that

> such term [handicapped individual] does not include any individual who is an alcoholic or drug abuser whose current use of alcohol or drugs prevents such individual from performing the duties of the job in question or whose employment, by reason of such current alcohol or drug abuse, would constitute a direct threat to property or the safety of others.[12]

As the statutory definition illustrates, the Rehabilitation Act does not mean that drug addicts and alcoholics are entitled to preferential treatment or that their addiction must be allowed to impact on their employer adversely. You can hold such persons to the same standard of behavior and conduct as other employees with regard to the essential functional requirements for their position, even if their unsatisfactory performance is caused by their drug addiction or alcoholism. This conclusion is reflected in the following extract from a Department of Health and Human Services (HHS) analysis of its own Rehabilitation Act regulations applicable to recipients of financial assistance from HHS:

> With respect to the employment of a drug addict or alcoholic, if it can be shown that the addiction or alcoholism prevents successful performance of the job, the person need not be provided the employment opportunity in question. For example, in making employment decisions, a recipient may judge addicts and alcoholics on the same basis it judges all other applicants and employees. Thus, a recipient may consider—for all applicants including drug addicts and alcoholics—past personnel records, absenteeism, disruptive, abusive or dangerous behavior, violations of rules and unsatisfactory work performance. Moreover, employers may enforce rules prohibiting the possession or use of alcohol or drugs in the work place, *provided that such rules are enforced against all employees* (emphasis added).[13]

This quotation highlights the skills required of a cautious supervisor: if the drug addiction or alcoholism results in a violation of your rules of conduct, the employee may be disciplined for breaching the rules pertinent to performance, conduct, and dependability, and not for being an alcoholic or drug addict.

If an employee defends a charge of drinking or drug abuse by admitting the problem and offering to participate in a voluntary rehabilitation or drug offender program, serious consideration must be given to this proposal. As one arbitrator has said, "although the modern view regards alcoholism as a sickness, it is an illness that only the patient can cure."[14]

Therefore, an employer who gives the employee an opportunity to get the problem under control generally will not be reversed by arbitrators if the individual subsequently is discharged for work-related problems caused by alcohol or drug usage. But again, you must balance the desire to aid an employee against the risk of the recurrence of on-duty problems from such abuse.

Theft of Employer's Property

Theft occurs when a person takes and removes property of another with the intention of depriving that person of its possession. Therefore, to constitute theft, three elements must be present:

1. The property must belong to another.
2. The property must have been taken against the owner's will or without the owner's consent.
3. The taker must intend to steal it.

It is an implied term of any employment contract that employees act honestly and respect their employer's property. A written policy or work rule is not necessary before an employee can be disciplined for stealing your employer's property. Therefore, you should be unwilling to retain an employee who has been proved by objective evidence to have stolen your employer's property. Nevertheless, as discussed in more detail later, arbitrators do reverse discharges for theft based on some of these factors:

- Has each element of the offense been proved by convincing and objective evidence?
- What is the value of the property taken? (Note that even stolen items of very nominal value have justified discharge.)
- How long has the employee been employed?
- What is the employee's prior record?

Aside from being a crime, theft also is a tort, which means the victim has a right to sue in the courts for the recovery of the goods or for their value. Thus, where the value of the goods stolen is significant, you should consider whether to institute a lawsuit. Such an action serves notice on other employees that you will not tolerate dishonesty and are prepared to go to some lengths to protect your rights.

Theft also is a crime punishable by the state. Again, where the value of the goods stolen is significant, report the theft to local authorities and cooperate with their attempts to obtain a conviction. However, you should not report such instances to the authorities nor insist that they pursue it actively unless you have reasonable and provable grounds for believing a theft occurred. To do otherwise simply creates the potential of exposing you and your employer to a damages action for malicious prosecution.

An employee who is discharged for theft often experiences great difficulty in finding another job. For that reason alone, you should assume that such a discharge will be challenged. For the same reason, be aware that arbitrators frequently bend over backward to avoid reaching a conclusion that a theft has occurred. They do this either by deciding that the offense was not proved, that it required more lenient treatment, or by supporting the discharge on other grounds. In handling theft allegations, therefore, you must assume that a greater degree of proof may be required than for other offenses and also assume that the presence of any reasonable doubt may be resolved in favor of the employee.[15]

All of these factors mean that your investigation must be thorough: your witnesses must be certain of their facts, their statements must be recorded in detail, the employee's version (or refusal to respond to the opportunity you give for responding to your known facts) must be obtained, and any factual inconsistencies or credibility issues must be resolved.

Apart from straight denials, some employees caught in the act of stealing will claim that they did not know the article was of any value or that they believed it had been discarded.[16] To avoid these difficulties, review your policies and make sure they clearly specify a procedure for the removal of discarded or waste property by employees and that the theft or removal of any property, regardless of its value or where it is located (even if it is in the trash), will constitute grounds for disciplinary action. Such a clear policy, adequately publicized to your employees, will help support your actions, deter grievances, and prevent reversals by arbitrators or other decision makers.

Fighting on the Premises

You have the right to expect that all employees will conduct themselves in a cooperative fashion without creating disturbances in the workplace or engaging in fighting or other aggressive misconduct.

Elements of Offense

Yet frequently it is not easy to decide whether an employee's behavior is fighting or related misconduct, such as verbal abuse (and remember that verbal abuse should be separately labelled for disciplinary purposes), or whether the behavior merely reflects the type of isolated flare-ups that can arise in a working environment. Thus, guidelines to assist you in making these determinations include these:

- Physical attacks clearly constitute "fighting."
- Attempts to engage another in a fight, throwing objects, attempted blows, etc., are "fighting."
- Abusive, obscene, or vulgar language, without any other overt action (such as insubordination, throwing a punch, etc.) will not justify disciplinary action for fighting.

However, also be aware that:

- The use of words sufficiently provocative to cause another person to fight or to resort to self-defense in fear that a fight will occur, qualifies the misconduct as punishable for "fighting."

- Abusive, obscene, or vulgar language by itself, whether toward other employees, supervisors, patients, or visitors, can be alternate grounds for disciplinary action, particularly where you have a specific policy, consistently enforced, that prohibits such behavior.

Identifying the Aggressor

When two employees fight and both end up delivering punches, there is a temptation to hold both to blame and to punish both equally (as discussed in Chapter 11). Avoid such temptations. Although it is difficult, your investigation should make every effort to identify who, if anyone, was the aggressor; your discipline then should reflect your findings.

This does not mean that you automatically must absolve the nonaggressor from all blame, but the fact that another employee threw the first punch frequently will be held to be a mitigating factor.[17] A key point to pin down is whether that person was goaded into delivering the first blow or did so in fear of being hit (discussed next). Again, however, this depends on your particular factual circumstances, e.g., if the nonaggressor continues to fight after the first employee unequivocally attempts to withdraw or uses excessive force (such as a tool for a weapon), then equal disciplinary action still may be warranted.

The Use of Self-Defense

There will be occasions when an employee's involvement in a fight can be characterized as self-defense. In such circumstances, you may find it difficult to sustain the employee's termination, even if you have a rule against fighting that requires the discharge of all involved employees, regardless of who started the fight.[18] In fact, one arbitrator reversed a three-day suspension where the attacker was a woman and the defender a man because the "victim" had acted reasonably in his own defense. Thus, if self-defense is raised by an employee, consider the following factors:

- Was there any other way of avoiding the attack (e.g., immediately available security guards, walking away, etc.)?
- Was the "victim's" response reasonable; that is, did the person limit the response to what was necessary to ward off the attack?
- Did the "victim" cease fighting upon succeeding in stopping the attack?
- Did the "victim" provoke the aggressor in any way?

Consequences If Proved

A health care employer should tolerate less physical aggression than many other employers because of its working environment. As a result, hospitals and other health care employers often are obliged to come down hard on fighting and other aggressive behavior after the following factors have been considered:

- What is the length of service and prior record?
- What was the nature of the act—was it an isolated, emotional outburst or a cool, deliberate attack?
- Did the employee use bare hands, fists, or a weapon?
- What effect did the incident have on coworkers, patients, physicians, visitors, etc.?
- Were there mitigating factors—provocation, stress, lack of sleep, serious personal problems, etc.?
- What does your employer's disciplinary policy say concerning fighting, and has the policy been followed consistently?

Even if you decide one employee is more to blame than another, this does not prevent you from disciplining both; just make sure your punishment reflects the different degrees of guilt. In addition, if there has been bad blood between the employees for some time but their immediate supervisor, with knowledge of the situation, has failed to take any corrective steps, at least one arbitrator found that such facts constituted mitigating circumstances justifying a lesser penalty.[19]

Possession or Use of Deadly Weapons

Quite apart from actual fighting, you may be faced with a situation where an employee is found in possession of a firearm or other dangerous weapon. In assessing this offense, review the following factors:

- Was the person in possession of the gun or other weapon on or off the premises?
- Does the employee have any reasonable explanation?
- Was this possession a criminal offense?
- Does the person have any record of violent behavior?
- Are there any special mitigating factors such as recent attacks or rapes in the neighborhood?
- Do you have a specific policy prohibiting the possession of guns (or any other weapon) on the premises?

While the use of a deadly weapon rarely will be tolerated, even if the act occurs off the premises, discharge inevitably will be the only appropriate response when it occurs on the premises. Again, you should report such incidents to the authorities and avoid locking yourself into a position where the employee's final discipline depends upon the results of a criminal prosecution. As always, conduct your own investigation and keep your options open.

Off-Duty Misconduct

What employees do on their own time away from work normally is their own business and not subject to discipline by an employer. This general principle was well stated by an arbitrator:

> [R]ecognition must be given to an accepted principle in arbitration, that the employer cannot properly discharge or discipline an employee for an act committed when the employee is off-duty. This principle holds generally, that to do so, would constitute an invasion of the employee's personal life by the employer and would place the employer in the position of sitting in judgment on neighborhood morals, a matter which should be left to civil officials specifically charged with such responsibility.[20]

However, every rule has its exceptions and those involving the above rule all have a common underlying theme, namely, does the off-duty misconduct have an adverse effect on the employer-employee relationship? Following are three major categories of exceptions.

1. Has the Employer Been Harmed?   In deciding harm to the employer by an employee's off-duty conduct, consider the following factors:

- Does the employee perform a job that is affected by the incident? An extreme example would be a pediatrician's assistant who is convicted of a crime involving immoral conduct toward a minor.
- How much adverse publicity or other negative public reaction has occurred that would directly and adversely affect your employer's standing in the community?
- Is the workplace situated in a small community and/or does your employer have a small work force?
- Would patients really refuse to come to your institution as a result of this misconduct?
- How serious are the charges?

Above all, avoid speculation. Minor scandals do blow over and the general public has a great capacity to overlook or forget minor transgressions.

2. Is the Employee Unable To Perform the Job Because of Misconduct?   An obvious example occurs when, as a result of the misconduct, the employee's license is taken away and the individual cannot continue to practice that profession. Another example: when the employee is sent to jail for a significant period (in which case you should handle the incident as an absenteeism problem; see section on "Handling Employee Excuses" later in this chapter) or when even probation or a temporary jail sentence constitutes a substantial interference with obligations to your employer.

3. Do Coworkers Refuse To Work with the Employee? Some of the cautions expressed earlier also are relevant here. In addition, use some healthy skepticism in evaluating employee complaints:

- Employees may express an initial reluctance to accept the wrongdoer back in their midst but frequently this is not a permanent attitude. In fact, employees frequently change their mind after you have taken disciplinary action, which means that obtaining written complaints or other written verification from employees may be wise.

- Other employees' fears or refusals to work with the offender may stem from reasons that have some basis in fact. For example, refusing to work with an employee who engaged in violent behavior is a realistic human response but a refusal based on a drunk-driving conviction, simply because it offends the refusing employee's own moral standards, is not so reasonable. These distinctions become important. Remember that if an employer generally is precluded from taking disciplinary action for an employee's off-duty conduct, then it is equally true that such action cannot be justified under the guise that other employees have refused, unjustifiably, to work with the offender.

Criminal Prosecution

One of your employees may be arrested and prosecuted for conduct either on or off your employer's premises. Should this happen, there is one golden rule: always conduct your own investigation and never condition your final decision on the result of the criminal proceeding.

As is well known, the criminal justice system is overtaxed and unable to cope with the volume of cases. As a result, district attorneys and other law enforcement officers frequently are obliged to reduce charges from serious to petty. Indeed, the caseload is so heavy that many cases are simply dropped, not because of the innocence of the defendant but because the system is too overloaded.

Standard of Proof

The standard of proof in criminal cases also is much higher than for disciplinary action. Thus, a criminal court judge may rule that an employee was innocent of any criminal wrongdoing in a case in which an arbitrator easily reaches the opposite result. However, remember that arbitrators generally do not consider themselves bound by the exclusionary rules that prevent the courts from considering important and very relevant evidence because the means of obtaining it are considered improper in the criminal and constitutional context.

In addition, the law enforcement agencies may have a different focus. You will be more aware of the aspects of the employee's conduct that affect the employment relationship so your own investigation may delve into areas not covered or emphasized by the police.

Finally, when you investigate an incident yourself you retain control of the case. Therefore, your record of the investigation will remain in your hands and can be referred to and used in any subsequent arbitration or other employee challenge. By contrast, district attorney or police files and witness statements may be difficult or impossible to obtain because of legal or practical obstacles unless a public record such as a trial transcript is made during the criminal proceeding.

Reliance on Criminal Prosecution

Even if the employee is acquitted of any criminal charges, or the charges are dropped, etc., you still may discipline the individual if your investigation reveals substantial evidence of wrongdoing[21] and if you have made it clear to the person, from the outset, that you will not be bound by the results of any criminal proceedings. As noted, criminal courts require a higher standard of proof and, given the crowded court calendars, a decision is made not to prosecute for reasons quite unrelated to a person's guilt or innocence.

A conviction in the criminal courts may, in itself, justify disciplinary action, including discharge. But you still must be sure you can justify your decision to discipline for off-duty misconduct under one of the three exceptions listed earlier.

Suspension pending a criminal trial is a common response by employers yet it is not always the best action. Long delays in criminal proceedings are common and, even after conviction, appeals may delay final resolution for years. Furthermore, this reaction (unless it is accompanied by contrary notice to the employee) may lead to a conclusion that you have tied your employer's response to the results and standards of the criminal proceeding, which exposes you to continuing liability for back pay if the employee is acquitted.

For these reasons, the better course of action may be to consider placing the employee on a "suspension pending investigation" (not a suspension pending the criminal proceedings). (See discussion in Chapter 12.) This investigatory action is appropriate where the employee allegedly engaged in serious misconduct (e.g., acts of violent behavior, such as murder, attempted murder, rape, robbery, etc.) or when a continuation of active employment could result in demonstrable potential harm to your employer (because of the relationship between the alleged misconduct and the employee's work, such as a bookkeeper and embezzlement, etc.). But even under these circumstances, be sure to conduct your own investigation, to the fullest extent possible, while the employee is on suspension. Then, when you subsequently decide whether final disciplinary action is appropriate, it may be based on the results of your investigation and your own employer's standards.[22]

Disloyalty to the Employer

As noted, the law expects an employee to be honest in dealing with an employer—and to be reasonably loyal. While disloyalty is much harder to define than dishonesty, a review of arbitrators' decisions suggests that the following definition reflects the general view: "An employee owes a broad duty of loyalty to her employer. This means that . . . the employee may not publicly denigrate her employer's business or give harmful information or do other acts impairing the employer's relations with her customers."[23]

Again, as in the case of off-duty misconduct, avoid speculation. Remember that mere criticism of an employer rarely will support discharge or other serious disciplinary action unless there is a real potential for harm to your employer. Also, if the employee's statements constitute protected concerted activity (see Chapter 3 and this chapter's next section on "Perils and Pitfalls"), then termination or other disciplinary action cannot be taken.

An employee who engages in direct competition with an employer may be subject to discipline. For example, a part-time nurse who establishes a registry and tries to solicit R.N.s who work for you is engaging in the sort of competition that is objectionable. However, do not confuse such activity with mere moonlighting (discussed separately) since "competing with the employer" requires some real conflict of interest, such as where the employee's activities help a competitor obtain an advantage.

Perils and Pitfalls

Labor laws often protect an employee who engages in acts that generally would be considered disloyal—striking and picketing are two obvious examples. (Chapters 3, 9, and 10 discussed your rights and duties in this area in more depth.) Some of the more common protected activities you should not classify as disloyalty are:

- filing a complaint under the Fair Labor Standards Act or state wage-hour laws
- filing a workers' compensation claim
- filing charges or giving evidence before the National Labor Relations Board (your employer's rules cannot be used to limit or prevent an employee who has been subpoenaed from testifying at an NLRB hearing or to regulate the content of the employee's testimony)[24]
- filing charges or testifying under the Occupational Safety and Health Act (OSHA)[25]

- filing charges or testifying under Title VII of the Civil Rights Act or any of the other statutes outlawing job discrimination
- engaging in "concerted activities" protected by section 7 of the National Labor Relations Act, which would include derogatory statements made during a strike, during contract negotiations or grievance meetings, etc., or statements that have the purpose of "mutual aid or protection." (See discussion in Chapter 3 concerning protected activity.) Thus, a complaint to a state health department was considered to be protected, concerted activity not subject to discipline.[26]

These are just some highlights areas in which caution should be exercised. And since "protected activities" are varied and often not easily identifiable, you should consult a labor law specialist before taking disciplinary action if there is any basis for believing that an employee's action could be characterized as such.

Moonlighting

Before disciplining an employee for moonlighting, all relevant factors should be analyzed:

- Is the employee working full or part time? Imposing restrictions on other employment by part-time employees frequently is considered unreasonable.
- Do you have a clear, well-publicized rule against moonlighting and is the rule a reasonable one?
- Has the moonlighting resulted in poor performance, absenteeism, or tardiness? If so, discipline for these resulting problems, not for the moonlighting.
- Has the employee been dishonest? For example, has the employee been claiming sick leave while performing outside work?

Remember the general rule: what an employee does outside working hours usually is the employee's own business unless it affects work performance, is competitive with the employer's business, or results in other demonstrable harm.

HANDLING ATTENDANCE PROBLEMS

Your Need for Dependability

Your rights to maintain attendance policies controlling absenteeism have long been recognized. As one arbitrator has stated: "The right to control unnecessary absenteeism is the most basic and essential of management rights. Certainly an employer can require employees to attend upon their work. Without this require-ment all other management rights would be meaningless."[27]

For a number of reasons, you, as a supervisor in the health care industry, have a right to expect a high degree of dependability from your emplyees. State law frequently mandates minimum staffing levels and the JCAH imposes similar restrictions on accredited hospitals. Excessive absenteeism may hamper your ability to meet these requirements, interfere with the timely provision of needed services by your work area, and place an increased workload on other employees. These consequences, particularly since health care facilities cannot always respond to a low turnout of employees by simply reducing services, make a lack of dependability by your employees a priority for your supervisory efforts.

Absenteeism. This is habitual or repeated failure to report to the job during scheduled work periods. Absenteeism, in this sense, is a neutral term since it includes absences for legitimate reasons such as sick leave, injuries, personal problems, etc.

Tardiness. Tardiness, as distinguished from absenteeism, occurs when an employee is late in reporting to work or in returning to work from authorized breaks.

Extended Absences. Another attendance problem arises when employees fail to return from authorized absences, such as leaves and vacations, on their appointed date. Such a practice can be extremely disruptive and is grounds for discipline.

Reporting Procedures. To maintain a systematic means of responding to inevitable absences, you may implement a policy specifying that employees must (1) report their absences by a fixed time prior to (or at the start of) their shift where such absences are unavoidable, and (2) submit an adequate advance request for approved time off for vacations, leaves, time off for holidays worked, etc. Where an employee has been absent on sick leave or medical disability, you also are entitled to implement a reasonable policy requiring adequate proof of illness. Before any such polices are implemented or revised, however, be sure to review any union contract provisions to ensure that your actions will not conflict with them.

Handling Employee Excuses. Some excuses or reasons given by employees who are absent (or who are requesting absent time) require particular attention:

- Imprisonment: Remember to focus on the reason why you are contemplating discipline. If you are concerned by the employee's criminal conduct, then apply the principles pertaining to such misconduct. If it is the employee's absence that causes the difficulty, then focus on the length of the absence, the previous attendance record, the employer's policies, and how you have treated previous absences for these and other reasons.

- Religious Beliefs: This area is filled with potential problems. If an employee asks for leave on religious grounds, Title VII considerations (and perhaps state discrimination law issues as well) may arise since employers are required to make reasonable allowances for an employee's religious beliefs (see Chapter 7). As a result, and if your employer's existing policies prohibit the requested leave or are silent on the subject, your wisest course is to consult hospital administration or obtain expert advice before the employee is given a response.

- Alcoholism: While alcoholism generally is viewed as an illness, an employer is not required to retain an employee whose condition prevents functioning within acceptable limits. As a result, and even on those occasions where an employee's prior record or other consideration warrants attempts at rehabilitation, still continue to expect the individual to comply with your uniformly applied work rules, including your dependability requirements.

- Handicapped Employees: Caution must be exercised if you become aware that an employee's absences are the result of a handicap or medical condition. As noted in Chapter 7, you may be covered by either the federal Rehabilitation Act or state legislation that prohibits discrimination against handicapped persons. You are not required to throw all your rules out the window simply because a person is handicapped, and you can require such employees to adhere to your policies and procedures on applying for or returning from leaves, etc. However, where you are faced with a handicap situation, review the legal obligations it presents and, if you are uncertain, seek expert advice.

Illness, Sick Leave, and Leaves of Absence

Legitimate Use of Sick Leave

Most employers grant their employees a limited annual number of paid days off when they are unable to work for health-related reasons. Nationally, employees are absent from work because of illness, injury, and miscellaneous reasons slightly more than 3 percent of normal scheduled hours. Assuming an employee is working a five-day week and has ten working days vacation and ten paid holidays a year, this percentage converts to slightly more than seven working days per year. The figure rises, however, for employees covered by union contract.[28]

You should make it a policy to encourage legitimate use of sick leave in genuine cases. Sick employees who continue to work endanger their own health as well as that of other employees and of patients. Moreover, employees hampered by illness will be less efficient and more likely to commit errors.

On the other hand, discourage the use of sick leave for other purposes and insist that it be reserved for instances of genuine illness. Unless you have a union contract or policies that say otherwise, sick leave is not earned in the same sense as paid vacation leave; sick leave is "insurance" against wage losses because of illness and not an automatic entitle.ment to pay or time off.

Improper Sick Leave Usage

When you suspect that an employee is abusing your sick leave policies by using it for reasons other than genuine and significant ill health, try to determine whether your suspicions have any objective basis:

- Has there been a recurring pattern of sick leave by this employee (e.g., tending to be absent when preassigned to particular duties or when the person's spouse is off work, etc.)?
- Does the employee frequently take sick leave in conjunction with days off, weekends, holidays, or vacations?
- Does the employee try to avoid using your reporting procedures?
- Does the employee produce adequate proof of sickness such as a doctor's certificate, pharmacist bills, statements from spouse, etc.?
- Was the sick leave taken after the employee had been refused a leave of absence or other day off?

Be sure to check any union contract since it may spell out what constitutes an abuse of sick leave, what is sufficient proof, when sick leave may be used, etc.

An employee who has complied with all the conditions of your policies and/or of the applicable union contract is entitled to be paid sick leave for absence because of sickness. In other words, before you can deny payment of sick leave, you must be satisfied (and able to prove) that the employee is not eligible for the leave (e.g., was not sick) or is in breach of a significant rule or policy governing the use of such leave.

There will be occasions when abuse of your sick leave policies requires you to take disciplinary action. This is warranted where an employee (1) fails to comply with your reporting procedures, (2) takes sick leave when not ill, or (3) falsifies or otherwise acts improperly regarding any medical or other verification of illness that you request.

The first category is relatively easy to detect and, consequently, to handle. The second and third, which can involve dishonesty in the use of sick leave, are more difficult and require more caution.

Dishonest Use of Sick Leave. When an employee claims sick leave but actually appears to be absent for other reasons, you as supervisor must, as in all misconduct cases, make an adequate investigation of the facts before acting. Always allow the employee an opportunity to offer an explanation. For example, an employee who took part in a softball game was not necessarily abusing sick leave, according to one arbitrator. The employee was on a program of progressive exercise for back trouble; the arbitrator held that softball, while not wise, was not specifically prohibited.[29] As with theft, arbitrators are very reluctant to let stand a discharge for dishonesty, believing that an employee's career can be ruined. Thus you may have a substantially greater burden of proof to overcome in order to justify a discharge on this basis.

Excessive Use of Sick Leave. Just because an employee accrues ten days of sick leave a year generally does not mean the person is entitled to use all of those days or that you cannot take disciplinary action where the individual breaches an employer policy controlling excessive absenteeism. For example, you may already have, or propose to institute, a point system that gives credit for good attendance and that results in automatic discipline when a sufficient number of points are lost because of absence. Arbitrators frequently uphold such systems, even for legitimate illness, if all employees are given advance notice of the requirements and if they are treated consistently in conformity with the policy. Yet this type of disciplinary action is not taken "because of" dishonesty in the use of sick leave and should not be treated as such.[30]

Questionable Patterns of Sick Leave Usage. Some employees demonstrate questionable patterns of sick leave usage—for example, those who are always "sick" the day before or after a day off. Some absenteeism policies incorporate this type of usage in a point system, with more points being deducted for sick days taken in conjunction with other absences. If your employer does not have such a formal absenteeism policy, however, then remember that questionable patterns of sick leave usage are simply indirect evidence of abuse. In other words, a questionable pattern may support a conclusion that sick leave is being abused or is being used for occasions other than illness; then again, it may not support any such conclusion, depending upon other facts present. So caution should be exercised, with disciplinary action considered only after you have talked to the employee, asked for an explanation, and otherwise carefully investigated the surrounding circumstances.

The Legitimate Long-Term Absence

Many employers provide for both paid and unpaid sick leave. Consequently, employees suffering from an extended illness may exhaust their paid sick leave and seek an unpaid leave of absence. Your policies or union contract may provide for such a leave of absence subject to a qualifying period (for example, six months or a year of continuous employment) or subject leaves to other limitations (for example, they may not exceed six months). A few cautions are that:

- Federal law requires you to treat maternity leave in the same manner as any other physical disability leave[31] if your employer allows disability leaves (but note: both maternity and other disabilities may need to be treated differently from workers' compensation leave).
- An employee cannot be forced to take early maternity leave if she chooses to remain on the job and is able to work without risk to herself or others.

- State law may preclude termination and/or may assess penalties for terminations that result because the employee is not able to return by the end of the maximum leave allowed under your policy (for example, termination of employees on workers' compensation leaves may be unlawful).
- Other state requirements should be checked since some states provide greater protection for employees seeking maternity, workers' compensation, or other leaves (for example, California law provides that a maternity leave for the length of the disability, up to four months, must be provided).[32]

The Perpetually Absent Employee

Even if an employee comes up with appropriate reasons for each individual absence, and even if you do not contest their legitimacy, you still can respond to excessive absenteeism if it results in significantly diminishing the individual's value to your employer. The laws protecting handicapped workers from discrimination generally are not contrary to this principle. For example, employees whose illness prevents them from performing the job would not appear to be "qualified handicapped persons" for the purposes of the Rehabilitation Act since they cannot "perform the essential functions of the job."[33]

It must be noted, however, that it can be difficult to judge whether absenteeism has exceeded permissible limits. Consideration of the following factors may help you reach a decision:

- the previous attendance record
- the total length of service
- the nature of the absences
- the extent to which the absenteeism exceeds the norm
- the effect on the efficiency of other employees in the department
- the prospects for future improvement
- the question of whether medical education or assistance to the employee might aid in reducing the amount of absent time.

As always, when there is an unacceptable pattern of absenteeism, make sure that you talk to the employee to (1) review your expectations and any pertinent employer policy, (2) emphasize the unacceptability of the person's attendance record, and (3) inform the employee that continued absenteeism at that level will lead to progressively more severe discipline, including discharge. Such an approach is advisable for two reasons: it is fair to the employee, who is placed on notice, and it ensures that any subsequent disciplinary action is less likely to be challenged successfully through grievances or other proceedings.

One exception to the concept of progressive discipline also should be noted. Specifically, medical or other objective verification may disclose that the employee's health simply will not allow continued employment. In such a case, and although the employee should be given advance discussion, notice, and an opportunity to present contrary evidence, termination may be appropriate even though it is not preceded by lesser disciplinary action since it is nondisciplinary in nature.

Tardiness

Punctuality Requirements

Tardiness, while similar to absenteeism, has this distinguishing feature: it is almost always within the control of the employee. Generally speaking, therefore, you should approach tardiness in the same way as other deliberate infractions of the rules:

- The rule must be clear and fair.
- The employee should have adequate notice of the rule and its consequences.
- The policy should be applied consistently.
- The use of counseling and progressive discipline is an appropriate response.

It is tempting to deal with lateness by responding in kind such as by docking an employee's pay each time the person is late. While such a practice has been approved by arbitrators, caution is in order:

- Check any applicable union contract and/or employer policy since arbitrators and others will examine them closely to make sure a remedy is permissible.[34] Make sure that employees receive clear and adequate notice of what the rules are before you tighten up and start docking pay[35] if you have enforced the policy loosely in the past.
- Apply the policy uniformly, consistently, and without discrimination.[36]
- Make the tardiness the subject of progressive disciplinary action—warning, suspension, discharge—remembering that docking the employee's pay is not disciplinary action; instead, it represents refusing to pay for time not worked.

Some employers have a practice of docking wages for a unit of time, such as a quarter hour, even though the employee is only a couple of minutes late. This might seem to violate wage-hour law since the entire period an employee works generally is regarded as compensable working time (see Chapter 9). But the courts have approved such employer policies if your system uses the same units for overtime (for example, if employees are 8 minutes late, they are docked 15 minutes; and if they work 8 minutes overtime, they receive 15 minutes of overtime pay). The courts theorize that employee gains and losses will balance out in the long run and, in any event, the amounts involved are too trivial to warrant judicial action.[37]

Consistent with these wage-hour principles, the periods of time docked do not need to be included in an employee's total hours for calculating overtime. But be careful. Aside from federal or state wage-hour provisions, you must check any contractual provisions or employer policies that may limit your right to decline to pay for overtime. For example, in one case an employee arrived an hour late, then worked two hours "overtime" beyond his normal quitting time. In principle, the arbitrator said, the employer was entitled to pay for the first hour of "overtime" at straight-time rates. However, the language of that particular contract mandated payment at the rate of time and one-half for the first quarter-hour worked after the employee's regular quitting time.[38]

Employee Excuses

Tardiness can become endemic and often is difficult to eradicate. Nevertheless, you can start with the assumption that it is the employee's responsibility to arrive at work on time and that failure to do so should not be excused without exceptional circumstances. For that reason, the use of a predetermined point system has an advantage since it avoids the necessity of constantly examining the validity of excuses, a time-consuming and rarely satisfactory method.

Even if your employer does not use such a system, tardiness still can be handled if your response is consistent and evenly enforced. Do not try to judge the validity of the excuses or feel that you have to justify your expectations for dependability when you have been faced with the employee's tale of woe. Instead, use your own common sense. Give employees the benefit of the doubt if it is an isolated instance, is infrequent, or occurs under circumstances affecting many employees (a major storm, etc.). But if tardiness starts becoming a way of life, then inform the person that a continuation is not acceptable and that the personal reasons for arriving late must be resolved—by the employee.

Reporting Procedures

Calling In Sick

Because of the nature of the industry in which you work, you have a right to be concerned about punctuality and regularity and to insist that you receive advance notice, if the employee will be absent. Inevitably, employees need to be absent on some occasions but just as inevitably you should insist upon strict compliance with your reporting procedures and, if they do not comply, consider the following:

- Is your rule clear and has it been sufficiently published to your employees?
- Have all the loopholes been eliminated? For example, have employees been told to call *x* person at *y* time, or can they just call and tell "someone" at the

other end of the telephone who may or may not have authority to handle the call?

- What has been your prior practice?
- Does your rule specify whether employees have to call in for each day they will be absent, or just for the first day and then provide advance notice of the day they will return?

Even though the employee has a legitimate reason for being absent, you can and should consider disciplinary or other corrective action if your reporting procedures are violated.[39] If the employee made a good faith but unsuccessful attempt to comply, then consider whether a lesser penalty, or whether simply reviewing the correct procedure with the individual, would be a more appropriate response—but specify and document the reason for your action.[40]

Remember to focus on the actual offense. Do not impose an excessive penalty in response to a minor infraction of your reporting procedures when you really are trying to punish the employee for a suspicious illness. On the other hand, do not allow a legitimate reason for absence to distract you from the fact that an employee has violated your reporting rules.

Reporting Back to Duty

Some employees develop a habit of overstaying their absences, then offering a variety of excuses. Treat such cases as you would any other type of absenteeism. For example:

- Did the employee give adequate notice?
- Did the employee comply with any policies or procedures (i.e., that the employee must contact you personally to request approval of an extension and may not just leave a message or assume that an extension is acceptable)?
- Did you investigate the proffered excuse and decide whether it is legitimate?
- Has the employee shown a pattern of "emergency" leave extensions?
- Has your rule against extended vacations or other absences been applied consistently?
- Was a request for a longer absence denied before the employee left work on this particular occasion?

If you have been lenient in the past, make sure that you give clear notice before tightening up. If an employee fails to report back to duty without complying with your procedure for obtaining an extension of the leave, but the reason for the absence turns out to be legitimate, then consider some penalty less than discharge.[41]

Medical Verification

Insisting upon a doctor's statement is one means of controlling excessive sick leave. But can you do it for every instance, and what happens if you do require such statements?

A requirement for a doctor's statements for every sick leave, no matter how short, can appear unreasonable. Many employees may be genuinely incapacitated for a day or two without consulting a physician. This is particularly true among health care professionals who often feel competent to self-diagnose and self-treat minor ailments such as colds, flu, etc. The formal doctor's statements need to be balanced against the recognition, however, that it strains credibility to believe that these same individuals are genuinely incapacitated by one day of illness each month or each time their sick leave pay accumulation has been replenished.

Union contracts often limit medical verification to instances where sick leave has extended beyond a minimum period (for example, three days) or where an unacceptable or improper use of leave exists.

Where an employee has been off work for an extended period as a result of a disabling illness or injury and wants to return, medical verification of the ability to return and to perform the job should be obtained, generally from the individual's personal physician, although verification by employee health also may be required. Furthermore, as a general rule these consistent requirements should exist without regard to the original reasons for the leave (maternity, work-related injuries, elective surgery, etc.).

If you still have any doubts about an employee's ability to work, insist upon examination by a physician selected by your employer, whether it be one on staff or an outsider. However, the value of obtaining a second medical opinion will be lost unless the physician is made fully aware of the nature of the job, focusing upon any particular skills or efforts it requires.

Never refuse to reinstate an employee on medical or health grounds unless you have a documented medical opinion stating that the individual does not meet medical standards designed to ensure that the person is able to perform the job.

Be careful to state clearly in your policies and other communications that the physician's statement will not be controlling in all instances, even after it is submitted. For example, the statement may raise further questions needing verification, it may be inconsistent with other facts, you may want a second medical opinion or other verification, etc.

Finally, remember to check with your legal advisers on any applicable state law that regulates the disclosure and use of medical information. Some states, such as California, have heavily regulated this area and there are pitfalls.[42]

As always, check union contracts and your employer's policies for provisions spelling out the procedures you must follow in verifying illnesses or in reinstating employees after disabilities. These same documents also may govern the type of proof you can require.

Unauthorized Absences

Because of the potentially serious consequences to the health care facility that can arise from unanticipated employee absences, it is reasonable for you to be especially firm with those who absent themselves, even for short periods, without prior notification or authorization. In applying appropriate discipline, however, determine whether your employer's policies or any union contract mandate that you consider the nature of the employee's work.

For example, the absence of an R.N. assigned to a night shift that already is short staffed may be viewed more seriously than that of a clerical employee, although the latter still calls for some disciplinary action. You also should consider whether a specified supervisory response can be taken without regard to the employee's position; e.g., whether termination is to occur if the person has an unauthorized absence of three days or more. Because of the practical difficulties presented by varying standards based on an employee's assigned work area and/or classification, however, the use of such a distinction in response to unauthorized absence is not recommended for voluntary inclusion in an employer's policies.

There also is the question whether the unauthorized absence was accompanied by aggravating circumstances. As one example, your investigation may reveal that an employee asked for time off, was refused, but still took the time by not reporting for duty. You may treat such an unauthorized absence as more serious misconduct and in considering appropriate discipline you need not be restricted by your prior practice in handling "simple" unauthorized absences.[43]

NOTES

1. Potash Co. of Am., 40 LA (BNA) 582 (1963) (Abernathy, Arb.).

2. California; CAL. ADMIN. CODE. tit. 22, R. 70215 (1980).

3. Washington Hosp. Center, 75 LA (BNA) 32, 34–35 (1980) (Rothschild, Arb.).

4. Neches Butane Products Co., 62–2 ARB (CCH) ¶ 8723 (1962) (Coffey, Arb).

5. Charleston Naval Shipyard, 54 LA (BNA) 145 (1970) (Kosselman, Arb.).

6. Brown & Williamson Corp., 60 LA (BNA) 502 (1973) (Duff, Arb.).

7. Charleston Naval Shipyard, 54 LA (BNA) 145 (1970) (Kosselman, Arb.).

8. Cal Custom/Hawk, 65 LA (BNA) 723 (1975) (Ross, Arb.).

9. 13 AM. JUR. 1st ed, *Proof of Facts* § 420 (1963).

10. Fish & Wilson, *Identification of Cannabis Constituents in the Particulate Matter of Smoke*. FORENSIC SCIENCE SOC'Y J. 9, 37 (1969) cited at 22 AM. JUR. 2d *Proof of Facts* (Supp. 1973, n.18, identification of substances).

11. 29 U.S.C. §§ 701–794.

12. 29 U.S.C. § 706(7)(B).

13. 45 C.F.R. pt. 84, app. A, subpt. A–4.

14. Caterpillar Tractor Co., 44 LA (BNA) 87 (1965) (Larkin, Arb.).

15. H.R. Terryberry Co., 65 LA (BNA) 1091 (1975) (Hillman, Arb.).

16. Emge Packing Co., 61 LA (BNA) 250 (1973) (Getman, Arb.).

17. Affiliated Hosps. of San Francisco, 64 LA (BNA) 29 (1975) (Jacobs, Arb.).

18. Consolidated Vultee Aircraft, 11 LA (BNA) 152 (1948) (Hepburn, Arb.).

19. Zinsco Electrical Prods., 65 LA (BNA) 487 (1975) (Erbs, Arb.).

20. Menzie Dairy Co., 45 LA (BNA) 283 (1965) (Mullen, Arb.).

21. Chrysler Corp., 53 LA (BNA) 1279 (1969) (Alexander, Arb.).

22. Plough, Inc., 54 LA (BNA) 541 (1970) (Autrey, Arb.).

23. Moore Business Forms, Inc., 57 LA (BNA) 1258 (1971) (Lawson, Arb.).

24. John Wanamaker, Phila., Inc., 199 N.L.R.B. 1266 (1972).

25. 29 U.S.C. § 660(c)(1).

26. 29 U.S.C. § 157; Mushroom Transport. Co. v. NLRB, 330 F.2d 683, 685 (3d Cir. 1964); Walls Mfg., 137 N.L.R.B. 1317, *enforced*, 321 F.2d 753 (D.C. Cir. 1963).

27. Celanese Corp., 62 LA (BNA) 1175, 1177 (1973) (Wolff, Arb.).

28. 1980 BUREAU OF LABOR STATISTICS REPORT, cited at 107 LAB. REL. REP. (BNA) 195–196 (1981).

29. Goulds Pumps, Inc., 74 LA (BNA) 818 (1980) (Paley, Arb.).

30. Le Blond Mach. Tool, Inc., 76 LA (BNA) 827 (1981) (Keenan, Arb.).

31. 42 U.S.C. § 2000e(k).

32. CAL. GOVT. CODE § 12945(b)(2) (Deering, 1982), *but see* Ch. 6, n.44.

33. *See generally* 45 C.F.R. § 84.3(k)(1); 28 C.F.R. § 41.32.

34. Mallinckrodt Chem. Works, 70–1 ARB (CCH) ¶ 8118 (1969) (Goldberg, Arb.).

35. Hellenic Lines Ltd., 62–1 ARB (CCH) ¶ 8276 (1962) (Loucks, Arb.).

36. Eastern Color Printing Co., 62–1 ARB (CCH) § 8161 (1962) (Scheiber, Arb.).

37. Abel v. Morley Mach. Co., 10 F.R.D. 187 (S.D.N.Y. 1950), 9 WAGE & HOUR CAS. (BNA) 414; Smith v. Cleveland Pneumatic Tool Co., 173 F.2d 775 (6th Cir. 1949).

38. Van Camp Hardware and Iron Co., 68–1 ARB (CCH) ¶ 8336 (1968) (Willingham, Arb.).

39. Whitaker Cable Corp., 63 LA (BNA) 1262 (1974) (Yarowstey, Arb.); Celotex Corp., 60 LA (BNA) 680 (1973) (Nicholas, Arb.).

40. Goodyear Clearwater Mills, 11 LA (BNA) 419 (1948) (McCoy, Arb.)..

41. Packaging Corp. of Amer., 42 LA (BNA) 606 (1964) (Sherman, Arb.).

42. CAL. CIV. CODE §§ 56–56.37 (Deering Supp. 1984).

43. Dixie Belle Mills, Inc., 43 LA (BNA) 1070 (1965) (Dworet, Arb.); Kroger Co., 24 LA (BNA) 593 (1955) (Slavney, Arb.).

Chapter 14

Using Your Knowledge and Skills

INTRODUCTION

The following case studies are designed to allow you to practice and apply a systematic approach to typical employment problems. The emphasis, as you review the cases, should be on developing the skill of analyzing the problems and identifying the strengths and weaknesses. In this process, and after you have read the facts for a particular case study, it would be helpful for you to review the checklist in Appendix 11–A (*supra*) before moving on to the suggested responses in each situation.

Do not be discouraged by the detail or the number of potential issues presented. Remember that all problems, no matter how complex, are resolved easily if you break them down into their constituent parts and approach each part in a careful and systematic manner. Remember also that you cannot, and will not, be expected to know the intricacies of labor and arbitration law.

These studies are designed to develop your awareness of potential problem areas. In a real-life situation you almost always will have an opportunity to consult with others before making a decision. However, approaching the problem in the right way will decrease the chances of making an error. If you do consult an adviser, using the correct approach will enable you to present your recommendation and the pertinent facts in a meaningful way. (All of the names used in these studies are fictitious and the facts of each case have been disguised to protect those actually involved.)

Good luck, and remember:

- Procedure!

- Substance!

CASE STUDY #1: SUBSTANCE VS. PROCEDURE

Facts of the Case

Judy Ramirez and Sally Smith were two housekeeping attendants who often socialized outside of working hours. As usual, on Thursday, May 5, they had lunch together in the hospital cafeteria that was open to the public and to ambulatory patients. While finishing their meal, they started to discuss absences from work by certain employees, including themselves, that had followed a party at Judy's house. Judy complained that she received a written warning for her absence, she was still upset that she had been singled out, and she was resentful toward Sally who had received no disciplinary action. As Judy and Sally continued to talk, their voices rose and eventually a loud argument erupted with the women yelling at each other. Suddenly, Judy stood up, called her a "fat-assed bitch," and leaned over the table to get her purse. Sally replied by shoving Judy, who fell to the floor.

As Sally started to leave the table, Judy struggled to her feet, while yelling at Sally and reaching for her purse that had fallen to the floor. Sally quickly grabbed Judy's purse, crying, "You're not going to shoot me with your gun." At that point, a supervisor who had overheard and observed the incident from several tables away, hurried over and physically restrained Judy from lunging at Sally. The supervisor calmed Judy down, returned her purse, and told both employees to "cool off" and return to work.

The day after the incident, the department head and the personnel director asked Judy what had happened. In that interview and later at the arbitration hearing, Judy's explanation was limited to saying that she did nothing to antagonize Sally, that she did not hit her, and that Sally unexpectedly pushed her to the floor. Judy also vehemently denied ever carrying a gun in her purse. The supervisor subsequently confirmed that Sally shoved Judy, but he also said that Judy was a troublemaker who had provoked Sally by cursing at her. The supervisor's interview did not take place until May 15, since the supervisor was on vacation the week after the incident.

The department head and personnel director also tried to schedule an interview with Sally, but when she demanded that a union representative be present, the interview was cancelled. Sally admitted during a telephone conversation with the department head that she had shoved Judy. Sally also said she had seen a gun in Judy's purse within the two months preceding the incident, that she was afraid of her, and that she shoved Judy because she was reaching for the purse.

Two days after the incident, Judy and Sally were terminated for fighting, and on the following payday, May 13, they were paid for all hours worked. Each asked the union to file a grievance on her own individual behalf. Only Judy's went to arbitration since the union, in Sally's case, forgot to file the request within the time limits prescribed by the union contract.

The issue for decision by the arbitrator was whether just cause existed for Judy's termination. The grievant (Judy), the department head, the personnel director, and the supervisor all testified at the hearing, but neither the union nor the employer called Sally as a witness. Sally's version was presented at the arbitration hearing through the department head's testimony. On cross-examination by union counsel, the department head confirmed that Sally had not told him of Judy's cursing, and that he was unaware of that fact when he and the personnel director decided that both employees should be discharged.

In the last two years, the hospital has dealt with similar incidents in the following manner:

1. Shirley Weeks, housekeeping attendant, abusive language, warning.
2. Harry Palmer, physical therapy aide, fighting on hospital premises, seven-day suspension.
3. Ramon Ruiz, occupational therapist, fighting and causing disruption on hospital premises, discharge.
4. George Carpenter, stationary engineer, abusive language, threatening behavior, 14-day suspension.

Questions To Consider

1. What are the weaknesses in the employer's arbitration case?
2. What are the strong points of the employer's arbitration case?
3. Would you, if you were the arbitrator, sustain or deny the grievance, and why?
4. What claims could be brought against the hospital by Judy Ramirez in addition to the arbitration of her grievance under the union contract?

Suggested Responses to Case Study #1

Weaknesses of the Employer's Case (Question 1)

Analysis of the weaknesses of the hospital's case shows clearly that the employer failed to follow certain important procedural and substantive steps in its investigation.

Procedural. First, no decision to take disciplinary action should have occurred until after the supervisor had been interviewed, and had prepared a report as to the incident. This did not occur, and as a result, the arbitrator might exclude the supervisor's testimony as to Judy's cursing at Sally and might not allow that misconduct to be used as support for the discharge. Why? Judy's cursing (her provocation to Sally) was not known to the employer until May 15, when the supervisor returned. Since Judy was terminated on May 7, any provocation created by the cursing obviously was not relied upon by the employer in reaching the disciplinary decision. Thus, it cannot be argued that Judy was terminated because the hospital believed at the time that she was equally culpable for fighting.

Second, it does not appear that the department head or the personnel director reviewed the hospital's policies regarding terminations for fighting on the job or checked to see how similar incidents had been handled in the past. If they had done so, they would have found that the hospital had been inconsistent in dealing with similar situations in the past. For example, while one employee (Ruiz) had been discharged for fighting, another (Carpenter) had been given a suspension from work.

Third, the supervisor who broke up the fight did not act appropriately. Instead of ordering Judy and Sally home pending an investigation, immediately calling another supervisor or the personnel office for advice or assistance, or returning the employees to work after notifying them that the matter was not closed, the supervisor told both employees to return to work. At that point, therefore, neither Judy nor Sally had been put on notice that they might face disciplinary action. Furthermore, the supervisor overheard Sally's remarks about the gun, yet no search of the purse was requested; instead the purse was handed back to Judy without further comment.

Substantive. The major problem is that Judy was terminated for fighting which she did not do. Judy definitely engaged in misconduct by her verbal abuse toward Sally, and it is a close call as to whether such cursing is sufficient provocation to result in Judy being equally culpable for Sally's response. However, as noted previously, since the cursing was not known to the employer when Judy was discharged, it cannot be relied upon to support a conclusion that Judy was equally at fault by provoking the incident.

Any argument that Sally shoved Judy in self-defense because of Sally's immediate fear that a weapon would be used also should be unsuccessful because a reasonable basis for Sally's fear cannot be established. Only hearsay evidence (the department head's testimony as to what Sally said during the telephone conversation, where Sally is absent from the hearing and not available for cross-examination) exists to the effect that Judy ever carried a gun in the past. Absolutely no evidence exists, moreover, that Judy was carrying a gun on May 5, particularly since the purse was returned to Judy with no request for an inspection of its contents. In contrast to the department head's version of what Sally said, Judy is present at the hearing to personally give her own denial. When an arbitrator is faced with two contrary versions, and one is from an absent witness, the resulting substantive facts generally are found in favor of the witness who is personally present, available for cross-examination, and whose demeanor can be judged.

Strong Points of the Employer's Case (Question 2)

Strong points could have existed as Judy's actions definitely supported disciplinary action and perhaps, even a termination. These facts were not relied upon in reaching the decision to terminate Judy, however, and so the hospital would be limited to stressing the following.

First, and perhaps most importantly, Judy engaged in disruptive behavior by loudly yelling and cursing at Sally in an area (the cafeteria) that was frequented by both visitors and patients of the hospital. The hospital can contend that such behavior is so totally inappropriate that Judy need not have received prior discipline of any kind before being terminated, and that the conduct is equivalent in severity to fighting and should support her discharge. In addition, the hospital could argue that since Judy had to be physically restrained from attacking Sally (the supervisor had to restrain Judy from lunging at Sally after regaining her feet), she could be viewed as a participant in the fight. Again, however, the same flaws described above (that Judy was terminated for fighting and not for engaging in other misconduct) would undercut the hospital's reliance upon her actual misconduct as a basis for disciplinary action.

The Arbitrator's Decision (Question 3)

An arbitrator in this case probably would rule in favor of Judy, the grievant. Judy testified that it was Sally who shoved her, and that Judy never hit her back, or even touched her. Furthermore, Judy's provocation (her cursing at Sally, and the claimed presence of a gun) would be rejected as a basis for her termination since the cursing was not known to the employer and the existence of a gun (or a realistic and reasonable basis for Sally's assuming that Judy carried a gun) was never proved. Given these facts, it appears that Sally was more at fault than Judy *for the offense charged.*

In addition, the arbitrator would note that the hospital had not maintained a consistent policy of discipline in incidents involving fighting, nor did it appear to have a clear definition of "fighting."

As a result of not following correct supervisory procedures, and not analyzing the situation substantively, the hospital would be faced with an arbitrator's award to reinstate Judy. The award might not include back pay for the period she was off work, however. Equitable considerations that might lead the arbitrator to deny back pay are Judy's misconduct that helped precipitate the incident and her less-than-forthright explanation of her own provocative statements toward Sally.

Other Claims

In addition to a grievance under the union contract, other claims that might ensue include the following:

1. Judy might file a charge of national origin discrimination with the EEOC or a state agency since Hispanic employees seemed to be disciplined more harshly. Judy was the only person who received a written warning for her absence after a party at her house. In addition, she and Ramon Ruiz were discharged, while non-Hispanic employees (Shirley Weeks and George Carpenter, both of whom engaged in abusive language as did Judy, and Harry Palmer) received less severe penalties.
2. Judy could file a charge of sex discrimination, alleging that she was discharged while other males who engaged in similar conduct (Harry Palmer, George Carpenter) were only suspended. The fact that Shirley Weeks, another female, also received a lesser penalty than did Palmer or Carpenter tends to reduce the sex discrimination aspect of the case, however.
3. Judy could file a complaint with the state agency (such as the labor commissioner) concerning the hospital's six-day delay in paying her if she worked in a state that had a law providing that employees must be paid their final wages upon termination. (Of course, Sally would have the same claim.)

CASE STUDY #2: THE RELUCTANT PATIENT

Facts of the Case

December 29, 1983 Incident

On the morning of December 29, 1983, the night supervisor reported to the patient care coordinator for 4 east-med/surg that a "serious" patient incident had occurred on the night shift. Both the hospital attendant on duty, a 10-year employee, and a patient, a 23-year-old flight attendant, apparently gave the night supervisor the same general story:

> The patient, who had an infected broken jaw, was scheduled for surgery in the morning and was given a sleeping pill. The patient wanted to read without disturbing her roommate, so the attendant allowed her to sit in the hall immediately outside of her room, adjacent and visible to the nursing station, where the hospital attendant remained to watch for patient lights. Shortly thereafter, the R.N. came by and ordered the patient to bed. When the patient protested, the R.N. lifted the patient out of her chair by her arm and pushed or steered her into the room, with the patient still protesting. The resulting commotion awakened her roommate and was very upsetting to her. When the hospital attendant attempted to calm the patient, the R.N. told her to mind her place and that she (the R.N.) would handle it.

Incident reports, which covered both patients' complaints and all of the facts observed, were made out by the hospital attendant and the night supervisor, who had been called by the hospital attendant immediately after leaving the patient's room. The nursing supervisor's report noted that both patients were so agitated she stayed with them for 15 minutes and then instructed the hospital attendant to sit with them until they fell asleep. The supervisor also noted that while it was against policy to allow patients out of bed if they had been given sleep medication, policy also allowed an R.N. to exercise independent judgment by allowing such patients to move about.

After hearing this report the next morning at the change of shift, the patient care coordinator went to her office, where she found a note from the R.N. The note expressed the R.N.'s anger at the hospital attendant for her intervention and at the attendant and night supervisor for "coddling" a patient, and requested that the attendant be admonished for her actions. When the patient care coordinator spoke to the patient two days later, the patient confirmed the same basic facts that had been reported by the nursing supervisor and the attendant.

Prior Record

The hospital attendant's personnel file included no record of any prior disciplinary action or counseling sessions and her performance evaluations did not reflect any unsatisfactory ratings. The R.N., who had been employed since 1973, had various documents in her personnel file. One was a warning in February 1983 for "poor work due to neglect," based on observations by the patient care coordinator. Attached to the warning was written documentation of "employee counseling" that occurred in 1982 for numerous incidents of poor reporting and four of poor nursing judgment. The reporting deficiencies primarily involved inadequate information while the instances of poor nursing judgment included allowing a patient to go 12 hours without medication (the R.N.'s position was that the patient had refused the medication), and an alleged misreading of fluids that drained from a post-op hip patient during the R.N.'s shift (the R.N. stated that the prior shift had not marked the bottle properly).

A performance report to the director of nurses in October 1983 concerning the R.N. cited reporting errors, including misinformation concerning late medications, and failure to properly report a significant change in blood pressure readings taken by an attendant. The October report also enumerated certain charting deficiencies.

Two incident reports dated December 1, 1983 and April 25, 1983 also were present in the personnel folder. The December 1, 1983, report documented that the doctor's orders for patient Smith included urinary measurements, vital signs, and intake-output since the sedated patient also was receiving medication for respiratoₗy problems. The R.N.'s IV credit did not match that left in the IV bottle, however, and while the urine output was charted, the R.N. acknowledged during her report that she was unaware that the patient had a catheter and, when reminded, said she would have to recheck the output measurement. The second incident report, dated April 25, 1983, reported that the R.N. had given patient Jones' medication to another. The patient also was noted to have complained of not having received any of the ordered medication since his day shift admission. A cover memo noted that the nursing care coordinator had no first-hand knowledge of the April 25, 1983, incident.

The R.N. gave her version of the December 29 incident in a meeting held January 3, 1984. The R.N. denied laying a hand on the patient, repeated her concern at the hospital attendant's intervention, and stated that the patient was a difficult person who was being seen by a psychiatrist. Nursing administration expressed dissatisfaction not only with the December 29 incident as reported by the night supervisor and the attendant but also noted that the R.N. had received a warning less than a year previously and had exhibited unsatisfactory performance as reflected in the December 1 and April 25, 1983 incident reports, and in the 1982 counseling reports. The R.N. denied any unsatisfactory performance, disputed all of the facts referred to in the written warning, counseling and incident reports. She also stated that she was unaware of the October 1983 performance report to the director of nursing and could not recall experiencing any problems at that time.

Questions To Consider

1. If you ignore the R.N.'s prior work record and base your action solely on the December 29, 1983, incident, what disciplinary steps, if any, would you recommend for the R.N.? For the hospital attendant? Why?
2. If you were making the decision for the hospital, what disciplinary action, if any, would you take based on that incident and the R.N.'s prior work record, and why?

Suggested Responses to Case Study #2

December 29 Incident (Question 1)

The R.N. Basing your discipline decision only on the incident of December 29, you might give the R.N. a written warning for physically handling the patient (who had a broken jaw) in the manner that she did, for using poor judgment (the R.N. did not ascertain why the patient was in the hall before the R.N. acted), for awakening the patient's roommate at that late hour, and for causing both patients to become so upset that they were agitated and unable to sleep. The facts necessary for sustaining a written warning can be proved and an adequate investigation was done—the key factors in evaluating proposed disciplinary actions. The use of a suspension is much more susceptible to challenge by an R.N. since unsatisfactory performance generally should be handled by progressive discipline. The prior warning was almost one year earlier, and the R.N. had been with the hospital for more than ten years.

The Hospital Attendant. The attendant made an error in not receiving the R.N.'s permission to allow the patient who had a broken jaw, and who had taken sleeping medication, to remain sitting in a chair outside her room. However, the attendant did remain at the nearby nursing station where she could watch the patient. The attendant's attempted intervention also was in an effort to assist the patient and calm a disturbing situation. Since the attendant was a long-term employee with no prior disciplinary or other performance difficulties, a counseling session to remind the attendant of pertinent policy and appropriate protocols would be sufficient.

Cumulative Records of the R.N. (Question 2)

The R.N.'s cumulative record changes the type of disciplinary action you can take. However, you must take care to separate disciplinary steps from other types of actions. For example, if you outlined the content of her personnel file, it would disclose that during the past year the R.N. had one warning of poor work because of neglect, two incident reports concerning patient care, a recent performance report that listed a number of problems (reporting errors and charting deficiencies), and a number of counseling sessions for poor reporting and poor nursing judgment.

However: (1) incident reports and counseling sessions are not considered discipline; (2) discipline occurs only if certain incidents or facts result in issuance of a written warning, suspension, etc.; (3) an employee may not be aware of an incident report in the personnel file; and (4) incident reports themselves generally should not be in personnel files anyway since they relate to potential malpractice issues, and legal privilege may be lost by their inclusion. Looking at disciplinary actions, then, your outline would disclose only one prior written warning for poor work because of neglect.

The Appropriate Decision

In summary, factors to consider in making your decision are:

1. The R.N. was a long-term employee.
2. She had only one written warning in her personnel file.
3. She was partly justified in her actions because the patient should have been in bed, under hospital policy, unless the R.N.'s approval was obtained.

Or, to look at it another way, she may have done the right thing, but in the wrong manner. Based on her record as a whole, and these considerations, a short suspension seems appropriate. A termination, by contrast, would subject the hospital to unnecessary liability since the incident, by itself, is not so serious as to warrant discharge.

CASE STUDY #3: THE DELAYED LAB REPORTS

Facts of the Case

Exhibit 14–1 consists of three documents referring to an incident involving two employees, Mrs. Wolfe, a senior laboratory technician who sometimes relieved the assistant department head, and Mr. Lamb, a new laboratory assistant in his first month of employment. The supervisory personnel involved are Kramble, the department head, and Jones, the assistant department head.

Questions To Consider

If you were an arbitrator hearing the case and the testimony is consistent with the three documents, would you uphold the department head's suspension of Mrs. Wolfe, and why or why not?

Suggested Responses to Case Study #3

Based on the documents in the file, and no other information, an arbitrator most likely would sustain the grievance and order the hospital to pay Mrs. Wolfe back pay for her five-day suspension.

The Employee Conference Note

The Employee Conference note to Mrs. Wolfe concerning the June 19 incident is confusing and contradictory. First, if the room was dark, how did department head Kramble know for sure that Mrs. Wolfe and Mr. Lamb were asleep? Perhaps he assumed they were asleep because of their reclining position, and because they didn't respond to him when he first arrived. This is speculation on Mr. Kramble's part, however, not evidence that they actually were asleep. Right away, the document he himself wrote throws doubt on the accuracy of his observations and conclusions. Second, what was Mrs. Wolfe actually suspended for? It certainly isn't made clear in Mr. Kramble's note. The only clear warning mentioned is that Mrs. Wolfe had been told previously that the corridor door was to remain open at all times and that on June 19 Mr. Kramble found it locked. Third, his memo did not account for the fact that the employees may have been on their break: an

Exhibit 14–1 Personnel Documents for Case Study #3

First Document:

Employee Conference

Employee Name: *Mrs. Wolfe*   Date: *June 20*

Department: *Laboratory*   Time: *10 a.m.*

From: *D.H. Kramble*

Those Present: *D.H. Kramble, A.D.H. Jones, Mrs. Wolfe.*

Subject for Discussion:

On my arrival at the hospital on June 19, 1984, 6:30 a.m., I found the door leading from the ground floor corridor into our area was locked. When I unlocked the door, and then proceeded to my office, I found the lights out and you and Mr. Lamb asleep. Even in the darkness I could see both of you sprawled in the chairs with your feet on the desk, and you didn't say a word to me until I turned the lights on. Both of you were on a scheduled shift and paid hours. In addition, in May I instructed all personnel that the corridor door is to remain unlocked and open at all times.

Your action leaves me no choice but to suspend you for five working days, starting June 23. I must warn you that in case of a reoccurrence, your employment will be terminated.

Comments inserted by D.H. Kramble: I reviewed the above with Mrs. Wolfe but she refused to sign and refused to say anything about what happened on 6/19.

Second Document:

Interoffice Memorandum

To: Department Head Kramble   Date: June 23, 1984
From: Assistant Department Head Jones
Re: June 5 Incident

On Friday morning, June 5, 1981, at 6 a.m., I came to work two hours early. When I reached the department's office area, I found the door locked. At that point, I used my pass key and entered. As I approached your office, I saw the lights were out in there and two employees were sitting in the chairs by your desk with their feet on your desk. The two employees were Mr. Lamb and Mrs. Wolfe.

Both Mr. Lamb and Mrs. Wolfe were warned by me not to let this happen again.

Several days later, Dr. Smith complained to me that, on occasion, the reporting of results of emergency lab tests was extremely slow on the night shift.

Exhibit 14–1 continued

Third Document:

To: D.H. Kramble   Date: June 23, 1984
From: Mrs. Wolfe
Re: June 19, 1984

I was *not* sleeping. You know we always take our breaks in your office. Besides, I should be commended, not penalized, for my energy conservation efforts. I don't think this is *fair!*

Juanita Verago Wolfe

P.S. Dr. Smith agrees with me.

obvious consideration that should have been determined before writing the conference report or deciding to take disciplinary action.

The June 23 Interoffice Memo

The June 23 memo from Mr. Jones, the assistant department head, is another problem.

Although Mr. Jones describes a similar incident concerning Mrs. Wolfe that occurred June 5, the date of his interoffice memo is June 23, the day on which Mrs. Wolfe began her suspension. This raises a number of questions. Why was the documentation prepared so long after the fact? Did Mr. Kramble know of the June 5 incident at the time he made his decision to suspend Mrs. Wolfe, thus affecting the severity of the disciplinary action taken? Was Mr. Jones' memo prepared after Mrs. Wolfe was suspended to provide support for the hospital's decision?

Mr. Jones' memo also is confusing as to "what" he previously had warned the employees not to do. Was Mrs. Wolfe warned not to take breaks in Mr. Kramble's office, not to turn off the lights, not to lock the office door, or not to sleep—all of which is only implied in the memo?

Mr. Jones refers to a complaint by Dr. Smith that lab tests were being delayed. This additional comment is of no help to the hospital's case, because disciplinary action was not based on unsatisfactory performance or inattention to duty. There also is no evidence that Mr. Jones ever talked to Mrs. Wolfe about that complaint, or that anyone else made similar complaints. Although it is natural to think that the delayed lab tests could have been caused by Mrs. Wolfe's sleeping on the job, or other inattention to duty (if in fact they were late—a fact nowhere proved), this is not sufficient proof, by itself, for the hospital to build a case against her.

Mrs. Wolfe's note of June 23 raises additional problems. Not only does she deny sleeping, she states that taking breaks in Mr. Kramble's office was a known and accepted practice. If this is the case, this seriously weakens any impact Mr. Jones' prior warning may have had.

In sum, this is a case in which inadequate and unclear documentation (and perhaps the underlying facts as well) would prove fatal to sustaining the hospital's disciplinary action.

CASE STUDY #4: THE CASE OF THE SALARY INCREASE

Facts of the Case

Multisystems (the Employers) was a multiemployer bargaining group of hospitals that had negotiated a series of master union contracts with the Better Health Care Workers Union (the Union) for several decades. Every contract since 1965 contained the following provision in its compensation section:

Section 3—Pay Periods

It is understood that any employer may elect to pay employees under this Agreement on the basis of monthly pay periods or two-week periods, and if an employer changes its pay system it shall give the union advance notice.

Section 4—Wage Changes

Wage changes will be implemented by the individual employers commencing as of the payroll period nearest the date of the increase.

The various employers' pay periods did not coincide and it had been a practice at most hospitals to implement salary adjustments at the beginning of the pay period nearest the effective date of each new contract. Under this practice, employees sometimes received salary adjustments before the effective date and sometimes some days afterward. Although the hospitals had been following this method for a number of years, the union never had complained about it.

The collective bargaining agreement expired March 31, 1981. Negotiations for a new contract began early in 1981 and continued late into the year. At the initial negotiation session, there was some discussion concerning the implementation dates of future salary increases. A union spokesperson said the date should be the "stated" effective date in the contract.

For example, the wage portion of the prior contract stated that housekeepers would receive $5 an hour effective April 1, 1979, and $5.25 effective April 1,

1980, and the union believed these dates, not section 4, should govern. The employer spokesperson responded that in accordance with the agreement and prior practice, the employers would continue to implement increases beginning with the payroll period closest to the stated effective date in the contract wage section. This issue was not discussed again and the union did not present a proposal to change the language.

After a tentative settlement had been reached, the parties started drafting the actual contract and during this process the union proposed deletion of section 4. The employers refused to do so and the union submitted the matter to arbitration.

At the arbitration, the union argued that the parties' settlement stated that wage increases would be effective as of April 1981 and that this required implementation of the increases on the stated effective date. The employers argued that the language of the contract and the prior practice of the parties permitted each of the hospitals to implement the wage changes at the beginning of the pay period nearest to the "stated" effective date, regardless of whether it fell before or after the date of the agreement.

Questions To Consider

Assuming that the arbitrator applied traditional principles of labor contract interpretation to the dispute between the parties, would the union's grievance succeed?

Suggested Response to Case Study #4

Since no facts of any substance were in dispute, the arbitrator should rule against the union, based on the following considerations:

1. Since the tentative settlement contained only changes in the expired contract, and since section 4 was not mentioned, the disputed provision would properly be incorporated in the new contract.
2. The language of section 4 clearly permitted individual hospitals to implement wage increases as of the payroll period nearest the date of the increase.
3. The language of section 4 would not be required, in fact it would have no meaning, if the dates in the wage section governed the exact date on which increases would be implemented.
4. The practices of most of the individual hospitals are consistent with the argument that the contract allowed implementation of wage increases at the beginning of the nearest pay period.
5. The union, during the negotiations, had not proposed changes in the contract language that, if agreed to, would have changed the hospitals' prior practice. This fact is consistent with a conclusion that the hospitals could implement

wage increases at the beginning of the payroll period nearest to the date of the increase.

6. The hospitals' practices had extended over a number of years without union dissent.

CASE STUDY #5: QUIT OR DISCHARGE?

Facts of the Case

June Reston, an experienced medical-surgical (med/surg) nurse employed in 1979 was a float or relief nurse on the night shift and was routinely assigned to various units. Whenever she was assigned to the ICU, however, she expressed dissatisfaction with working in that unit to Irene Kimball, the night supervisor. On September 21, 1982, she requested a transfer to the med/surg unit adjacent to the ICU (Unit 2–E) and was reminded by Supervisor Irene that if she transferred there she also would be required to perform basic nursing duties in the ICU on an as-needed basis.

Although fully qualified ICU nurses were permanently assigned to that unit, the hospital on occasion assigned staff nurses on the 2–E Unit to the ICU to act as support or backup when necessitated by staffing needs. Support nurses had been oriented to the ICU and assisted the primary nurse by providing basic med/surg nursing; support nurses were not expected nor required to perform any specialized ICU functions such as reading the monitors, responding to the patient alarm system, or administering emergency medicine.

Although this policy was explained to June, she nevertheless declared she wanted the transfer. The transfer occurred on October 15, 1982. Shortly afterward, June reminded Supervisor Irene on several occasions that she preferred not to be assigned at all to the ICU because she could not read the monitors. Soon thereafter, upon being assigned to the ICU, June tearfully explained to Supervisor Irene that working in the ICU unit around equipment that she did not understand made her extremely nervous and upset. In response, Supervisor Irene stressed that June was responsible only for performing her regular med/surg nursing duties.

June also expressed her dislike for the ICU to Carol McKnight, the administrative nurse in charge of that unit. When Carol asked her if she had been aware when she transferred to Unit 2–E that her responsibilities would include functioning as an ICU support nurse, June Reston confirmed she had but that she still did not like working there.

After June's conversation with Supervisor Irene, the hospital did not assign her to the ICU for the next seven months. However, on May 6, 1983, when she reported to work on the night shift, she learned that she had been assigned to the ICU. Angered, she called the p.m. supervisor and declared vehemently that she would not work in the ICU. She explained that it made her uneasy because she could not read the monitors and she felt she was not competent to work there at all. The p.m. supervisor advised her to wait until Irene, the night supervisor, arrived.

When Irene reported in, the p.m. supervisor told her of June's refusal to work and Irene immediately telephoned her. During their conversation, June emphatically stated that she would not work in the ICU that night. In response, Supervisor Irene instructed her to remain on Unit 2–E until she could come to the unit to discuss the situation further. After a pause, June replied that she would work in ICU that night but it would be against her will; Supervisor Irene informed her that her conduct could subject her to disciplinary action.

While waiting for Irene, June spoke to several nurses leaving the p.m. shift and learned that the ICU supervisor had just been called by Supervisor Irene and was coming in to work the night shift. When June heard this, she was relieved that an experienced nurse would be working in the unit. Since she still felt agitated and upset, however, she decided to go home, as she concluded that she had been replaced in her assignment and there was no further need for her services.

The following morning, May 7, Lynn Harley, the assistant director of nursing, called June at her home. Lynn told her that she was suspended "pending further investigation" of the prior night's incident and that a meeting had been set up with the director of nursing later that week.

June responded that the hospital did not have to suspend her because she had thought about it overnight and had decided to quit. She explained that although she had informed Supervisor Irene that she did not wish to work in the ICU, she again had been assigned to work there as a support nurse. Since she felt there was no guarantee that she would not be assigned there again, she had decided to leave the hospital. In response, Lynn asked that she submit a written letter of resignation since hospital policy required that resignations be in writing, and June agreed to do so. She wrote out a letter of resignation that same day and gave it to a friend, who delivered it to the director of nursing on May 9.

Upon reflection, June later decided to take the case to arbitration on the ground that her resignation was not voluntary but forced, that it really was a discharge, and that the hospital did not have just cause to discharge her.

At the arbitration, she contended that she always had enjoyed her work with the hospital but felt it was a dangerous practice for the hospital to have her, an unqualified ICU nurse, work in that unit at all, regardless of her assignment. Thus, when abruptly assigned to the ICU the night of May 6, the pressures became unbearable. When informed that she was being placed on suspension, she stated that she felt she really was being given the ultimatum of resigning or being terminated and that she had had no choice in the matter.

In contrast, the hospital submitted that it had tried without success to obtain an experienced ICU nurse to work the evening of May 6. When all attempts failed, the appropriate measure was to assign June to the ICU as a support nurse since all

Unit 2–E registered nurses were considered backup nurses for the ICU. In addition, the hospital pointed out that June's med/surg duties in the ICU were identical to those of a staff nurse in Unit 2–E. The hospital also explained that June had been told on several occasions that she was to perform only basic nursing duties in the ICU, and that the monitoring systems or other duties she could not perform would be taken care of by the primary ICU nurses.

Thus, the hospital's position was that the assignment was proper, that it had reached no decision concerning termination, that June had not been suspended in fact, and that her resignation was entirely voluntary.

Questions To Consider

1. What are the weaknesses in the employer's arbitration case?
2. What are the strong points of the employer's arbitration case?
3. Would you, if you were the arbitrator, sustain or deny the grievance, and why?

Suggested Responses to Case Study #5

Weaknesses of the Employer's Case (Question 1)

First, while June clearly was not experienced as an ICU nurse, she nevertheless was assigned to that specialized unit as a support nurse.

Second, after she had informed her supervisor on several occasions that she did not wish to be assigned to the ICU, and after her last complaint, she had not been so assigned for seven months. Thus, she could argue that her lack of assignments was an implicit agreement on the part of the hospital not to put her on the ICU.

Finally, since Supervisor Irene informed June that her actions could subject her to discipline, even after June had agreed to work in ICU that night, she could contend that implicit in the supervisor's statement was the threat of termination: that June either could resign (because of the threat of either termination or a continuation of ICU assignments) or be discharged.

Strengths of the Employer's Case (Question 2)

First, June voluntarily requested a transfer to Unit 2–E and was well aware that R.N.s there routinely served as support nurses in the ICU when needed.

Second, June's supervisor explained to her that she need not perform any duties other than routine med/surg nursing duties in the ICU—that the primary ICU qualified nurses were responsible for reading the monitors, etc.

Third, after June had refused to work in the ICU, Supervisor Irene advised her to stay at the hospital so the two could discuss the matter; instead, June chose to leave in direct contravention of her supervisor's instructions.

Fourth, when telephoned at home the next morning, June was informed by the assistant director of nursing that she was merely suspended pending an investigation and that a meeting had been arranged with the director of nursing later that week. It was at that point that June chose to announce her resignation and declined the hospital's request to discuss the matter further.

Fifth, June sent in a written letter of resignation later that day but still had the chance to change her mind as she did not put it in the mail but gave it to a friend, who did not deliver it until two days later. Thus, she had ample opportunity to reverse her decision, which she chose not to do.

Finally, June could have grieved her work assignment through the union to arrive at a resolution of the contract dispute; instead, she chose to leave her job without first having filed any grievance at all.

The Probable Decision (Question 3)

The grievance should be denied, basically for the reasons identified in the response to Question 2: the facts establish a clear, conscious decision on the R.N.'s part to resign from the hospital, which was made after a long enough interval of time from the incident to allow her to reflect upon her actions.

CASE STUDY #6: THE CASE OF THE SCHEDULE CHANGES

Facts of the Case

The housekeeping employees at St. Augustine Hospital had been covered by a series of union contracts for a number of years. The housekeeping department head, after reviewing his staffing, concluded that the current work schedules of his employees no longer suited the needs of the hospital. In particular, he noted that too many were scheduled to work on certain weekdays and too few on weekends. After reviewing the issues with supervisors in his department and other members of the hospital's administration, including the personnel department, he decided to implement new schedules with new assignments that involved more weekend personnel. He realized that many of his staff considered weekend work undesirable.

Although the hospital notified the union of its proposed changes and tried to give those affected preferred shifts, particularly where they were senior employees, it was not possible to please everyone and some were assigned weekend work against their wishes. Some of the more senior of the disgruntled employees filed grievances under the union contract, challenging the hospital's action.

Relying on the contract, the union agrued that the hospital was obliged to assign shifts according to employees' seniority and, therefore, the more senior ones had to be permitted to select the work schedules they preferred. During the grievance procedure and at the subsequent arbitration, the hospital raised a number of arguments:

1. The express language of the union contract provided that seniority must be respected only where there was a "job change."
2. "Job change" was expressly defined by the contract as either the total elimination of a position or a decrease or increase in hours that changed it from one category to another (e.g., regular full time to regular part time).
3. All the employees in the housekeeping department continued to work a 40-hour schedule so no "job change," as that term was defined in the contract, had occurred and thus seniority principles were not applicable.
4. The union, during contract negotiations, had tried to insert a provision to expand the term "job change" to cover shift reassignments. The hospital had refused to agree to such provisions and the union had dropped its proposal.

The union countered by raising the following arguments:

1. The radical changes in the schedules and reassignment of work obviously involved "job changes" and all "job changes" triggered the seniority provisions of the contract.
2. The hospital's changes resulted in employees' working entirely different shifts, on different days, an action that had in fact "eliminated" some positions and created others.

Thus, the union argued, the seniority provisions of the contract were applicable and employees should be permitted to bid by seniority for the shift, or the days off, that they preferred.

Question To Consider

Assuming the arbitrator applied traditional principles of labor contract interpretation to this dispute, would the union's grievance succeed?

Suggested Response to Case Study #6

Since no facts are in dispute, the arbitrator's sole duty is to interpret the contract and apply commonly accepted rules of interpretation. Under this approach, the arbitrator could deny the grievance and rule in favor of the hospital for the following reasons:

1. The arbitrator could not look beyond the express terms of the contract unless the disputed language was ambiguous—that is, capable of more than one meaning.
2. The words "job change," whatever their meaning in ordinary language, are given a specific and clear definition in this particular union contract. As a result, the term was not ambiguous but meant the sort of change that resulted in a complete elimination of a position (e.g., as in the abolishment of a position, resulting in a layoff) or the changing of the hours to convert it from a full-time to a part-time job, or the reverse.
3. All affected employees continue to occupy full-time positions after the implementation of the shift revisions so this obviously was not a "job change" as defined in the contract.
4. The negotiating history of the "job change" unequivocally supports the hospital's position. Therefore, even if the contract language were ambiguous, which is not the case, the grievance still should be denied.
5. The doctrine of "reserved powers" states that an employer has the right to manage its business as it chooses—including making work assignments—and that the right is limited only by legislation or the terms of a collective bargaining agreement. Since there is no clause in the union contract regulating changes in shift assignments or days off, the right to make such changes in employees' work schedules was reserved to the hospital. Therefore, the hospital could devise appropriate schedules at its own discretion unless it acted arbitrarily and capriciously, a factor not presented by these facts.

Index

A

Absenteeism
  case study of termination (Title VII)
    and, 176-77
  legitimate and dishonest sick leave
    and, 342-44
  long-term absence and, 344-45
  medical verification and, 349
  need for dependability and, 340-42
  perpetually absent employee and,
    345-46
  reporting procedures and, 347-50
  unauthorized absences and, 350
Administration, supervisor and, 10
Administrative law judge (NLRB)
  hearings and, 48
  termination case example and, 4
Advancement, age and, 206
Advertisements (help-wanted), 179-80,
  203, 213
Affiliated Hospitals of San Francisco,
  94
Affirmative action, 184-85
Age discrimination, 6, 155. *See also*
  Discrimination
  advancement and, 206

aptitude tests and, 204-205
classification and, 204
employment benefits and, 201-203
employment selection procedure and,
  203-204
federal act covering (ADEA), 20, 21
  defining discrimination and,
    197-200
  jurisdiction, requirements, and
    procedures and, 196-97
  protected age group and, 195-96
FLSA and, 227
help-wanted ads and, 203
medical examination and, 206
state laws and, 197, 200-201
statistics and, 205
supervision and, 206
Alaska, 142
Alcoholism, 217-18
  as misconduct problem, 325-26
  rehabilitation and, 330-31
Ally doctrine, strikes and, 60
Ambulance duty, 120
Apprenticeship programs, 156-57, 163
Arbitration, 76-81
  contract and, 94-97, 130-33
  final and binding, 99-104

"interest," 110, 145-46
    mandatory mediation and, 59
    prior awards and, 108-109
    public employees and, 147-48
    refusal to take part in, 97-98, 104
Arrests and convictions, 185
Assault charge, detention and search
    dilemma and, 268
Assistance programs, discrimination
    and, 156-57, 164
Attacks (fighting on premises), 333-36
    case study of, 353-57
Attendance problems. *See* Absenteeism;
    Tardiness
Attitude classification, 314-15
Attorney General's office, 209
Authority
    arbitrator, 96, 132
    emergency, 18
    exceeding, 18
    head nurse and, 51
    ratification and, 18
    supervisor and professionals and,
        12
    supervisor as management
        representative and, 16-18
Authorization cards, 32
Awards
    arbitration, 102-103
    contract and prior arbitration,
        108-109
    public employees and, 147

B

Bargaining. *See* Collective bargaining
Bargaining contract. *See* Collective
    bargaining contract
Bargaining work jurisdiction, 90
Billing, contract example and discounts
    and, 134
Blacklisting, 265
Blood banks, 52
"Blue flu" strike action, 147
Board of Inquiry (BOI), 59-60

Bona fide occupational qualification
    (BFOQ)
    age discrimination and, 199
    help-wanted ads and, 179
    patient preference and male nurses
        and, 186-87
Boycott (secondary), 44
Buddy system (supervisory
    characteristic to avoid), 8
Bulletin boards, 134
Byrnes Act, 266

C

California, 141, 143, 146-47, 158, 200,
    214, 267, 303
California Licensed Vocational Nurses'
    Association, Inc., 94
    contract example and, 115-37
Callback duty, 120
Calling in sick, 347-48
Case studies
    employment problem, 353-71
    Title VII, 176-78
Cedars-Sinai Medical Center case, 49
Charge. *See* Unfair labor practice charge
Child-care arrangements, 6
Civil Rights Act of 1871, 152-53, 162
Civil Rights Act of 1866, 152, 162
Civil Rights Act of 1964.
    See Title VII of the Civil Rights Act of
        1964; Title VI of the Civil Rights
        Act of 1964
Civil service laws, 143
Civil Service Reform Act of 1978,
    139-41
Claims
    disability, 258
    unemployment insurance, 260-61
Clinical fellows, training program and,
    49-50
Clinical supervision, 50-51
Collective bargaining
    agency responsibility and, 140-41
    employees and, 28

employment law and, 54-57
negotiations and, 82-85
refusal to take part in, 42, 44
scope of, 35-38
states and, 142-43
strikes and, 84, 85-87
supervisors as union members and, 53
typical provisions
defining, 75-76
legal framework and, 76-82
subjects of, 79-82
union contract negotiations and, 76
union's fair representation and, 66
Collective bargaining contract
association membership and, 116
common provisions in, 89-99
enforcement and, 99-104, 147-48
example of, 115-37
FMCS and mandatory mediation and, 27
interpretation and, 104-109
language used in, 105, 109
legal framework and, 76-82
negotiations and, 76
notification and, 292
past practices and, 105-107
probation period and, 111
professional and technical
classification and, 12
states and, 147-48
tardiness and, 346
terminable-at-will, 264-65
termination notice and, 27, 58
time limits and, 95, 97
writing of, 88-89
Colorado, 189, 214
Commission on Graduates of Foreign
Nursing Schools, 182
Communication
supervisor and policy and, 10
Title VII and skills in, 181-82
Communication journals or logs, 289-90
Comparable worth theory, 188-89
Compensatory time off (CTO), 244-45
"Complainer" method of supervision, 9
Concluding work activities, 242

Conduct problems. *See* Misconduct
problems
Connecticut, 142, 267
Constitution of the United States
detention and search and, 268-69
discrimination and, 151, 162
Contract. *See* Collective bargaining
contract
Contractors
discrimination and federal, 154-56,
163
employees of independent or
subcontractors and, 87
Section 503 of Rehabilitation Act and
federal, 215
wage-hour laws and, 230-31
Corrective action, notification of
employee and, 287
Cost-of-living statistics, 83
Counseling, 2
documentation and, 294
notification and, 292-93
County of Washington v. Gunther, 189
Court appearances, 124
Criminal prosecution, 337-38
Criminal record, 185

D

Decision-making methodology, 275-79
checklist for, 281-84
Denver, 189
Department of Health, Education, and
Welfare (HEW). *See* Health and
Human Services (HHS, formerly
Department of Health, Education,
and Welfare)
Department of Justice, 209
Department of Labor (DOL), 196, 198,
204, 215
Detention and search dilemma, 268-69
Disability programs, 257-59
Disaster clause, 96
Disciplinary action, 2
contract and, 110-11

contract example and, 128
progressive
    exceptions to, 302
    oral reprimands and, 298-300
    suspensions and, 300-301
    termination and, 301-302
    written warnings and, 300
public employee, 147
R.N.s and, 51
supervisor
    and physician example and, 11
    and professionals and, 12
tardiness and, 346
Discrimination, 6. See also Title VII of
the Civil Rights Act of 1964; specific
types of discrimination, e.g., Age
discrimination; Sexual
discrimination, etc.
    contract example and, 117
    disproving, 175-76
    federal requirements and, 150-57
    handicapped and defining, 209-13
    "no cause" and, 173-74
    proving, 174-75
    remedies for victims of, 178-79
    states and, 157-59
    supervisor and employee and, 20-21
    union membership and, 41, 43-44,
    117, 145
District of Columbia, 159
Dress codes, 183-84
Drinking. See Alcoholism
Drug abuse, 217-18
    as misconduct problem, 326-30
    rehabilitation and, 330-31

E

Early Litigation Identification Program
    (of the EEOC), 171
Educational requirements, Title VII
    and, 180-81
Education leave of absence, 126
Employee preference, Title VII and,
    185-86

Employee Retirement Income Security
    Act of 1974 (ERISA), 202, 203,
    262-63
Employees
    bargaining issues and, 54-57
    contract and categories of, 117-18
    contract probation period and, 111
    defining status of, 49-50
    detention and search of, 268
    employment law and unionization
        and, 27-30
    employment terms and conditions
        and, 29-30
    misconduct problems and, 320-40
    notification of
        groups and, 287, 288-92
        importance of, 285-86
        individuals and, 287, 292-302
        purpose of, 286-87
    performance problems and, 315-21
    replacing striking, 86
    resignation from union and, 60-61
    restraining or coercing of, 40-41
    schizoid supervisors and, 9
    strikes and questioning of, 86
    supervisor as, 14-15, 20-21
    supervisor's discussions with (during
        organization of union drives and
        elections), 72-74
    union dues and, 27
    union elections and, 33-40
    union fair representation and, 66
    union organizing and, 30-31
    union restraint and, 43
    union solicitation and distribution
        policies and, 62-64
    violence against (by union), 43
    Weingarten Rule and, 64-66
Employers (health care). See also Public
    employment
    access to files of, 267-68
    contract and, 75-76, 82-85
    defining health care, 26
    disability programs and, 257-59
    disloyalty to, 339-40
    employment law and unions and, 24-25

picketing and neutral, 60
residing on premises of, 242
restraining of employee union activity
and, 40-41
R.N.s and, 51
sexual harassment and, 190, 191
supervisor and employment law and,
25
supervisor as representative of,
14-15, 15-20
supervisor's legal framework and, 2-7
theft of property from, 331-33
Title VII and, 176
unfair labor practices and, 40-42
union recognition and, 31-33
union restraint and, 43
vocational programs and, 52
Employment agencies, 203
Employment law (NLRB Act)
bargaining unit issues and, 54-57
defining terms and, 49-53
employee rights (Section 7) and,
27-30
fair representation and, 66
health care institutions and, 26-27
professional organizations and, 53
public employment and, 138-48
solicitation and distribution policies
and, 62-64
strikes and, 57-61
structure of
basic, 24
employers and, 24-25
evolution of, 23-24
supervisors and, 25
supervisors and, 2-7, 25
unfair labor practices
employer (Section 8a) and, 40-42
NLRB and, 45-49
union (Section 8b) and, 42-45
union representation (Section 9) and,
30-40
Weingarten Rule and, 64-66
Employment problem case studies,
353-71
Employment references, 267

Employment selection procedure.
See also Hiring
age discrimination and, 203-204
Title VII and, 179-80
Enforcement authorities, drug offenses
and, 330
Equal Employment Opportunity
Commission (EEOC), 6, 165, 196, 202
access to records of, 178
age discrimination and, 197, 198,
199, 200, 201, 204
Civil Rights Act of 1866 and, 152
state fair employment and, 157-58
Title VII and, 166-67
filing a charge and, 167-74
Equal Pay Act of 1963 (EPA)
defining equal work and, 237-38
discrimination and, 153, 162
FLSA and, 227
scope and coverage of act and, 236-37
supervisors and, 20
Executive Order 11491 (1964), 155, 163
Executive Order 11246 (1965), 155, 163

F

Fair Labor Standards Act (FLSA),
153, 196
deductions and, 232-33
disloyalty and, 339
enforcement and, 227-31
hours worked and, 233
minimum wage and, 231-32
exemption from, 235-36, 251-56
overtime and, 233-35
exemption from, 235-36, 251-56
scope and coverage of, 226-27
False imprisonment charge, detention
and search dilemma and, 268
Family, Title VII and, 183
Fannin, Paul J., 54
Federal Labor Relations Authority
(FLRA), 140
Federal Mediation and Concilation
Service (FMCS)
contract negotiations and, 27

strikes and, 58, 59-60
Federal regulations. *See also* State
   regulations
   discrimination and, 150-157
   handicapped and employment and,
      206-213, 215
   public employment and, 139-41
   supervisory legal framework test
      example and, 5-7
   unemployment insurance and, 259
Federal Unemployment Tax Act,
   259-60
Fighting on premises, 333-36
   case study of, 353-57
Financial injury, supervisor and, 19
Fringe benefits, 83, 212
   contract and, 91
   contract example and, 121-27
   veterans and, 220-21
Funeral leave of absence, 126

G

Good faith bargaining, 77-78, 265
Grievances, 76, 83. *See also* Unfair
   labor practice charge
   contract and, 94-97, 109, 130-33
   federal employees and, 141
   insubordination and rule for, 323
   no-strike clause and, 98
   R.N.s and, 51
   state public employees and, 147-48
   union's fair representation of
      employees and, 66
   wage-hour laws and, 243
Gunther prison guard case, 189

H

Hairstyles, 184
Handbooks (employee), 291
Handicapped
   data confidentiality and, 216-17
   defining, 209-210
   drug and alcohol problems and,
      217-18
   federal contracts and, 215
   federal employment and, 215
   medical examination and, 216
   preemployment medical inquiries
      and, 216
   Rehabilitation Act of 1973 and
      defining dicrimination and, 209-13
      HHS and, 208-209
      overview of, 206-207
      Section 504 and financial assistance
         and, 207-208
   state laws and, 213-14
   tests and, 217
Health care employers. *See* Employers
   (health care)
Health care institutions. *See also*
   Hospitals
   defining, 52
   defining employer and, 26
   employment law and, 26-27
   supervisors and complexity of, 10
Health and Human Services (HHS,
   formerly Department of Health,
   Education, and Welfare)
   disability programs and, 258
   handicapped and, 208-209, 215
   rehabilitation and, 331
Health, insubordination and, 323
Health and welfare program, 126-27
Hearings (NLRB)
   arbitration, 101
   employment termination example
      and, 3-5
   holding of, 48
   supervisor and physician and, 11
Help-wanted ads, 179-80, 203, 212
Hiring, 2, 212. *See also* Employment
   selection procedure
   R.N.s and, 51
Holidays
   contract and, 91
   contract example and, 121-22
Homosexuality, 179
   sexual harassment and, 190

Hospital and Institutional Workers'
  Union, AFL-CIO, Local 250, 94
Hospitals. *See also* Health care
  institutions
  contract and rights of, 116
  defining health care employer and, 26
  grievances and, 131-32
  union solicitations and, 62-64
  wage-hour laws and, 226-27
Hours. *See* Wage-hours laws; Work
  hours
House staff, 49-50

I

Illinois Fair Employment Practices
  Act, 158
Immigration and Naturalization Service
  (INS), 182
Indiana, 200, 214
Insubordination, 320-24
Insurance. *See also* Unemployment
  insurance
  contract and, 87, 91
  supervisor as employee and, 21
Interns, training programs and, 49-50
Investigation
  EEOC and Title VII, 170-71, 172
  wage-hour claims and, 227-28

J

Jury duty, 124
Just cause, 110-11, 128

K

Kennedy, John F., 139

L

Laboratory reports delay case study,
  361-64
Labor Management Relations Act, 24

Labor Management Reporting and
  Disclosure (Landrum-Griffin) Act, 24
Lakeside Community Hospital
  (Lakeport, California), 94
Landrum-Griffin Act, 24
Language skills
  English fluency requirements
    case study, 177-78
  Title VII and, 181-82
Larkin, John Day, 104
Layoff, 129
  unemployment insurance and, 261
Leaves of absence, 124-26, 212.
  See also Sick leave
Lectures, 243
Liability, supervisor and personal,
  19-20
Licensure laws, 266
Lockouts, 58, 81, 132
  unemployment insurance and, 261
Lodgings, 87

M

Maine, 267
Management. *See also* Supervisors
  supervisor as part of, 14-15, 15-20
  union organization drives and
    elections and, 72-74
Manuals (policy and procedures),
  290-91
Marital status, 6, 183
  pregnancy and maternity and, 188
Maternity, 187-88
Meal periods, 241-42
Medicaid, 208
  affirmative action and, 184
  discrimination and, 156
Medical examination
  age discrimination and, 206
  handicapped and, 216
Medical verification (absence), 349
Medicare, 208, 209
  affirmative action and, 184
  discrimination and, 151, 156

Meetings
    contract and, 120, 134, 135
    notification and group, 288-89
    R.N.s and, 51
    wage-hour requirements and, 243
Michigan Civil Rights Act, 158
Michigan State Public Employment
    Relations Act, 144
Minimum wage. See Wage-hour
    laws
Misconduct problems
    alcohol and, 325-26
        rehabilitation and, 330-31
    case studies and, 353-71
    criminal prosecution, 337-38
    disloyalty to employer, 339-40
    drug abuse, 326-30
        rehabilitation and, 330-31
    fighting on premises, 333-36
    insubordination, 320-24
    moonlighting, 340
    off-duty employees and, 336-37
    performance problem differentiation
        and, 313-14
    poor attitude and, 314-15
    problem identification and, 313
    sleeping on duty, 324-25
    theft of employer's property, 331-33
Moonlighting, 340

N

National Labor Relations Board
    (NLRB). See also Employment law
    (NLRB Act)
    discrimination and, 154
    employment termination
        example and, 3-5
    supervisor as management
        representative and, 15-16
    unfair labor practice proceedings
        and, 45-49
    union election process and, 32, 33-40
    union petition processing and,
        34-35

Nation of origin discrimination,
    165-66
Nebraska, 143
Negotiations
    bargaining sesssion conduct and,
        84
    contract and history of, 107-108
    "impasse," 78-79, 141, 145-47
    participation on committee for,
        83-84
    planning, 82-83
    professional standards, 109-110
    spokesperson and, 83
    strikes and, 84-85
    union contract, 76
New York, 142, 146, 214
Notification
    contract termination, 27, 58
    group, 287, 288-92
    importance of, 285-86
    individual, 287, 292-302
    insubordination and, 322
    purpose of, 286-87
    of resignation from union, 61
    ten days' advance strike, 27, 58
Nurses
    bargaining units and, 55, 56-57
    collective bargaining example of
        LVNs, 115-37
    disloyalty example and, 339
    foreign training and, 182
    patient preference and male,
        186-87
    professional organizations and, 53
    quit or discharge case study and,
        366-69
    supervisory status of, 50-51
Nursing homes, 26
    patient preference and male
        nurses and, 186-87

O

Obey now—grieve later rule, 323
Occupational Safety and Health Act
    (OSHA), 339

Office of Civil Rights (OCR), 209
Office of Federal Contract
  Compliance Programs (OFCCP),
  155, 184, 215, 219
Oral reprimands, 298-300
Orientation sessions, 291-92
Overtime
  contract example and, 119
  federal law review and, 6, 7
  FLSA and, 233-35
    exemption from, 235-36, 251-56
  head nurse and, 51
  state wage-hour laws and, 239

P

Passing the buck (supervisory
  characteristic to avoid), 8
Patient care issues, 135
Patient intervention case study,
  357-61
Patient preference, 186-87
Patient triaging and transferring, 85
Pay. *See* Wages
Pennsylvania, 141
Pension plan, ERISA and, 263
Performance Appraisal and
  Development Form, 303-311
Performance evaluation, 2
  contract example and, 127
  notification and, 294-98
  R.N.s and, 51
Performance problems
  case studies and, 353-71
  corrective action and, 319-21
  dealing with
    attempting to improve, 315-16
    deficiency identification and,
      315
    employees and, 316-17
    group problems and, 317
  distinguishing between conduct
    problems and, 313-14
  poor attitude and, 314-15
  problem identification and, 313
  standards for, 317-19

Personal liability (of supervisor),
  19-20
Personnel. *See specific personnel
  category, e.g.* Employees; House
  staff; Physicians; Nurses;
  Supervisors, *etc.*
Personnel manual, 135
Petition for NLRB decision
  enforcement, 49
Petition for union, 34-35
Pharmacy discounts, 134
Physical attacks (fighting on
  premises), 333-36
  case study of, 353-57
Physical examination. *See* Medical
  examination
Physical injury, supervisor and, 19
Physicians
  bargaining units and, 55, 56
  supervisors and, 11-12
Picketing, 57. *See also* Strikes
  employee rights and, 28
  fines for crossing lines and, 60-61
  illegal, 44-45
  neutral employers and, 60
  unlawfulness to deter nonstrikers
    and, 43
Policy
  notification and, 285-86
    manuals for, 290-91
  supervisory behavior and, 10
Posted notices, 289
Pregnancy, 187-88
Preparatory work activities, 242
Problems of supervision. *See*
  Misconduct problems;
  Performance problems
Procedure
  case studies and, 353-71
  decision making and, 276, 277
    checklist and, 281-82
  defining, 8
  notification and, 285-86
    manuals and, 290-91
Professional disputes (as
  irsubordination), 323-24

Professional organizations, 53
Public employment
  characteristics of, 138-39
  federal employment and, 139-41
  state laws and, 141-48
Public Employment Relations Board
  (PERB, California), 146

R

Racial discrimination, 151-53, 165.
  See also Discrimination
Records
  access to
    contract and, 132-33
    EEOC, 178
    employer, 267-68
    grievance procedure and
      employee's, 96
    handicapped and confidentiality
      of, 216-17
    keeping of (wage-hours), 245-46
References (employment), 267
Regulations. *See* Federal
  regulations; State regulations
Rehabilitation Act of 1973, 6
  Section 504 of, 156, 164
    financial assistance and,
      207-208
  Section 501 and federal
    employment and, 215
  Section 503 of, 156, 163
    federal contracts and, 215
Rehabilitation, alcohol and drug
  use and, 330-31
Religious discrimination, 166.
  See also Discrimination
Reporting to work time, 244
Residents, training programs and,
  49-50
Residual rights theory, 104-105
Rest period, 241
Retirement
  contract and, 91, 127
  federal law review and, 6-7

  mandatory, 201
"Right to sue" letter, 173-74
Right-to-work provisions, 94
Roosevelt, Theodore, 139
Rules enforcement, 292

S

Safety
  employee rights and, 28
  employee transportation and,
    87
  insubordination and, 323
Salary. *See* Wages
Salary increase case study, 364-66
Secondary boycott, 44
Seniority, 89
  contract and, 92, 106
  contract example and, 128-30
  veterans and, 220-21
Sexual discrimination, 157, 166.
  See also Discrimination
  comparable worth theory and,
    188-89
  patient preference and, 186-87
Sexual harassment, 189-91
Sexual preference, 179
Shift work. *See* Work shifts
Sick-ins, 147
Sick leave, 212. *See also* Leaves of
  absence
  contract bargaining and, 87, 91,
    104, 105
  contract example and, 121
  legitimate and dishonest, 342-44
Sickness, calling in to report, 347-48
Sleeping on duty, 324-25
Sleeping time, 244
Standards, 2
  bargaining unit, 54-55
  negotiation and professional,
    109-110
  performance problems and,
    317-19
Standby duty, 120

Standby time, 241
State regulations. *See also* Federal
  regulations
  age discrimination and, 197,
    200-201
  discrimination and, 157-59
  handicapped and, 213-14
  licensure laws and, 266
  public employment and, 141-48
  unemployment insurance and,
    259
  wage-hour laws and, 238-39
Strikebreaking, 265-66
Strikes. *See also* Picketing
  collective bargaining
    issues and, 87
    negotiation and, 84-85
    no-strike clause and, 81, 98, 132
    questioning employees and, 86
    replacement of strikers and, 86
    triaging and transferring and,
      85
  contract and right to, 99
  employee rights and, 28
  employer prohibited conduct
    and, 42
  employment law and, 57-61
  health care industry and, 57-61
  illegal picketing and, 44-45
  nonstrikers and picketing and, 43
  public employee recognition and,
    144
  public employees and, 145-47
  unemployment insurance and,
    261-62
Substance
  absenteeism and tardiness and,
    340-50
  case studies and, 353-71
  decision making and, 276, 277
    checklist and, 282-84
  defining, 8
  misconduct problems and, 320-40
  performance problems and,
    313-21
  supervisory issues and, 313-15

Supervision, age discrimination
  and, 206
Supervisors
  absenteeism and tardiness and,
    340-50
  arbitration and, 101-102
  clinical, 50-51
  commitment and, 1
  as combination of management
    and employee, 14-15
  dual status reconciliation and,
    21-22
  as employee, 20-21
  as manager, 15-20
  employees and
    what you cannot tell and
      discuss with, 73-74
    what you can tell and discuss
      with, 72-73
  employment law and, 25
  functions of
    daily use of principles and, 7-8
    defining, 272-75
    legal framework and, 2-7
  health care institution
    complexity and, 10
  labor union membership and,
    52-53
  methodology of decision making
    and, 275-79
    checklist for, 281-84
    defining functions of, 272-75
    overview of, 271
  misconduct problems and, 320-40
  performance problems and,
    313-21
  personal liability of, 19-20
  physicians and, 11-12
  professional and technical
    classifications and, 12
  sexual harassment and, 190
  specialized problems of, 12-13
  status definitions and, 50-51,
    139-40
  styles of supervision to avoid
    and, 8-10

Suspension, 300-301

T

Taft-Hartley, 24
Taft, Robert, Jr., 54
Tardiness, 341, 346-47
Tax Equity and Fiscal Responsibility
    Act (TEFRA) of 1982, 202
Tenure step movement, 119
Terminable-at-will contracts,
    264-65. *See also* Collective
    bargaining contracts
Termination
    absenteeism case study (Title VII)
        and, 176-77
    contract example and, 128
    employment law example
        (supervisor) and, 3-5
    no-strike clause and, 98
    professionals and supervisors
        and, 12
    progressive disciplinary action
        and, 301-302
    public employee, 147
    R.N.s and, 51
    supervisor and physician
        example, 11
    terminable-at-will contracts and,
        264-65
    vacation pay and, 123
Tests
    age and aptitude, 204-205
    blood, breath, urine, and other,
        327, 329
    employment, 180
    handicapped and, 217
    supervisor and federal law, 5-7
Theft of employer's property,
    331-33
Time off (compensatory, CTO),
    244-45
Title VII of the Civil Rights Act of
    1964
    access to EEOC records and, 178

affirmative action and, 184-85
case studies
    English fluency requirements,
        177-78
    termination for absenteeism,
        176-77
communication skills and, 181-82
comparable worth theory and,
    188-89
countering employer's defense
    and, 176
criminal records and, 185
disproving discrimination and,
    175-76
dress codes and, 183-84
educational requirements and,
    180-81
EEOC and, 166-67
employee preference and, 185-86
employment selection procedure
    and, 179-80
family members and, 183
filing claim charges and, 167-74
foreign training for nurses and,
    182
government and, 151-52, 162
language skills and, 177-78,
    181-82
maternity and, 187-88
nation of origin and, 165-66
patient preference and, 186-87
pregnancy and, 187-88
protected classes and, 165-66
proving discrimination and,
    174-75
religion and, 166
remedies for victims of, 178-79
sexual harassment and, 189-91
sexual preference and, 179
Title VI of the Civil Rights Act of
    1964, 156, 164
Trainees, wage-hour laws and, 230
Training programs, 243
    house staff and, 49-50
Transferring of patients, 85
Transportation, 87

Travel time, 242-43
Triaging, strikes and patients and, 85

U

Underemployment,
  unemployment benefits and, 262
Unemployment benefits, 28
Unemployment insurance, 259-62.
  See also Insurance
Unfair labor practice charge. *See
  also* Grievances
  employment termination
    example and, 3-5
  filing and processing of, 45-49
  supervisor and, 25
  Title VII and filing of, 167-74
Unfair labor practices
  agency responsibility and public
    employment and, 140-41
  employers and, 40-42
  NLRB and, 45-49
  states and public employment
    and, 145
  union and, 42-45
Uniforms, 183
  wage-hour requirements and,
    247-48
Union contract. *See* Collective
  bargaining contract
Unions
  bargaining order remedy and, 40
  closed, union, and agency shops
    and, 93
  contract and, 75-76, 93-94
  discrimination and membership
    in, 41, 43-44, 117, 145
  employee rights and, 27-30
  employees resigning from, 60-61
  employer assistance to, 41
  fair representation and, 66
  membership maintenance and, 93
  NLRB secret ballot elections and,
    32, 33-40
  organizing question and, 30-31
  petition requirements and, 34-35

public employees and, 143-44
recognition of, 31-33, 115
restraining of employees and,
  40-41
rival union and, 33
schizoid supervisory behavior
  and, 9
solicitation and distribution
  policies (employment law) and,
  62-64
supervisory discussions during
  organization drives and
  elections and, 72-74
supervisory personnel and, 52-53
ten day strike notice and, 27, 58
unfair labor practices and, 42-45
visitation rights and, 98-99, 133-34
Weingarten Rule and, 64-66
Union security, 93-94, 144-45

V

Vacations
  contract bargaining and, 87, 91
  contract example and, 122-23
  veterans and, 221
Veterans Readjustment Act, 218-19
Veterans' Reemployment Rights,
  154, 163, 219-21
Vietnam Era Veterans'
  Readjustment Assistance Act of
  1974, 155, 163, 218
Visiting nurse associations, 26
Vocational programs, 52
Volunteers, wage-hour laws and,
  229

W

Wage-hour laws
  Fair Labor Standards Act (FLSA)
    alternative hours and, 248
    deductions and, 232-33
    enforcement and, 227-31
    hours worked and, 233,
      239-44

minimum wage and, 231-32
    exemption from, 235-36, 251-56
overtime and, 233-35, 239
    exemption from, 235-36, 251-56
scope and coverage of, 226-27
state and overtime, 239
payment of wages due and, 239
scope and coverage of laws for and,
    238
Wages. *See also* Equal Pay Act of
1963 (EPA); Wage-hour laws
age discrimination and, 204
contract and, 80, 83, 87, 89, 90,
    91, 118, 137
disability programs and, 258
employee rights and increases in,
    28
Equal Pay Act and, 153, 162
handicapped and, 212
head nurse and, 51
reporting, 120
salary increase case study, 364-66
supervisor as employee and
    equal, 20
Waiting time, 240-41
Weapons
    case study of fighting and, 353-57
    possession or use of, 335-36
Weekend provisions, 92

Weingarten Rule, 64-66, 293, 298
Witnesses, 101, 102, 170
Women, 6, 166. *See also* Sexual
    discrimination
    comparable worth theory and,
        188-89
    dress and, 183-84
    employee preference and,
        185-86
    fair employment and, 157
    pregnancy and maternity and,
        187-88
Workers' compensation, 28, 87
Work hours. *See also* Wage-hour
    laws
    compensation for, 118, 137
    contract and, 80, 90
    standby and callback, 120
Working conditions, contract and,
    92
Work schedules, 2
    contract example and, 127
    schedule change case study and,
        369-71
Work shifts
    contract and, 106
    contract example and, 119-20
    holidays and, 122
Written warnings, 300